The Rise, Fall & Resurrection of
Brian Wilson

The Rise, Fall & Resurrection of
Brian Wilson

David Leaf

OMNIBUS PRESS
London / New York / Paris / Sydney / Copenhagen / Berlin / Madrid / Tokyo

Copyright © 2025 David Leaf Productions, Inc.
Except 'Inspiration' © 2024 Tom Nolan and 'Columnated
Ruins Domino' © 2024 Charlotte Martin

Published by Omnibus Press
(A Division of Wise Music Limited
14-15 Berners Street, London, W1T 3LJ)

Cover designed by Mark London
Picture research by the author

ISBN: 978-1-9158-4131-5

David Leaf hereby asserts his right to be identified as
the author of this work in accordance with Sections 77 to 78
of the Copyright, Designs and Patents Act 1988.

All rights reserved. No part of this book may be reproduced in any
form or by any electronic or mechanical means, including information
storage or retrieval systems, without permission in writing from the
publisher, except by a reviewer who may quote brief passages.

Every effort has been made to trace the copyright holders
of the photographs in this book but one or two were unreachable. We
would be grateful if the photographers concerned would contact us.

A catalogue record for this book is available from the British Library.

Printed in the Czech Republic

www.omnibuspress.com

CONTENTS

1. The Curtain Rises — vii
2. (Re) Introducing Brian Wilson — ix
3. *SMiLE*: 'In A Nutshell' — xvii
4. Foreword by Melinda Wilson — xxi
5. 'Leaf' by Howie Edelson — xxiii
6. Author's Note: *The Reason I Had to Write This Book* — xxv
7. A Child Is Born — 1
8. In His Room — 5
9. God Only Knows — 8
10. Dumb Angel — 33
11. Don't F★★★ With the Formula — 69
12. Can't Wait Too Long — 91
13. Raising the Titanic — 117
14. Dreams Do Come True — 165
15. I WAS THERE: *My Fellow 'Brianistas' Look Back* — 201
16. The Critics Chime In — 210
17. The Album & The Documentary — 214
18. *SMiLE* on Tour — 230
19. The 'Brianistas' Part Two — 236
20. Grammys, Lawsuits, and Box Sets — 244
21. Reports From Here, There, & Everywhere — 249

Tom Nolan   *Inspiration*   251

The Witnesses	*School's in Session*	259
Harvey Kubernik	*Honour the Incarnation*	263
Debbie Keil-Leavitt	*The Night of the World Premiere*	266
Gary Pig Gold	*The SMiLE That You Send Out*	268
Sylvie Simmons	*Hallelujah!*	271
Peter Carlin	*'It'll Knock Your Socks Off'*	274
Sean O'Hagan	*'Cabin Essence' Comes Alive!*	277
David Scott	*'The Old Master Painter'*	279
Andrew G. Doe	*A SMiLE Returned*	285
Domenic Priore	*DIY . . . The SMiLE Pot Boils*	287
Dr. Daniel Harrison	*A Sacred Oratorio*	295
The Band & Friends	*Twenty Years Later*	298
Charlotte Martin	*'Columnated Ruins Domino'*	303

22. Epilogue	311
23. Acknowledgements	315
24. Selected Bibliography	319

THE CURTAIN RISES

'I live my daydreams in music. I see my life in terms of music . . . I get most joy in life out of music.' **Albert Einstein**

'If music is math, Brian Wilson is Einstein.' **Anonymous**

'If I had to select one living genius of popular music, I would choose Brian Wilson.' **Sir George Martin**

'I have to tell you that Bach was easily the greatest musical innovator in the history of the world. He was so advanced for his time. There's a spiritual depth to his music.' **Brian Wilson**

'God is nearer to me than to others. I approach him without fear. I have always known him.' **Ludwig van Beethoven**

'I'm writing a teenage symphony to God.' **Brian Wilson**

(RE) INTRODUCING BRIAN WILSON

Dennis Wilson: 'Brian Wilson is The Beach Boys. He is the band. We're his fucking messengers. He is all of it. Period. We're nothing. He's everything.'

Sir George Martin: 'As the leader of The Beach Boys, he composed the songs, made the arrangements, performed along with all his mates in the band and produced the sounds in the studio. His genius seemingly encompassed everything.'

Carol Kaye, *legendary bassist, studio musician:* 'If you worked for Brian, you knew you were working for the best . . . He couldn't go wrong . . . To him, music was his life and his breath, and we understood that.'

Chuck Britz, *engineer, United Western Studios, Hollywood:* 'Brian, as far as I'm concerned, he *was* The Beach Boys.'

Bob Dylan: 'Jesus, that ear. He should donate it to the Smithsonian. The records I used to listen to and still love, you can't make a record that sounds that way. Brian Wilson, he made all his records with four tracks. But you couldn't make his records if you had a hundred tracks today.'

Case closed? Well, not entirely. As we embark on this journey, there's more we need to know about the artist at the centre of it.

Brian is regarded by his peers and the generations that have followed in his musical footsteps as a sui generis genius. And the music of *SMiLE* is a big reason for that.

I have devoted a significant portion of my adult life to proselytising for his remarkable artistic accomplishments which were often buried under tabloid stories that focused on mental illness and drugs and a bad, 'mad doctor' and intra-group squabbles, all of which overshadowed the public perception of who Brian Wilson actually is – an artist.

My focus has been on his artistry, and this is a book about a specific work of art. So before we head back into the mists of time, let's hear from those who know far better than I why Brian Wilson is so important to musical history: members of the Rock & Roll and Songwriters Halls of Fame, Grammy Award–winning producers, those he's musically inspired as well as respected music journalists, all of whom have boundless admiration for what Brian did as a composer, arranger, and producer.

We begin with those with whom he shared a bedroom, the stage, and a recording studio microphone, his late brothers Dennis and Carl.

Dennis Wilson: 'The first time I really got what he was doing was 'God Only Knows' . . . He was able to organise his thoughts to a point where they're hypnotic yet entertaining. Meaningful and spiritual, too . . . The thing I wonder about is where does Brian's creative spark come from? Not his subjects or anything, but his spark. What makes it so great for me is that I really don't know. There's a mystery behind Brian, even to me.'

Carl Wilson: 'I asked Brian one time, "Why do you think we succeeded in such a big way?" He said, "I think the music celebrated the joy of life in a real simple way."'

Elvis Costello: 'There's a continuum that goes George Gershwin, Cole Porter, Richard Rodgers, Burt Bacharach, Brian Wilson, Paul McCartney.'

Burt Bacharach: 'Brian's music mattered then; still matters now. When you hear those records – sophisticated harmonies, vocal blends . . . Some of those songs, like 'Good Vibrations,' 'God Only Knows.' So fresh, and kind of made you smile.'

(RE) INTRODUCING BRIAN WILSON

Roger Daltrey: 'Who pushed the musical boundaries [in the 1960s]? I really thought, "This guy's a genius." And obviously, as you get older and you get wiser, then you suddenly realise you are listening to what, in the equivalent century, would be a Mozart, a Beethoven, a Bach. He's got this immense humanity about him. You just kind of wanna run up to him and embrace him.'

Sir George Martin: 'Brian is, to me, on a peak with John and Paul. In a way, although it's a completely different era, he's on a par with Porter and Gershwin and Jerome Kern.'

Roger Daltrey: 'He is the greatest writer of the 20th Century.'

Sir George Martin: 'Well, he's up there with the greats, isn't he?'

Van Dyke Parks, songwriter, artist, producer: 'He knew how to make a record better than anybody. He reaches perfection.'

Terry Melcher, record producer: 'As a record producer, somebody who knows what goes on as far as mixing, EQs, things that make a balance sound right, there isn't anyone better. He's as good as anyone I've heard.'

Don Randi, legendary keyboard player, studio musician: 'Musically, he's probably one of the greatest composers . . . His brilliance will be with us forever.'

Lenny Waronker, record producer and former president of Warner Brothers and Dreamworks Records: 'He cast a giant shadow over L.A. during his time as a producer and a music man. Brian was very much Gershwin-esque. [He was] a one-of-a-kind musician, artist, songwriter, producer [and] he could sing. [He had] just this amazing gift [and was] a competitive artist who had and has big, big, big ideas about what music can be. Enormous talent. Our children's children's children will be learning about him. And he looked good, too.'

Danny Hutton, Brian's best friend and founding member of Three Dog Night: 'He's driven by the love and need to create music. Be around it. I thought he could do anything. He was the hottest, most plugged-in person in music in my opinion. Above The Beatles. Above any other act. On a pure musical level, he was the man. And I think people like Dylan and McCartney and everybody caught on to it, and all were looking at him to see what he was going to do next.'

Jimmy Webb: 'There's no doubt in my mind that Brian could have been a classical composer.'

Phil Ramone, *fourteen-time Grammy Award–winning producer:* 'And it would have been called modern classical. Great music sometimes has such comparatively simple ideas. And you say, "Why I can't I do that?" Well, go and try to write one of those things. It's impossible. But he doesn't do it because it's clever. He does it because emotionally, he wants to take you somewhere.'

David Crosby: 'The most highly-regarded pop musician in America.'

Neil Young: 'He's like Mozart or Chopin or Beethoven . . . This music will live forever. There's very few writers I feel the emotional and spiritual contact with that I feel with Brian.'

Lindsey Buckingham: 'As a writer, and craftsmen, the way he puts chords together he's up there when any of the greatest writers of the 20th century.'

Art Garfunkel: 'He is rock and roll's gentlest revolutionary . . . our Mozart of Rock 'n' Roll.'

Randy Newman: 'Brian Wilson is one of the greatest creative artists in the history of popular music.'

Sir Elton John: 'I have so many great memories of listening to his music, of being inspired by it, crying.'

Bruce Springsteen: 'American masterworks . . . The beauty of [Beach Boys music] carries with it a sense of joyfulness even in the pain of living.'

(RE) INTRODUCING BRIAN WILSON

In his song, 'Love Again,' **Little Steven** sings, 'Got a picture of Brian Wilson that I pray to every night.'

Terry Melcher: 'Of all the people I ever met in the rock and roll business, no one ever approached Brian Wilson in terms of talent or complete unpredictability.'

Bono: 'The genius of his music is the joy that's in it. I know that Brian believes in angels. I do too. But you only have to listen to the string arrangement on 'God Only Knows' for fact and proof of angels.'

Sean Lennon: '*SMiLE* is unbelievable. It's the most amazing thing I've ever heard.'

Questlove: 'He's a modern-day Stravinsky, the way he constructs his music. He was doing stuff [over forty years ago] that modern people do now, looping his work and stuff. There's [a *SMiLE* outtake] with a whole bunch of tubas having a conversation with trumpets. It's great.'

Sylvie Simmons, *UK music journalist:* 'You can understand why rock critics just fall all over this. He has everything that we want. There isn't just the story about the human being that's so kind of tender and crazy. But there's just this music that has so many different levels. So many layers.'

Richard Williams, *UK music journalist:* 'With The Beach Boys, it was one guy, Brian Wilson, who was creating this fantastic music for his group. [It put him in a class with] Charles Ives, Aaron Copeland, Duke Ellington, Moondog, Howlin' Wolf, all kinds of people. And it seemed we were getting something, a real American statement, best of America, in my view.'

Stephen Page, *Barenaked Ladies:* 'There's a sense in that [*SMiLE*] era of Brian's music that there's a search for something deeper in the music.'

Kevin Hearn, *Barenaked Ladies:* 'His music hits me in an emotional way. The melodies are haunting.'

Rufus Wainwright, *musician, singer/songwriter:* 'What I've always loved most about him is his harmonic sense. His melodies – incredibly sort of a free-flowing sophistication that reminds me a lot of [Erik] Satie. Very impressionistic. I'm a big opera fan, that's mostly what I love. If I was to make a correlation between Brian's work and that music, it sounds very French.'

Raphael Saadiq, *Grammy Award–winning singer/songwriter, producer:* 'Brian Wilson is a brilliant arranger of vocals and harmonies, but he wasn't just about the songs. I've always loved [the instrumental 'Let's Go Away For Awhile']. The instrumentation, the harmonies, the bells, the chimes, the strings, the tympani . . . every sixteen bars, something happens. The orchestration is brilliant and unique.'

Jeffrey Foskett, *musician and singer (member of The Beach Boys and The Brian Wilson Band for nearly thirty years):* 'Brian is the singularly most successful, unconventional writer musically and vocally. Have Mozart and Puccini and others written unconventional music? Yes, with a melody line. But not with five-part harmony on top of it.'

Alan Jardine, *The Beach Boys:* 'He's a musical visionary.'

Linda Ronstadt: 'I don't think there is anyone his equal in pop music.'

Tom Petty: 'I don't think you would be out of line comparing him to Beethoven.'

Guy Webster, *photographer:* 'It'll be like Beethoven is to us now, three hundred years from now, that's what Brian Wilson will be to what he was discovering musically. I can compare Brian to Michelangelo in the sense that Michelangelo suffered greatly for his art.'

Lindsey Buckingham: 'Brian Wilson was my greatest example of how to follow my own heart and ideas as a musician, producer, and song-writer. I admire many things about him, but that's the thing I admire most.'

(RE) INTRODUCING BRIAN WILSON

In 2022, for Brian's eightieth birthday, a video compilation was put together featuring, amazingly, Bob Dylan singing 'Happy Birthday.' Here are a few other messages from that tape.

David Crosby: 'I love your music. I always have.'

Sir Barry Gibb: 'I've followed you all of my life since the first time I heard you. Your inspiration, your insights into chord changes, your insights into harmony, has been overwhelming to me. Has always been . . . I love you very much.'

Sir Elton John: 'You've inspired me all my life. To me, you're the only real pop genius in the world, and I love you very much.'

Sir Elton John and Brian Wilson begin a complete performance of *Pet Sounds* with a duet on 'Wouldn't It Be Nice', March 29, 2001 at *An All-Star Tribute to Brian Wilson,* Radio City Music Hall, New York City. That night's performance of 'Heroes And Villains' by Brian and his band was a major turning point in the story of the completion and presentation of *Brian Wilson Presents SMiLE.*

THE LIPPIN COMPANY LIMITED
16-19 SOUTHAMPTON PLACE, LONDON WC1A 2AX
TEL +44 (0)20 7745 7189 FAX +44 (0)20 7745 7190

BRIAN WILSON TO APPEAR AT LONDON'S ROYAL FESTIVAL HALL PERFORMING HIS LOST MASTERPIECE "SMILE" LIVE FOR THE FIRST TIME

2004 Concert Tour To Include Performances in the U.K. And Europe

Los Angeles, CA -- Brian Wilson, co-founder of the Beach Boys, will return to London's Royal Festival Hall in February 2004. For the first time in his 40-year career, Wilson will perform his mythical unreleased masterpiece, "Smile." In addition, the concert will include classic Beach Boys and Brian Wilson favourites as well as selections from his new solo album (details forthcoming).

The concert tour announcement comes on the heels of the 2003 Ivor Novello Awards at which Brian was presented with the Special International Award. Following the Awards ceremony Brian was honoured at a reception hosted by his publishers Rondor Music, celebrating his achievements on the occasion of the Beach Boys' 40th Anniversary.

In 2002, Brian Wilson performed sold out concerts to stellar reviews at Festival Hall in January and June. The four January 2002 concerts sold out immediately and when Wilson returned to London later that year to perform at the Queen's Jubilee Concert, he sold out another two nights. Among those who attended Brian's Festival Hall performances were Eric Clapton, Roger Daltrey, Elvis Costello, Richard Ashcroft, and others. The gigs were cited as the concerts of the year by most UK critics. Brian Wilson and the Royal Festival Hall were honoured with the prestigious 'Live Event of the Year Award' by Time Out Magazine."

> "Blame Brian Wilson. Eleven months to go and we already know the gig of the year." – TIME OUT 6 February 2002

> "...there could only be one Gig Of The Year. No one knew what to expect from former Beach Boy Brian Wilson's first-ever dates in Britain, but to see this icon...as spectacularly as any of those other sixties heroes here and alive and in the flesh was astounding." THE EXPRESS

> "Best Gig: Brian Wilson, Royal Festival Hall, London, January 27. The greatest songs in the history of pop music, exquisitely performed before an emotional, involved audience. What else do you want from a gig?" THE GUARDIAN

The stunning 2003 press release announcing that Brian would be performing SMiLE in 2004. Only four February concerts were originally scheduled for the Royal Festival Hall, but they sold out so quickly that two further dates were added. Nobody knew what a challenging journey it would be to the first show.

SMiLE: 'IN A NUTSHELL'

Sir George Martin: 'I've never known anything like this before. We heard about *SMiLE* being made at the time, when we were in the sixties. And we were so excited. Rumours were it was great. But we never heard anything. And it was coming out. And we were waiting for it. And it never happened. We waited in vain. I never thought we'd hear it. And now we've got it. And it's fantastic.'

The dramatic story of *SMiLE* – the tragedy and the triumphant presentation of the work in 2004 – is what gives this book its subtitle: a book born to celebrate the twentieth anniversary of a legitimate artistic miracle.

As the late Sir George Martin noted above, in 1966, The Beatles and everybody in the music world knew about *SMiLE*. And were waiting for it with eager ears.

But what makes the *music* of *SMiLE* worthy of a book? Why was it – why *is* it – such a big deal, something that people still listen to, talk about, wonder about with fascination?

Very simply, the music was exquisite, beautiful, stillborn, *and still somehow revolutionary.*

If, over four hundred years ago, you had walked into church and somebody was playing 'Surf's Up' or 'Wonderful' at the organ, you might think, 'Wow. That must be Bach's latest piece.' That's the kind of music Brian Wilson was composing during the *SMiLE* era. Timeless.

Until 1966, The Beach Boys were known for 'Fun in the Sun' music. But bubbling underneath, if one listened to the album tracks, was something else. Something profound. Songs with an intimacy that gave the listener a sense of the troubled heart and mind of the creative force behind the group.

In 1966, working with lyricist Tony Asher, Brian Wilson composed, arranged, and produced *Pet Sounds;* the album stunned the music world. 'God Only Knows' became a standard. Nobody in popular music had revealed their inner thoughts and feelings like this before – so powerfully, so deeply, and so artistically successful.

Sir Paul McCartney: 'I've often listened to *Pet Sounds* and cried. It's that kind of album for me.'

Bob Harris, *legendary British DJ:* 'I know from Paul himself that having heard *Pet Sounds* it was . . . "If Brian can do this, we can do this."'

Alan Jardine, *The Beach Boys:* 'He grew immensely during that time.'

Dennis Wilson: 'He opened a lot of doors for people. Especially me.'

Pet Sounds almost instantly became the new standard by which albums would be judged.

David Wild, *pop culture writer, author:* 'For lack of a better term, *Pet Sounds* is where rock and roll becomes a religious experience. Over a half century later, we're still reckoning with this record because Brian went as deep as pop music can go.'

Or so we thought.

A few months after *Pet Sounds* was released, Brian finished production on a new single. For the first time, rather than recording a song, he used the studio in a radical way. He recorded pieces of music. Lots of pieces. Some would fall by the wayside as he stitched it all together to create 'Good Vibrations.' *That* was ground-breaking. And a million-selling number one hit single.

That one-two punch (the landmark *Pet Sounds* album and the earth-shattering single, 'Good Vibrations') had amazed everybody listening, especially in England. But long before 'Good Vibrations' was released, in the summer of 1966, Wilson began work on new music, using the modular technique he had pioneered on 'Good Vibrations' *for an entire album.*

This, too, was unheard of. Were Brian's new compositions up to the task? Were the lyrics of his new collaborator, Van Dyke Parks, equal to the musical invention?

Everybody in Brian's inner circle who heard the *SMiLE* music at the time believed so. Passionately. They were constantly being astonished.

What was Brian playing them? Very simply, in a matter of months, he and Van Dyke Parks had written and recorded a half-dozen remarkable songs (including 'Heroes And Villains,' 'Surf's Up,' 'Cabin Essence,' and

SMiLE: 'IN A NUTSHELL'

'Wonderful.') Unfinished recordings worthy of note (e.g. 'Do You Like Worms'), tracks which didn't yet have lyrics. Work had begun on an 'Elements' suite. The 'Prayer.'

To hear the music, you had to be on the inside. A few journalists were welcomed into the inner sanctum to have their minds blown. In the late fall of 1966, stories about *SMiLE* began to appear regularly in the rock press.

All these tales only increased anticipation. Then, in April 1967, on CBS, Brian himself appeared on a network television special hosted by maestro Leonard Bernstein! On *Inside Pop: The Rock Revolution*, Brian, *alone* at the piano, performed 'Surf's Up.'

Finally, a piece of the *SMiLE* music could be heard. And anybody watching instantly 'got' that the press reports weren't hype, that Brian was indeed operating in a new musical realm. Like Bernstein, viewers immediately recognized that something 'Important' with a capital 'I' was happening. Unquestionably, *SMiLE* was part of a completely new direction in popular music.

In 1957, Leonard Bernstein was nearly forty when he and Stephen Sondheim, then in his mid-twenties, collaborated on the stage musical masterpiece, *West Side Story*. That changed the theatre forever. A decade later. Wilson and Parks – much younger but perhaps even bolder – were on the verge of radically transforming popular music.

Bernstein understood this and included 'Surf's Up' on his television special.

But neither Capitol Records nor The Beach Boys' business model recognized or celebrated or supported Brian's progressive work.

Ray Lawlor did. Ray, who would become one of Brian's best friends, remembers that hearing 'Surf's Up' in 1967 left him 'flabbergasted. I'd never heard anything like it. It was obviously a departure from *Pet Sounds* into another stratosphere or universe.'

We didn't get to travel to that universe, at least not in 1967.

It seemed that *for the third time in one year*, Wilson was rewriting the rulebook on what pop music could be. 'Surf's Up' on TV coming through a three-inch speaker only whetted appetites. When would we hear all of it? And how would we respond? One person who was hearing the work-in-progress, who was *singing* on it, left little doubt about how incredible it was.

SMiLE

Dennis Wilson: 'In my opinion, it makes *Pet Sounds* stink. That's how good it is.'

True? What could *SMiLE* have been? All evidence would ultimately suggest a musical revolution.

But we never found out because in the spring of '67, Brian stopped work on *SMiLE*. In the lyric of 'Surf's Up,' he was 'a broken man too tough to cry.'

And from that moment on, hearing *SMiLE* became a seemingly impossible dream, one that many of us chased for nearly forty years. We *had* to hear this music. Some, including me, were driven, became obsessed.

An almost unimaginable series of events led to the creation of *Brian Wilson Presents SMiLE*. And in 2004, when it came into the world, we could hear it. Own it. Revel in it. Twenty years after its birth, we celebrate it. But for the longest time, that seemed an impossibility. And that is the story of this book.

Brian at work on *SMiLE*, Western Studios, early January 1967.

Brian: 'Every time I hear [Gershwin's 'Rhapsody in Blue'] it reminds me of falling in love with music and knowing that's what I wanted to do with the rest of my life… I hear music in my head… I think I was born to compose music… I saw in the future a vision of music in a dream I had one night… I heard all kinds of celestial, heavenly sounds. It just blew my mind.'

FOREWORD

BY MELINDA WILSON

February 20, 2004.

At last, the day was here.

The past six months had been filled with stress, the roller coaster of life as I watched my husband grapple with the idea of finding a way to assemble his *SMiLE* music so it would make sense to him . . . and to an audience.

In May of 2003, while he and David Leaf were in England when Brian got the prestigious Ivor Novello award, that's when we first announced that Brian would be back in London in 2004 with the world premiere of what, for artistic and legal reasons, would be called *Brian Wilson Presents SMiLE*.

The media went wild. The fans were in disbelief. Could this be real?

But the joy that accompanied that moment quickly, for Brian, turned into despair. It was like, 'Oh no. How am I going to do that?'

Fortunately, he had his team to help him figure out how to present this most beautiful music. Darian Sahanaja – Brian's most sensitive collaborator since he started touring – helped Brian make sense of it all, helped him figure out a sequence for the songs. They worked closely together as Brian decided which pieces of music from the original sessions from 1966–1967 had to be included and which could be left out.

Then, Van Dyke Parks came to the rescue. There were still a few songs that needed lyrics, that needed some repair work. Van Dyke was 'Johnny on the Spot.'

Brian wanted David around while he was doing all this work, and as David was becoming an accomplished documentarian, it made sense for him and his team to capture all that was happening on video. His film, the remarkable *Beautiful Dreamer: Brian Wilson and the Story of SMiLE* had it all. The ups and downs. And the uncertainty.

SMiLE

What none of us knew was what was going to happen. It was like being on the high wire at the circus. One slip and 'Boom.' And would the net be strong enough to catch Brian?

What I saw was a determined man, using what he calls his famous 'Will Power.' It seemed that nothing was going to stop him. Even as the date approached, even as he admitted how scared he was, he kept moving forward.

When we got to London, all we could do was watch and wait for that fateful moment when Brian walked up the stairs to confront his destiny.

For more than thirty-five years, people had been waiting to hear *SMiLE*. Would *Brian Wilson Presents SMiLE* meet their expectations? Could it?

If you watch *Beautiful Dreamer*, you can feel every moment of tension. Brian just sitting and meditating, wondering what will happen when the music is played.

I sometimes wonder if maybe we were all nervous for no reason. After all, he knew how great the songs were. Why would an audience who was there to see him and his band play them think any differently?

And, of course, the rest is history. The world premiere of *Brian Wilson Presents SMiLE* went off without a hitch. Ending with maybe the biggest standing ovation he's ever received. Sure, Brian was nervous. You can see that in his face. But by the time it was all over that night, it was one of the greatest moments I ever experienced. *We* ever experienced. And I was so happy for him. He had accomplished what seemed impossible, and *he* was happy.

After the world premiere, when he was asked how *SMiLE* compared to *Pet Sounds,* the album that was routinely called one of the greatest albums ever made, Brian said, 'On a scale of one to ten, I give *Pet Sounds* a seven and *SMiLE* a ten.' I almost fell off my chair.

But I knew he believed that.

And now, twenty years after that very special moment at the Royal Festival Hall on the South Bank of London, it all seems like a beautiful dream. Except it wasn't. It really happened. As you'll read, the road wasn't smooth. But it was a drive I wish we could take again.

So smile as we relive the journey to my husband's greatest work, *Brian Wilson Presents SMiLE*.

Melinda Wilson
August 2023

'LEAF'

Nobody really does what they say they will. It often *seems* like they do – but it's rarely the case. Deadlines come and go; projects begin, end, and time changes everybody. Who can even remember last Tuesday?

David Leaf didn't travel West in search of stardom or some wide-eyed industry dream. He actually came to California for an answer and ended up directly part of the process in realising it. The cut-to-the-quick headline of why we're talking about David at all is that he literally left his life to discover 'What happened to Brian Wilson and where is *SMiLE*?' It's really as simple (and complex) as that.

David didn't want to write songs with Brian. He didn't make a bid to manage The Beach Boys. He didn't view any of this as some opening to a career in 'the business.' He came at this thing for the same reason we all did: The music. David, who loved The Beach Boys and The Beatles – along with all the best music of his time – was a historian and a storyteller who saw a gaping hole in the narrative: How and why does Brian Wilson, one of the figureheads of popular *and* progressive rock, abandon his masterpiece, fade into the shadows, and wind up an overlooked cultural curio?

But above all else, David just wanted to hear *SMiLE* completed.

Along the way, *SMiLE* has had many angels in its midst; obviously its creators – Brian Wilson, Van Dyke Parks, and The Beach Boys, as well as the engineers, numerous studio musicians featured on the original recordings and 2004 performances. We remain forever indebted to the 'outsiders' that shepherded, chronicled, collected, studied, revered, and facilitated its eventual completion – namely, David Anderle, Domenic Priore, and last but certainly by no means least, a true friend to us all – Darian Sahanaja.

SMiLE

Yet it was David Leaf, who over the decades (both figuratively and literally) was always whispering to Brian, 'So, what about *SMiLE*?' Luckily for us, Brian's wife and most ardent supporter, Melinda Wilson, alongside manager Jean Sievers ALSO had the foresight, curiosity, and gumption to finally ask, 'Yeah Brian – *what about SMiLE???*'

It would be absurd to suggest that *SMiLE* alone is the reason for David Leaf's existence – but it's absolutely the reason for David Leaf being in OUR lives. He was doing all that work for us *(undoubtedly* long before most of us even knew what 'Barnyard' sounded like).

Modern art's most infamous untied shoelace and uncrossed 't' was finalised due in large part to David Leaf giving a shit about Brian Wilson and his music for all the right reasons. Perhaps David Leaf's by then thirty-plus years of love and friendship for Brian was just the thing needed to jimmy this music free for the good of the planet. Maybe not, but knowing what I know, I just don't see one happening without the other.

As a fellow New Yorker, who was in heaven (and tears) both nights at Carnegie Hall in 2004, I'm proud of what David Leaf accomplished by leaving us behind all those years ago to go and find *SMiLE*.

Howie Edelson
New York City
September 2023

(Howie Edelson is a Beach Boys archival producer and creative consultant for Brother Records Inc. & Iconic Artists Group.)

AUTHOR'S NOTE:

THE REASON I HAD TO WRITE THIS BOOK

There are many reasons and only one that truly matters: this book is the celebration of a genius revealed, the twentieth anniversary of *Brian Wilson Presents SMiLE* . . . the genuine *liberation* of music that had once been the most tragic burden any artist has ever had to bear. The anniversary being observed focuses on one of the most extraordinary and significant accomplishments in musical history.

And a miraculous personal rebirth, too.

When it comes to *SMiLE,* Brian Wilson, and the music he created with The Beach Boys, I'm a fan. Short for fanatic. I also love much of his solo work, and his vocals on Van Dyke Parks' brilliant *Orange Crate Art* helped make that a big favourite too. The sounds Brian has created have an emotional depth that touch me profoundly.

In 1962, when Brian Wilson first walked into Capitol Records in Hollywood, he was nineteen years old, a slender stork, a man child, a boy who had written a handful of songs. There was nothing about him that would make you think that within five years, he would create a body of work that would almost and somehow forever change popular music.

And now, over sixty years since that day in 1962 – as we look back on the music he created in that 'annus miraculous' 1966 – we can appreciate what a monumental achievement it was and could have been. For those of us who worship at the Church of Brian Wilson, the story of *SMiLE* – the promise, disappointment, and ultimate completion of *Brian Wilson Presents SMiLE* – is our bible. It's a moment of unparalleled significance in musical history, too. There has never been anything quite like it: a piece of music first created in 1966 and finally 'born' in 2004.

SMiLE

L.A. Times pop music writer Randy Lewis puts it into historical context: 'Mozart was born, lived his entire life, and died in less time than it took this work to come to fruition.'

SMiLE was the most famous unfinished album in popular music history, the most thought-provoking unfinished piece in all of music history. For over thirty years, I doubt Brian Wilson ever did an interview in which he wasn't asked about it. He often would say nothing. Or that it was an inappropriate subject. When he did address it, nothing he said satisfied anybody. And this went on for *decades*.

Meanwhile, as pieces of *SMiLE* appeared on Beach Boys albums, as *SMiLE* session tapes leaked out, *SMiLE* took on a life of its own. Beginning in the 1980s, there was a wave of bootlegs available at independent record stores. Countless fan-created *SMiLE* recreations on cassette. The thought amongst fans might have been, 'If Brian and The Beach Boys aren't going to finish *SMiLE*, then I'll have to create my own version.'

DIY (Do It Yourself) *SMiLE*, combined with Domenic Priore's classic compilation, *Look! Listen! Vibrate! SMiLE!* – the music *and* the mystery – fuelled a new generation of young *SMiLE* fans.

And then, on February 20, 2004, Brian Wilson completely changed the narrative. From backstage right, he walked deliberately and purposefully out of the darkness and into the spotlight, waved, bowed (right and left) to the audience, then took his place centre stage behind his keyboard at the Royal Festival Hall on the South Bank of London. And on a stage stuffed with nearly twenty musicians and all manner of instruments, Wilson and company performed *Brian Wilson Presents SMiLE*.

The World Premiere was one of the emotional and artistic highlights of Mr. Wilson's life. It was certainly one of mine. It was a dream I had spent nearly thirty-three years chasing, sometimes wondering if my pursuit – like Brian's artistic one – might be a little insane. Was a finished *SMiLE* remotely possible? Were we all just chasing a ghost?

'World Premiere Week' – six shows on London's South Bank – became nightly visitations for true believers who had made the pilgrimage from as far away as Tokyo and Cape Town. The seats were also filled with our musical heroes (including Sir Paul McCartney, Sir George Martin, Roger Daltrey, and Jeff Beck) who had come to cheer Brian on. There were Beach Boys fans too. And the media-inspired curious as well. *If* they could get tickets for those SRO concerts.

THE REASON I HAD TO WRITE THIS BOOK

The reviews were, almost without exception, ecstatic. The audience response ultimately led to a multi-continent tour, an album that sold nearly a million copies worldwide, and Brian's first Grammy Award.

Then the music historians began to take notice. A 2005 book by Mark Paytress – *I Was There: Gigs That Changed the World* – included such events as Monterey Pop, Woodstock. Wattstax, Live Aid, and Lollapalooza. The Moondog Coronation Ball, too.

This incredible compendium of legendary concerts featuring music greats from Frank Sinatra to Miles Davis to The Beatles and beyond includes almost everybody of significance in pop and rock. There's even a nod to hip hop (Public Enemy and Eminem).

And the last chapter in *I Was There* focuses on the aforementioned world premiere of *Brian Wilson Presents SMiLE*. An excerpt: 'A staggering thirty-six years after it had been written off as an unworkable vanity project by a crackpot prodigy, *SMiLE*, Brian Wilson's great unfinished mid-century symphony, was unveiled in a series of instantly legendary shows in London . . . There were few dry eyes left in the house.'

'Instantly legendary'? Clearly, our collective souls had not been chasing a ghost.

In 2007, a *Rolling Stone* article titled 'The 50 Greatest Concerts of the Last 50 Years' included the momentous show at the Royal Festival Hall. As Andy Greene wrote, 'For decades, Brian Wilson avoided even talking about *SMiLE,* the psychedelic follow-up to The Beach Boys' *Pet Sounds* he shelved . . . After poring over the old *SMiLE* tapes, Wilson walked onstage and finally delivered on his decades-old promise of "a teenage symphony to God," bringing rock's most famous unheard album back to life. From the first celestial harmonies of 'Our Prayer' much of the audience was in tears.'

In 2011, in Paolo Hewitt's *'Scuse Me While I Kiss the Sky: 50 Moments That Changed Music*, the world premiere of *Brian Wilson Presents SMiLE* is one of those 'moments.' Here's how Paolo ended his piece: 'The musical vision that Wilson had tried to realise was now a reality . . . able to do what its creator always wanted. It made the world smile.'

Finally, *Brian Wilson Presents SMiLE*'s place in musical history had been secured. And now, twenty years after its London debut, this book is a commemoration of the music's deliverance – the story of a body of work created by a musical genius that we nearly never got to hear – music so different that it almost defies description.

Not only had Brian triumphed against all the odds, but presenting *SMiLE* led to many other wonderful moments in his most unexpected career renaissance.

Brian Wilson's story has been told and retold almost ad nauseam – in newspapers, magazines, on TV, in numerous films, documentaries, and books (including mine, 2022's *God Only Knows*). In the massive update to the original 1978 edition, I admitted that my passion for his music is what brought me to California: to write a book about Brian, become his friend, and help him finish *SMiLE*.

As I *was* there in 2004, *this book* will give us a special peek behind the scenes. Our cameras followed Brian and his band for my feature documentary, *Beautiful Dreamer: Brian Wilson and the Story of SMiLE*, a Grammy-nominated film which culminates (spoiler alert) with the World Premiere concert in London.

Since 1971, in my work, especially 1993's *Good Vibrations* box set and 2001's *An All-Star Tribute to Brian Wilson* at Radio City (which I wrote and produced with the late Chip Rachlin and Phil Ramone), and *Beautiful Dreamer*, my focus was on *SMiLE*. I've more than had my say on the subject. Some would say too much, or believe I've told the story unfairly, that I wasn't impartial in my analysis. They aren't necessarily wrong. OR right.

So, it's time for everybody else to have *their* say: Brian's musical family, his closest friends (then and now), other musicians, The Beach Boys, family members, record company executives, journalists, music historians, and fans. What does Brian Wilson and *SMiLE* mean to *them*? To the world?

We'll hear from the people who created it back in the day, as well as how in 2003-4 it was finally put together. Courtesy of the 'flies on the wall,' we'll hear how they experienced this most convoluted saga. We'll get ever closer to the truth – as close, that is, without being able to read Brian's mercurial mind.

For the making of *Beautiful Dreamer,* I interviewed dozens of those who were there. Generous excerpts from the outtakes of that film – especially my 2004 interviews with Brian and his *SMiLE* collaborator Van Dyke Parks – will give us a sense of what this musical revolution meant to those two, as well as those who were just listening in wonderment.

THE REASON I HAD TO WRITE THIS BOOK

As perhaps nothing is as important as the fact that in 2004, we finally were presented with this music, the people who will have the most to say are those (especially Darian Sahanaja and Van Dyke) who worked closely with Brian to bring his unfinished masterpiece back to life, the devoted musicians who were there to help Brian with this epic re-imagining. I believe the brand-new interviews with Brian's 2004 band are a gift of revelatory remembrances about the art and the artist. There's much to learn from the people who were closest to (and love) this real Wizard of Oz.

And as the music of *SMiLE*, one of Brian Wilson's greatest gifts to the world, was received with the feeling with which he infused it, the book also includes reminiscences from dozens of fans who were at the Royal Festival Hall premiere or at another stop on tour, the people for whom *Brian Wilson Presents SMiLE* was a dream come true – even a life-changing event. As one fan said just before the first concert in *Beautiful Dreamer*, 'I'm going to have my life pre-*SMiLE* and my life post-*SMiLE*.'

The book ends with a *SMiLE* mini-anthology. Through all these voices, we can both celebrate this music and ultimately determine for ourselves what *SMiLE*, *Brian Wilson Presents SMiLE*, and Brian Wilson mean to us.

My role is to be the curator of this collection of quotes, anecdotes, and essays. Like a one-man Greek Chorus, I'll set the stage, contextualise events, and provide the connective tissue.

Unfortunately, several key figures from the first *SMiLE* era did not make themselves available to be interviewed for this book; fortunately, I did speak with many people who were there (some of whom have since passed away), and this is how they remembered it.

What I think is special about this oral history is that the world really doesn't know what Bach or Beethoven or Mozart were like as artists or *as people*. For me, when it comes to Brian Wilson, I can tell you that one-on-one, he is the kindest, sweetest, and funniest person and that his music comes from his pure soul.

In our extended conversation in 2004, Van Dyke Parks said, 'It's hard for me to say what Brian Wilson is really like. All I know is I like what I see in him. All I know is what it's like to work for him. Because that's what our relationship was. I've met Brian Wilson through his work. Andrew Carnegie said "My heart is in the work." I think Brian Wilson's heart is in the work. Now what drives that, I don't know.'

SMiLE

'The work' is our focus: the story of Brian Wilson's journey to create, abandon, and ultimately complete the most enigmatic *SMiLE* since the *Mona Lisa*.

In 2004, in the earliest outline of *Beautiful Dreamer*, there was a piece of voice-over narration that didn't make the cut. But I think it's instructive twenty years later. Here's what I wrote: 'The story of *SMiLE* is not one that can be told in a few glib sentences or a handful of soundbites. It's been thirty-seven years since the album was put on the shelf and became the most famous unfinished, unreleased album in rock history. So be patient. You're about to experience a miraculous artistic resurrection. And miracles take time . . .'

Brian in 1966, with what was – at least when this photo was taken – a much more famous smile. In 2005, on public television's *The Charlie Rose Show*, Brian was asked, 'Is it the greatest thing you've ever done?' Brian's response: '*SMiLE*? Oh, yeah. By far...I would say my genius showed a little bit on *SMiLE*.'

A CHILD IS BORN

'Creative minds have been known to survive any sort of bad training.'
Anna Freud

WE NEED TO GET TO 1966 AS QUICKLY AS POSSIBLE. SO HERE GOES.

Brian Douglas Wilson was born on June 20, 1942, Murry and Audree Wilson's first child. The Wilsons, an almost middle-class family, lived briefly in Inglewood and then in Hawthorne in the South Bay area of Los Angeles County.

Brian Wilson: 'When I was a little baby, I used to listen to [George Gershwin's] 'Rhapsody in Blue.' That's when it first started coming into my soul . . . I realized I had a musical gift at age 8. I was listening to my dad play the piano, and he taught me some piano, some boogie-woogie. I knew I had some musical ability then . . . Rosemary Clooney taught me to sing with love in my voice. She taught me how to do that. (*Sings*) "The evening breeze, caress the trees, tenderly." [. . .] My Uncle Charlie taught me how to write musical notations on music paper, with sharps and flats and naturals, and treble clef and bass clef, too . . . The Hi-Los turned me on to modern harmony . . . I learned how to make [vocal] arrangements from the Four Freshmen.'

As Brian eagerly remembered during an interview for *Beautiful Dreamer*, 'When I was about 14 years old, I started listening to rhythm and blues shows on the radio. And I felt a real strong affinity with records like 'Earth Angel' by the Penguins. 'In the Still of the Night' and 'Over the Mountain,' 'Rock Around the Clock.' I had such an affinity with those records that I knew in my heart that one day I would make music like that. I knew I would. I didn't know when and where or what, but I knew I would.'

In the laughter-filled bedroom he shared with middle brother Dennis and the youngest, Carl, he would teach them to sing in harmony.

Brian: 'We developed this special blend: (*Sings*) "Come down, come down from your ivory tower. Let love come into your heart."'

That 'Three Freshmen' blend would become the basis for The Beach Boys' sound.

It seems music was the easy, happy part of Brian's life. More controversial is what young Brian's home life was like. Murry Wilson infused his boys, especially Brian, with both loyalty to family and a strong competitive spirit. Murry, by most accounts, was a successful businessman, a failed songwriter, and a jealous bully.

Brian's best friend Robin Hood described Brian's dad as 'a drill sergeant.' In interviews, Brian and Dennis were less polite.

Brian: 'My father was a very, very hostile, messed-up man with a lot of hatred in him.'

Dennis: 'Our father beat the shit out of us; his punishments were outrageous.'

In our 2004 conversation for *Beautiful Dreamer*, Carl's first wife, Annie Wilson-Karges, added a different point of view.

Annie Wilson-Karges: 'I don't think Carl remembers it that way . . . I think "harsh" is a good enough word. Harsh with the boys. Just very emotional about his sons. Very protective.'

Brian's mother?

Annie: 'How do you talk about a mother and her oldest son? It's very special. She was so special. I think Audree and Carl were most alike. She was just [a] very evolved human being. And I think she transmitted that, and her sons picked up on that, each in their own individual way, on that sort of outlook on life that she had that was really very healthy.'

But did Audree protect her sons? Could she? Murry ruled the roost, and it seems he did that with the tools of a tyrant, sometimes punctuating his verbal blows with his fists or other forms of debasement.

Brian: 'I was a hero, and my father was a villain.'

What is unknowable is, how bad was the abuse and its impact? Did it instil within Brian a lifetime of fear, of always wondering, 'What will happen if I do the wrong thing?' In his childhood home, was there enough of what Brian would later call 'emotional security'? Impossible to know how this scarred the Wilson boys.

A CHILD IS BORN

Outside the home, Brian was a typical teenager: he loved sports, loved having fun, loved making people laugh. Tall, athletically-gifted, he played center field on the Hawthorne High baseball team and quarterback on the football team until he decided he would rather run track than get slammed to the turf.

Rich Sloan, one of his closest friends, fondly remembers Brian.

Rich Sloan: 'He wasn't a serious person like in 'In My Room.' He was out there to have fun and for everybody else to have fun at the same time. If he could get other people to laugh, he felt everybody would feel comfortable. He loved to draw attention to himself. With humour. He would do something comical, trip over a chair. He was happy, even if he was the butt of the joke. Brian loved to have people laugh.

'The parents loved to have Brian come over because he was a breath of fresh air. When Brian entered a room, he lit it up. People were always happy to see Brian. He brought so much happiness and joy with him. He just made everybody smile.' ☺

Robin Hood and Brian became best friends in the seventh grade; he remembers Brian with great warmth.

Robin Hood: 'We were joined at the hip . . . from the time I met him until the last time I saw him, we were trying to make each other laugh . . . But there's another side of him who's very shy. And it took a while for him to get to know people, and once he did . . . he gained a lot of friends, and then he could joke with everybody. But he had to know you first. There is a shy side to him.'

Brian was never shy about singing.

With his beautiful boy soprano voice, Brian always loved to sing – at Wilson family singalongs, Christmas carolling, hanging out with his cousin Mike Love, who loved R&B and doo-wop. Brian even performed at a high school assembly.

Murry Wilson recognised his son's gift, bought Brian a reel-to-reel tape recorder, and built a music room for Brian.

Carl Wilson: 'There were many years of his life where he did nothing but play the piano. Months at a time. Days on end. He'd listen to Four Freshmen records. Just all music.'

Brian spent countless hours obsessively deconstructing the harmonies of the Four Freshmen. Brian's musicality would soon pay off.

In September 1961, along with brothers Dennis and Carl, first cousin

Mike and a high school friend, Alan Jardine, the five not-yet-Beach Boys learned a song called 'Surfin'' (written by Brian and Mike). It was kind of primitive doo-wop, not the genuine guitar-driven instrumental music of Dick Dale and the Deltones. Rather, it was a vocal song *about* surfing.

Up until that mythical moment when Dennis said to Brian he should write a song about surfing, a coastline craze, there was no group. These weren't young musicians who were pursuing a career in music.

At the time, Brian was 19, at El Camino Junior College, studying psychology. Mike was 20, working two jobs to support his wife and young child. Dennis was 16, at Hawthorne High; Carl was only 14. Al was thinking of going to dental school.

But fate was on their side. The boys met an independent record label owner, went into a local studio and recorded 'Surfin''; it quickly became a hit on L.A. radio. They had wanted to call themselves The Pendletones; for better or for worse, music industry exec Russ Regan came up with their name: The Beach Boys.

To put their overnight success in perspective: Down Under, the brothers Gibb – the Bee Gees – would struggle for *nearly a decade* before they had their first hit.

On the other side of the Atlantic, in 1957, John Lennon asked Paul McCartney to join his group, The Quarrymen. Soon after, Paul suggested that George Harrison be added to the lineup. They eventually renamed the group The Beatles. And regardless of how much talent and charisma and ambition and determination they had, it would be *nearly five years* before they would get a major label recording contract.

For this baby band of Hawthorne Hotshots, it would be more like *five months*. It was as if The Beach Boys had won the lottery. Their good fortune would continue because the group had one member who spilled out catchy melodies like Niagara Falls.

IN HIS ROOM

'A great artist . . . must be shaken by the naked truths that will not be comforted. This divine discontent, this disequilibrium, this state of inner tension is the source of artistic energy.'

Goethe

BRIAN: 'WHEN THE BEACH BOYS AND I MADE MUSIC AND WE HEARD IT ON the radio, it was the biggest thrill in the world. I couldn't believe it.'

The Beach Boys would probably have been one-hit wonders if not for two things: Brian's growing and immense talent and his father's resolve to have success in the music business – if not for himself, then for his sons.

Beach Boy **David Marks:** 'Murry wasn't so much a manager as a promoter . . . He had faith in us. If there was no Murry Wilson, there would have been no Beach Boys.'

The Beatles and Beach Boys share several superficial similarities: Their names begin with the letters 'BEA,' their prolific melody-writing bass players were born two days apart in June of 1942, and they were signed to major record companies in 1962 and began to have hits immediately.

But, in the *SMiLE* story, perhaps the most significant difference wasn't in their makeup or their education or their comparable musical experience or talent or their aspirations or intellectual curiosity (or lack thereof) or their cultural impact, but in their respective managers.

The Beatles' manager in 1962 was Brian Epstein, a restless but artistically-educated man from a well-to-do family with an unshakable belief that The Beatles would one day be the biggest band in the world.

The Beach Boys' manager was Murry Wilson, a man who saw the group as a *family business*.

It was Murry's persistence that secured them a contract with Capitol Records, and he shrewdly held on to their publishing. In the early years, he promoted The Beach Boys tirelessly. But beyond being 'successful,' there was no bigger picture. The Beach Boys existed for the benefit of the Wilson family, meaning Murry, Audree, and their three sons. He ran Sea of Tunes as his own personal publishing fiefdom; nephew and lead singer Mike Love was often unfairly left off of songwriting credits.

More significantly, anybody who wasn't a blood relative was an outsider, to be regarded with suspicion. These 'outsiders,' Murry believed, were going to exploit Brian. This became a recurring theme. *Loyalty to the family band* was a priority.

However, in the early and mid-1960s, Brian liked writing with 'outsiders' (be it Gary Usher, Bob Norberg, Jan Berry, Roger Christian, or Russ Titelman) despite what Murry or cousin Mike (Brian's most successful hitmaking collaborator) might think was best for *the family business*. Brian could write a great song – a hit song – with anybody. Including himself. 'Surfer Girl,' the first song he ever wrote, featured words *and* music by Brian Wilson.

From 1962 through 1965, on his way to creating a body of work that would earn him a place in the Songwriters Hall of Fame, The Beach Boys' induction into the Rock & Roll Hall of Fame, and countless other awards – despite a childhood injury that left him almost completely deaf in his right ear – Brian composed, arranged, produced, and sang the high harmony (and the soaring, operatic lead vocals) on nearly a dozen Top 10 Hits (including three number ones) and almost forty Top 40 hits.

Richard Williams, *UK music journalist:* 'They were obviously fantastic pop records. In those days, you had a single with an A-side and a B-side. And very often on those early Beach Boys records, the B-side told you more about the group than the A-side, so you would hear these wonderful ballads like 'The Warmth of the Sun' and 'Kiss Me Baby.' And you'd stop to hear what richness there was in the music, that this was more than just a group putting out hit singles.'

What was going on behind the scenes belied their beautiful harmonies. With Murry Wilson as their hard-driving manager, being a Beach Boy was never a carefree existence.

In 1963, during early Beach Boys tours, Brian didn't enjoy going on the road; Al Jardine substituted for Brian, alongside David Marks.

IN HIS ROOM

David Marks: 'Everything Murry did was out of love for his sons; he wanted to see them succeed. The psychological approach he had towards Brian, the guilt was, "You're letting your brothers down. How do you expect the band to flourish if you're not out there doing all the tours . . ." I can see how that might have driven Brian a little bit crazy . . . to feel guilty about doing something that you love and that you're a genius at . . . that has to be really horrible. There must have been a lot of turmoil in Brian's head over that stuff.'

Annie Wilson-Karges: 'This was a man that was so emotional about his sons. There's a lot that's been said about him, but there's no doubt in my mind that he adored his sons, especially Brian. So, there's a lot there.'

In early 1964, The Beach Boys fired Murry Wilson as their manager. By then, David Marks's first tenure in the band had ended, but he had seen the dynamic at work.

David Marks: 'Here's what was going on in Brian's head. "Murry's getting in the way. It's messing me up. I can't produce. I can't write. This can't continue, and we're going to do it without you." And, of course, Murry was crushed, but what could he do? At that point, Brian really was in control, and he knew it. Without Brian, there wasn't going to be any more Beach Boys. Or anything else.'

In mid-1963, Brian took over formal, credited production of the records and began to churn out the hits. By the end of 1964, to exclusively do what *he* loved . . . write songs and make records . . . he knew he needed to stop touring.

In late December of '64, just three weeks after marrying sixteen-year-old Marilyn Rovell, the responsibility of being a Beach Boy on the road and then coming home to compose, arrange and produce their records had become overwhelming. The stress bubbled to the surface, and Brian had a breakdown.

GOD ONLY KNOWS

'I want to touch people with my art. I want them to say, "He feels deeply, he feels tenderly."'

Vincent van Gogh

WE CAN ONLY IMAGINE WHAT IT WAS LIKE TO BE IN THE BEACH BOYS IN 1965-1967, how it felt to be in the group and live in Brian's shadow, subject to his every idea or whim, musical or otherwise. Or how Brian felt as the leader of the group whose supremacy as the biggest band in America had been instantly overshadowed by The Beatles.

To understand exactly what happened in the world of Brian and The Beach Boys, one would need a time machine and a team of forensic psychologists. A lie detector?

But getting to the *absolute* truth? Well, that's impossible. It's kind of like looking at this saga through a kaleidoscope. Each time you turn it, you see Brian's life and the *SMiLE* story from a different angle.

For me, putting this oral history together was just a bit like *SMiLE*. Not in terms of its genius, artistry, or ambition, but in the sense of piecing together a story that has a million fragments and so many of them are missing.

There has always been an inexplicable aspect to this legend, which is one reason I named my last book *God Only Knows*. Because that is often the answer when trying to get to the truth of any aspect of Brian and The Beach Boys' history.

There are more than two sides to look at how the *SMiLE* era unfolded and folded up its tents. And what it meant to The Beach Boys' career. In literary terms, in interviews about *SMiLE*, Brian can sometimes be a most imperfect narrator, giving contradictory answers to how LSD affected him, why he may have felt the need to self-medicate as *SMiLE* was falling apart, why he shelved it and decided he would no longer be The Beach Boys' producer.

So, here we go. We will just follow a yellow brick road that is filled with highlights and roadblocks, potholes and detours, and eventually we will get to the promised land of 2004.

It begins in 1965, with a simple decision.

Brian: 'I quit touring because I wanted to write songs at home. I couldn't write on the road very good. I wanted to write at home, so I could produce tracks for "the Boys" to come in and sing to.'

For a while, after leaving the Wilson family home, before he married, Brian had shared a South Bay apartment with Bob Norberg (during his college days before he became a commercial airline pilot).

Bob Norberg: 'The main thing is that the Brian I knew is a *good* person at heart. I don't think he wants ill will for anybody. He's not malicious at all . . . I don't remember ever hearing him ever say anything that would hurt you . . . In the early days, the things that were unusual about [Brian] would be his kindness, his genuine interest in helping and having you participate in what he was doing . . . His openness.'

Echoing Rich Sloan, Bob remembers that Brian would 'do silly things to make you laugh. I think he was easily amused . . . but I think you have to realize, in his head, he's still way ahead of the people around him.'

Working at Hollywood recording studios, Brian was meeting a world of new people. Individuals who had different experiences, different thoughts about the world, different talents. He also spent time at the Rovell family home in L.A.'s Fairfax district where he was reportedly welcomed with open arms.

So, in 1965, as The Beach Boys toured without Brian, their musical leader was in L.A., recording the instrumental tracks for their next record. Inspired by his producing idol, Phil Spector, Brian had begun working regularly with the best studio musicians in the business; his increasingly sophisticated compositions needed these instrumentalists who were schooled in jazz and classical music. In Los Angeles, that could only mean one thing – a clique of 'first call' players who were at the very centre of the music business.

Carol Kaye: 'We were working for Quincy Jones. We were working for Phil Spector. There was something special about Brian.'

Hal Blaine: 'I don't know of any other artist that was doing the entire package by himself. Brian was doing everything. He was arranging, writing, singing. He was part of the group.'

Don Randi: 'You could see it in his eyes. He was a constant thinker. He was planning ahead. Always planning ahead.'

Hal: 'Brian knew exactly what he wanted. It was all in his head. And we were all amazed; we watched Brian really blossom into this incredible arranger.'

Don: 'You'd say to yourself, "God, I wonder where he's gonna take this?"'

Carol: 'Brian took chances. He didn't put it in a framework. He didn't try to do like other people. He had his own thing going.'

Don: 'Hip jazz chords and fusing 'em with the rhythm of rock 'n' roll – he was probably the first fusion artist.'

Hal: 'All of a sudden, I started hearing these things coming from Brian . . . over a period of records, months, maybe a year, his harmonies, his chord structures, were getting more sophisticated.'

Van Dyke Parks: 'Studios [back then] were very, very primitive compared to what is offered today. Except in one respect. You'd find musicians in them in those days. Competing musicians. A-list musicians. Playing real instruments really well. Either through reading or through their extemporaneous skills. And it took both to participate in Brian Wilson sessions.'

Carol: 'We wondered what [he] was gonna come up [with]. And so we could hardly wait to work for him.'

Brian: 'The musicians that I used, the studio musicians, helped me to get across my music because they were really good players.'

The records Brian produced in 1965 – for The Beach Boys and Glen Campbell – were becoming more emotionally expressive. With the help of these remarkable players, he was putting his heart on his musical sleeve.

Alan Jardine: 'Brian was growing exponentially.'

He was also growing as a person, hanging out with a new circle of friends. So not only was Brian no longer part of the touring group, but he had left his Hawthorne roots behind, becoming friends with people who did not necessarily meet with the Beach Boy family's approval.

This group of friends and eventual collaborators would ultimately include such key figures as Tony Asher and Van Dyke Parks, David

GOD ONLY KNOWS

Anderle and Danny Hutton (pre-Three Dog Night). David Crosby of The Byrds. Some were older and more experienced than Brian. Most were better educated. Except for Crosby, none had yet had significant success in the music business. It seems these 'outsiders' weren't welcomed with open arms if they 'threatened' to disrupt The Beach Boys' family business.

On a list all his own was Loren Schwartz, a Beverly Hills kid who became a William Morris agent. Like some in the L.A. music scene at the time, he was a follower of the spiritual practice of Subud; eventually he changed his name to reflect that and became Lorren Daro.

Brian: 'He was a very aggressive type of guy with a very, very egotistical attitude . . . He was a typical friend of mine . . . I liked his sense of humor. I thought he was a very funny guy . . . A sense of humour is important in life. With him, it meant a lot to be funny.'

Lorren: 'He was an innocent. He had no guile about him, no maliciousness about him. He was a truly good heart, self-effacing, humble, sweet as sugar, *try to please everybody all the time* . . . I never saw a glint of anything negative in him at all. He was an angel.'

To Murry Wilson, people like Lorren were 'Hollywood phonies.' Lorren's biggest 'crime' was turning Brian on to the drugs of the day. From the point of view of The Beach Boys family, Daro – one of Brian's new friends – was 'the wrong crowd.' In this interview from 2004, before his passing, Daro saw it very differently.

Lorren: 'Brian fell in with the wrong crowd. It was his family. That was what his problem was. He just lived in fear of bad reactions from [them] . . . I tried to tell him to make his own decisions and not be influenced by everybody, 'cause that's what was driving him crazy.'

Even though The Beach Boys had fired him as manager, as their father and publisher, Murry Wilson continued to show up at recording sessions.

Hal Blaine: 'Murry wanted to be the producer . . . But Murry became, as they say, a pain in the neck, and it really bothered Brian . . . the only time I ever saw anything that rubbed Brian wrong, I think, was his dad.'

At instrumental tracking dates circa 1965, while Brian worked in the studio with the musicians, Lorren recalled being in the booth, listening to the rants of Brian's father. It was almost like being in the middle of a Shakespearean tragedy.

Hal: 'Eventually Brian banned Murry from the studio, which was a very sad thing. I'm sure he loved him. I know he had built in certain things about his father hitting him as a child, things like that.'

Daro felt strongly that the biggest problem facing Brian wasn't the arrival of The Beatles, but of the ties that bind.

Lorren: 'He couldn't handle it.'

Brian's love/hate relationship with his father had seemingly established a pattern for his life. However, it wouldn't stop him from pushing forward, at least for a couple of years. In the mid-1960s, Brian was eager not just to grow musically but to learn about the expanding horizons of the decade.

Hanging out at Daro's West Hollywood apartment – something of a self-styled rock 'n' roll salon – Brian met a different, 'hipper,' universe of people. Daro exposed him to metaphysics, which Brian embraced.

Lorren: 'I told Brian [that] the highest calling is to be an individual who makes his own decisions, who is responsible for everything that happens to him, and chooses basically everything that happens to him. I got him to question the authority of his father and of his family . . . That's all you can really do . . . He was really finding himself through people like me . . . endlessly curious . . . The rest was just coping . . . All of them [his family] wanted him to be what he had been in Hawthorne. And they endlessly mourned the loss of the "old Hawthorne Brian."'

Drugs were prevalent in the music business. Brian wanted to smoke marijuana with Daro. Daro refused.

Lorren: 'He finally convinced me. He said, "Everyone's offering me pot, but I keep turning it down 'cause I wanna get high with you." . . . And Marilyn found out and Carl found out and Mike found out and Murry found out, and they all went fuckin' nuts.'

Were they right? In a sense, absolutely. They had witnessed first-hand Brian's insecurities. His breakdown in December 1964. But in the 1960s, Brian told everybody – The Beach Boys, his family, the musicians, and his friends – what he wanted *them* to do.

Carl Wilson: 'He's one of the nerviest people I've ever met. He does exactly what he wants to do.'

All across America, parents in the 1960s at 'the dawning of The Age of Aquarius' were terrified by the changing world. Drugs were part of the burgeoning counterculture.

GOD ONLY KNOWS

In the centres of popular music – London, New York, and L.A. – there was a constant search for what was new. Musically, Brian was always enthralled by new sounds; he could satisfy his artistic desires. But from everything he heard, he came to believe that his consciousness needed to expand too. Meaning a still legal drug called LSD.

Through the years, Brian's family blames Lorren for introducing Brian to LSD, which they blame for Brian and *SMiLE*'s downfall, earning Lorren the eternal enmity of The Beach Boys family.

Brian: 'Lorren Schwartz was the guy that gave me LSD.'

Lorren: 'He finally came to me and said, "I wanna drop acid." I said, "No way. I will not be responsible for that."[. . .] He finally said to me one day, "If you don't take me on a trip, I'm gonna take acid from" – and he mentioned another person. I had to – 'cause he knew I'd do it right. So I got him at my house one night and I gave him 125 mics [micrograms] of purple liquid Owsley, the real stuff. And I didn't take it. 'Cause you didn't do that . . . Someone is the guide and someone gets high, that's how it is.'

Brian: 'So I took it not knowing what it would do.'

How much LSD did Brian take in his life? How much damage did it do? Brian's answers on the subject are contradictory.

In a Fall 1966 piece for the *L.A. Times' West* magazine, Brian told writer Tom Nolan about his first LSD experiences.

Brian: 'About a year ago . . . I took a full dose of LSD, and later, another time, I took a smaller dose. And I learned a lot of things, like patience, understanding. I can't teach you or tell you what I learned from taking LSD. But I consider it a very religious experience.'

A decade later, during the infamous 'Brian's Back' debacle of 1976, he would appear on Mike Douglas's talk show.

Brian: 'I did my dose of LSD. It shattered my mind, and I came back, thank God, I don't know, in how many pieces.'

In 2004, during the making of *Beautiful Dreamer*, Brian told me he began experiencing auditory hallucinations after his first LSD trip. He also stated this:

Brian: 'After I took LSD, I was glad I did. Because it gave me a deeper understanding of myself and my music . . . opened up my ability to create music and sing and gave me a deeper feeling about music, a deeper understanding of my feelings, my musical feelings.'

In 2005, on *The Charlie Rose Show*, when asked what he might have done differently in his life, he said, 'I would not have taken LSD. It killed me. It ruined me. It put my mind away. It was a rough, rough drug.'

In another interview Brian said, 'I took the LSD and that just totally tore my head off. Acid was like everything I could ever be or everything I wouldn't be. You just come to grips with what you are and what you can do and what you can't do. And you learn to face it.'

Mind-expanding or mind-shattering? A religious experience or a psychological reckoning?

In Brian's story, it can all be true.

★ ★ ★ ★

In 1965, Brian was diving into new experiences – taking LSD, reading books on metaphysics and philosophy – moving in the opposite direction from the group and his family.

Lorren Daro: 'They were all saying the same thing to him. "What are you doing?" And he had to justify it both ways. But it was Carl that really upset him 'cause he could never explain it to Carl. I would listen to him say, "Don't worry. I'm not hurting myself. And everyone does this. This is good; I'm more creative."'

While this may be a touch self-justifying, Daro concludes: 'I believe that [first LSD] trip changed everything in Brian's life. Everything. And it did not make him crazy. He began to write all the best songs of his career right from that point, 'Good Vibrations,' *Pet Sounds*, all of it just emerged from there.'

★ ★ ★ ★

'Life is not a support system for art. It is the other way around.'
Stephen King

In 1966, Brian composed, arranged, and produced *Pet Sounds*, still considered to be one of the greatest albums in pop music history, and the earthshakingly innovative 'Good Vibrations,' perhaps the most revolutionary single of the decade.

Before recording sessions for *Pet Sounds*, both Carl and Brian remembered having prayer sessions. *They* knew there was a holy aspect to what they were doing.

GOD ONLY KNOWS

Carl Wilson: 'Brian was always more into music as . . . a sound feeling and vibration . . . a really heavy vibration says a lot more than a million words could in eternity say. As far as really holy sounds go.'

In our conversation in 2004 for *Beautiful Dreamer,* Carl's first wife, Annie Wilson-Karges, clearly recalled the divine aspect of the work.

Annie: 'Just to underscore, Brian's an incredible spiritual being, first and foremost, for me . . . Carl and Dennis were just always his little brothers. Carl was always his little brother who would just do what his big brother wanted him to. That dynamic of older brother/little brother was just so real . . . really neat to watch.'

Carl: 'The idea of making music that could make people feel better became like a crusade.'

Annie: 'That was just one of those things that went with their work, with Brian's work. There was more than one prayer session . . . Not every time. But to have a prayer session was not unusual. It's just where Brian was coming from, the depth of where he was coming from. And everybody was on the same page – [I'm] talking about the Wilsons. That was always the underlying theme.'

Guy Webster, *photographer:* 'When he was doing *Pet Sounds* and things like that, I think he was in competition, maybe with himself or with the world or with The Beatles, and he had to make it perfect.'

Brian: 'I smoked some marijuana and listened to [The Beatles' new album] *Rubber Soul*, and it blew my mind. It just totally took my mind away. I thought to myself, "God, they're so good, and I feel competitive about this." I said, "I want to do something good like *Rubber Soul.*" So, I went in and did *Pet Sounds* . . . I was trying to get across a feeling of love and depth in the background tracks. Love and depth.'

Musically, he was certainly successful. But for the ideas he needed to express lyrically, he wanted help – a new songwriting partner.

Brian: 'Lorren [Daro] told me that Tony [Asher] was an advertising agent and that he was good with words, and that I might want to write with him. So I called him up and he came over, and we started writing (*Brian snaps fingers*) right off the bat. We didn't even have to talk. We just started writing . . . I was very happy with Tony's lyrics. I thought they were very creative and very tender . . . 'God Only Knows,' we wrote in a half-hour, believe it or not. It took us a half-hour. That's all it took. And it was like experiencing "loveland."'

Tony Asher, *lyricist:* 'I can remember just being blown away by so many of the things he did . . . I was stunned sometimes by how much he had going on in his head that I never dreamed was there . . . It was staggering.'

Lenny Waronker, *record producer:* 'There were elements of Americana in that record. The string stuff I always felt was [Aaron] Copeland-esque in a way. It was clearly a young composer who was beyond his time and dipping into areas of music that pop music had never heard before. Always open and beautiful and heaven-like.'

For those to whom *Pet Sounds* would be shocking, especially at Capitol Records, there was plenty of musical and lyrical evidence of the direction Brian was heading in 1965. Beginning with Side Two of *The Beach Boys Today!*, he had shifted his focus, composing, arranging, and producing beautiful ballads that reflected his feelings about life and love.

But there is no question that 1966's *Pet Sounds* was a line in the sand of Brian's musical life and in the group's history. Van Dyke Parks elaborated on Brian's musical growth.

Van Dyke: '[With] the music of *Pet Sounds,* he almost got to the point of realizing what soloistic values there were in music and in what instruments could do to, in a solo sense, to bring certain strengths to a piece. And I talk about economy. He could do more with less. He was turning into a sage, wise beyond his years. And *Pet Sounds* gave him that vision, that revelation. He was ready to handle sounds. He was ready to bring more people into play. He was thinking outside the box. And at the same time, he was redefining what a song could be. Sexualized, yes, for sure. Less obsessed with dance all the time.'

Pet Sounds, primarily written and recorded in the winter of 1966, was the album that changed everything for Brian, The Beach Boys, and the world of popular music. The album would come to be regarded as one of the high-water marks of the rock era. But that wasn't immediately the case in America in 1966. Or in The Beach Boys' world.

The instrumental tracks were recorded while the group was on tour, and when they returned from Japan, they weren't all happy.

Brian: 'When they heard the tracks, they didn't like it, because it wasn't surf music anymore. It was a notch up, a step up, in creativity. I thought they'd like it. I thought they would really like it a lot. I was disappointed. Mike is the one who didn't like it the most. He's the one who made the most criticism, critical remarks. It made me feel a little bad, but I got over it.'

Mark Volman, *The Turtles, The Mothers of Invention:* 'Brian was trying to make an incredible record. And that was hard for the band to understand that Brian wasn't trying to do [a] Beach Boys [record]. And if he could've sat down and explained himself and said, "As soon as I'm done with this [*Pet Sounds*], we'll do a Beach Boy record." And it never really worked out that way. In fact, it got more and more disjointed.'

Tony Asher: 'Brian's ability to stand up for what he believed in depended entirely on who he had to stand against. Meaning, he had no problem with me or [engineer] Chuck Britz. I think the difficulty arose when he was dealing with family . . . I think Brian was uncomfortable with the notion that people felt that since most of the creative genius was coming from him that he was somehow better than the other guys.'

In early 1966, the listening public didn't know or really care that Brian was the musical leader. They just loved The Beach Boys.

Tony: 'He was interested in sharing the limelight . . . he was uncomfortable with the notion that he was great, and that the rest of the group were just sort of along for the ride . . . to keep the peace and to give the other guys in the group their due, he didn't want to bully them that much. He would bully them in terms of "You guys aren't singing it right," or "You're not trying hard enough," or "You're not listening to what I'm telling you."'

Mike Love, who had co-written more hit songs with Brian than anybody else, perhaps felt he had been cast aside for a stranger. He might have believed, 'These are beautiful songs. I can write lyrics for them.' But in 1966, that wasn't what Brian wanted. More problematic, Mike didn't hear this new music as commercial.

At the time, Brian explained the conflict to Asher.

Tony: '[Brian] said, "There's some feeling among the guys that this is not what they were expecting, and that they're fearful that it's too much of a departure," and he said exactly that. "Don't worry about it. I'm committed to this, and I think it's terrific." And they were saying, "This is not what we've done before." So, he saw that as a kind of a validation.'

Brian: 'I told the guys, I said, "Look, we're going to go through this. We're going to get this done."'

Brian repeated it for emphasis. 'We're going to go through it, and we're going to get it done. And they did it.'

Brian was a taskmaster, with perfect pitch, and it was his pursuit of 'the feel' that made recording the group's background vocals challenging. In a 2023 interview on *The Vinyl Guide* podcast, Mike Love admitted that the vocal sessions weren't 'always pleasant.'

That's putting it mildly.

Tony: 'During one session, when Mike was in the studio on mic and I was in the booth, and he knew I was there, he made some comments about some of the lyrics that suggested that he didn't think it was appropriate. He never was critical of what it was, he was just saying it wasn't right for The Beach Boys. He was very aware of what he referred to as "the formula."'

Beach Boys' vocal sessions were hard work, and for Tony Asher, not a happy memory.

Tony: 'I was beginning to feel uncomfortable there. People didn't talk to me. Brian did. And Carl did. Carl wanted everything to be friendly and warm and loving. And so, he always smiled and sort of patted me on the back and said, "Hey, this is great." But there were other people in the room who were not cordial to me, so . . . I decided not to go to more of the sessions with The Beach Boys.'

Danny Hutton, *Three Dog Night:* 'Brian could have sung all the parts on *Pet Sounds* himself. It probably would have sounded almost the same . . . so it wasn't a thing where he was dismissing them, didn't want them in there.'

With two instrumentals, two tracks which featured Brian's solo lead vocals, and 'God Only Knows,' which has just Carl, Brian, and Bruce Johnston, *Pet Sounds* was indeed very different. Brian sang most of the leads, and excluding 'Sloop John B,' it has less than ten minutes of Beach Boys background harmonies.

Brian: 'They thought it was a little bit too arty and a little bit too much, explorative in music. And after they got their vocals done, they really liked it.'

Both Capitol Records and the group were concerned that their fans would not embrace the new direction. Despite those concerns, Brian couldn't wait to get his new music out to the world.

GOD ONLY KNOWS

Tony: 'From time to time, Brian would say, "Wow, this is not what people expect when they buy a Beach Boys album. This is going to surprise people."'

There were lots of surprises ahead.

Brian: 'As soon as we got 'Caroline, No' recorded, I said to myself, "That might be something to explore a solo career with . . ." Not a career, but a solo release under my name. So, we tried it, and it didn't sell very good.'

Actually, Brian's first solo single went to number 32, one of four singles from the album to reach the Top 40. 'God Only Knows' went to number 39 in the US, where it was the B-side of 'Wouldn't It Be Nice,' which peaked at number eight. 'Sloop John B' hit number three. The album itself reached number ten.

Brian: 'A lot of people told me they liked it a lot. It was a very successful industry album.'

Burt Bacharach: 'I think *Pet Sounds* is one of the great albums, pop records.'

Eric Clapton: 'All of us [in Cream] – Jack Bruce, Ginger Baker, and I – are absolutely and completely knocked out by *Pet Sounds*. I consider it to be one of the greatest pop LPs to ever be released. Brian Wilson is without doubt a pop genius.'

Lenny Waronker: 'You really felt like you were in another world when you were hearing that record . . . He was investing these sounds that were absolutely unique and "right on" in terms of what they were doing for the song. He seemed to have a great sense of how to make a song very, very special [and] not take away from the song with fancy production. [It was] much more about adding colours that were unique, fresh, newly-developed, and it all added up to this amazing thing that I'm not sure anybody's done it since, quite like that.'

Randy Newman: '*Pet Sounds* is a remarkable achievement.'

Jimmy Webb: 'I think *Pet Sounds* was probably the most significant record of our generation.'

Lenny: 'It was a massive record, and it was thought of as this very, very special amazing record that covered incredible ground . . . the respect that people had, musical respect that it had with musicians and other artists was such that you knew it was going to be a classic.'

Jimmy: 'We're suddenly faced with the inescapable conclusion that without *Pet Sounds*, we would be looking at a much different musical landscape . . . So we're really talking about something that kind of took on an awesome significance.'

Lenny: 'The record itself had a beauty about it that I don't think we'd heard before. There was just something spiritual about it, forgetting the title.'

Brian: 'John [Lennon] and Paul [McCartney] called me after they heard *Pet Sounds* and told me how much they liked it. And it was quite an honour for me. I was at my house on Laurel Way in Beverly Hills, and I got the call from them one night. That was the first time I had ever talked to them. It was an actual thrill for me. It really was. I told them, I said, "I'm looking forward to hearing your new records, something new." And they said, "Well, expect something good."'

How big was *Pet Sounds'* influence, then and now?

Sir George Martin: '*Sgt. Pepper* was our *attempt* to equal *Pet Sounds*.'

Sir Paul McCartney *(in 1990)*: 'I love the album so much. I've just bought my kids each a copy of it for their education in life—I figure no one is educated musically 'til they've heard that album.'

Questlove: 'The day I moved to London in 1993, side one of *Pet Sounds* was playing at a record store. I had never heard this music in my life, but I felt like I had known those songs forever. I never had music really penetrate a layer of my soul like this.'

But back in the day, the lyrical subject matter, as well as the songs themselves, were a fundamental departure for the regular Beach Boys fan who was expecting songs about girls and cars and surfing. The formula.

Pet Sounds would sow the first significant seeds of creative dissension within the group as to the direction they were going in – or should go in.

Looking back, it was but 'a tempest in a teapot' compared to what lay ahead in the *SMiLE* era.

★ ★ ★ ★

'It is cruel, you know, that music should be so beautiful. It has the beauty of loneliness and of pain: of strength and freedom. The beauty of disappointment and never-satisfied love. The cruel beauty of nature and everlasting beauty of monotony.' **Benjamin Britten**

Brian (*Beat* magazine, 1966): 'I try to seek out the best elements of people. Because, after all, people are part of my music. A lot of the songs I write are the result of emotional experiences, of sadness and pain. And you don't get those experiences except in association with people.'

From almost the very beginning, Brian had been writing melancholy music (e.g., 'The Lonely Sea,' 'In My Room,' 'The Warmth of the Sun,' 'Don't Worry Baby,' 'Guess I'm Dumb,' and 'Please Let Me Wonder'), but there had never been an entire Beach Boys album of emotional music ('Sloop John B' excepted).

So what went wrong? Why did *Pet Sounds* not sell well? Why was it their first album in three years to not 'go Gold'?

One theory was that the cover photo, shot at the San Diego Zoo, led some to believe it was a children's album and not buy it. But most significantly, it was Capitol Records' lack of belief in the album. An album with four Top 40 hits might have been a much bigger success had Capitol Records given it their full support.

To wit: *Pet Sounds* was released in mid-May of 1966. Reportedly, 300,000 copies were pressed and shipped. However, when record stores sold out and ordered new ones to stock their bins, they didn't necessarily get more copies of *Pet Sounds*. Instead, *within two months*, Capitol Records released *Best of The Beach Boys*. Greatest hits albums were often an indication that the record company didn't think there would be any more hits.

Mike Love, on the 2023 *Vinyl Guide* podcast: 'Brian and I presented the album to Capitol. Our A&R guy [Karl Engemann] played it for their marketing team, and Karl came back and said, "Gee guys, this is great. But could you do something more like 'California Girls' or 'I Get Around' or 'Fun, Fun, Fun' . . ." In other words, they wanted that 45 RPM hit formula to continue ad infinitum. But we were interested in breaking boundaries and experimenting, getting a little complex in the orchestration.'

We were? Interesting.

Carl Wilson picks up the story, in a 1974 BBC documentary interview with Bob Harris, explaining that setting up their own label, Brother Records, in 1966, was, in part, a response to Capitol's reaction.

Carl Wilson: 'It was freedom from limitations and restrictions working with Capitol. They're a very big company, but it was difficult to get the ideas across and have them be receptive to what we wanted to do. It goes back to *Pet Sounds* being different from the things we'd done. I think some of the people there didn't think it was commercial. That direction. They were just real resistant to it, so that sort of led to a sort of dissatisfaction.'

Al Coury, a Capitol executive, on that same BBC documentary: 'Some of the people were carried away with the album and felt it was an important album. Other people probably couldn't relate to it. Because I think the album was probably ahead of its time. I think most people today realize it was.'

England didn't feel that way.

Al Coury: 'The album did receive good exposure at the time. But it didn't sell. Retail activity on the LP was not as good as previously released Beach Boys albums.'

How could it sell if it wasn't in the stores?

Coury didn't think that *Pet Sounds* helped pave the way for *Sgt. Pepper*.

Sirs McCartney and Martin would certainly disagree. John Lennon, too. In December 1965, in *Melody Maker's* 'Blind Date' article, Lennon had this to say about 'The Little Girl I Once Knew,' the last studio single before *Pet Sounds*. And one that musically foreshadowed what was to come.

John Lennon: 'This is the greatest! [. . .] It's fantastic . . . It's all Brian Wilson. He just uses the voices as instruments. He never tours or anything. He just sits at home thinking up fantastic arrangements out of his head.'

But was the album, as Coury said, too early? Or was it that Capitol didn't know how to sell it?

Karl Engemann: 'Capitol Records loved The Beach Boys. They didn't criticize them in any way. Except they thought that maybe going in the direction of *Pet Sounds* was [not] going to be as wonderful [translation: sell as many copies] as . . . hot rod records, the surf records. Those kinds of things.'

Today, *Pet Sounds* might be described as 'off-brand.' Back then, Capitol was more directly dismissive.

Brian: 'They said, "It's not commercial music."'

In Capitol's eyes, its 'only' reaching number ten on the charts in the US made it a comparative failure.

Karl Engemann: 'It hadn't [immediately] gone to the same heights on the charts as some of the prior records, so Capitol, right away, in order to make [sales] quota, they hurried and put out *Best of The Beach Boys*.'

GOD ONLY KNOWS

Bruce Johnston: 'We have *Pet Sounds* out. By the way, we're going to put out *Best of The Beach Boys* . . . can you believe that?'

Mike Love: 'We were in competition with our history.'

In Don Was's revelatory documentary, *Brian Wilson: I Just Wasn't Made for These Times,* Marilyn Wilson, Brian's first wife, said when *Pet Sounds* wasn't as successful as Brian expected it would be, 'It really hurt him . . . He couldn't understand it. "Why aren't people willing to expand and accept more and grow as I'm growing?"'

Karl Engemann: 'And it didn't do as well as some of the other albums, and it might have had there been more of a spirit within the company, "This is great, and we're going to push this and take it where it should be."'

With *Best of The Beach Boys*, what Capitol did was almost a self-fulfilling prophecy, as if the label was sabotaging Brian's new creative direction.

How did it feel on the inside when this was all happening?

Annie Wilson-Karges: 'It was disapproval and then fear. In the middle of all of that, I remember the guys getting negative feedback from Capitol Records about the songs they were recording on *Pet Sounds*. Just a whole lot of disapproval, and then fear of the acceptance of where the music was going. And I think it affected the group.

'The disapproval from Capitol put questions in The Beach Boys' heads. Especially Brian's head, since he was creating it and pulling it in the direction he was pulling it. I think that doubt was definitely in his head, transmitted to him. The rest of the guys – I think it was really confusing for them. I really do. In so many different ways. Just group unity, and "Where are we going?" All of that. It just made everything be a question. I think it was lack of support from the record company, and then dissension among the guys. I think it transmitted that fear and doubt and insecurity into the group.'

In England, it wasn't an issue.

England embraced *Pet Sounds* – thanks in part to promotional work done by recently-minted Beach Boy Bruce Johnston – where it was a big critical and commercial success.

The late rock journalist Ray Coleman wrote in the *Disc and Music Echo* in June 1966: 'A superb, important and really exciting collection . . . they seem to have found their direction under the clever guidance of Brian Wilson and this should gain them thousands of new fans . . . *Pet Sounds* has brilliantly tapped [into] the pulse of the musical times.'

Did Capitol read this? Did The Beach Boys? Did they understand the magnitude of what Brian had achieved?

Richard Williams, *music journalist:* 'It was very competitive in Britain in the mid-sixties – The Who, The Beatles, The Rolling Stones, The Kinks, The Yardbirds and so on . . . Each [new] record was a challenge to the other groups.'

Bob Harris, presenter, *The Old Grey Whistle Test:* 'I was 20 in 1966 . . . We were very much enamoured with the sort of arriving psychedelic sounds. The Beatles had already given us a taste . . . certainly on *Revolver* . . . I think, there was just an open mind to where *Pet Sounds* was coming from. Plus . . . the reviews were good.'

Richard Williams: 'When *Pet Sounds* came out, people were used to the idea of pop music advancing at an unprecedented speed . . . *Pet Sounds* fit very, very clearly into that pattern, that was a quantum leap, something that really sounded new . . . it was *Pet Sounds* that made [The Beach Boys] important.'

Important *and* popular in England.

Bob Harris: 'We appreciated the layers and layers of creative genius that had gone into it . . . much more imagination in their creative work . . . Particularly in Britain, we, for a short time, really were the centre of music, art, film, fashion. It was an amazing moment.'

Sir Elton John: 'When you heard *Pet Sounds*, it blew your head off.'

Elvis Costello: 'I heard *Pet Sounds* and knew that was a great record . . . It's the fearlessness of it. It's still got a lot of the harmonic signatures . . . but the sensitivity of the lyrics being about a young man who is not entirely at ease with himself and his place in the world . . . a beautiful complement to the sensitivity [in] the music.'

Andrew Loog Oldham, *Rolling Stones manager:* 'I did snap to when I actually heard him say, "One day I will write songs people will pray to . . ." [. . .] I was raised in an agnostic family. And *Pet Sounds* actually gave me faith.'

Roger Daltrey: 'You suddenly realize that this man's music is about a lot more than what's in the lyrics. It's about what's going on in the music . . . he's just the master of counterpoint, so many things going on that it's always a journey . . . It was a milestone.'

GOD ONLY KNOWS

Right around the time of *Pet Sounds*' release, Brian hired Derek Taylor as the group's publicist.

Brian: 'We hired Derek because he was The Beatles' publicist and we wanted to have somebody good like him.'

Bob Harris: 'Once Derek Taylor got involved, it felt like a huge endorsement of them as a creative force.'

Credibility. And interest in what was coming next.

Richard Williams: 'Messages started coming back from America about these fantastic recording sessions . . . Derek Taylor had good contacts with the British music press . . . He probably sent some fairly teasing and tantalizing bulletins back. And Brian began to be a presence in those.'

The music world was changing, rapidly, and Brian was leading the way. But is that what Capitol wanted?

Brian: 'After *Pet Sounds* came out, my company, Capitol Records, wanted The Beach Boys to make more commercial records . . . Mike said we should get back to The Beach Boys' formula. He mentioned that to me one time in 1966. I told him I agreed with him. I said, "Yeah, you're right. We should make records that are more commercial for the public."'

What followed was their most experimental and avant-garde record. It would also be The Beach Boys' biggest hit of the decade and their first million-selling single.

Brian had originally recorded a version of 'Good Vibrations' during the *Pet Sounds* sessions but had put it aside. After *Pet Sounds* was finished, he turned his attention to that song. He had big ideas for it.

Brian: 'With 'Good Vibrations,' that was the first time I had ever written a record in sections . . . I didn't have it in my head the way it was going to come out. We had to keep going to the studio and doing it. Writing it in sections was very easy, and we strung them all together after we were done with the sections . . . and it worked out just great.'

Hal Blaine: 'I can't honestly say that I saw a major change [in Brian], except for 'Good Vibrations,' which all of a sudden became a trilogy, a quadrilogy, a sixtilogy. The word is kicked around with so many people – genius, genius, genius. Brian Wilson, no doubt is a genius. He was a young genius then; he was doing things that were not possible. He was writing songs that were not possible.'

Dennis Wilson: 'When [it] was all I could do to struggle to learn one melodic line, Brian had eight or nine going.'

Don Randi: 'There was no way to tell where that was gonna go . . . it was like a classical piece of music the way it was thought out, put together, pieced together, and arranged. Just marvellous.'

Brian: 'And Mike came up with (*Brian plays "I'm pickin' up good vibrations" on the piano*). That was the [lyrical] hook of the record.'

Hal: 'Whatever we could come up with, he wanted to hear something different, something new. He always liked it.'

As Hal noted, Brian wanted 'something different, something new,' and that applied to his new friends, too. They recall hearing his music in 1966, just as they were joining Brian's team.

David Anderle: 'The thing that was so exciting is, it reminded me of nothing that I had been hearing in popular music. My real love is classical music and jazz. And there were all those elements in there. And it was just the feeling of Brian . . . a certain feeling that got to me.'

David Anderle was a painter and artist manager, and he brought Danny Hutton, one of his artists, to meet Brian at the Wilson home on Laurel Way.

Danny Hutton: 'The first time I was just very shocked because I had a little turntable at home. And then to go to Brian's house and there's these massive speakers. And he played me some instrumental tracks. I was amazed that he'd gone to another level. Phil Spector's stuff, to me, was always like just a dense layer of sound, a wash. Brian's, to me, had a lot of depth to each sound. I wouldn't say each instrument because he many times would combine two instruments, three instruments, and create a fourth sound. It was a combination of the sounds, but also the arrangements – stunning, clever, well-produced, beautiful, different, unique.'

Why was Danny there?

Danny Hutton: 'I didn't know what 'Good Vibrations' meant, but he had a song he was interested in me maybe recording. So, he played me a version of 'Good Vibrations.' And it almost sounded like a Spector version. It had that big wall of sound, washy thing with a big baritone sax on it, too. It was great, but . . . it was more of a flowing one-piece song that I heard. Whereas I think the final version was entirely different, cleaner with all sorts of individual parts you could hear.

'The whole evening, I was just stunned by everything. It was amazing . . . I think he was sizing me up; it was our first meeting. I think it was also that thing of a guy being really proud of his stuff too, an excuse to play everything for me. I was under the assumption that I was gonna be one of the first artists with Brother Records. So, I think he was just throwing stuff out. "Maybe this is the song for you. And I'm just going to write another one." (*Laughs*) They were flying out. 'Good Vibrations' was one of the songs he just brought out.'

Danny was recording at Gold Star, so he had seen Spector and Brian there.

Danny: 'When Brian walked in, he just had that little sly, seemed like a sly smile. And he was just very direct. He asked "How old are you?" "Do you sing well?" Just (*laughs*) to the point. He's never been known for that Hollywood nice routine. But I sensed a real nice guy – the description I'd use is, "completely in command of the room." The guy was the best in the land.'

However, their relationship quickly went from potential artist to something else.

Danny: 'How do you become friends with someone? We had an instant thing of feeling relaxed around each other. I was sincere.'

Friends. So, if Danny was up at the house or they had gone bowling and Brian was heading to the studio, Brian would invite Danny to hang out. He was there for, among many other sessions, 'God Only Knows' and 'Good Vibrations.' Danny recalls Brian playing 'God Only Knows' for him, at an upright piano in a studio hallway.

Danny: 'He would start with a great song. But usually, in his head. Most of the people – the musicians and the recording engineer – didn't know what the song was 'cause he would start with the track. That's what was magic for me because he would start doing a track with these odd counter melodies, odd tempos. And he'd be working to get combinations of sounds together. It was just very magical.'

Working with the musicians, Danny would watch as the instrumental track evolved.

Danny: 'I felt he knew exactly what he wanted to hear. But you didn't know where he was going. It would be like a secret he had. And all you could do was sit and watch this guy just say "Okay, let's try that again." "Hold it, hold it." "No, no. You gotta be faster." "Look, you guys have gotta play a little more this way or that way." And then they'd start, and he would just go over and over and over, "No. One more time." [It could be] Take Twenty on one part 'cause lots of times he didn't have a lot of tracks so everything was locked in. So everybody had to get that *feel*. He was so into it being about *the feel*. And he would sit there with his engineer Chuck Britz, and Chuck would do a lot of it. But all of a sudden, Brian would do a little thing and tweak it, and the sound would just pop, blossom, and get bigger and better.'

The sessions were always full of surprises.

Danny: 'You would watch it just get better and still, magically, I'd hear things and say "What? What is that about?" And then maybe later, when it was almost done, he might hum the melody. Then, it was like the puzzle would be complete and I'd go, "Ah, now I see what he's doing." I still wouldn't be hearing all the magical vocal parts that he'd be putting on later. It was a guy at the top of his form in complete command with an incredible song, arranging, and production ability . . . I can't think of many that can hit every area and sing everything himself.'

Often, there were more than a dozen session musicians in the studio.

Annie Wilson-Karges: 'At times, just the volume of people that he was directing, the excitement that he projected, how infectious that was. His communication skills were amazing. Very clear, very precise. And energizing for his brothers and for the rest of the guys. He is the big brother. So those were his little brothers, and they did what he said.'

Outside the studio, a new team was taking shape, and the key players were all connected in one way or another. David Anderle, who was managing both Van Dyke Parks and Danny Hutton, came aboard to create Brother Records, ostensibly to manage non-Beach Boys projects. And Brian was eager to play his latest creation for them.

Brian: 'When I finished 'Good Vibrations,' in August of 1966, I first played it for David Anderle, and he goes, "That's so where it's at, Brian. That's so where it's at." Then I played it for Van Dyke, and he liked it. And then I played it for The Beach Boys. They loved it. They thought it was a great record.'

Van Dyke Parks: 'I was totally knocked out about the way Brian used sounds that were not considered governable in recorded music.'

Released in October 1966, 'Good Vibrations' was almost an instantaneous number one smash. With the success of 'Good Vibrations,' The Beach Boys, at least in England, were going 'toe-to-toe' with The Beatles for artistic supremacy. And Brian was the breakout star. By the end of the year, a *New Musical Express* readers' poll amazingly placed The Beach

GOD ONLY KNOWS

Boys ahead of The Beatles for World Vocal Group (albeit by a slim 100 vote margin) and Wilson as the fourth-ranked 'World Music Personality' — about 1,000 votes ahead of Bob Dylan and 500 behind John Lennon.

New Musical Express couldn't choose an 'Album of the Year,' so they gave co-album of the year honours to The Beatles' *Revolver* and *Pet Sounds*. Just ahead of Dylan's *Blonde on Blonde*. Unbelievable.

In a business where publicity is paramount, The Beach Boys had the best.

Danny Hutton: 'Derek had a lot of "juice" because of The Beatles.'

Derek Taylor: 'The bloody *Pet Sounds* album was undoubtedly a very great work of art . . . Possibly with my connection to The Beatles, but certainly later [Brian was] taken with me as good listener, for whatever it was he wanted to say. Because in addition to being a great producer, he was a great talker. It put strains on [my] marriage 'cause his hours were not ours. He lived like a vampire. He got up at night, and he wanted to talk. It seems later now that he was also taking rather more acid than I would suppose . . . But he was fine. It was a privilege to work with him.'

Derek was taken with what Brian was doing.

Derek: 'They were [now] getting recognition from people who'd previously despised them. The so-called intellectuals. The so-called hipsters, people who said it was "kids music" previously were now seeing . . . that it represented more than pop.'

Derek explained that in the wake of *Pet Sounds* and 'Good Vibrations,' 'It was the easiest thing in the world to get space in the papers about the follow-up. [If] anything, [it] was, '"When's the next record coming out?"'

Derek: 'In a town where everyone's a goose or swan, I thought he was a genius . . . it seemed to me a way of making people sit up and pay attention to him . . . The way he orchestrated the voices. His ability to marshal things inside his head, without benefit of a producer and appearing to be, in the best sense of the word, "crackers." He had an extraordinary gift for knowing how to do a song. 'Good Vibrations,' 'Heroes And Villains,' and 'Surf's Up' are just breathtaking. Breathtaking.'

Joan Taylor, *Derek's widow:* 'Derek had huge respect for The Beach Boys as a group. And for Brian as an individual and as an artist. I think he always knew genius. And that was one of things he brought to the job . . . very good taste. Whether it was Noël Coward or Danny Kaye or Al Jolson or Frank Sinatra, he recognized the special ones. And Brian was one of those special ones in his area. But Derek was also someone who could toss a phrase around because it sounded good. But when you go back and look at it, you realize that it wasn't just tossed. He said "Brian Wilson is a genius, I think." He meant, "I think Brian Wilson is a genius." But who am I [to interpret]?'

Joan Taylor 'found him [Brian] quite intimidating. A little bit like John Lennon was intimidating. And he was funny. He was a very big presence. But there was something about him that you sort of [felt], "Don't mess with me."' But overall, Joan remembers Brian 'as very sweet and friendly . . . and I probably got to know Brian better than the others. Because he would come and visit us . . . he would be in the kitchen talking about his relationship with Phil Spector. Or whatever he'd been doing that day musically. Or we'd be in bed asleep and there would be a knock on the door, and it would be Brian wanting company or to play some music. I also remember going to his house and him being very friendly and very hospitable.'

'Good Vibrations,' the epic single, which had been created in more than a dozen sessions, unleashed on the world over fifty years ago, was an immediate and absolute milestone in recording history. Derek Taylor was probably the one to call it 'a pocket symphony'; given its movements, it was an apt description, as Wilson demonstrated the breadth of his musical vision as well as how the recording studio could be both an artist's garret and a key instrument in creating his art.

In the UK, as Bob Harris explains, a big factor that was very different from America was pirate radio.

Bob Harris: 'Fleets of boats out in the North Sea beaming 24-hour-a-day music into Britain . . . Radio Caroline. Radio London, in particular. They were forward thinking. You were hearing perhaps the first tracks by Cream or The Yardbirds, and you were certainly hearing The Byrds. And they were playing The Beatles. On Radio London, Kenny Everett, one of the greatest DJs of all time. He would play 'Norwegian Wood,' and then stuff from *Revolver*, 'Tomorrow Never Knows.' So this was all kind of paving the way for the arrival of 'Good Vibrations.' [That record] seemed to capture a spirit of [that] moment in that time. Radio London was absolutely playing it to death. It's such a fascinating record; it sounded

GOD ONLY KNOWS

so different from everything around it, and yet everything around it seemed to have prepared us for its release.'

In the fall of 1966, The Beach Boys headed to the UK for their first British concert tour, where London was, in the words of one headline, '"VIBRATING" FOR THE BEACH BOYS.'

Annie Wilson-Karges: 'It was amazing. Great to be in England. After all the questions about the acceptance of *Pet Sounds* in America, it was just what the doctor ordered. To go on that tour and to have it be so visibly, one hundred percent accepted, the adulation and all of that.'

The 1966 combination of *Pet Sounds* (which reached number two in the UK) and 'Good Vibrations' (number one both stateside and in England) was so potent that, thanks in large part to Derek Taylor's work, The Beach Boys were received as rock royalty. But there was another article headlined: 'Brian Wilson's Puppets?' That probably didn't go down well.

Brian, who was back in L.A. working on the follow-up to *Pet Sounds*, monitored the music media.

Brian: 'When I saw all the press we were getting, I felt very honoured and proud.'

His two 1966 masterpieces had set the stage for what was seen by Brian as 'the next step.' This production quickly became one of the most anticipated works of the rock era.

Brian (in *Beat* magazine, 1966): 'Wilson is growing, I hope, as a producer. I don't see any end to the experiments.'

In the October 8, 1966, issue of the UK's *Melody Maker,* in a monthly 'Word Association' called 'Pop Think In,' in response to the word 'album,' Brian said this:

Brian: 'Our next album will be better than *Pet Sounds*. It will be as much an improvement over *[Pet] Sounds* as that was over *Summer Days [and Summer Nights!!]*.

No self-imposed pressure there, eh? But he knew what was coming.

★ ★ ★ ★

'Art is the most intense mode of individualism that the world has known.'
Oscar Wilde

Music lovers wanted more. Everybody in the industry was asking 'How did he do it?' Danny Hutton remembers that there was absurd talk that Brian must have some special equipment, a secret 'black box.'

SMiLE

The answers to all these questions would take shape through a new collaboration, this time with an inspired and poetic lyricist, arranger, young studio musician, and burgeoning songwriter.

Brian (in *Beat* magazine, 1966): 'I'd like to make all song lyrics completely free-form. By that I mean, anything goes . . . you don't get hung up on looking for words that rhyme. And I want to write hymns . . . yeah, real hymns but ones which will appeal to kids.'

Enter Van Dyke Parks, the most important new figure in the *SMiLE* story.

Brian explains why he chose his new collaborator.

Brian: 'I really had enough of getting too far into music. After we were done with *Pet Sounds*, I said, "It's time to not get quite so far into music." The emotions got a little bit too intense for me. Feelings. The songs were very personal. Working with Van Dyke was a way that the words weren't quite so personal for me. My wanting to work with Van Dyke was intellectual. I didn't tell "the Boys." It was a decision I made.'

So as 'Good Vibrations' headed from final mix to master to pressing plant to number one, Brian and his brilliant lyricist began work on his third major production of '66. Those who heard the 'work in progress' would soon be hailing it as the cutting edge of a 'new' sound. It was music that combined classical composition, inventive harmonies singing Van Dyke's wondrous wordplay, *Beach Boys harmonies*, all with an experimental sensibility. It was somehow going to be both ahead of its time and timeless.

Brian: 'I never felt like, that I could do something better creatively by myself than The Beach Boys. I always liked doing it for the group.'

So interesting – 'For The Group.' As if he wasn't quite one of The Beach Boys. He felt responsible for them but didn't exactly feel like he was a Beach Boy. Looking back, *Pet Sounds* is almost a solo album under The Beach Boys' name. The music of the *SMiLE* era would be from another world.

DUMB ANGEL

'True art is characterized by an irresistible urge in the creative artist.'
Albert Einstein

'That which is static and repetitive is boring. That which is dynamic and random is confusing. In between lies art.'
John A. Locke

'Shall I tell you what I think are the two qualities of a work of art? First, it must be indescribable, and second, it must be inimitable.'
Pierre Auguste Renoir

'They teach you there's a boundary line to music. But man, there's no boundary line to art.'
Charlie Parker

DAVID ANDERLE: 'IF *PET SOUNDS* WAS HIS BLUE PERIOD, THEN *SMILE* WOULD HAVE been his Cubist period. It would have been that radical a move from one form of art to another and would have influenced music at that time as much as Picasso's Cubist period influenced art.'

What was *SMiLE* going to be? If its predecessor, *Pet Sounds*, feels like Brian's emotional autobiography then *SMiLE*, in its most basic terms, was to be an American story told by America's greatest pop composer and the lyricist he had chosen, Van Dyke Parks.

Van Dyke: 'Clearly, from the first, we both understood it, is do something particularly, peculiarly, positively American.'

Through the decades, there have been countless depictions, descriptions, and informed guesses of what *SMiLE* was supposed to be. What it was going to be. How the songs and song fragments might be sequenced.

Back in 1966, the *SMiLE* sessions were just one project on Brian's plate. There was talk of a humour album. Other ideas. Ultimately, it all became just one piece: *SMiLE*.

Probably the earliest sketch of *SMiLE* that surfaced was that it was going to be a musical trip taken by a bicycle rider, flying from east to west, looking down upon America. It would be a musical travelogue from Plymouth Rock to Diamond Head. *SMiLE* would include an Elements suite (Earth, Air, Fire, and Water).

Alas, in 1967, after much turmoil, the project was shelved. But this chapter and the next are the historical context we need . . . the rise and (self?) crucifixion before we get to the resurrection in 2004.

We'll have lots of help in unravelling this impossible-to-solve mystery, and along the way, we'll try to answer this question from one famous American fan who was paying attention.

Rob Reiner, *writer, actor, director:* 'What is that great, crazy genius doing?'

Let's start with the principals, those who were at the centre of the *SMiLE* universe.

Brian: 'David Crosby used to come to my house and listen to my records. He wanted to see what we were up to. He came by, and he really liked *Pet Sounds* and 'Good Vibrations' a lot. They were waiting so they could figure out what they were going to do next. I was aware I was kind of a leader in the industry, to show people where things were going. It felt good to be a leader, to be a "prime mover."'

To remain the 'prime mover,' Brian needed and wanted a new collaborator for his next production.

Brian: 'I remember Crosby bringing Van Dyke and Durrie [Parks's first wife] up to my house – that was the first time I met him. I thought he was a character . . . a very cute character. [He] was a little more creative than other people, had a little more talent than other people. Van Dyke had a very good education – a musical education, too. I thought his ideas, his lyrical ideas were advanced enough for something really good. I wanted to advance. Everybody wanted me to get back to the basic format, but I ignored them. I ignored them because I wanted to try something new, something different. Working with Van Dyke Parks was a new direction.'

DUMB ANGEL

Durrie Parks: 'Van Dyke and I were at the Troubadour one night. David Crosby was there and said, "Come on, man. You gotta come hear something." And we got in his black Porsche and drove up to Brian's house. He was mixing 'Sloop John B' in the living room.'

Van Dyke sets the scene.

Van Dyke: 'Two four-track tapes up there and, by the way, a fluorescently lit room, very bright, not too many love beads. TVs in the house, no sandboxes. It was just white-on-white, two [tape] machines. His house, like his studio, was his laboratory and he was making up sounds, discovering ways to make sounds and put machines in synch and finding synchronous situations which were not even designed for synchronous . . . opening up the possibilities of multi-tracking. This was all phenomenal to me, as much as Harry Partch or Stockhausen. I thought, "This was it."'

What Van Dyke was hearing, as he recalls, was 'also happier than John Cage, better music, as a matter of fact. Legit, lowbrow legit . . . using rhythms to bring people along and persuade them into the thing but with so many voices going so many wonderful places. So that was the first time I met Brian. 'Sloop John B,' as good as that number could sound. Of course, I'd been introduced to it by the Kingston Trio.

'He deconstructed the tune; he got into its innards. And it was better than riding the carousel at a county fair. It was better than winding up Grandma's music boxes. It was every bit as good as all of that at the same time. Also [you've] got to remember, folk music was out of fashion. Brian wasn't interested in fashion, wasn't looking at what somebody else was doing. He wasn't interested, really, in what The Beatles were doing. He was more taken by the mania, that The Beatles discovered everywhere they performed. Wild women screaming *during* the music. Why was that? . . . Brian didn't want anything to do with that. Interested in music, that's all. No mystery.'

Durrie Parks: 'Brian was bigger than life, as was what we were hearing . . . in his huge house, sort of overwhelmed by the whole thing and 'Sloop John B' on those huge speakers . . . to be in his presence was really exciting.'

How did that night affect Van Dyke?

Van Dyke: 'I was absolutely floored. I was probably at his house for I would say an hour-and-a-half, two hours. Just enough for the cranial deformation, just enough to get my nose bloodied by all of this talent and positivity. And that such raw talent had nothing to do [with] The Beach Boys or really anything to do with the particular style . . . but [it] represented kind of a more epic ability, that he could handle more things.'

Could he?

Brian: 'I loved doing everything; it was great. I composed. I arranged. I did the background parts, and I did the tracks. And I sang. It didn't come out of pressure at all. I was loving it. I was compelled to make music; I really was. I was compelled to do it.'

Reportedly, there was another meeting between Brian and Van Dyke, a conversation on the lawn at record producer Terry Melcher's house.

When Brian made the decision to collaborate with Van Dyke, that is the beginning of the *SMiLE* story.

In the late summer of 1966, The Beach Boys' leader began work on the follow-up to *Pet Sounds*, an album briefly named *Dumb Angel*. Because Brian believed in laughter – loved to laugh and make people laugh, believed in the healing power of laughter – *SMiLE* was almost the only choice.

Brian: 'Van Dyke and I wanted to make a title that would catch people's ears, so they would want to hear it. So we said "*SMiLE*."'

With Van Dyke providing the incredibly imaginative lyrics, Brian worked on the music for nearly nine months . . . composing, arranging, re-arranging, and producing more than an hour's worth of new and, by all accounts at the time, startling music.

With *SMiLE*, Brian set out to do something unprecedented: an entire album to be created in the modular style of 'Good Vibrations.'

Danny Hutton: 'I'm the heretic here, okay? I'm allowed to do that. Everybody tries to compartmentalize that there was a *SMiLE* album in his head. I don't think that's what happened. I think he created all this music at a certain period, and if it had been all packaged at the time, it would have been called *SMiLE* . . . But I never heard him say, "My next album is going to be called *SMiLE* . . ." I think there were all of these beautiful pieces . . . maybe some of them were lost or they ended up being put piecemeal on different albums and in different forms. But that was kind of what would have been *SMiLE* if it had all been put together.'

Danny, Brian's best friend for over fifty years, isn't the only *SMiLE* sceptic.

David Anderle: 'When I was involved, it was pieces of music. But just from the musical point of view, there never was a *SMiLE*.' David adds, 'I never viewed 'Good Vibrations' as being part of *SMiLE* I thought it was this stepping stone from *Pet Sounds* to *SMiLE*. It never was part of the conversation of *SMiLE* for me.'

For historical purposes, those distinctions matter. But let's put them aside.

What we need to first know is, how did these seemingly unlikely collaborators come together? Re-enter Mr. Parks, who sat down with me in 2004 for a most extensive conversation before the world premiere in London.

Van Dyke, at that point, was well known in the L.A. music business, and had enjoyed some success. But for him to be central to 'What's Next' with Brian Wilson was a big deal. A very big deal. However, if you expect him to tell the story clearly and concisely, as if you were reading a report in *The Guardian* or *The New York Times*, you evidently haven't ever listened to Mr. Parks's lyrics or solo albums.

But if you read the lines – and read between them, too – you'll be graced, as I was, to hear Van Dyke talk about their process and his creative partner with affection and tremendous insight – and heartbreak too. You might also want to have Google or a dictionary handy.

Van Dyke: 'I've never met anybody brighter than Brian in terms of his mathematical skill. His musical ability. And where the rubber hits the road is in voice leading. And his harmonic sensibilities that come from that. A powerful "melodian." All I can say is, he reaches perfection, as far as I am concerned. That is, there is nothing better than *that*. Now, there are other kinds of music . . . they are perfect and beautiful, and supportable by the presence of some personality. Which is another ace the kid has up his sleeve.'

Which is to say, when they met, Brian had a lot of personality.

What drove Brian to create the *SMiLE*-era music with Van Dyke?

Van Dyke: 'I don't know what makes somebody write music or think up music or want to provide music for others. I'm guessing a need, more than a hunger, a need to communicate something. And I really think that that's what drove Brian.'

Clear enough. So far.

Van Dyke: 'Now, it's true that as his comedic forces developed and

[in] *SMiLE*, there is some comedy. There is as much comedy as error in it. It's obviously intentional. But it could have come from a very despondent place . . . Brian was providing a great deal of beautiful music [at] a time when he was really in terror. So what makes a person want to do that? To keep that intrepid veneer of some kind of hopefulness. And be able to wipe some of it off on a communicant? I don't know where that comes from.'

For certain, Van Dyke was not expecting to be Brian Wilson's collaborator.

Van Dyke: 'It was funny to me that Brian asked. I was startled that he suggested I write lyrics for him. I think he wanted to do it because, honestly, in a small pond, I was a big fish, I was recognized as somebody who worked hard on lyrics and music and so forth. I was in the loop. I don't think that could have mattered to him. He was an industry [himself]. The music he was selling [with The Beach Boys], he was selling by the ton. I don't think he could have been [less] interested [in my credits].'

Straining to find *the* answer, Van Dyke admits, 'I have no idea why I had that opportunity.' Then, he comes to a conclusion. 'I think that it was just Brian's instinct, and that's why I liked it. And I had nothing to lose is the way I figured it.'

Suddenly, Van Dyke was again on his way to the Wilson home on Laurel Way in Beverly Hills.

Van Dyke: 'To see him in that house which represented everything good about the American dream . . . Steam rising out of the swimming pool. And a string of pearls [the city lights] below, showing the grit of the Los Angeles basin. It was really something. It was the California dream. Now, it surprised me [that] he asked me to come up. I loved 'In My Room.' I thought it was a beautiful thought. I loved that song. It came out of that contemplative place. Innocent but not mawkish to me. I was totally high and dry. Wonderful dream.'

Durrie Parks: 'Van Dyke and I are musical snobs in a way and in different ways probably. We do like all kinds of music and different kinds of music but *Pet Sounds* had cut through all of that . . . was really important to us and so it was a very big deal for us to be there.'

What would their collaboration entail?

Van Dyke: 'I didn't know exactly what he had in mind. But I think he recognized me as a good fellow who was interested in the American

Dream, and that's what we discussed in passing . . . details, nuance beyond my memory.'

David Anderle: 'I'm not certain anyone sat down in the beginning and said, "This is what we're going to do." I mean, Van Dyke *is* Americana . . . To the max. He's Aaron Copeland. He's Charles Ives. He's all those guys. So, he brings that. And Brian is clearly West Coast Americana. So, it's obviously an Americana album.'

Van Dyke: 'Harmonica . . . banjo . . . those were the things I liked. Those were articles of faith. It's almost like we're looking into the same trunk of precious little things. Here's an old seashell with some algae on it. "Remember where we picked this up? No. Me neither, let's use it." Whatever it was that he brought into play, musically. It was a refreshment for me and a real step away from the mighty wind of that folk-rock that I had just come from.'

A meaningful digression from a close observer that night.

Durrie Parks: 'I have to say that Brian has the most amazing left hand I've ever heard, and it just doesn't matter where he is or what he's doing. If he sits down and touches a keyboard, something magical happens. And I know it's a really lame word. It's like saying 'Genius.' It's hard to explain exactly but he can do something that nobody else can do. Because Brian sits down at a keyboard and something happens that's just unbelievable. And Brian was so excited. He was really excited. This was so much fun for him and so it was fun for anybody else who was around it to watch. Van Dyke perhaps had a little less fun 'cause he had to work.'

Van Dyke: 'When we got together, it was . . . "Your Honour, may I approach the bench?" And he would say, "Yes," and I would go over there and approach the [piano] bench and I would sit next to him on the bench. And he loved that. Just great fraternity. It was wonderful. It was just great, [a] fair-minded guy, no-nonsense, top-of-the-heap, saying, "Come on in."'

Brian explained that the songwriting partnership would be that of equals.

Van Dyke: 'Fifty-Fifty, oh my God, what does that mean? The way he approached me, simply on a handshake. And, also to this day, unique, individual in my life, because we both came through what is famous now in memorabilia as the sixties. The line being, "If you were there, you can't remember." Well, I was there, and I can remember a lot about it.

[Brian] says he can't. This will make any discussion that we have that approaches that line between myth and history very interesting.'

Indeed. What was the first song they worked on?

Brian: "Heroes And Villains'.. In the key of C#. That was one of *the* highlights of my life.'

Van Dyke: 'We did that one and knocked that out in a day. That was the first thing we did. And that gave us a lot of wind at our backs.'

How did they write?

Brian: 'He'd be sitting on my left. He would think about a rhythm and give me a [musical] bag. "I need a bag," and then I'd take it from there. He'd say, "How about something like . . ." (*Brian snaps fingers*). He would say, "How about a rhythm like . . ." (*Brian plays rhythm on piano*) And then I'd go like, (*Brian sings melody line*), and he would immediately start writing lyrics. Immediately. I'd immediately translate his ideas into a piano figure.'

How did 'Heroes And Villains' take shape?

Brian: 'So then we'd get . . . (*Brian plays the first verse on the piano*) and he would write lyrics to the melody . . . Like that, with that many bars. Then I'd sing his lyrics to the melody, and then we'd go a step farther. (*Brian plays piano and sings*) "I've been in this town so long that back in the city . . . home of the heroes and villains."

'So we'd go that far, and then we'd start the same thing [with the next verse], and the same thing, until we were done with the song . . . He came back a week later and then we did 'Cabin Essence' . . . He kind of inspired me to come up with new licks and new melodic ideas.'

Because he has infrequently talked about the thought or meaning behind the *SMiLE* songs, Van Dyke had much to offer in this 2004 interview. He expands upon that day: "Heroes And Villains' was the first thing that emerged. And it emerged as a ballad and a great refreshment to me, I'll tell you why. Because I love Marty Robbins. I love country music because country music had to do with telling a story. I like the age of the balladeer.'

Can we get back to 1966, please?

Van Dyke: 'I asked him what the title was. He told me, 'Heroes And Villains.' I knew that he wanted to write a song that talked about good guys and bad guys. And maybe do some work where good would triumph over evil, and I like all that, see. This was the longest song I'd ever heard, certainly the longest introductory sentence. I remember how satisfied we both were when I wrote, "And I've been taken for lost and gone and unknown for a long, long time." And he was so happy, that he didn't ask [me] to remove one syllable. And I was grateful to my Maker that we came in to such a provident beginning. That we just started out on the right track. And I didn't mind as we got into it his sense of farce, because . . . anything that Brian was interested in, even farce, was great.'

Durrie Parks: 'It was fairly evenly balanced. Brian was very deferential to Van Dyke. He never gave up his own point of view and neither did Van Dyke, and I think that's why the collaboration was so strong. It was a [fascinating] process to watch . . . The most exciting thing is when you see people creating. And they were fairly relaxed about it.'

The partnership fit Brian's needs and his schedule. He liked to work at night.

Van Dyke: 'When I was working with Brian, I was available to him twenty-four hours a day . . . Every time I went up to his house, we worked. We always got something done.'

Durrie: 'They did write fairly quickly, and they had a chance to sit and write and then go to sleep and [the next day], review what they had done and see if they liked it. If Brian had an idea or Van Dyke had an idea, they could make an adjustment at that point before they went any farther. And they did a lot of "[let's] sleep on it." But it did seem to go very quickly.'

As to what song they wrote next, memories contradict slightly here, but let's go with Van Dyke's.

Van Dyke: 'The next song was 'Surf's Up.''

Brian: "Surf's Up'? He wanted to write pure poetry, and I wanted to write pure music. So we put pure music and pure poetry together, and it went real well. [Van Dyke] said 'Surf's Up' was one of the best songs ever written. He did. He liked it a lot. I felt honoured, I felt very honoured, I [thought], "He really thinks that?" I couldn't believe it. It gave me confidence that we were [going] in the right direction with our music.'

Van Dyke: 'Then, I think, 'Wonderful' or 'Cabin Essence.' Then, I think maybe 'Vega-Tables.' But not sure of the order after that . . . I probably worked up at his house two or three times in a week. And then we would go into the studio and work on that for a week or two . . . And then we would go back and repeat the process. So, there were intervals between my going up there.'

The surviving session sheets seem to tell a different story regarding the writing/recording schedule, but what's indisputable is that in a matter of only a few months, Brian and Van Dyke had written a half-dozen terrific songs. And in the studio, Brian arranged and produced the instrumental backing tracks for them.

Brian had first recorded pieces of songs during the 'Good Vibrations' sessions. Some beautiful sections would be left on the cutting room floor for the final single version of the record. For *SMiLE*, that process accelerated. Titles might change too. 'Home on the Range' might become part of 'Cabin Essence.' The piece called 'Child Is Father Of The Man' might find a new home . . . or remain homeless.

Mark Volman, *The Turtles:* 'Danny Hutton and I were very close, and he opened the door for me to go up with him to [Brian's house] and become one of the listeners of the record on a day-to-day basis. Brian was doing a lot of testing, and he tested with all of us.'

Mark explains that at the long dining room table, Brian had installed headphones at each seat. Mark describes Brian walking around to 'make sure every headphone was perfect . . . he pulled the headphones up and kind of listened.'

Brian would then play the latest piece.

Mark: 'He was always watching how we were reacting . . . And it was hard to have a perspective [because] it was just lots of pieces, and that was disjointed, but also very, very fun to hear where he was headed . . . you could just hear he was doing [something] that was really "out there." He'd play a minute of something and say, "This is from 'The Elements'." What's 'The Elements'? . . . It was like a scene, a movie, searching for gold. And [it] eventually would get all tied together. I remember when we heard pieces that kept getting assembled and put together, and it was confusing. It really was.'

The dining room was just one place for those listening sessions.

Mark: 'When Brian got even more comfortable, we'd end up in the bedroom, sit in the bedroom listening, and Brian would look at us as we were kind of watching him. It was a really a unique situation, and you were beginning to see Brian's idiosyncrasies.'

DUMB ANGEL

Annie Wilson-Karges: 'We lived really close . . . two or three miles away. And I just remember, we were there every day or every night . . . there would be lots of people and ideas and talks, and Van and just all kinds of sessions, all kinds of creativity. So there were plenty of ideas flying around the room.'

David Anderle: 'Brian would come back from the studio sometimes with little pieces he had recorded . . . stacks of demos, little acetates. And we would sit around in a circle. And he would play these bits of music . . . endlessly. And we would go, "Oh, my God." . . . Brian would say, "This piece is 'Cabin Essence.'" And [we would say], "Oh, no, Brian, that's perfect as 'Wonderful.'" So we would argue with him. "You can't make that change." And then he would make the change and we'd go, "Oh, man, that is so cool." So that's what I did. I said a lot of, "That is so cool."' (*Laughs*)

The process was fast but not furious.

Van Dyke: 'He always was astounding me . . . the best, most invigorating kind of a social force in what I felt I should do with my musical curiosity. And I was so happy serving his flawless ideas without being sullen or slow. And everything to me was to try to facilitate his musical decisions. Didn't question them. 'Cause I'd seen the power of rationality, what was "Reasonable" was that we were in the Gulf of Tonkin.'

A reference to the disastrous and tragic Vietnam War.

In describing their work together, Van Dyke chose the opposite course.

Van Dyke: 'Simple, straightforward, uncomplicated, collaborative Heaven. It was Heaven on Earth. Going on blind faith was enough. And that's what I did. And I didn't question it. And you might look at a relationship like that as irresponsible or even folie à deux, where two people share their own private madness. And that's the way it was [later] characterized by the dissenting parties, as folie à deux.

'I saw it as Brian's opportunity to develop music, a codified musical experience. It would take work doing it. And it would take a certain sovereign kind of like noblesse oblige, a privilege of his accomplishment, that he had enough portfolio behind him to go out and experiment with a record album. And I was happy to do it, and continued it, until its bitter conclusion, which was when I had to absent myself because of so many counter-productive forces. Basically, it was an overpopulated result.'

We're not there yet. It's still the fall of 1966. And Van Dyke explains, in retrospect, what he came to understand.

Van Dyke: 'Brian Wilson was delivering a project through The Beach Boys, Incorporated. And a very eager press. An incredible amount of surface tension immediately became associated with the project, that it would be a very important project. Because *Pet Sounds* . . . was not the big money maker that The Beach Boys really expected of Brian Wilson.'

Van Dyke understood there was pressure from the record company for Brian to 'bring something of greater commercial appeal. And Brian Wilson knew that it should be of equal aesthetic appeal. So all of those things were hopping around in everybody's head. And all that sense of anticipation' was building.

Brian, in the fall of 1966, was at the height of his powers, as a composer, arranger, producer, and singer. And visionary leader.

Annie Wilson-Karges: 'He incorporated all of that. All systems go. He was on. It was happening.'

Would anybody question what was happening?

Annie: 'Why would you want to challenge it, when it was more fun to do it his way? So I don't think a lot of challenging happened, that I saw.'

The songs that Brian and Van Dyke had written were *unlike anything* that had been on a previous Beach Boys album. Which is what was causing so much excitement in his house and in the press. Especially if a reporter was allowed into the studio to see Brian at work. A frequent question might be, 'What is *SMiLE*?'

Durrie Parks: 'In terms of a theme, 'Child is the Father to the Man' and 'Heroes and Villains' clearly was Brian's . . . in large measure was Brian trying to say some things. As was Van Dyke. I don't feel I know exactly what he was trying to say, but absolutely, it had to do with the whole Americana trip across the United States.'

Contextualizing it, Durrie notes, 'It was a very exhilarating time. Not only with *SMiLE* but what was happening in the rest of the musical world and in what people were finding and discovering and opening themselves to. And I'm a big believer in gestalt and I think everybody's life was being changed by being around everybody else.'

Van Dyke recalls that *SMiLE* was American music aimed at a very specific target.

DUMB ANGEL

Van Dyke: 'There was an aggressive attempt to hang onto our egos. *(Laughs)* To hang on to our American egos. There was a definite desire to do that. It was a direct result of the British Invasion. That's what it was about. Absolutely. Bob Dylan dominated the advancement of the American popular song. There's no question of it. Bob Dylan became the real hipster . . . just leading [to] new possibilities in songwriting. That is topicality of songs, what they would say – that songs were allowed to be popular, even danceable, and still have a sensibility of vox pop politics. Still thinking about things. Not necessarily hitting them all dead-on, but, but those were part of the words that came into play, the Grand Coolie pattern.'

Van Dyke was well-aware that the word 'coolie' was racist. That it was offensive. That it was derogatory. That was the point of using it. Because America's past (and present) is filled with that kind of racism. In the midst of that song, he was giving a history lesson.

This was a reference to the indentured Asian Coolie labourers that would do the most dangerous work, making them essential to the building of America's Transcontinental Railroad.

Van Dyke: (*Reciting the lyrics to 'Cabin Essence'*) '"Hey mister, have you seen the Grand Coolie working on the railroad." We can't say dam. We might as well say railroad. So, I'm sorry to tell you that the pun is the most vulgar of all the utensils available for a humourist. That's according to Shakespeare. But it certainly isn't something that scared me off during this *SMiLE* thing. There are a lot of attempts to entertain with punditry and puns.'

The listener would need to know – or learn – that Van Dyke wrote 'railroad' and not 'dam' because there was a Grand Coulee Dam, but that the Coolies were working on the railroad.

It's an example of why Van Dyke's lyrics weren't easily grasped on first (or even tenth) listen.

Van Dyke: 'I think that a good lyric should be revisited. Should be interesting. Repeatedly. It should be well designed. There should be the same number of syllables, indicated in the melody. Not certainly, not absolutely. But, generally, that's the rule.'

Van Dyke's goal was to 'try to arrive at words that could be interpreted different ways, if anybody wanted to. And I see now that that's been a very good and a very bad thing. The bad thing is that people tell me what I mean . . . by what it is that I said and expect me to confirm it. And if I don't, I am messing with their icons. And this whole project has become iconic. It's really become something of an icon to a select choir.'

So even though Van Dyke knew what inspired the lyrics, he was generally reluctant to reveal. But not in our conversation. Illuminating further the song's connection to the Transcontinental Railroad, Van Dyke explains that the lyric 'alluded to the Chinese working force that made the railroad possible, that actually made the Golden Spike a reality. It connected this entire place . . . Because [with the railroad], we got as far as we could go. We got to the [California] beach. Now, it was time to look, turn around, and see what we've done . . . At the same time, we started to think about . . . the genocide of the American indigenous people, about the Indians themselves.'

Each song had a different origin story.

Van Dyke: 'He [Brian] wrote [the title] 'Heroes And Villains.' I just started writing words. I got the scene set there, and I think it was because I was dutiful, didn't interfere with his musical process that he was so relieved. So we got to the second [verse]. "Fell in love years ago with an innocent girl." Got a cat up the tree, in a kind of a dramatic sense. Got some gunplay. Got some losers and some winners, all put into this thing. Which suggested an anecdote, an incident, with a westward heave and ho, something that moved West, thought about Americans. Expansionist pains and so forth. Just started to think about these things. He was happy with them.'

The lyrical process, as Van Dyke recalls, could occasionally be interactive. On 'Surf's Up,' Van Dyke wrote 'a broken man too . . .' '[Brian] said, "Tough." I said, "Fine, '[too] tough to cry . . ."' That was his word. It was his "tennie" that flew right off in 'Vega-Tables.' Fine. But very, very infrequently would he change a word because I was always trying to make it at least, good for the ear, a good word . . . so that it felt like the melody and the lyric were coincidental discoveries. That was my plan. Win some, lose some, but that's where I was going. I wanted him to be happy.'

Brian was.

Van Dyke: 'And I think that he found, in a way, more satisfaction in the serviceability of the lyrics to his intent, the feeling. "Let me look at this thing." What is a song? A song is music, a melody and lyrics. Now, the melody and the harmonies that surround it dutifully . . . that's called feelings. That's making feelings. The lyrics are thoughts. With thoughts and feelings, as we look at history, for example, in the making of the songs, you see King David made the Kingdom of Israel with the power of his songs. Bob Dylan was changing America with the power of song. A song is a very powerful thing, very potent political force. But I didn't wanna talk about the same politics. I wanted to talk about the causes of the things that brought us here.'

In writing about America's past, Van Dyke could make his points, and even if he wrote quickly, he thought very deeply about what he was doing. What *they* were doing together.

Van Dyke: 'I wanted to get outside the box myself. I wanted to get out of the present tense. I found the present tense odious. I wanted to run from it. I wanted to go to another place, an idealized place. And he did, too. It was a matter of fact. He [Brian] led that. It wasn't like I felt that I had to go in and teach Brian something. I had to simply go in and service his music.'

Writing side by side, Brian and Van Dyke worked in perfect harmony.

Van Dyke: 'I made up the lyrics to 'Heroes And Villains' right there with him that first day that we worked together. That day, he came away with 'Heroes And Villains.' Not the "Cantina" thing, but the other stuff. The body of the song. "Ribbon of concrete" . . . It was, "Just see what you've done to the church of the American Indian." It was kind of like skewed Woody Guthrie.'

Anybody allowed to listen to the work in progress *in the studio* was in awe.

Van Dyke: 'I don't think I had a role in the studio. I can clearly remember, without doubt, the fact that I never made up a note. I [had] suggested the cello on 'Good Vibrations.' [Brian] liked that . . . that cello and the fundamental triplets, that was my idea.

'After I got in the tent, I decided to shut up. No musical ambitions at all. I did nothing except play the marimba. He'd come over and show me the part to play. I played those notes. I played what I was told if I played at all. But beyond that, I had no purpose in the studio with Brian Wilson, except to learn what he was doing and to observe him . . . It was really an illumination for me.'

Working with studio musicians, the best players in town, Van Dyke saw that Brian 'got all willing agents. Everybody . . . whether it was a cellist or a bassist or a drummer. Everybody was prepared to do something that was like [an] experiment with gaucherie. Maybe even to state the obvious. But, beyond all of that, everyone trusted him completely, absolutely. Because they realized the sobriety of his intent. The guy was absolutely earnest in everything he did.'

Annie Wilson-Karges: 'Brian was electric in the studio. He was endless energy. He was commanding. He was absolutely take-charge of everything. He got everybody going. He got everybody inspired. Quickly. Not just the guys, but the musicians that were there . . . So he was very much in charge. He was "The One."'

Van Dyke: 'So there's this great synchronicity of interest. Everyone was totally synced up to what it was that he had in mind. [Brian] had a great sense of leadership and this infectious enthusiasm . . . after all was said and done, all of this, this question of design, it has to serve the emotive strength. In this case, it's vocal music, so it's the singer . . . but he was so adept at it. I'm saying this as a rapid learning curve for everybody in the studio.

'Each one is like working as a [Flying] Wallenda, without a net. It's like a high-wire experience. Very hazardous. Doing things with your instrument that you're not supposed to do. Maybe playing out of range to reach some kind of a nasal quality. Doing something that just isn't done. [The] musicians were prepared to look into those areas . . . no reluctance. [Brian] asked things that require rethinking to get reform, and it will work with each person for a matter of seconds. And we get eight bars at a time, would get done and in no time flat. Everyone is in synch.'

An example of what Van Dyke means, a wonderful memory from one of Brian's favourite studio musicians:

Don Randi: 'We were going over one section over and over because he wasn't getting what he wanted out of it. And we had already been in there, at United Western for about eight hours. I was playing Hammond B3 organ on this one. And there's a real low note on the *bawww*, really that you hear and then he goes into this wild chord. And then they start the middle section of that thing. He kept doing that over and over and over and he couldn't quite hear what he wanted. And I was exhausted at this point. And he was working it out. All I was doing was playing with my foot on the low bass keys of the B3. I took a pillow and laid down with my head compressing the low key and I took a nap. (*Laughs*) I think I must've slept for a half-hour or more ... somebody came, kicked me and said "Wake up." And I woke up, and he had gotten that section [while] I was asleep on the key on the floor, under the organ.'

Van Dyke: 'He brings the best out in the people around him. So [there was] this kind of enthusiasm, [an] inclusionary process.'

The project quickly became all-consuming; Durrie and Van Dyke moved into a spare bedroom at the Wilsons' home.

Durrie Parks: 'Being with Brian and Marilyn was a lot of fun for us because we were young marrieds. They were young marrieds. There was that context which I think is really important.'

Mark Volman: 'Marilyn was very special.'

Marilyn Wilson (from the Don Was film): 'He was a pretty far-out guy to be married to, let me tell you. Life was somethin' else.'

Annie Wilson-Karges: 'Brian was just very cute with her. He called her Mary sometimes. Brian had a million names for things and people. They were very compatible. She was so good-natured and such a good sport. Laughed easily. It was a really good combination. It really was.'

Brian wasn't your typical husband.

Durrie Parks: 'He was out someplace and saw some Tiffany lamps and could not make a choice. And so home came fifteen or sixteen Tiffany lamps which strung across the living room. And the Madame Alexander dolls – I remember very clearly because they were in these wonderful display cases ... and they stood in the living room.'

Work and fun. And everything in between.

Brian has been described as dominating, intimidating, wilful. At the height of The Beach Boys' success, at the height of his creative powers, he did what he wanted when he wanted to. In the mid-1960s in the studio, at the control board, working with his musicians, he was in charge, an incomparable maestro. Outside, nobody said 'No' to him either. He got what he wanted, especially during the *SMiLE* era.

For example, when he returned from Michigan, where he'd gone to record a live album and supervise The Beach Boys' first live performance of 'Good Vibrations,' he had summoned family, friends, and photographer Guy Webster to LAX to meet his returning flight. To promote physical fitness, he suddenly filled the living room with tumbling mats. He had an Arabian tent custom-made for meetings.

There were all-night conversations about whatever was on his mind: astrology, astronomy, numerology. Ping-Pong. A cageful of mice. His reaction to David Anderle's portrait of him. These, and other legendary anecdotes, would later be looked back upon as examples of how eccentric he was. His behaviour might raise eyebrows, but it was mostly just fun, 'the commander' ordering his 'troops' into action, looking for release from the enormous self-imposed pressure he felt to beat The Beatles.

David Anderle: 'Numerology was huge with Brian – I think he actually stamped me "OK" based on a numerological evening. I had all the right numbers . . . I had that illogical part of my life too. I'm a marshmallow man, I guess. I believe in a lot of that stuff myself.'

Danny Hutton: 'He got into the I Ching and astrology and spent hours just looking for different planets.'

Brian's energy was boundless, and he was tireless in all pursuits, release from the uncompromising work. The Rolls-Royce had tinted windows, so nobody could see in during, in David Anderle's words, their 'adventures around town.' Which probably meant they were smoking a joint. And Brian might be the 'chauffeur' on rides to get burgers at Dolores Drive-In, a favourite West Hollywood twenty-four-hour coffee shop.

Were these unconventional episodes that have been endlessly recounted elsewhere (including in *God Only Knows*), just a bunch of young men, having fun? After all, it wasn't a nine-to-five work life. In the studio, Brian was creating sounds that were unprecedented. Why wouldn't everything else in his life be just as exceptional and unusual?

In that regard, perhaps nothing was more inventive or relevant to the creative process than that sandbox built around his piano.

Danny: 'He's saying . . . "I'm gonna get a sandbox in the living room." I'd look at him. "Is he testing me?" Very unique guy.'

Ron Swallow, The Beach Boys' road manager in the mid-1960s, recalls one time at Brian's house, 'Brian [said], "I'm having trouble. I feel if I could put my feet in some sand, maybe I'll be able to write some surfing music again." And [I asked] "What do you want?" [Brian said,] "I'd like to put the piano in some sand." It was no big deal.'

Ron called the lumber yard, 'got some two-by-six material, mitred the edges, and put it together. And then . . . I ordered enough sand to fill up this frame that we made . . . it seemed right. It seemed normal. Creativity comes in so many different ways.

DUMB ANGEL

'So we got the load of sand dumped out on Laurel Way . . . we got a couple wheelbarrows, and started wheeling it inside the house, and filled it up, picked up the piano and put it in it. And he was happy. And then he sat in it and started playing . . . And he'd be bare-footed and he'd be playing with his feet in the sand. And it turned out to be really a neat thing.

'But it wasn't like, "Oh my God, this is a strange thing." . . . It was the way that everything evolved. It was just so normal with him . . . He was always doing something kind of off-the-wall, and we just kind of went, "Oh, okay, no problem. We can do that." . . . If Brian wants something, you give him what he wants. It was no problem.'

Annie Wilson-Karges: 'We did every adventure. Every idea. The idea of the sandbox was just another creative idea. It wasn't like it was unusual for Brian. That's the thing that's hard to talk about, is that, at the time, it was a Brian idea. He thought of it; he could execute it. The sandbox was to the right of the front door, as I recall. I don't remember how long it lasted . . . It was just one of those creative ideas . . . He did it. And I think he tired of it. But it was there for the moment to do whatever it did for him. It was another tool . . . a tool in search of creativity.'

Mark Volman: 'The sandbox was just kind of a visual thing that when you saw it sitting there in the house . . . We'd look at each other from across the room and kinda go "Right. This makes perfect sense." And when you're looking at it, it was unbelievable.'

Durrie Parks: 'I just remember the sandbox appearing . . . and in fact, I remember Van Dyke not being really thrilled about it . . . This was a house with pets.'

David Anderle: (*Laughing*) 'The problem was the dogs crapping in the sandbox.'

Durrie Parks: 'And Van Dyke was not happy tiptoeing through the sand to get to the piano bench but that's the way it was, and it seemed to work for Brian's creative process.'

Indeed it did. It's where Brian and Van Dyke together began to construct a brand-new landscape for popular music.

Brian: 'Van Dyke and I worked on songs sitting [in] the sandbox. My piano was right in the sandbox. We sat barefoot in there just to give us a feeling that we were, like, on the beach . . . When people would come over and see it, they would say, "What in the heck are you doing? That's very creative."'

Brian remembers that among the songs they worked on in the sandbox were 'Heroes And Villains,' 'Cabin Essence,' 'Surf's Up,' and 'Wonderful.'

Brian: 'It was a great sandbox.'

An album with just those four songs alone would have been staggeringly original. Add 'Wind Chimes' and 'Vega-Tables.' 'The Elements' suite. And, almost certainly at the record company's insistence, the recent number one hit, 'Good Vibrations.'

(Author's Note: If you haven't listened to it recently [or ever], I would suggest that it might be a good time for you to stream Disc 1: Tracks 1-19 of *The Beach Boys SMiLE Sessions*.)

Van Dyke: 'I think Brian Wilson's singular works validated pop music. Certainly, in my way of thinking – without comparison to The Beatles – validated popular music and reconstituted [it]. The melodic force put . . . melody back in play.

'But what Brian did that was very interesting and what you like to think of as sui generis. He did it himself. Designed the package . . . he didn't turn to a George Martin to do this. He didn't have a building full of moles writing out notes, anonymously. He did the work himself . . . The reason his work appeals to me, fundamentally, is because it's sharp stuff, bright stuff. It's got great voice leading. That's the ticket. It's the voice leading. Everybody goes somewhere . . . and this was the first interactive popular music I've ever heard.'

Brian was open to anybody's ideas, but especially Van Dyke's. Their creative relationship was unlike any other Brian had ever had. Or would have.

Annie Wilson-Karges: 'It was like Brian had a peer. He was *so* excited about working with Van Dyke. He was so infused with this collaborator. It was head-and-shoulders above anything else I'd seen. I think part of it was Van Dyke being a wordsmith, and Brian, as well, loving words. Audree [Brian's mother] was a wordsmith. I think Carl, as well. Just the love of the language. The love of the language and how to put words together, say something in a more unique way or in a memorable way. I think their love of words, to me, was part of this interest that they shared. Something that simple.'

Danny Hutton: 'Van Dyke is also incredibly musical. He's a master of the piano. I'm sure he maybe pushed Brian in certain ways, even musically. But I think he also, on a "hip" level, intellectual level – opening up Brian to a much larger vocabulary. Literally. And thinking – Van Dyke is very worldly in the best sense of the word. And I think that, on some level, influenced the writing in the melody. Van Dyke's knowledge of classical instrumentation. Along with the lyrics.'

Annie: 'It just seemed like Brian really loved Van's ideas and was sparked by that. Really back-and-forth, with that creative spark between them. But my recollection of Brian is they were his ideas, and he really made you want to do them. It wasn't any negativity about it, it was like, "Come on! We're doing this." It was very positive. And it was fun . . . . Brian – he's very, very persuasive. So you got into it.'

Van Dyke was, as Annie remembers, 'like nobody you'd ever met before. Just so charming. His look and his sound. I think it was very exciting for Brian to have someone like that to interact with, stay up all night with. Talk to and exchange ideas. It was very exciting.'

In the sandbox and in the studio, the songs Brian and Van Dyke were writing, then recording, created sounds that were unprecedented. And they often fit the prescription that laughter is the best medicine.

Durrie Parks: 'Brian had a wonderful sense of humour. I think he's very childlike; I think that played into the whole thing with "The Elements."'

In listening to certain *SMiLE*-era songs, such as 'Wonderful,' it isn't immediately obvious that laughter was at the heart of *SMiLE*. Outtakes such as the 'Surf's Up' version with the dissonant horns might have offered a glimpse. Or another outtake, which *SMiLE* obsessives know as 'George Fell Into His French Horn', offered a more straightforward 'clue' to Brian's pursuit of laughter.

Van Dyke: 'He is a funny man . . . I'm talking about vasovagal. Laughing so hard that you just might die. Fighting for air, that's how funny the guy can be. And that's what I found in his music. "You can't do *that*." Oh my God. That is what appealed to me. And the force of his personality in the music.'

As Danny Hutton noted above, it wasn't immediately evident when Brian might be putting them on. Musically, that was invaluable.

Van Dyke: 'I don't know when he's kidding. That's one thing about [him], a very deceptive man. His music is filled with deception too, [a] lot of deception. You think he's gonna go one way; he goes the other.

That's what I think; he got me snookered so much. But it's without malice. The kind of humour that doesn't take a victim.'

As we spoke in 2004, Van Dyke continued to try and explain Brian, perhaps as much for himself as for my cameras.

Van Dyke: 'We're not talking about the age of irony. We're not talking about [a stand-up comic] making a living out of talking of family dysfunctions or any other kind of dysfunctions. Brian's humour is just off-the-wall and it's a matter of timing . . . I just hear it all over the music. He just goes from one attitude to another and place and contrasts them, and that's not the stuff of pop music really. It's not what pop music is supposed to be. A sense of futility and still an informed optimism, which is what his work has. And that's good. That's quality people where I come from. That's church people. That's somebody believing in something, knowing that it costs nothing to believe.'

Stay with him.

Van Dyke: 'And the belief in anything, like it's a value that will accrue to the principal invested so you invest in something, and you get some interest from your investment, and that, in terms of somebody who believes as much as Brian does in things, made it very momentous for him to get into *SMiLE*, to take that moment to do that. His own project, and to take possession of it . . . and not be encouraged.'

Again, Van Dyke is a bit ahead of the story, but let him continue.

Van Dyke: 'That's why it was momentous because he had always been encouraged to follow his dream, his belief, and in fact, never took the audience too far from record to record. And if you look at these pop artists of the sixties and seventies you see some great careers being made, The Beatles, Joni Mitchell, Harry Nilsson, different artists going from one record to another with greater faculties of performance, of songwriting ability, or communication skills.

'And with each project, pulling that audience, yanking them forward into another thing entirely. With the onus of having to drag their audience as if they care about an audience, and I believe Brian did. [He] was not just shouting into a vacuum. He didn't wanna do that. I don't think he was out to make art. I think he was out to communicate something, the sensations, the residue of his own beliefs. And, as I said, *informed optimism*.'

A deep breath as we take in Mr. Parks's insights.

And now, back to the collaboration. The pace of work, in Van Dyke's view, was strong.

Van Dyke: 'Don't let the marijuana confuse the issue here. If you look at the amount of work that was done, and the amount of time it took to almost finish it, it's amazing. [It was a] very athletic situation. And very focused.'

Danny Hutton: 'Brian was obsessed, what you'd call a workaholic now. But he never professed, "I'm doing this," because he had to kick The Beatles' ass, or "I've got a deadline and they're [meaning the record company] bugging me." It was always just about the music. It was always just exploring. He just constantly wanted to do things that no one else had done. And probably part of that was the competition with the other groups. Lyrically, maybe with Dylan and musically, performance-wise with The Beatles. But that was just mixed in with his love for and the obsession with music.'

For months on end, Brian recorded and, for his friends, played songs or pieces of music: 'Heroes And Villains.' 'Surf's Up.' Wonderful.' Songs with tantalizing, inexplicable titles like 'Cabin Essence.' Another called 'Do You Like Worms'? What in the world could that be about? 'Wind Chimes.' Just the title evoked a picturesque vibe and sound. A song about 'Vega-Tables' on which Paul McCartney reportedly chomped on a celery stalk. 'Song For Children,' 'Holidays,' and more. There was 'The 'Elements' suite that included 'Mrs. O'Leary's Cow,' a water chant – 'Da Da'/ 'Love to Say Dada,' and 'Vega-Tables.' 'Workshop,' 'Barnyard' and pieces of covers (e.g. 'I Wanna Be Around,' 'Gee,' 'The Old Master Painter,' and 'You Are My Sunshine.')

Brian found a way to constantly make music that continued to shock his collaborator, friends, and observers.

Danny Hutton: 'I remember him playing 'You Are My Sunshine' for me. Great happy, happy lyrics and he just put it all in the minor [key]. The saddest chords, and it was great. The irony of doing that. (*Singing*) "You are my sunshine." Turning it into a dirge. I thought it was very clever. I thought it was fabulous. I thought it was incredible . . . more wonderful, great stuff that he was gonna put all together.'

In the studio, Van Dyke watched as Brian recorded the backing tracks (and sometimes the lead vocals too) for their 'sandbox songs.' There was the acapella 'Prayer.' With everything on tape, once The

Beach Boys had added their vocals, there would easily be an album's worth of music.

Much of this was done well before 1966 had ended. So, in retrospect, it wasn't surprising that the publicity for *SMiLE* had begun in earnest.

Reports about the album started to trickle out, then became something of a deluge, thanks to the work of Derek Taylor. Before becoming the group's publicist, while he was still in England, Derek remembered: 'I would be listening without taking an interest as a fan [until] The Beatles told me I should stop being a bigot. And Lennon said, "They really are great."'

It was Derek's work that led to the first major stories in the US on Brian, and in the UK press taking The Beach Boys seriously. Derek opened the door to the inner sanctum. Journalists Tom Nolan, *Crawdaddy*'s founding editor Paul Williams, and Jules Siegel were among the select few who were handed the keys to the kingdom – access to Brian, to the *SMiLE* sessions – so they could spread the word. And they did just that, not knowing that their work would become the founding documents of the myth.

But in 1966, it wasn't a myth. It was a reality. When Nolan visited Brian in the studio, he remembered that Brian 'spoke with the happy anticipation of a taskmaster about how he was going to work them [The Beach Boys] until they got the perfect blend for this record he was going to make.'

Brian and *SMiLE* were everywhere. In one interview, Dennis Wilson blessed *SMiLE* in his typically bold fashion, one worth repeating here.

Dennis Wilson: 'In my opinion, it makes *Pet Sounds* stink. That's how good it is.'

In the studio, Brian continued to create sounds that were unprecedented. His studio musicians were constantly astounded.

Don Randi: 'He never stayed safe. He always took chances. He always put a major seventh where nobody else would have. Or put the seventh in the bass, instead of on top.'

Carol Kaye: 'He heard sounds, a combination of sounds that were not written before at all. And I think because he didn't have any rules. But he had heard it in his head and you knew that he was creating something really, really big and broad and beautiful. So, something very rare.'

Don: 'It all was in his mind. He was so resourceful. He didn't run out of ideas . . . he was amazing. We didn't hear it . . . but Brian was hearing those things as we were doing them.'

Astonishing music and lyrics. Laughter. And for Brian something perhaps even more significant. Something he had not yet shared publicly. Right around the time 'Prayer' was first recorded, Brian told Tom Nolan for the *L.A. Times' West* Magazine that *SMiLE* 'will be a teenage symphony to God.'

Brian: 'I feel very spiritual when I'm making music. I feel very godly and spiritual. In 1966 I felt the pinnacle of my spiritual-ness. It's hard to describe how it felt. It just felt very emotional and spiritual.'

Spiritual and comical? Brian's musical developments and experiments continued. With his own band of merry pranksters, he continued to pursue the limits of his talents. 'Fun, Fun, Fun?' How about beets and carrots?

Van Dyke: 'Very important. Now, of course, it's farcical. Now, this is kind of [the newspaper comic] 'Far Side,' but I've been taught that farce is the highest form of humour. I've read Jonathan Swift. I knew *Candide*. I've read some stories. And farce, to me, was a very difficult, rarefied, theatrical arena. So 'Vega-Tables' is fine.'

The origin story of this song is two-fold, with a side order of Zappa.

Durrie Parks: 'Brian took to coming over, eating with us, and we were having a lot of salads . . . And [as "The Project"] slowly became more and more intense, we started staying at their house. We spent a great deal of time sleeping in a bedroom [there]. One of the things I remember most clearly is that Van Dyke and Brian would stay up all night writing.'

Perhaps during a break in one of these all-night sessions was when Brian and Van Dyke connected with a non-Wilson 'social influencer.'

Van Dyke: 'There was a guy on a small station out in the [California] desert, in Zzyzx Mineral Springs. His name was Brother Curtis Springer. And he'd talk about the redemption of sound nutrition. And the vegetarian diet. And that's what started this whole thing with vegetables. Curtis had an evangelist approach to his message. He was totally charismatic. And he needed a lot of money to continue his campaign. And, of course, it may be that we contributed to it somehow. We wanted to connect with this guy, maybe even meet him. We were sold on his health kick. That was the beginning of that.'

SMiLE

Durrie: 'Van Dyke had [worked] with Frank Zappa for about a minute and a half . . . Zappa at that point was working on a song about vegetables and when Van Dyke and Brian were working on a song about vegetables, we thought, "This is a natural." And we took Brian to meet Frank . . . I'll never forget the two of those guys shaking hands, talking about vegetables.'

A 'Kodak Moment' indeed. A rock 'n' roll summit for the ages.

As to the work itself, according to the session sheets, when The Beach Boys were in town, e.g., on September 19, they would be in the studio to record their vocals for the stunning, wordless, acapella 'Prayer' which became 'Our Prayer.'

Van Dyke: 'I didn't participate in the 'Prayer.' It's my favourite piece. My favourite lyrics are on the 'Prayer.' Right down to the last *hum.* And kind of an "aw, shucks" ending. Just add a little, a modest button, if you will, at the end, still within the work itself, is a great deal of contemplation. And that comes from a mind at rest. Able to be alone and designing something. Receiving a message, as it were. I don't want to get spiritual on you. But I think it's [a] very spiritual power. And a healing power. And I think music has that potential. Has that opportunity. And you find that from Brian. And that came from Brian Wilson singly. No lyricist was involved in those moments. But it sure made a lot of people happy to participate in its coming together. And on a performance level, so many people did come together.

'It was Brian Wilson who created that opportunity for those voices to pray like they pray together. When people used to get together in a room and sing at each other, with each other. I still got that from The Beach Boys' experience of Brian Wilson. Those are events that go somewhere. They have an exposition, and they satisfy . . . like a good hymn. And if you've spent enough time on some of these aspects, you find great pockets of contemplation. Now, how do you [as an artist] get to those places of contemplation? That was of interest to me. Those were radical things to think.'

For somebody whose ambition was to write 'a teenage symphony to God,' that piece of music might be an ideal way to musically set the stage.

★ ★ ★ ★

Through the fall and early winter of '66 and into '67, recording sessions continued, perhaps two or three a week.

Durrie Parks: '[Brian] could hear things that nobody else could hear. [In the studio], he knew what he wanted, and he knew how to get there. I think it really is a gift with him . . . As self-conscious as he is in some ways, he's just totally un-self-conscious when he's working. He knows what he's after and he's going for it . . . and he gets it.'

Work and fun. Vegetables. God, prayer, and laughter.

Brian: 'The idea of SMiLE was to make people SMiLE and be happy and feel very good.'

Hal Blaine: 'Brian was a happy guy, man. And I don't think it was because there were checks coming in. Musically, it made him so happy, he . . . felt [like] a human being as opposed to a kid in high school or [somebody who] couldn't find his way. He enjoyed laughing. He loved to laugh.'

Michael Vosse: '[At our first meeting], he started talking about the divinity of humour and I liked what he had to say, because humour is basically mean-spirited. We laugh at others' misfortunes. We laugh at our own. We laugh when somebody falls down. Brian was more interested in the exact moment when somebody laughs. Saying that that [at that] moment, he feels it was kind of like sneezing. You have no control. And at that moment you have every possibility of having a divine moment. I think he meant an epiphany. Which may have been an extreme way to look at it, but I thought, "This is really fascinating."'

In our 2004 conversation, I asked Annie Wilson-Karges if anybody at the time pointed out to Brian that some of the SMiLE songs weren't happy, or was that typical of him, always a contradiction?

Annie: 'I think that was typical of him. I think that SMiLE denotes, for me, joy. And joy is an inner thing. "Happy" is something else. But SMiLE is more the inside job.'

Brian believed when you laugh, you lose control. And when you lose control, you can have a spiritual experience. I asked Annie, 'Is that the kind of unique thinking you were hearing all the time in that period?'

Annie: 'In every period. He's capable of coming up with things like that. That's just always been Brian.'

Michael Vosse came aboard the team as Brian's personal assistant. One of his main jobs was to always carry around a Nagra tape recorder for when Brian might want to record sounds. Brian's ideas might not always get realized, like when he wanted to start a fight in a bar so they could record the sounds of the fight. Otherwise, Vosse was omnipresent.

David Anderle: 'Michael [was always] walking around with the Nagra, recording sounds for Brian . . . up at our place recording water sounds for Brian (*laughs*) out of our tap. I think Michael played a very key role for a short period of time in this whole Brother Records thing or this whole *SMiLE* saga. He's the guy that had the eight-millimetre camera running around, taking the films. And Michael was recording everything. He was the documentarian.'

Brian: '[Michael] was a very funny guy, and he had a great sense of humour, a wonderful sense of humour. He produced a short for 'Good Vibrations,' a movie short. We went out on a fire truck. We got on the back of a fire truck . . . running up and down stairs and riding on the fire truck. Just being funny. Sliding down the fire pole, where the firemen would go from their beds down to the fire truck. We were trying to make people laugh. We thought we'd be funny.'

Brian's *SMiLE* 'posse' included his friend Danny Hutton, Michael Vosse, Van Dyke Parks, and David Anderle.

Mark Volman: 'David and Van Dyke were very articulate, and they both had crazy senses of humour. They were both very funny, and their brains jumped from thing to thing really quickly . . . David was probably the smartest of all of us . . . Durrie Parks was a very smart person.'

Durrie: 'David Anderle, during *SMiLE* was, I think, very vital. He was always a positive influence. David likes order, and he tries to present an orderly situation and is a cool head when it is less than orderly. And I think his intention was to have it be a business for Brian's sake. I don't think David ever worked for his own sake in this; I think it was always for Brian and Van Dyke.'

David Anderle: 'All this incredible energy. We started formulating the idea of how we could do a record label that would just be about spreading love and humour and happiness in the world. And that's what Brother Records was supposed to be. That's how I got involved in it. And the next thing I knew, I was Brother Records.'

Brother Records, David explained, was initially created for Brian's side-projects. That's not what ultimately happened, and the exact chronology of Brother Records is difficult to determine, other than to note that Articles of Incorporation were filed in January of 1967.

DUMB ANGEL

David: 'I was so consumed with trying to make Brother Records happen the way Brian wanted. [I was] so stoked by this *SMiLE* stuff going on that I probably didn't really see much beyond that world of Brian and the house, the studio. So I probably missed a lot of the bigger stuff going on around it.'

Supporting Brian's artistry as an individual was Anderle's first call of duty. Which would not necessarily sit well with Capitol Records (who The Beach Boys sued in early 1967) or The Beach Boys, at least one of whom would have a hard time relating to *SMiLE*.

Brian: 'I thought [David] had a lot of brains. He's a very smart guy, and I thought he was good for the job.'

Brian explains, 'I felt like I was in control. In control of myself and on top of my game at that point. I felt like I was in control of my creativity. I never have a hard time concentrating. I never did. I never felt like I was losing focus.'

By December 1966, everything was moving forward. Artist Frank Holmes, a friend of Van Dyke's, created a *SMiLE* shop design for the album cover. He also did a series of imaginative illustrations for a booklet that would be included with the album.

In Capitol's in-house magazine, *Teen Set*, *SMiLE* was featured. Anticipation was building.

Ray Lawlor*, Brian's friend:* 'Before Christmas 1966, the issue of *Teen Set* came out with the *SMiLE* cover. That's when I started calling record stores, hitching to record stores. Somebody had to have that record. Naivete, eh?'

Indeed. Nobody had it. Yet.

And what happened next was a big deal for *SMiLE*.

In December of 1966, filmmaker David Oppenheim was working with Leonard Bernstein – the composer (*West Side Story*, *Candide*, et al), impresario and musical director of the New York Philharmonic – on a television special about 'pop music.' Oppenheim came to Los Angeles to document what was going on with Brian and The Beach Boys.

The 'highbrow' New York music world wanted to know what Brian Wilson was doing. While nothing filmed with the group would become part of the program, when Bernstein and company heard the song 'Surf's Up,' they understood that something new and different was happening. That song would be featured in his 1967 CBS-TV broadcast, *Inside Pop: The Rock Revolution*.

Here's how it was introduced:

David Oppenheim: 'There is a new song, too complex to get all of the first time around. It could come only out of the ferment that characterizes today's pop music scene. Brian Wilson, leader of the famous Beach Boys, and one of today's most important pop musicians, sings his own 'Surf's Up."

Over the fade-out of Brian's performance, Oppenheim said, 'Poetic, beautiful even in its obscurity, 'Surf's Up' is one aspect of new things happening in pop music today. As such, it is a symbol of the change many of these young musicians see in our future.'

Brian had been singled out as one of the rock revolutionaries. What did it mean to be included in this special?

Van Dyke: 'When David Oppenheim came out from New York to Southern California on behalf of Leonard Bernstein to do this thing, to look at Brian Wilson . . . because of Bernstein's view that the validation that he gave Brian's 'Surf's Up,' it just notched everything up, in terms of the possible importance of that project. Because it took The Beach Boys out of the teen world that they'd served so faithfully.'

As always, Brian sums it up more succinctly.

Brian: 'Leonard Bernstein validated what I was doing.'

Van Dyke recalls playing 'Surf's Up' for Dennis.

Van Dyke: 'I came over and played this song that begins, "A diamond necklace played the pawn," and he asked me what it was. In front of Brian. I said, "This is called 'Surf's Up,' Dennis." Because I was determined that we would use that continuum of their image, the surf image. I didn't know how that might be taken, but it was immediately taken enthusiastically . . . And then you notice that [at the end of the Bernstein performance, Brian] goes into a non-verbal kind of a deal, kind of a vibe. We just left that there. It was like a sand painting with something missing . . . we couldn't have imagined that that song would be taken so favourably by Leonard Bernstein.'

Being filmed for Bernstein's CBS program was so important.

Van Dyke: 'It was a thrilling benchmark in the process to get some attention from the tux set. I realized that it put any dispute about Brian's musical relevance to American popular music to rest. Brian had made it with that endorsement. That he brought a validity to the recording process that gave the classicist pause, a reason to stop and look. [Brian] was the first one out of the box.

'That gave us some kind of validation that we were doing the right thing to explore, to try to get outside the box . . . All of that just reinforced in Brian's mind and my own mind the potential for what it was that we were going to do. And it also isolated us a great deal from the rest of the group. The light was on Brian, see? So, I remember that.'

In retrospect, being included on the special became even more significant. But at the time?

It was good for Brian and Van Dyke. Good for *SMiLE*. Was it good for The Beach Boys?

David Anderle: 'So we have the *SMiLE* thing going on. We had the Brother Records formation going on. We had the Beach Boys returning from England, wondering what the hell is going on . . . they don't want anything rocking the boat, as they shouldn't. And so, it got very, very confusing. I mean, I understand why Brian got so confused. I got confused.'

Confusing for sure. But there was a bigger issue. What was this new music and how did The Beach Boys fit into it? And was it right for them?

David Anderle: 'To say "no" or not to support Brian, particularly at that time, 'cause he had so much energy going, was a real detriment. Ergo, when "The Boys" got back from England, I mean, that was "the major no." And doubt. Brian needed a lot of support . . . Support is really important. For Brian, it was critical. I mean, 'no' to Brian was really not a good thing.'

Danny Hutton: 'I think it was the start of him having doubts. Which he never did.'

Regardless, into the winter months of 1966/1967, sessions continued. There were all sorts of recordings, including work on 'The Elements' suite, covers (e.g. 'I Wanna Be Around'), pure fun ('Workshop') and endless sessions for 'Heroes And Villains.'

A proper chronology of the *SMiLE* era includes key non-musical events: In January of 1967, Carl was drafted, and declared 'conscientious objector' status. In February, the group sued Capitol Records.

Determining how, when, and why *SMiLE* began to fall apart is much more difficult. Actually, it's impossible.

Looking back (in our 1977 interview), Derek Taylor recalled, 'I got very muddled by *SMiLE* . . . All I know is that it was goddam hard to publicize them 'cause I didn't know what was coming out. What were they releasing? As I wrote in some paper, 'Heroes And Villains' was certainly the most famous single *never* released up to that point.'

But weeks before the Bernstein taping, there was one moment that is often singled out as brilliant, terrifying and the turning point, the moment when the joy of *SMiLE* becomes something else.

Just after Thanksgiving, on November 28, 1966, a piece of music was recorded. The AFM (Musician's union) log called it 'The Elements-Part 1.' The 'Fire' music. 'Mrs. O'Leary's Cow.'

As a composition, as an arrangement, as a production, there can be little doubt that it was and is brilliant. But what did it mean? What was going on in Brian's head when this howling sound emerged?

★   ★   ★   ★

'The more horrifying the world becomes, the more art becomes abstract.'
Paul Klee

The 'Fire' session occurred just days after The Beach Boys had returned from England. In the UK, the media, the fans, and the world of pop were all going wild over *Pet Sounds*, an album that was a big step forward in Brian's *artistic* evolution. 'Good Vibrations' was on the radio everywhere.

Brian: 'Recording 'Fire' . . . we've got fire helmets for the musicians, little toy fire hats. And I brought in a bucket of fire, and it made the mood come, a little bit, and it would go real good.'

Danny Hutton: 'Brother Julius hung around Gold Star. And, as a bit of a goof, he rolled in a big a garbage can with a flaming fire inside. Then he rolled it out. It was just for fun.'

Hal Blaine: 'Now, remember, there would have been five, six, seven of these going on, at once. Everybody had a whistle. (*Makes noises with various slide whistles.*) It was almost like a New Year's Eve party, to parallel it that way. Everybody was just having fun. And the guys loved it.'

Brian: "Fire' was a little bit bizarre for me to go through . . . But we did it. It's very different, off-the-wall music, so it's not like, 'Surfer Girl' or 'Be True to Your School.' . . . I'm feeling unhappy so I thought 'Fire' would express the crazy, weird thoughts I was going through.

Van Dyke: 'It was like, all of this was so much fun. And I was watching the guy in crisis. And I knew that all of a sudden, if this was a joke, it was at someone's expense. And whose expense was it but Brian's?'

Los Angeles was in the midst of one of its frequent droughts, and shortly after the 'Fire' session, a building near the studio reportedly burned down. Dennis Wilson apparently put the idea in Brian's head that his music was the cause. Was this the first example of creeping paranoia? If so, there would soon be fuel added to the fire.

It was time for The Beach Boys to dive into the vocal sessions for *SMiLE*. And if they had regarded *Pet Sounds* as a departure, they didn't know what to make of these news songs.

Could The Beach Boys sing the parts Brian was teaching them to his satisfaction? Yes. *But did they want to sing the parts Brian had written?*

Brian: 'I knew how good it was, but I thought they would think it was too far into a new creative bag."

Brian knew his bandmates very well.

Brian: 'They said, "Hey, that's too creative. We don't like that." [I said] "Give me a break. I'm trying something new . . ." I thought maybe they wouldn't like it at first, but I knew they'd get used to it as soon as they heard it all . . . When they said they didn't like it, it hurt my feelings a lot. Really, it did. It really killed me inside.'

Could it all come together? In a mid-1966 interview, Brian had explained, 'The thing is I write and think in terms of what The Beach Boys can do. Not what they find easy to do but what I know they are capable of doing which isn't always the same thing . . . I have a governor in my mind which keeps my imagination in order . . . But I don't like to be told, "It can't be done," when I know it can. That's the point. It mostly can.'

What were the issues? Remember, we're talking about very young men. Mike Love was the oldest, at 25; Carl, the youngest, was 18. In a sense, all they had ever known was being a Beach Boy and the fame and fortune that came with that. Perhaps, they thought, this new music threatened their livelihood.

Brian: 'I'd done the tracks, but I needed their voices on the tracks. Even though I could sing all the parts, I still needed them to do it. I needed that Beach Boy blend. I knew they were right; they didn't know. But I knew. They didn't think they were right for it; but I knew they were right for it.'

David Anderle: 'It was awful to watch because the procedure was always Brian going into the studio with the guys and going over the parts with them in the past. And he was [now] doing that with these [Van Dyke Parks'] lyrics ... There was a huge amount of frustration. And you could see Brian becoming very frustrated ... Mike was trying to make sense of it. Carl was being diplomatic about it and Dennis was going, "We can do it, Bri."'

Were the lyrics the sole cause of the problem?

Elvis Costello: 'If you're writing music that is almost completely without precedent, then why wouldn't you have words that are the same?'

Was it just the lyrics? Or was Brian imploding? Was The Beach Boys world itself imploding? Had the relationship between the touring group and Brian as the musical leader in the studio reached a breaking point? Had Brian reached a breaking point?

Did they resent Brian for getting so much media attention? Did Brian feel badly that he was the focus of the press's attention? Or were The Beach Boys just scared? And did their response to the new music amplify Brian's fears and insecurities? Shake his confidence?

It was clear in December that the album wouldn't be finished anytime soon, so Capitol Records postponed the January release date of *SMiLE*. But the pressure to finish the record must have been intense.

In the studio, The Beach Boys worked hard to master the vocal parts Brian was teaching them. And they did so, beautifully. But the words? What were these songs about?

Van Dyke: 'We just continued, as you can see, with a passion ... and made mistakes. [We] should have accommodated all of The Beach Boys. Somehow, I feel that that was my responsibility too, and I didn't do it. Somehow. But honestly, I didn't do it because I wasn't able to do it. I wasn't able to serve all the masters. But I knew this, that if you don't aim high, you don't get anything ... so to achieve what I'd say are the transcendental moments of the work, I was perfectly happy to reserve the right to be wrong, that was okay with me. If we continued the project further, I think we would have come up with some more durable goods.'

★ ★ ★ ★

DUMB ANGEL

'No artist is ahead of his time. He is his time. It is just that the others are behind the time.' **Martha Graham**

'The job of the artist is always to deepen the mystery.' **Francis Bacon**

'The music business is a cruel and shallow trench, a long plastic hallway where thieves and pimps run free, and good men lie like dogs. There is also a negative side.' **Hunter S. Thompson**

Brian did not think of himself as a genius. He thought of himself as 'ingenious.' He believed the music of SMiLE was jovial, that it would bring joy to people. But events were about to take such a dark turn that even in retrospect, the emotional, psychological, and record-business turmoil surrounding the project is hard to clearly define.

With SMiLE, Brian was aiming for the cosmos. Since childhood, he'd always been fascinated with the stars. Could his music take him (and the listener) into the furthest reaches of the galaxy? Would The Beach Boys happily board this rocket ship that he and Van Dyke had been constructing?

Unfortunately for Brian, for The Beach Boys, for the SMiLE project and music lovers everywhere, that's not what happened. Artistically, Brian seemed to have been about to change the course of music history. But Brian, as competitive as he was, had a loyalty ingrained in him.

And so, we return to 'Fire.'

Van Dyke: 'I was probably unhappy with 'Mrs. O'Leary's Cow' because . . . there was no room for lyrics. Damn it. And the other was that it was very abstract.'

Van Dyke believes the 'Fire' music 'was a product of Brian's own anxieties. All of that in the face at the same time everyone had . . . an obsession for jollity. That there was . . . so, so much fun. And I was watching a guy in crisis. It's like watching a falling man. He was a falling man . . . And so, I had great reservations about exploiting his psychological dilemma. That's the way I looked at it, anyway.'

Van Dyke soldiered on. 'I've always been a Pollyanna. I've always wanted something to be totally positive. I always want a better world. I always wanted to disquiet the confident and make comfortable those who are not comfortable. To upset those who are comfortable, bring agitation to those. So, I am looking for a way out of the status quo.'

The 'Fire' music was, to Van Dyke, not aligned with the confirmational spirit behind the *SMiLE* project.

Van Dyke: 'All of a sudden, Brian's music was taking a turn for a kind of a deeper and despairing quality.'

Reconsidering this in 2004, Van Dyke had a different point of view. And how that relates to what was happening back in 1966/67: 'It's no longer a concern to me. As I am just listening to this stuff. It seems to me it's a necessary ingredient. Man's problems aren't with himself. They are with society.'

In late 1966, as Van Dyke made clear in 2004, 'It's the exterior stuff, which brings psychological distress to an individual. It's those events around an individual that feed into his psychological well-being or problems ... And that's the [why] I dismiss all this stuff with Brian's "problems." They are not Brian's problems at all. They are the problems of people around him. And it's too damned bad that so much time was lost in his being able to recognize that. But it's no time for regret. It's time for celebration that [in 2004] he has the stamina and the interest to do this. And it's a defining moment of the project.'

In 1966, 'Mrs. O'Leary's Cow' seems to have been a defining moment of the project too. At least for some people.

In the 1966 'word association' interview Brian had done, when asked to respond to the word 'Fear,' he had said: 'Not knowing what to expect is the only reason for fear.'

Brian did not know how The Beach Boys would react to the *SMiLE* songs. He had confidence in the work. He believed it was important and cutting edge. But he feared how the record company would react, how the group would respond.

Lindsey Buckingham: 'He was taking chances, bucking the system, so to speak, when everyone around him was expecting him to make a certain type of music. Brian had to create his own support system to do that.'

But would that be enough?

Jeff Bridges, *actor:* 'Sometimes, an artist will leave his comrades in the dust.'

Artistically, Brian Wilson had done that. But how would his family band respond? And would Brian choose to be loyal to his creation or to his family?

DON'T F*** WITH THE FORMULA

IF *BEAUTIFUL DREAMER: BRIAN WILSON AND THE STORY OF SMILE* WAS TO succeed as a documentary, I had to find out why Brian stopped working on *SMiLE*.

SMiLE was as far from formula as a Beach Boys record could be. But why did he stop working on it? Was it record company pressure? Was it resistance from within the band? Had he lost his way artistically? Was it drugs?

In my lengthy interviews with Brian, I asked him repeatedly about the *SMiLE* era.

One time, he said, 'David, ask better questions.'

The question remained in the air. 'Why did you stop work on *SMiLE?*'

Finally, perhaps definitively, Brian answered. It was, it seemed to me, with a weary sigh, as though, if he told me now, he would never have to answer the question again.

Brian: 'I'll tell you from my heart. In 1967, the reasons why I didn't finish *SMiLE* was: Mike didn't like it. I thought it was too experimental. I thought that the "Fire" tape was too scary. I thought that people wouldn't understand where my head was at, at that time. Those are the reasons.'

What did that mean? Despite The Beach Boys commercial concerns, he had finished *Pet Sounds*. So even if they weren't completely behind the *SMiLE* project, why couldn't he finish it?

'Too Experimental?'

Michael Vosse recalled the first time Brian heard The Beatles' 'Strawberry Fields Forever,' their most experimental single ever. Brian said, 'They've done it . . . what I wanted to do.' Vosse was unsure if Brian was serious, but that record, while advanced, was unlike the *SMiLE* music. Maybe that record should have confirmed for Brian that being experimental was the right direction.

But in Brian's head, there seems to have been a production race between *SMiLE* and The Beatles' new album. This was a creative rivalry. And hearing their new record had an impact on him.

Van Dyke: 'Paul McCartney was only the adversary. But this was a nationalistic, a chauvinistic warfare in the truest sense, of the musical competition between The Beatles and The Beach Boys, and it was set up by The Beatles' regard for The Beach Boys.'

In part, that's why Derek Taylor had been hired.

Danny Hutton: 'Derek saw the big picture. He understood Brian's stuff right away . . . And I think he was almost the conduit or the spy. (*Laughs*) I think he was the guy letting The Beatles know, "You guys better watch out. You had better work a little harder. Because he's doing stuff that's going to blow your mind." Probably one of the reasons why Paul came out to check out what was going on.'

Joseph Heller, *Catch-22:* 'Just because you're paranoid doesn't mean they aren't after you.'

There were so many things for Brian to deal with.

Danny: 'I remember being at the 'Barnyard' session . . . with all the animal sounds. Then there was the session where they had all the laughing instruments. And I just think [The] Beach Boys heard that stuff and said, "What the heck? What is that all about?" I think he started getting pummelled mentally. And I think that's when he started having pressure, probably, laid on him.'

Brian: 'The resistance was something I didn't like. I didn't like the resistance at all. I didn't like it.'

There were so many magnificent pieces of music. The Beach Boys sang beautifully and brilliantly on them.

Mike: 'We did some really hard stuff, hard to do. And it took a lot of focus.'

But how did it all fit together?

Danny: 'Only he knew where he was going with it.'

Did he? With 'Good Vibrations,' Brian had to fit the pieces into one song. That wasn't done in a day or a week. Or a month. For *SMiLE*, it was an entire album, with many more pieces. How long would it take to finish *SMiLE* to his satisfaction? Brian thought he might need at least a year.

Brian: 'And I figured no one would give me a year to complete it.'

From an 'outsider's' perspective, how did Van Dyke's lyrics fit into the puzzle?

Danny: 'Van Dyke was just such an interesting person to sit with. And his form of communication, his pun on a pun on a pun, and then you'd say [to yourself], "What did that guy just say?" Because Van Dyke would say something, and as he was saying it, he would make a joke on what he'd said that was so clever. You were trying to figure out that joke, and then he'd put another joke on the joke. And if you didn't know him well, this guy just rambled at you.

'But if you sat there and listened to him – the complex lyrics, and the structure – which I think really, for an outsider, or someone like Mike Love, to come in off a tour after singing about hamburger stands and cars, must have been an incredible shock. And as much as I don't agree with Mike, I do see that, that for him it must have been an incredible shock.'

In the video promotional campaign for the 2011 *SMiLE* sessions box set, the Beach Boys had this to say about the project:

Bruce: 'I know he knew he was covering brand-new ground.'

Brian: 'I said, "You know what, Mike? I like car songs and I like surf songs . . . But we have to grow musically now . . . Just trust me. Just do your tours, and I'll get the music together."'

Mike: 'My thought process was exactly this: "Our fans in Omaha . . . Are they going to be able to get with this product of West Coast seeking?"'

Brian: 'When this is done, everybody's gonna love it.'

As this story evokes the description 'Rashomon,' there were way more than three ways to look at *SMiLE's* demise.

Perhaps most simply, Mike didn't find Van Dyke Parks's lyrics relatable, didn't think the Beach Boys concert audiences would 'get' them.

Annie Wilson-Karges: 'I remember that was another notch in the disapproval factor that was happening. It was Capitol Records with their feedback, and then the lyrics were too wordy now, and it wasn't simple like the old days. Yes, I definitely remember that.'

Brian: 'Mike did not like SMiLE at all. He hated it. He hated it.'

Could Brian shrug it off?

Annie: 'I don't think Brian shrugged anything off. I think everything pierced him at some level. I don't think he was able to shrug too many of those things off.'

Brian: 'I didn't know how to deal with it. I really didn't. I didn't know how to deal with it.'

So much pressure. Was time running out?

Perhaps Brian in January 1967 wasn't the same person he was a year earlier. Maybe he didn't have the same strength, certainty, and power. *SMiLE was* unquestionably avant-garde, a giant step into the unknown for a pop group. But these were Brian's experiments. Was somebody telling him they were 'too experimental?'

The issues surrounding *Pet Sounds*, including its relative commercial failure in the US, may have planted the seeds of doubt. Or perhaps just seedlings. But in the emotional turmoil of his life in 1967, perhaps exacerbated by drugs, that may have been enough. Given how Capitol Records had received *Pet Sounds*, would *SMiLE* have been a giant step too far for them?

Considering their response to *Pet Sounds,* Brian had good reason to be concerned.

Brian: 'I thought people wouldn't understand where my head was at, at that time.'

Did he mean the record buyers or did he mean The Beach Boys? Or did he mean members of The Beach Boys were telling him that their fans wouldn't want *SMiLE*?

A close observer who had witnessed *SMiLE* from its birth, has strong opinions and specific observations on how it devolved, what went wrong.

Durrie Parks: 'There were recording sessions where people wouldn't participate. There were meetings where it was discussed that this wasn't going well . . . or the feeling was that this was maybe not the best move to make and that maybe it should not come out in its present form at that time. And this was even after the Oppenheim thing, which was a blessing – I think in several ways – and gave Van Dyke and Brian at last some positive feedback from people outside of the immediate realm who felt that it was good [. . .] and useful to pursue. But there were clearly people who did not enjoy participating. And when somebody doesn't enjoy participating and you're dealing with a kind of family – "Hey, gang, let's put on a show" kind of thing – it makes it very difficult.'

Van Dyke: 'I do know that Brian sought confirmation or validation from a lot of people . . . There were a lot of opinions about different ways of presenting the project. And I think that that undermined the project a great deal.'

Was there a point where Brian's behaviour started to change?

Annie Wilson-Karges: 'I think we started to observe more mood swings with Brian at that time. One could only guess what they were directly correlated to. But that wasn't particularly part of his personality, that I had witnessed. They just started to occur. Then they became more familiar than not. So, the tide definitely turned with all of that. It didn't start out that way.'

Van Dyke: 'Brian [had] made it clear to me that he wanted to do something without restraint or apology or explanation to the rest of the group. And he honestly felt that I was a big enough guy to handle the door. There is no question of that. I wasn't a big enough guy. I tried to defend . . . to guarantee his right to continue this project. I had a very sceptical view about industrial largesse.

'I thought that it was crazy when people talked about how record company presidents had so much vision and so much patience and so much interest in the art. All of this [talk] about corporate largesse, the idea that a record company patiently waited for Brian to finish 'Good Vibrations' is horseshit. The fact is that he fought mightily day and night to change the way the record business viewed record production.

'Nobody had the moxie, the cheek, the nerve, the crust . . . to give the kind of special attention that Brian did to [a] perfectly produced record. Nobody had that. And Brian made that possible. There was a sense of relief in California among all the people at the gate [meaning other recording artists] – ready to run, to race – that Brian had just done something for everybody.'

Including The Beach Boys.

Durrie Parks: 'Carl Wilson . . . a beautiful, gentle, soul. Carl just always seemed vulnerable to me . . . and boy, could he sing. Dennis was very thoughtful. He was very concerned about people, and he just always got in trouble for whatever he did. There was just nothing that went on that Dennis didn't get blamed for, and he always was great. Mike Love is a challenging person, I would say.'

Mark Volman: 'Mike had a lot to say about it, 'cause Mike wanted to be The Beach Boys. Mike was a star in the way that he [took] it on stage. I liked Mike a lot ... he had a good sense of humour about it all, even though he'd say one thing to Brian, and then kind of turn around and go, "This is nuts. This is crazy stuff." And he had an opinion on everything that Brian was doing, and it wasn't good.'

As for Murry Wilson, Mark recalls that 'when we were there at the house, [Murry would] say, "Get rid of them. Send them home. We have business," and Brian would be, "But these are my friends." Murry [would say] "Get rid of 'em."'

Murry Wilson, as his father, as The Beach Boys' publisher, was still bullying Brian.

With pressure to finish a single, Brian and The Beach Boys were constantly in the studio in February recording vocals pieces of 'Heroes And Villains,' pieces that Brian would have to assemble as he'd done with 'Good Vibrations.' There were instrumental dates too. In February, a dozen sessions for just that one song.

Ambition without precedent.

In the sessions, he was in charge, knew what he wanted. But he was seemingly unable to find a way to finish the 'Heroes And Villains' single to his satisfaction. Were there record company deadlines he couldn't meet?

At the start, Durrie Parks felt that Brian 'just had an exuberance and things were a lotta fun for him; he was getting to do some things he'd never had a chance to do before. I think that was important to him, and he saw humour in what they were doing. And some other members of the group missed the humour element of it. And I think that's true of Van Dyke's humour in large measure. People often miss the humour, and I think in this case they missed Brian's humour.'

It was all slipping away.

And so, we return to Brian's reason number one.

Durrie: 'Mike Love didn't, at the time, really appreciate *SMiLE* ... Mike was not shy about letting people know that he didn't like it. Didn't like the lyrics, didn't like what was happening, didn't like Van Dyke really. I don't know if it was [that he] didn't like Van Dyke in the role he was playing with Brian in the *SMiLE* creation or if he just didn't like what was happening to what he saw as The Beach Boys' legacy, but he definitely made it difficult.'

In sharing her opinion, Durrie offers a surprising assessment.

Durrie: 'I think that it was fairly clear, fairly early on, that this was not going to be a process that got completed. It was clear to me that there was some real opposition from Mike Love and perhaps from other people. I don't know. Mike could easily have been the front person for a strong feeling from The Beach Boys . . . But there was opposition. And it was felt really early on, and it made it very difficult.'

Was there an identifiable reason?

Durrie: 'I think family is important to Brian . . . I don't think that he would've fought anybody who felt really strongly about it, who had a professional impact on him. I think it was the whole Beach Boys organization kind of thing that was more difficult for him to deal with in the family aspect. Because Dennis and Carl were never a problem for Brian. In my witnessing, they were always very honest with each other and everybody spoke out . . . I think it was other influences.'

Why and how did the producer of *Pet Sounds* and 'Good Vibrations' reach a place where he needed constant approval from everybody's opinions to boost his confidence? Was he now beginning to become unsure about the direction that he was taking? Did this contribute to an increase in a need to escape through self-medicating drug use? Was he having a mental and/or emotional collapse?

Whatever those influences were, Durrie believes that 'great art does not need unconditional support. I think great art survives against great opposition . . . I think that Brian was under immense pressure. And for a while they wouldn't do work every day . . . [But] I didn't ever see [an] "Okay, I quit, I'm done. I'm through" [moment].'

Van Dyke: 'I don't think that it's fair to say that Brian needed unconditional support. I don't think he is that much of a sissy. I think that, quite frankly, the guy had a lot of self-reliance . . . He was totally self-reliant; he could go into a studio and just make music with nothing there. He could do it unaccompanied.'

Van Dyke elaborates: 'I don't think he needed anything. He didn't get the support that he could have used. I think the issue wasn't what he needed or could have used. But I think the question is that he didn't get what he should have had. And that bugged him, deeply. He had had it, of course.

He was in the habit of getting all of the support and cooperation he needed until it went beyond the designs of [a] five-man group.'

Durrie: 'Brian's behaviour started changing in the process of *SMiLE* as he encountered opposition, and it became more and more difficult to proceed and he began to, again in a child-like context, act out . . . I couldn't even define for you exactly what that means. But I think it was clear that Brian was unhappy and wasn't sure exactly how to channel this unhappiness or how to correct for it . . . I think Brian is a very gentle soul and . . . that did not necessarily serve him well here.'

Durrie saw that 'he let himself be discouraged in the process but that he's so creative that you saw it coming out in other ways . . . I never saw a time when Brian stopped creating . . . I didn't really recall a day when I felt that . . . the project had reached its shelving because Van Dyke and Brian continued to see one another and to work.'

So, did Brian's Reason number one cause Reason number two?

Durrie reaches her conclusion.

Durrie: 'My sense was that Mike Love felt that this *SMiLE* thing was too far out for The Beach Boys. It's not where he wanted The Beach Boys going. He knew that The Beach Boys had a winning formula, if you will, in what they did and what they wrote about, and he didn't want to go this other way. He didn't want to sing those lyrics. He wasn't sure what they meant, and he didn't want to be part of it. And this is totally subjective, my feeling is that Mike would've had the same response to Bob Dylan. It wasn't necessarily that it was Van Dyke although I think that may have created a little extra friction, but he didn't want to be doing aerated or brainy or that kind of double entendre humorous or any of those things. My sense is he wanted to stay straight where they were . . . surfer girls, California, that thing. That was what he wanted to do.'

In 1995, a few years before he passed, Carl Wilson would confirm this.

Carl: 'I know there's been a lot written and maybe said about Michael not liking the *SMiLE* music. As I recall, his main problem was that the lyrics were not relatable. They were so artistic and to him, "airy fairy." Too abstract. Personally, I loved it.'

Fair enough. They certainly weren't what The Beach Boys' audience was used to. Or pre-1967, the mainstream pop audience.

DON'T F*** WITH THE FORMULA

In a 2011 interview for the *Mojo '60s SMiLE* article, one Beach Boy added his point of view.

Alan Jardine: 'I loved Van Dyke's lyrics. I just saw them as art for art's sake. These wonderful couplets. Mike [Love] didn't like 'em, because he didn't understand them. But you're not supposed to understand 'em. It's like a Lewis Carroll novel. But maybe it was out of context for a band called The Beach Boys. That's really what it's all about. But you have a lead singer who is fragile and needs to express himself, and things change.'

What about Capitol?

Alan: 'The label didn't dig it. I know that.'

Brian: 'I presented something, and they go, "That's not appropriate music." I said, "OK, well, I'll talk to you later about it." And that was that.'

Was the record company listening to what was happening in 1966? How rapidly the major forces in pop music were evolving? Had they heard The Beatles' *Revolver* and Dylan's *Blonde on Blonde*, both released in 1966, and realized the times were indeed changing?

Mike Love (in the 2016 *Pet Sounds* documentary): 'Anything and everything The Beatles did was worth paying attention to and was an inspiration.'

In retrospect. But what about fifty years earlier?

Did anybody at Capitol or within the group grasp that in *three years*, The Beatles had dramatically gone from 'I Want to Hold Your Hand' to 'Strawberry Fields Forever'? Why couldn't The Beach Boys go from 'Surfin' U.S.A.' to 'Surf's Up' in a similar stretch of time? At this crucial moment, did the group cheer him on and say, 'Brian, you've got the music to keep us competitive, to keep us in the game'?

Was anybody at Capitol listening to contemporary music?

Releases in 1966-1967 included The Kinks' *Face to Face*, *Fresh Cream*, The Rolling Stones' *Aftermath*, Donovan's *Sunshine Superman* and the first Buffalo Springfield and Young Rascals albums. *Jefferson Airplane Takes Off*. Yes, there was, indeed, something happening here.

There were vocal harmony groups that were new rivals too, notably The Mamas & the Papas and The Association. I am not talking about out-of-the-mainstream creations like Frank Zappa and The Mothers of Invention's *Freak Out*, or those that didn't connect with the bigger pop audience like Love or The 13th Floor Elevators. I am talking about artists who were in the Top 10. The competition.

What would have happened if somebody (i.e., Capitol and/or The Beach Boys) had said to Brian, 'These are the most beautiful, remarkable, and unusual compositions you've ever created. How can we help you complete it and bring it to the marketplace?' Did anybody say or think, 'We know Capitol wants "formula" hits. Why don't you release this as a Brian Wilson album, and then we can make a Beach Boys record?'

As to Brian, Durrie Parks thinks 'Brian was in an experimentation. He was enjoying this so much . . . Whether it was building the sandbox or experimenting with sounds, feeling the elements. And I think that had a spiritual aspect for Brian, probably more for Brian than for Van Dyke or for the rest of us. But I definitely thought that it had a spiritual aspect for Brian. I felt that the whole elements, the whole connectedness, this whole experience was very important for Brian.'

Some of the experimental recordings – such as when 'George Fell Into His French Horn' or when Brian insisted that he was inside the microphone – were (in the parlance of the sixties) 'far out.'

Those experiments were fun or funny or fascinatingly strange or a waste of time or 'What's wrong with Brian?' depending upon your point of view. If you didn't have the big picture, perhaps certain sessions might not have made sense either.

Brian had recorded the terrific songs he and Van Dyke had written. Did anybody, listening to how the music world was changing, understand that these songs and Van Dyke Parks' lyrics were indeed right for that moment? Brian would have kept The Beach Boys 'ahead of the curve.' If the record had been completed. If the record had come out.

However, this is all theorizing, because we don't know how the record-buying audience would have received the *SMiLE* music in 1967, because it wasn't released. Should it have been?

The publicity about *SMiLE* had *music* fans very excited. In the US and the UK, those anticipating *SMiLE* had embraced *Pet Sounds* and 'Good Vibrations.' They may not even have been the regular Beach Boys concert fans. But through Derek Taylor's work, excitement had been building for months.

Again, **Sir George Martin:** 'We heard about *SMiLE* being made at the time when we were in the sixties and we were so excited, we were waiting . . . and rumours were, it was great. But we never heard anything. And it was coming out and we were waiting for it. And it never happened. We waited in vain.'

Was the bullying in 1967 too much for Brian to resist? Was Brian's drug use to blame?

Danny Hutton: 'I think he was probably doing speed, some kind of uppers at the time. And drinking. But I think they helped him just work longer hours. I don't think they got in the way at all.'

This part of the story is rarely mentioned, but apparently, Murry Wilson hired a private detective to follow Brian, to find out how he was getting drugs. The paranoia Brian had about his father wasn't necessarily in his imagination.

Michael Vosse: 'I just think whatever the hell Murry did about getting private detectives to look into Brian's drug use, that drugs is the biggest red herring in the Brian Wilson story I've heard so far. I just don't buy it.'

So, if it wasn't drugs, what was it? You'll have to read this next quote very carefully. I read it several times before I completely got the import of it, understood what Mr. Parks was saying *about the end of the project.*

Van Dyke: 'It's only when the people around him stopped being interested so much in what he was doing and [more] how it affected them that problems happened. And that's all understandable, 'cause I don't think anybody is inherently evil. I don't think anyone inherently wanted to stop Brian Wilson's creativity. I think that Mike Love is the most famous instrument of restraint in the situation to the point that he defeated the process, but he didn't do it maliciously . . . he couldn't understand what it was all about. And ultimately, I got to the point where I couldn't understand what it was all about.

'It's not because of Mike Love that I walked away. It was because of my own irrelevance that I walked away. There were too many things conspiring against the record . . . and that's not just related to [the lawsuit] settlement with Capitol Records, 'cause, believe me, that [money] didn't come out of Capitol Records without a lot of hostility and adversarial incident. The Beach Boys were having a terrible time, both within and without, and I felt like an intruder. I don't feel like that anymore . . . That's why I [prefer to] keep talking about [2004's] *SMiLE*, Part Deux.'

Trying to understand what ended the project is like trying to survive in a circular firing squad.

What, we have to wonder, were The Beach Boys really thinking *in 1967*? On tour, they were big stars, headlining shows, playing the hits to adoring crowds. Did they see *SMiLE* as a disaster for them? When it came to Van Dyke Parks, was it just jealousy that Brian had chosen this outsider . . . a man who Brian has called his favourite collaborator? Was it fear that you might be out of a job if *SMiLE* was released by Brian as a solo project? Perhaps drugs can be blamed too, but why do people take drugs?

★   ★   ★   ★

As the early months of 1967 passed, Brian's rooting section . . . his new friends . . . were slowly vanishing, leaving, or (as in the case of David Anderle) essentially being banished by Brian when he wouldn't come out of his bedroom for a meeting.

One 1966 British headline about 'Good Vibrations' had read, 'They've discovered the new sound at last!'

Capitol wanted a new single and a new album and they wanted it NOW. They had begun actively promoting *SMiLE* in early 1967. Capitol wanted 'product.' And Brian needed time. The pressure to 'hurry up and finish *SMiLE*' just added to his anxiety.

In February, Brian's focus was on 'Heroes And Villains,' which was to be the follow-up to 'Good Vibrations,' the first single from *SMiLE*; it became all-consuming. But as the Ides of March approached, Brian still hadn't completed it to his satisfaction. It had to be perfect. And The Beach Boys, wanting to please Capitol, their fans, and Brian, were unsure of whether *SMiLE* was the right 'career move.' As if 'art' is a 'career move.'

And still, amidst all the push and pull, The Beach Boys sang beautifully on the *SMiLE* songs: stunning melodies combined with the sheer inscrutable brilliance in the lyrics by Van Dyke Parks. Who had written joyously with Brian for months before it was time to record the group's vocals.

The key problem for Brian seemed to be that his complete control was being questioned. The division of labour between the touring group and his work in the studio no longer had a clear line. And he wouldn't or couldn't stand up for himself. And Van Dyke Parks began to feel there was nothing left for him to contribute.

DON'T F*** WITH THE FORMULA

Van Dyke: 'As time went on, I got less able to provide lyrics because the music became more abstract. I noticed that. Like I say, I went out through the barnyard [referring to a piece of *SMiLE*]. I didn't understand all he was doing. But it was clear to me, I think, probably before anyone else, that Brian was headed for an emotional collapse. I knew that.

'I wasn't about ready to announce that. Because . . . Which came first, the chicken or the egg? Did he fall apart because the project was perceived with such reasonable doubt by the group, for example. First of all, because, of course, Brian's autonomy was putting the same people out of work that he'd already made millionaires. See? And that would be troubling, to me.

'It wasn't so much like being able to know Brian Wilson. It wasn't that, because I think that there was a great sense of "good fences make good neighbours," as Robert Frost said. There were good fences between me and Brian. I always respected him and his marriage and his family. And he respected me. We were not guppies in a fishbowl. We weren't just hanging out and feeling good.

'There was nothing hedonistic about the experience, by the way. It was tough to keep up with this fellow, in his pursuit of a musical ideal. And it's obvious . . . his love for music was driving him. But it was the people around him and the crowded house it became that generally made it hard for me to get my snout in the trough. My ideas were less and less relevant, it seemed to me, or useful for his purposes.'

And then Van Dyke sadly admitted, 'I believe there came a time when I was irrelevant. And I think that the words, the better the words that I put down were the product of his "time to get alone" [a reference to a solo song Brian wrote in 1967] . . . So, it wasn't so much a collaboration to me.'

Van Dyke: 'Those are [Brian] songs where the words are good. Where you can hear his extemporaneous flare in the melody or in the progression. The more sectionalized things became, later on, the more difficult it was for me to find out where the words should focus and how. I was perfectly happy [with the lyric "over and over, the] 'crow cries uncover the cornfield."' . . . I liked that image. To tell you the truth, I think it's a wonderful image. And I think that it was perfectly set to the music.

'But, Hell's Bells, it sure is tedious to have to explain lyrics to people. And it wasn't something I wanted to do for a living . . . And there was nothing I could do. Nothing that my staying involved with the project would do to make it an any more fruitful experience for Brian, which was the only obligation I had, was just to try to do my best.'

Van Dyke felt he had no place in Brian's world anymore. So he left. Van Dyke recalls thinking: '"Maybe Tony Asher might come back. Or Brian might continue himself. Or Mike Love might step up to the plate to facilitate Brian's emergence as a recording artist and songwriter." But that didn't happen. And, after all was said and done, after all this time, I would say that, yes, there is a question about the fragility of my own contribution to the project. But I will say this. "In the land of the blind, the one-eyed is king," and I was there, looking straight ahead and doing a good job, a faithful job, as a lyricist.'

As *The Beach Boys SMiLE Sessions* box set, released in 2011, showed, there were lots of complete songs, some terrific tracks without lyrics, some pieces of music that hadn't necessarily found their place in a song line-up. That puzzle was the producer's challenge. Meaning Brian's. Could he do it?

And still, the recording sessions continued.

An April 22, 1967 piece for *Disc and Music Echo* was headlined 'Paul drops in at a Beach Boys recording session.' As in McCartney.

It may have been the last positive moment of the *SMiLE* saga. The legendary 'Vega-Tables' session. Afterwards, Paul played the as-yet unreleased 'She's Leaving Home' for Brian.

Derek Taylor described the summit meeting between Brian and Paul: 'Somehow it was like Van Gogh meeting Constable meeting Turner meeting Rembrandt in a time machine fuelled by a compound of adrenalin and Dexedrine in unequal parts depending on the necessary speed.'

Derek's article also detailed ongoing changes: "Heroes And Villains' is not going to be a single . . . The talk now is that it will be an album track on *Smile*, the also famous album also not yet complete. Please understand that the Beach Boys' delays with product are the result of painful self-criticism. The mirrors into which Brian Wilson looks for reassurance are not always kind. Sometimes there is no reflection at all . . . It was ever thus with great men.'

One last thought about that meeting with Paul – Did hearing that beautiful ballad from *Sgt. Pepper* put in Brian's head the thought, 'They've won. I'm done.'?

DON'T F*** WITH THE FORMULA

This lightly-edited sequence from *Beautiful Dreamer*, from the people who knew Brian best at the time, gives us a sense of what was happening:

Michael Vosse: 'I think he was becoming confused emotionally. I think a lot of issues that had been festering inside this guy, that he had managed to compartmentalise so that he could make his music, may have burst out of their boundaries.'

David Anderle: 'God, the forces he was fighting — the guys, his dad, the label — I don't think he could've done it alone. He would've needed his little army to help him.'

Van Dyke Parks: 'He didn't lose his sense of control or purpose until well after I'd found my exit. But I knew that was the death knell.'

Narrator: 'Brian Wilson's musical revolution wasn't to be. Despite all of the wonderful sounds that had been composed and recorded, despite all of the publicity that had the world waiting for this incredible album, Brian put it on the shelf.'

Lou Adler: 'Knowing Brian, it doesn't surprise me at all that those pressures and whatever other chemicals or influences that he was having to deal with, that he would shut down. It seems like the natural thing to do under those circumstances.'

Brian Wilson: 'It's just that I felt personally beaten up by . . . 'cause I didn't complete it. I felt beaten up.'

David Anderle: 'He just went somewhere else. He checked out. Or it checked out. I don't know if he made a conscious decision to get sick the way he did. He just got sick.'

Brian Wilson: 'I did have a breakdown. I had a nervous breakdown.'

★   ★   ★   ★

Why? In one interview, Brian made it very clear.

Brian: 'I wanted to do my kind of music, and they wanted to do their kind of music.'

All he needed was voices who would follow him anywhere. All he needed in 1966 was for them to say, 'This is amazing. What do you need me to sing?'

Brian: 'I felt like I was being pulled to pieces.'

Is that what precipitated his breakdown?

The Beach Boys' world has always pointed towards the 'Fire' session and the drugs. But were those just symptoms?

Again unanswerable questions. But the main issue is, did the Beach Boys support Brian's artistic vision? Yes, we know how hard they worked. How difficult it was. What a perfectionist Brian was. And we know that their vocals on the *SMiLE*-era recordings are incomparable.

Did the group bring joyfulness to the studio? Or did they grumble, saying things like, 'Sure doesn't sound like the old stuff.' And complain about the hard work, nicknaming Brian 'the Stalin of the Studio.' So witty.

Bruce Johnston: 'Brian was between a hipster and one of your famous British generals. He was tough. He demanded everything from everybody.'

Yes, Brian was indeed a musical dictator. Unfortunately, it seems there was a revolution brewing. And, yes, I write here with (self-)righteous indignation and genuine sadness, how different Brian's life, The Beach Boys' career and even the world of popular music might have been had The Beach Boys just done what he asked with a *SMiLE* on their faces.

The Beatles, the biggest cultural phenomenon of the day, didn't worry about evolving. Revolving. Did Capitol pay attention to what The Beatles had done on 'Tomorrow Never Knows'? Did The Beach Boys?

The Beatles were fearless, understood that their new music might cost them some of their older fans, but believed that it might simultaneously bring them new fans too.

John and Paul heard what Brian was doing. He was, as Sir George Martin has said, their primary artistic competition. But perhaps 'just' being Brian's vocal instrument wasn't enough for 'the boys.' If that's the case, what a shame.

Mike Love has been singled out by Brian as the number one reason he stopped work on *SMiLE*. Mike says it wasn't his decision. It most assuredly wasn't.

Brian made the choice; he shelved the tapes out of loyalty, to save the group.

Brian: 'I realized that I had to stop. *SMiLE* was killing me. It might have killed The Beach Boys too if we had kept going.'

The doubters. The pressures. The real paranoia. The drugs. A recipe for failure. Were there people who failed Brian? Did he fail himself? And in 1967, when the artist called Brian Wilson abandoned *SMiLE*, perhaps it seems he had no choice. This bears repeating:

DON'T F*** WITH THE FORMULA

Brian: 'SMiLE was killing me.'

Was Brian justified in his paranoia?

Van Dyke: 'Oh, sure, absolutely. They say that the British kids who went through the bombing of London in the early forties that they came away with lifelong phobias. I think a whole bunch of extraneous baggage was hitting Brian, the musician.'

None of The Beach Boys had anything to do with the actual decision to kill *SMiLE*. But at that point, it was almost like artistic Russian Roulette. So sure, nobody but Brian pulled the trigger. But who loaded the gun and put the bullets in? Are you partially responsible if you help load a few rounds into the chamber?

When Brian looked at his alternatives, there weren't any. He had to put it on the shelf. But not finishing it, well, that might be his creative death. Talk about a Hobson's Choice. He was about to artistically touch the sun . . . and then, he fell into it. His ambition was scorched. His talent was intact, but within a matter of months, he was no longer *driven*. His energy became focused on survival.

Mike Love's objection to *SMiLE* seemed to have been focused on commerce. He might have thought, 'What are our fans going to think of these lyrics?' Lyrics that weren't his.

Perhaps Sir George Martin summed it up best. 'Artists shouldn't listen to record companies. And you shouldn't listen to frightened members of the band.'

But Brian didn't have a George Martin by his side in 1967. And as his new group of friends disappeared, as Van Dyke retreated, Brian was left alone with The Beach Boys to answer the question, 'What happens when art comes before commerce?'

In this story, we'll never know. To save himself, Brian decided to impale himself on his sword. Work on *SMiLE* ended.

Is this what happens when you don't follow the artist's vision? Brian was the musical leader of the group, but Mike was the frontman for the touring Beach Boys. Our witnesses make it clear that he believed the lyrics of *SMiLE* weren't right for the group's fans. Was he right or wrong? Could these new *SMiLE* songs be performed live in 1967? Would fans squirm in their seats if they were? We'll never know.

The problem for Brian was that his complete control of the recordings was being questioned. And he couldn't and didn't stand up for himself.

So, The Beach Boys didn't stay ahead of the curve, and he and they got steamrollered.

Van Dyke explains what he saw near the end.

Van Dyke: 'There are two things: There were the social and drug experiments. Both of those things got too much for me. And I never thought I was a coward. I'm still amused by the aroma of marijuana. I think it's a great adjunct to an adult, creative process, as much as Satchmo [Louis Armstrong] did. Don't disagree with Satchmo. I think Satchmo was right on.

'I don't think it's a necessary ingredient. And I think that with the detergent agitation of the psychotropic experiences, that just helped push Brian over the edge.'

Van Dyke continues, clarifying in his own way, leaving as many questions as he answers: 'There's no question in my mind that Brian Wilson was duped. He fell in with a bad crowd. I would say that. But there was no malice in it, I don't think. But I think that it just got too much for him ... The people who were surrounding him were more and more interested in their own positions with him. I want to try [and] distinguish myself in that.'

Van Dyke doesn't identify who he thinks 'the wrong crowd is,' and this next admission is startling. And not quite clear either.

Van Dyke: 'And as soon as I felt physical danger, felt like perhaps I would get hit, that's when I left ... I didn't realize that somebody was going to get me out [in] the parking lot, if I continued with this madness.'

Was it an idle threat?

Van Dyke: 'I felt threatened by [being] in that experience. Because as the project continued and the expectations for its success increased, all of a sudden, I realized that there were folks out there who wanted my gig. They wanted to be doing what I was doing, which was make words for Brian Wilson's songs. That hadn't occurred to me. That was news. That was a new thing for me to realize that somebody might resent my working for him. That was really beyond my imagining when I got into this.'

What exactly does Van Dyke mean? Presuming Mike Love is quoted accurately in this 2014 interview, it may give us an even deeper insight into how he viewed *SMiLE* and Van Dyke Parks working as Brian's lyricist.

'I have mixed feelings about it,' Love told the *Austin Chronicle*. 'I think there was some great music on *SMiLE*, some incredible tracks. But at that point in time, there were so many drugs being taken by Brian and other members of the group, and there was a lot of collaborating with people other than myself. I had literally nothing to do on anything on the *SMiLE* album, so naturally I was a little upset.'

Van Dyke: 'I think that the circumstances around the production of *SMiLE* turned into a Machiavellian disorder or anything you might read about . . . or any place where there's a great deal of concern for power and how it's distributed. And all of that . . . had nothing to do with music and it was very sad. It was devastating. It was devastating. And it continued to be devastating.

'For all those years, it was locked up and surrounded by all the sinister, the infamy that was heaped upon it. When in fact, it was a twenty-three-year-old and a twenty-four-year-old lad, they were getting together to work on some material. Now, this guy raised the money for the event, generated the money, he *was* the industry. He brought new records to tonnage to the rapidity of cash flow in the music business.

'I think that the sixties produced the perfect sentence setting for The Beach Boys situation entirely, provided a classic case of the collapse, his industrial collapse. I think all of the things there conspired against him at that time. And I think that it's like saying, "No good deed goes unpunished." That, to me, he was severely punished for doing the right thing.'

With sadly-bowed head, Van Dyke adds, 'That's what I find regrettable about the whole incident.'

All that was left was for an obituary to be published. Derek Taylor, who had brought news of *SMiLE's* brilliance to the rock press in 1966, was left to write a death notice. Just two weeks after he wrote about McCartney coming to the studio, he filed this report in the May 6, 1967, edition *of Disc and Music Echo.*

Derek Taylor: 'In truth, every beautifully-designed, finely-wrought, inspirationally-welded piece of music made these last months by Brian and his Beach Boy craftsmen has been SCRAPPED. Not destroyed but scrapped. For what Wilson seals in a can and destroys is scrapped.'

★ ★ ★ ★

Brian's decision to not complete *SMiLE* was catastrophic for all concerned. While they did not know it at the time, could not know it, The Beach Boys career as relevant and important record makers was essentially done.

For the next half-dozen years, through 1973's *Holland* LP, every Beach Boys album had truly worthwhile music on it. They just weren't commercially successful. And in 1974, with the release of the *Endless Summer* greatest hits compilation, they would become big stars again. 'America's Band.'

For the most part, it wouldn't matter what they did for the next fifty-plus years. The vast majority of contemporary music listeners had moved on, no longer cared.

David Anderle: 'I never saw [*SMiLE*] as a competitive piece with the industry. I just saw it as a new way to express music. As the first true pop classical piece of music ... Maybe if I'd have [still] been around when it was being finished, I'd [have] had to start thinking about it in terms of helping make it commercial or take it to the street or take it to the radio ... I would have maybe been more conscious of it in terms of [it] being that radical. I just was consumed with the fact that it was radical within itself.'

In 2004, Anderle summed up the past with a surprising statement.

David: 'I wish he would have stayed healthy, but I'm glad the record didn't come out as a Beach Boy record.'

Two other observers share similar conclusions.

Lorren Daro: 'Brian martyred himself. Absolutely. He immolated himself. That's what he did. Poured gasoline over himself and lit it. For them. He loved them. As mean as they were to him, he loved them. Even his father. Probably loved his father more than anyone. That bastard.'

Rob Reiner: 'He would rather take the pain and inflict the pain on himself than either his mother or father be hurt. Or his brothers or friends be hurt. And so for that reason, I think he never fully was able to become his own person. That personality trait seems to have been what doomed the project.'

By the spring of 1967, there was more than enough incredible music to fill an album. Yet Brian decided not to go forward with it. He decided not to release an album called *SMiLE* filled with the beautiful songs and sounds. Why?

Brian: 'Personally, I felt beat up.'

Was it a breakdown? If you were there, could you see Brian having a breakdown when he stopped working on *SMiLE*?

Annie Wilson-Karges: 'It was easy to see the correlation. So that's real easy to witness. Somebody completely just really beginning to isolate so totally. So, in that way, it's very visible. There's no guess-work in that. That was pretty physically visible.'

Do we know exactly why he stopped work on *SMiLE*? Let me try it a different way.

It wasn't because The Beach Boys had sued Capitol Records. It wasn't because The Beach Boys were afraid that Brian might abandon the group for solo work. Nor was it that *SMiLE* music wasn't the right direction for the band. It wasn't because Mike thought Van Dyke Park's remarkable lyrics were too poetic for the fans. It wasn't because the album would not have met with Capitol Records' approval. It wasn't because Mike wanted to be Brian's sole lyricist. It wasn't because Brian couldn't figure out how to sequence the music. It wasn't because *Sgt. Pepper* came out. And it wasn't because anybody doubted the beauty and brilliance of the sounds Brian had created.

To one degree or another, it was all of these reasons. But Brian sums it up strongly and simply: 'They knew it was good music, but they didn't think it was right for them.'

Perhaps that was at the heart of this confluence of events and circumstances and all the issues swirling around that led him to abandon the project. Through the years, there have been so many inconsistencies in the story of *SMiLE*; this isn't like a court case that can have a brilliant summation for the jury. It is, as the cliché goes, a mystery wrapped inside a riddle wrapped inside an enigma.

Does this response from Brian wrap it all up?

Brian: 'I got tired of it . . . I just got tired of the direction we were going in. I didn't like it.'

Brian has expressed being afraid that he was going to lose the group — and his family — by putting out *SMiLE*. Is that true?

Annie Wilson-Karges: 'I think he was probably just afraid of his own power. Just of his own power. I don't think he really wanted to know what that would do or not do. That's a real look in the mirror. The responsibility of letting it out into the world and being the revolutionary. Now you've got to take responsibility for the revolution. To risk the disapproval. It's just too big.'

Brian: 'I fell to pieces.'

For nearly thirty-seven years, *SMiLE*, like its creator, would remain in mostly ruins.

For Brian and The Beach Boys, it was if you owned a Baccarat crystal

SMiLE

store and there was an earthquake that shattered everything on the shelves into little pieces. *SMiLE* was left in fragments. Beautiful pieces, but shards nonetheless. We know, in retrospect, that an album with just the *SMiLE*-era versions of 'Heroes And Villains,' 'Wonderful,' 'Cabin Essence,' 'Wind Chimes,' and 'Surf's Up' (plus 'Good Vibrations') alone would have been a stunningly beautiful record. But it wasn't to be.

There is also no definitive answer as to what *SMiLE* was going to be, what it could have been. How it would have been received by Beach Boys fans, by music lovers. One would think that many who had bought and loved *Pet Sounds* and/or 'Good Vibrations' would have bought *SMiLE*. And in 1967, as FM radio became more popular, as the use of recreational drugs began to increase during the late 1960s, *SMiLE* would have been a welcome soundtrack.

But there are only questions. And the eternal sadness and regret that it wasn't finished . . . at least not in 1967. Because regardless of how one might want to write or rewrite history, the death of *SMiLE* was the end of The Beach Boys as a ground-breaking musical aggregation.

Brian Wilson decided to put the *SMiLE* tapes 'on the shelf.' And because he did, for the following thirty-seven years, *SMiLE* became the most famous unreleased album in rock history . . . an enormous artistic albatross for The Beach Boys and especially for the man who had decided he was no longer going to be their leader . . . Brian Wilson.

Terry Melcher had produced The Byrds' biggest hits in 1965/1966, so he was very much part of the L.A. music scene, and understood Brian Wilson's position in The Beach Boys and importance in the pop music world at large. Because of his relationship with Bruce Johnston, he was also privy to the inside world of the Beach Boys. In Tom Nolan's landmark 1971 *Rolling Stone* article on the Beach Boys, he saw *SMiLE* . . . and Brian . . . coming apart.

Terry Melcher: 'The guy never asked for any trouble . . . and everyone nailed the motherfucker to the wall. They really nailed him. That poor motherfucker.'

If you're feeling exhausted at this moment, you should be.

Imagine how Brian Wilson was feeling when he knew that to survive, he had no choice but to stop working on what was to have been his revolutionary masterpiece.

That tragedy is what would set the stage for 2004's triumph. The intervening years, however, would be extraordinarily difficult ones for Brian.

CAN'T WAIT TOO LONG

In May of 1967, it was reported that Brian had shelved *SMiLE*. *Strike one.*

On June 1, 1967, The Beatles' production masterpiece, *Sgt. Pepper's Lonely Hearts Club Band,* was released in the US. *Strike two.*

That same month, The Beach Boys cancelled their appearance at the Monterey Pop Festival. *Strike three. And you're out.*

CARL WILSON: 'WE WERE SUPPOSED TO HEADLINE THE MONTEREY POP Festival, but at the last minute, Brian backed out. Monterey was a turning point in rock 'n' roll. Overnight, the whole scene changed, and we felt as though we've been passed by.'

As for Brian, the ambition – the drive to make the greatest record ever – seemed to have been squeezed out of him. He no longer felt he had to beat The Beatles. The competitive spirit – instilled in him from childhood, fostered at Hawthorne High, developed through five years of ever-evolving classic Beach Boys records – was now gone.

Annie Wilson-Karges: 'I didn't think of it in terms of Brian losing his competitive drive, as much as I thought of it in terms of Brian becoming more fearful. Just Brian being overtaken by his fears. They're irrational, and they're rational. Certainly, the drugs and the fears and the disapproval . . . Bad combination.'

How did it feel when Brian shut down?

Annie: 'It was a loss. It was very sad. It was depressing. It was depressing for Carl. I think it was depressing for everyone. Having this leader not willing to lead. Not knowing where to go. Or not being willing to go there. The risk.'

Terry Melcher: 'I think he was pressured by the group. And knowing that everyone in that group was married, and had children, and a house. I think he felt like more of a benefactor than an artist. I picked that up a few times, that he felt like he was expected to do certain things on time: We'll have a hit record every three months, a tour every two months, and an album every four months. He was the creative force, and there were five other people – five other families – relying on his creativity. Which sort of puts a . . . I don't suppose any musical genius ever operated on a time-clock basis. He was feeling it a lot. So, I think he just went to sleep for a couple months. Just went to his room and went away.'

On a *Pet Sounds* outtake, Brian had once sung, 'Hang on to your ego, but I know you're going to lose the fight.' Was he prescient or just scared? Or both? Regardless, he felt he no longer had to be the leader of the pack.

But the loyalty instilled by his father was still there. In shelving *SMiLE*, Brian put the group first. Had they put Brian first?

And as all of this swirled around the band, they became almost desperate to get a record done. They went to Hawaii to record a live album. Capitol Records needed 'product' so they released *Best of The Beach Boys Volume 2*. A familiar story.

Brian: 'After I put *SMiLE* on the shelf, I was depressed, and then I got back into it.'

But for the fans who were eagerly awaiting *SMiLE*, fans who were waiting for anything new from the group, what would come next? It was *Smiley Smile*, an album with 'Good Vibrations,' a hurried single version of 'Heroes And Villains,' and low-fi remakes of three *SMiLE* songs as well as several new songs.

Noteworthy is that having called a halt to the *SMiLE* sessions, Brian decided that no longer would the credit 'Produced by Brian Wilson' grace Beach Boys records like a benediction from above.

And even though for the next few albums, Brian remained the primary songwriter, arranger, and producer, he didn't take the credit. Instead, the more democratic 'Produced by The Beach Boys' would formalize the fact that after nearly five years of hard work, Brian Wilson would not or could not take complete responsibility for the group's studio work.

The result of Brian's abdication, at a time when neither Carl nor any of the other Beach Boys was yet prepared to assume his role, was an album that sounded like a *Beach Boys Party* if everybody was stoned.

How did Carl Wilson describe *Smiley Smile*, the barely-baked replacement for *SMiLE*?

Carl: 'A bunt instead of a grand slam.'

For those of you who don't follow baseball, that's a disaster.

Van Dyke: 'I loved Carl. I think that I understood what Carl was saying . . . The final edit, the final cut [of 'Heroes And Villains'] . . . it wasn't the cut that I expected. It was a disappointment to me. So that 45 [single] that I heard on the air, that first time I heard it, I was shocked and saddened because it was almost like a schnauzer coughing up a hairball. It wasn't the thing I expected. It was part of a project that had great potential to me.'

As for the album released in *SMiLE*'s stead, Beach Boys historian Andrew G. Doe calls *Smiley Smile* 'the single most weird album ever put out by a major group.'

Ray Lawlor, who would be a key figure in Brian's personal and professional resurrection, remembers waiting for *SMiLE* in 1967 and being so disappointed by *Smiley Smile* that he tried to sell it to one of his friends for a quarter. He had no takers.

Domenic Priore, *SMiLE and pop culture historian:* '*Smiley Smile* is not without merit . . . Actually, the reason most people didn't care for *Smiley Smile* is that it came out in place of *SMiLE*.'

Exactly. And that what makes the album so disappointing. What we *could* hear was how great a song 'Wonderful' was. Just not a fantastic recording, which would become abundantly clear once we heard the *SMiLE*-era version.

Smiley Smile was, as Brian told me, the result of 'smoking a lot of marijuana, so the songs were light-hearted.' After *Smiley Smile* came out, Brian explains, 'I wanted to make pretty music,' which he would do on subsequent records, especially *Friends* (his personal favourite) and *Sunflower*.

Nevertheless, for The Beach Boys, *Smiley Smile* was the beginning of their march through the desert. And even though their popularity in England would not be significantly diminished throughout the remainder of the decade, there was no getting around the fact that at home, The Beach Boys were almost outcasts in the world of rock.

To fill out their albums, songs originally recorded for *SMiLE* turned up on their next five records. *Smiley Smile* had 'Heroes And Villains,' as well as modest versions of 'Wonderful,' 'Wind Chimes,' and 'Vega-Tables.' The *SMiLE* fragment 'Mama Says' is on *Wild Honey*. 'Our Prayer' and 'Cabin Essence,' two mind-blowing *SMiLE* outtakes, reached us on *20/20*. 'The Elements' water chant from *SMiLE* was part of 'Cool, Cool Water' on *Sunflower,* and the title song on *Surf's Up* is that album's high point.

Musically, one could really begin to hear what we had missed. But as to what had happened to *SMiLE*, what had gone wrong?

Back in the day, so the story goes, powerful newspaper magnate William Randolph Hearst once sent a telegram to a leading astronomer asking: 'Is there life on Mars? Please cable 1,000 words.' The astronomer replied with 'Nobody knows' – repeated 500 times.

Andrew G. Doe, *Beach Boys historian:* 'I've read all the books, and virtually every article and interview on the subject, over and over. Listened to the [*SMiLE*] bootlegs, repeatedly. Saw Brian perform *Brian Wilson Presents SMiLE* eight times. Devoured the official *Beach Boys SMiLE Sessions* box set. Used all of my knowledge to construct, with invaluable help from others, as accurate a timeline for the *SMiLE* era as I think is possible. Built a website to contain all that information (and more). Had endless conversations with fellow fans as to what happened to the project. Why it didn't come out. What the final sequence would have been in 1967. And I come back to that story. "Nobody knows." Nobody.'

As to understanding why it had happened, *Crawdaddy* magazine was filled with a heart-breaking conversation between editor Paul Williams and David Anderle, trying to make sense of it all. Trying. They really couldn't.

David Anderle's initial purpose in setting up Brother Records was that it would be a home for Brian's non-Beach Boys projects. Brian's first (and last?) Brother project would be with a group he named Redwood. It was a vocal trio featuring his great friend Danny Hutton and two other powerful voices, Chuck Negron and Cory Wells.

These singers were ready and eager to follow Brian anywhere. In October of 1967, Brian produced the instrumental tracks for what would be Redwood's first single – 'Darlin,' backed with 'Time to Get Alone,' a song he'd written at end of the *SMiLE* era. That title is telling.

Brian took Redwood into the studio, and Chuck Negron recalled that the problems started when 'Mike Love and Carl and I think Al came by . . . the whole thing changed; [Brian's] demeanour changed. He was uncomfortable. He was like more of a child; he was intimidated by them.'

CAN'T WAIT TOO LONG

'Time To Get Alone' is a remarkable song. This meeting with The Beach Boys was memorable for all the wrong reasons.

Chuck Negron: 'I came to believe it was because he was being a bad boy working with us; he was writing and sharing his gift outside the family. They weren't happy . . . it was almost like he was doing something wrong.'

The day of the vocal sessions, Chuck recalls that when Mike and Carl returned, perhaps with Dennis, 'The conversation was almost like he was being scolded . . . he became meeker and very uncomfortable . . . Brian almost started . . . crying . . . welling up . . . he was being emotionally abused . . . he came out to the studio and he said, "Listen, I can't do this . . . I'll give you any money you want to finish it" . . . We felt so bad for him. We said "No, Brian," and we left.'

Explaining what he saw, Chuck believes Brian 'was so important to their lives, they weren't about to let him go . . . my feeling was that this man was blossoming with us, spiritually and emotionally . . . removing himself from this chain and anchor . . . the burden he had to support all these people . . . was something very special to him but he also did it in the [Brother Records] framework to help his family . . . he was being bullied . . . abused . . . and they knew they were doing it . . . they knew how to get to Brian . . . it was family stuff. All I know is I saw a big man become very small and crumble right in front of our eyes . . . [like] this boy being scolded by his father . . . it was very obvious to anybody that this man was in distress . . . I am sure Carl loved his brother with all his heart . . . Mike was running that machine that day.'

Looking back, Chuck believed that Brian 'needed to be set free . . . he needed to grow.' From Chuck's perspective, they didn't say, '"God bless you, Brian . . . do what you want to do." They didn't do it.' To Chuck, 'That was a very big step in making his life very hard and changing happiness to sadness.' Chuck adds, 'Can you imagine having Three Dog Night on Brother Records? These guys would never have any money problems.'

Perhaps. But more likely, Redwood wouldn't have succeeded on Brother. And maybe it was their karma to have that success after witnessing what had happened with Brian.

The other song Redwood was to record was 'Darlin'. When I asked Danny Hutton about all of this, he understood why The Beach Boys wouldn't want Brian to give away a hit record. But it seems the way

Brian was treated makes it one of the worst moments in the story of Brian Wilson's pursuit of his artistry.

Is Negron's story the truth, the whole truth, and nothing but the truth?

Did The Beach Boys fear they were losing their leader to another group?

Redwood left the studio and soon after, changed their name to Three Dog Night. From 1968-1975, they had twenty-one Top 40 hits and three number ones. During that same period, The Beach Boys had two singles creep into the Billboard Top 20.

How does this relate to the *SMiLE* story? It goes to Brian's control (or lack thereof) of his art, his inability to stand up to his family, and his psychological state in that most unsteady year of 1967. It's also another example of the one-sided loyalty Brian had for the group. They demanded he not work with 'outsiders'; he meekly acquiesced. The Beach Boys' commanding leader had been neutered.

★ ★ ★ ★

In 1967, even after *SMiLE* had been shelved, Brian continued to make incredible music. Brian recorded a melodic piece that remained in the vaults for way too long. It wouldn't see the light of day for over twenty years, but in my opinion, it was almost as beautiful and inventive and amazing as anything intended for *SMiLE*.

In my tape collection, it was marked 'Can't Wait Too Long'/'Been Way Too Long,' long a favourite of hard-core fans as evidence that Brian hadn't lost his desire nor ability to express himself beautifully. He was just not going to take charge. It remained an unfinished masterpiece.

The tracks Brian cut for Redwood both ended up on Beach Boys records.

To me, the message from The Beach Boys to Brian seems clear. Work with us. Or don't work at all.

For the next twenty years, excepting work with groups that included his wife and sister-in-law and a spoken word record with lyricist/poet Stephen Kalinich, Brian would choose both options.

As to *SMiLE,* the story grows ever more tangled from here on out.

Dennis Wilson (in a December 21, 1968, *Record Mirror* article headlined 'I Live With 17 Girls')*:* 'A couple of years ago, we got paranoid about losing our public. We were getting loaded, taking acid, and we made a whole album which we scrapped . . . Drugs played a great role in our evolution, but as a result, we were frightened that people would no longer understand us musically.'

That was about as close as any Beach Boy got to explaining why *SMiLE* was shelved.

Or as Brian said in 2011, 'It took me a long time to come down off *SMiLE*, when we were working on it. 'Cause we were taking drugs, for one thing, right? And (*deadpan*) we were taking drugs. And drugs . . . We were taking too much drugs and we were unable to concentrate very good. We got stoned and couldn't unstone ourselves.'

There is one remaining *SMiLE* moment worthy of mention. Following quickly on the heels of *Smiley Smile*, 1967's *Wild Honey*'s low-key production seemed to be the opposite of the lost brilliance of *SMiLE*.

Curiously, during the 1967 sessions for that album, Brian went to the piano one day and recorded 'Surf's Up.' It was finally released in 2011 on *The Beach Boys SMiLE Sessions* box set. Just Brian solo at the piano, it's magnificent, perhaps the best version of all.

For me, it raises several questions. Why was Brian playing and recording 'Surf's Up' during the *Wild Honey* sessions? Was it because he had let go of *SMiLE* but *SMiLE* had not let go of him?

★   ★   ★   ★

On each new Beach Boys album, from 1967-1973, there would be new music from Brian. Much of it brilliant. And with a studio downstairs, just below his bedroom, he could record almost whenever he wanted. The question became, 'Did he want to?'

Was Brian's withdrawal as simple as him thinking, 'I've done my best work ever, and it was met with doubt and fear. So maybe it's time to sit back?'

In the aforementioned Don Was documentary, Marilyn Wilson explained that Brian's relationship with the group suffered in part because he felt guilty for being the focus of all the media attention. That they resented him for it.

Marilyn: 'I think it was very hard for them to understand, "Why is Brian Wilson singled out?" But anybody with a brain would know why.'

Marilyn, his first wife, observed as Brian slowly backed away from recording, would stay upstairs in his bedroom while the group worked downstairs, in his home studio.

Marilyn: 'It was very tough for him because he thought that they all hated him. I think it was like, "Okay, you assholes. Think you can do as good as me? Go ahead . . . You think it's so easy, you do it.'"

In that same film, Marilyn sadly admitted that The Beach Boys 'slowly tore him down. I hate to say it, but they did.'

★   ★   ★   ★

My *SMiLE* story began in October of 1971. My life was changed by a two-part cover feature in *Rolling Stone* magazine by Tom Nolan (with David Felton) about the group, timed to promote the new Beach Boys album, *Surf's Up*.

The title song of the record, the last song on Side Two, was the cornerstone composition of *SMiLE*. Simply put, 'Surf's Up' is stunning. And about ten other adjectives to describe its indescribable beauty.

The piece that preceded it, "Til I Die', was brand-new: exquisite, heart-breaking, and important. Terribly sad, the song's autobiographical lyrics let the listener know that Brian Wilson felt adrift, that he'd basically given up on life. Also significant in that it told anybody listening closely (i.e., me) that he could still write beautiful new music that would touch a listener's soul. Even if, as engineer Steve Desper would later recall, The Beach Boys didn't like the original lyrics. Thought they were too depressing. But as Brian admitted in the released version of the song, 'I lost my way.'

This *Rolling Stone* article was where I first read about *SMiLE*. Learning about the lost promise of the record, and then hearing the song 'Surf's Up' (which was evidence of how great *SMiLE* was going to be) turned me into an obsessive fan. I needed to hear *all* of *SMiLE*. That fall, seeing The Beach Boys in concert, with Carl performing a fabulous version of the song, cemented it.

In that article, Terry Melcher explained how he saw it: 'He left the music, yes. He left it, it never left him. For years I spent my nights at Brian's house, sitting around, not saying a word, not getting into any conversation, just hearing him play the piano and write some melodies once in a while. It was just fantastic. The guy's . . . he's better than anyone. It's really true. He just knows everything there is to know. It's unfortunate. He was born too late or something. If Brian Wilson were born 500 years ago, he'd be one of those giant classical figures that we all revere so much.'

★   ★   ★   ★

Brian at Western Studios #3, November 1966.

Van Dyke Parks at Western Studios, January 1967.

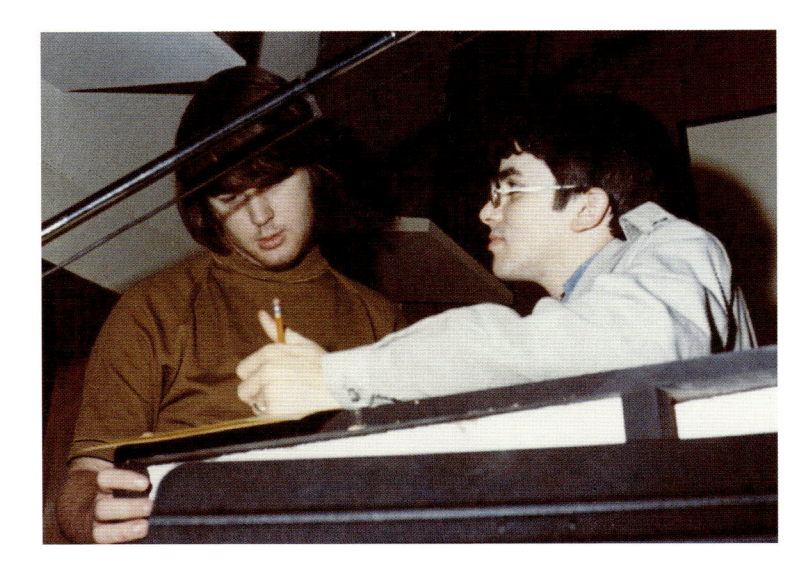

Brian and Van Dyke, writing (or re-writing) at Western Studios, January 6, 1967. It was Van Dyke who suggested the title *SMiLE*.

(All photos on this page by Jasper Dailey © David Leaf Productions, Inc.)

Chuck Britz, Brian, and Van Dyke, Western Studios, January 1967.

Below left: At the start of a session, Brian would play that night's song for Hal Blaine. Western Studios, January 1967.

Right: Once Brian had given everybody their part, he would conduct the session. Other than the fragments of cover versions, Brian was the sole composer, arranger, and producer of the *SMiLE* sessions. Gold Star Studios, November 1966.

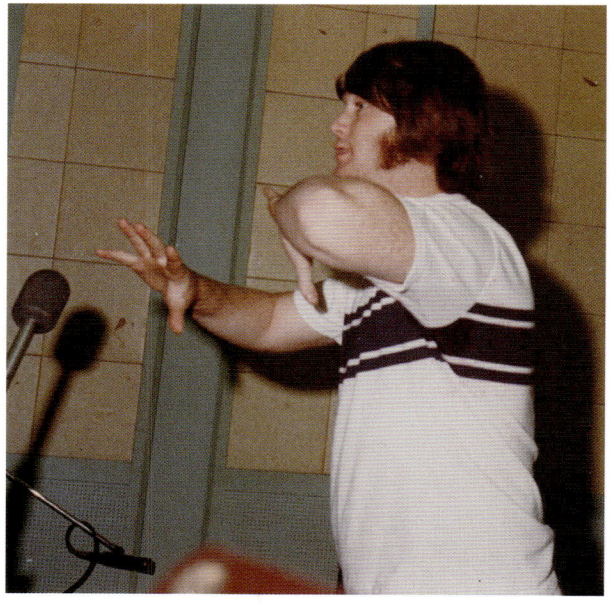

Below right: Carl Wilson, January 1967.

(All photos on this page by Jasper Dailey © David Leaf Productions, Inc.)

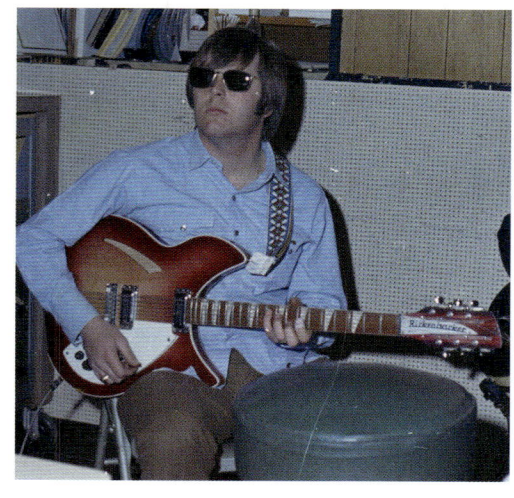

Brian at the piano in his sandbox. Photo taken at the Wilson's Laurel Way home in Beverly Hills, 1966. (Courtesy of BriMel Archives.)

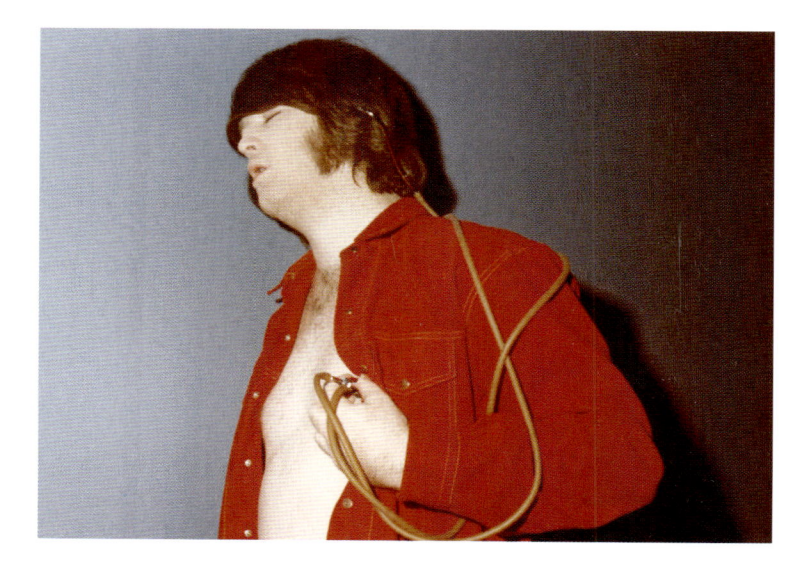

Is *SMiLE* already on life support? Brian checking on *SMiLE*'s heartbeat. At KHJ-TV Studios, November 1966.

Dennis Wilson at Western Studios, January 1967.

The hat must fit just right. Brian (wearing a fire helmet) on the day he directed the 'Good Vibrations' promotional film, October 1966.

(All photos on this page by Jasper Dailey © David Leaf Productions, Inc.)

October 1966, Brian Wilson's 'crew': Back row, L-R: Danny Hutton, Dean Torrence, David Anderle, Mark Volman, and Brian. Middle (L-R): Sherril Anderle, Michael Vosse, Robin Lane, Annie (Hinsche) Wilson, Diane Rovell, and Marilyn Wilson. Front (L-R): June Fairchild, Gene Gaddy, Barbara Rovell, and Dick and Carol Meir. In front, journalist and *SMiLE* mythologist Jules Siegel. (Photo by Guy Webster.)

Above: Fall, 2003. Clowning around for Melinda Wilson's camera during the reconstruction of *SMiLE*. Brian, Darian Sahanaja, and Van Dyke Parks.

Below: Vocal rehearsals for *Brian Wilson Presents SMiLE* at Brian's home, January 2004. L-R: Jeffrey Foskett, Darian Sahanaja, Taylor Mills, Nelson Bragg, Nick Walusko, and Scott Bennett. Standing is Probyn Gregory.

(All photos on this page courtesy of BriMel Archives.)

February 20, 2004, the night of the world premiere, on stage at the Royal Festival Hall, the first ever performance of *Brian Wilson Presents SMiLE*.

Above: The Brian Wilson Band. Encircling Brian, L-R: Jim Hines, Darian Sahanaja, Scott Bennett, Probyn Gregory, Bob Lizik, Nelson Bragg, Taylor Mills, Nick Walusko, and Jeffrey Foskett. They began with 'And Your Dream Comes True,' a musical 'Easter Egg' for what lay ahead. Paul Von Mertens can't be seen, but is behind Darian. (©Tim Whitby/Getty Images.)

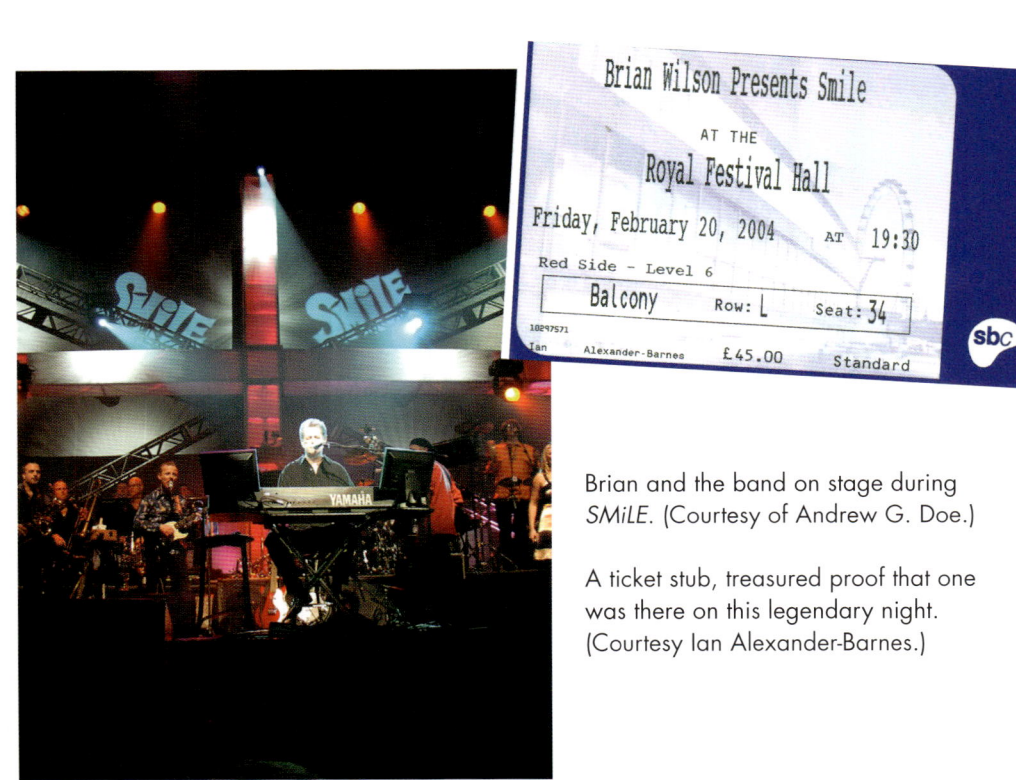

Brian and the band on stage during *SMiLE*. (Courtesy of Andrew G. Doe.)

A ticket stub, treasured proof that one was there on this legendary night. (Courtesy Ian Alexander-Barnes.)

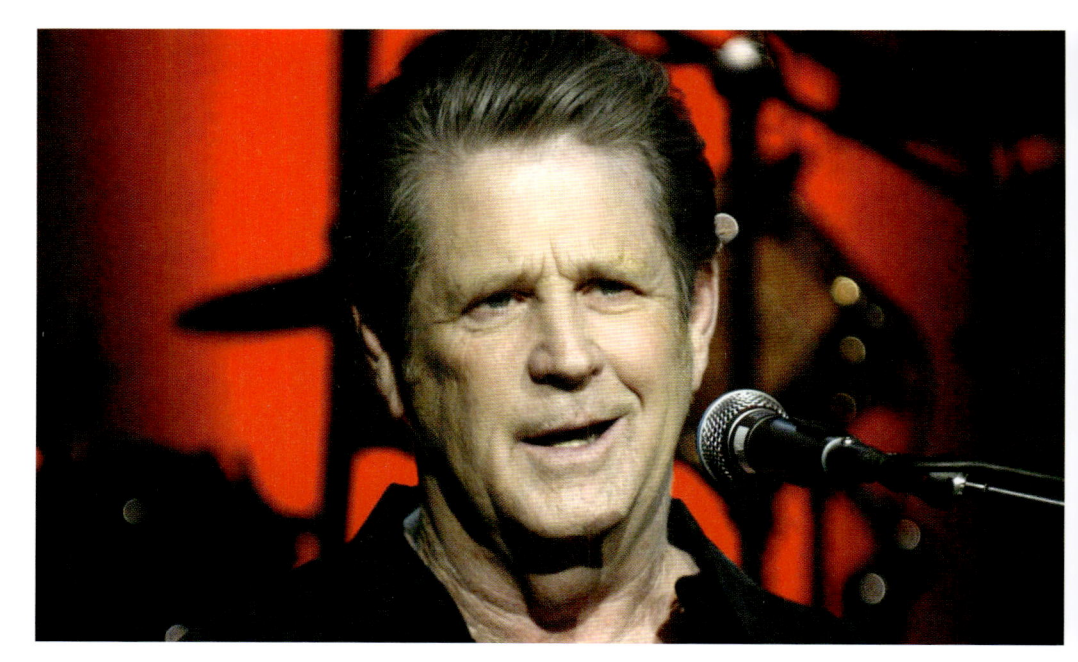

After an enormous standing ovation, Brian brought Van Dyke Parks onstage to take a more than well-earned bow. Darian and Paul Von Mertens can be seen behind Van Dyke and Brian.

(Top photo © Tim Whitby/Getty Images; Bottom pictures from *Beautiful Dreamer: Brian Wilson and the Story of SMiLE*. The film was directed by David Leaf in 2004.)

CAN'T WAIT TOO LONG

For decades, stories endlessly circulated as to why *SMiLE* was never finished. And Brian's eccentric behaviour (in public and private) made it unlikely that there would ever be another great Beach Boys or Brian Wilson record.

However, there was a *SMiLE* cult growing. From the time Brian performed 'Surf's Up' on the Leonard Bernstein special, many were eager, almost desperate for *SMiLE* to be finished.

Probably nobody both waited longer *and* made as important a contribution to its completion than Ray Lawlor, who began as a fan and became one of Brian's closest friends.

Ray and I bonded in 1976 (*SMiLE* was the glue), but as a series of Beach Boys albums came out in the second half of the decade, it was clear that Brian wasn't 'the old Brian.'

Ray Lawlor: 'What I remember about [1976's] "Brian is Back" [publicity campaign] is that I bought into it. But I was dismayed by his singing. I loved the production on *15 Big Ones* and the songs on *Love You*. There was enough in those records to let me know that he was intact musically. It was just a matter of putting it all together.'

But as Brian lost his way (again) in the late seventies and early eighties, finishing *SMiLE* was no longer what his friends were concerned about.

Ray: 'I saw him at the Westbury Music Fair in 1981 . . . Brian weighed about 325 pounds, was chain smoking at the piano. Only reason I went was that Carl wasn't there and Brian was going to be singing 'God Only Knows' and 'Good Vibrations.' I wanted to see if he had anything left in the tank. He didn't. I left at half-time.'

The bigger question soon became, 'Is Brian going to die?' And so, in late 1982, 'Dr.' Eugene Landy was hired (again). This time, his employers were The Beach Boys. They couldn't (emotionally, spiritually, or economically) afford for Brian to die.

Could they have employed somebody else to do the job? Perhaps.

Would it have been a kinder experience for Brian if somebody else had been hired? Unquestionably.

Would another psychologist have been able to quickly control Brian and bring him back so that he would soon be publicly presentable as a Beach Boy? Almost certainly not.

But looking back on what happened, Landy's hiring had significant intended and unintended consequences.

If Landy hadn't been hired, Brian might well have died.

SMiLE

Maybe most relevant to the *SMiLE* story, anybody else who The Beach Boys hired to save Brian would have kept him a Beach Boy.

That matters because after Brian worked on the group's 1985 album, Landy realized that he couldn't control The Beach Boys but did have total control of Brian. So, when an offer for a Brian solo album presented itself, he grabbed it.

It was Landy's power-hungry madness and greed (as well as his delusion that he was a great lyricist) that led to what I still regard as Brian's best solo record of all new material, 1988's self-titled *Brian Wilson*.

As that album relates to *SMiLE*, when Warner Brothers Records President Lenny Waronker encouraged Brian and collaborator Andy Paley to work on a *SMiLE*-like suite, the result was artistically successful and shockingly good: 'Rio Grande.' It had pieces of music – melodic pieces and beautiful harmonies – strung together. And the Indian chant even had a hint of 'Fire' music.

Perhaps most significantly in that era, if Landy doesn't get hired, Brian doesn't (at Landy's insistence) start to date Melinda Ledbetter. They dated a lot. Of great import, when Melinda realized what was going on and began to question it, Landy stopped Brian from seeing Melinda. Melinda led the charge to get rid of Landy.

Unintended and unexpected consequences.

Brian would describe his time with Landy as being like 'nine years in prison.'

Melinda would ultimately help get him out of jail.

Melinda would be the one to encourage him to perform live.

Melinda would be the one who helped make the *Pet Sounds* tour a reality.

And without all of those big steps – and lots of baby steps in between – there would never have been *Brian Wilson Presents SMiLE*.

The most unexpected consequence.

Of course, we're not quite there yet.

★   ★   ★   ★

As the early 1990s began, and Brian began to get back to work, writing regularly with Andy Paley, he was clearly 'Brian.' Who enjoyed making music. Just not the driven, 'going to make the greatest record ever' Brian. He wasn't crazy. He was just different, as his friends often said, 'just Brian being Brian.'

CAN'T WAIT TOO LONG

Would he ever be an artist again? Did he even want to build a career? As the psychodrama of the Landy era had played out, maybe the most surprising event of that time was the growth of a new, youthful *SMiLE* cult.

SMiLE bootlegs and Domenic Priore's passionate work was appealing to a generation who didn't know (or necessarily even care) about The Beach Boys. And some members of that faction would not just make *Brian Wilson Presents SMiLE* possible but were essential.

***Darian Sahanaja**, The Brian Wilson Band:* 'I was one of the kids who was introduced during the [1974] *Endless Summer* campaign. The first time I heard 'I Get Around,' I thought it was a current song . . . So, the very first album I owned was *Endless Summer*. I remember loving that music and the spirit in it.'

Darian told *Rolling Stone* that liking The Beach Boys could be hazardous to his health. 'I used to take physical beatings from neighbourhood boys for being a fan.'

Darian: 'I was just so into that stuff, and I wanted more. I remember hearing 'Wouldn't It Be Nice' in the movie *Shampoo*. And it just had this, "Wait a minute, this is music that I'm familiar with, but it's one step evolved . . ." [Then,] I got the David Leaf book, *The Beach Boys and the California Myth*. And it really opened me up, opened the door to the whole Brian Wilson world. Obviously, I picked up *Pet Sounds*. That was further evolved Brian Wilson. And that became my favourite album . . . I heard about *SMiLE* – what was in [Leaf's] book – but I'd never heard any of it.'

That was about to change.

Darian: 'I went to my very first Beach Boys convention, which was in Oakland, probably 1983. And they played 'Wonderful.' The [*SMiLE*] harpsichord version. And I just remember listening to this, frozen in my chair. This music was just hypnotic. And it was a similar kind of evolution, going from the early stuff to 'Wouldn't It Be Nice' . . . it was one further step beyond *Pet Sounds*. I also knew that it was about the same period as 'Good Vibrations.' And I thought to myself, 'Wow. If the album is anything like this, my God. What a great album it might be.'

The dominoes were beginning to form a column.

Darian: 'That's about the time I met Nick Walusko and Probyn Gregory, based on our mutual love for Brian Wilson. I remember being so into the *SMiLE* mythology that I made these custom handmade shirts with a *SMiLE* album cover. I was wearing it once, and a friend said, "I know somebody who would just die if he saw that shirt. He'd kill to have a shirt like that." I was later introduced to the guy. He was Probyn Gregory . . . and it was just instant friendship.'

Probyn Gregory, *The Brian Wilson Band:* 'When I was 8, I got my first transistor radio and heard 'California Girls' which astounded me . . . 'Good Vibrations' was inescapable the next year. And then the year after that, 'Heroes And Villains' was on the radio, which actually blew my mind more than the other songs. It was so different. Later on, when I was in high school, some friend said "I have a tape of a song, 'Cabin Essence,' you need to hear it." Finally, someone played me 'Surf's Up.' That was the end. The END. I burst into tears the first time I heard it. It was so powerful; it still gets me. I used to analyse the tag end of that song. When I was a senior in high school, I wrote out the vocal parts. That song was very influential to me. After that, when I got into college, more and more [Beach Boy] things came through, like *Pet Sounds* which also made me cry right away.

'I came to Los Angeles in 1980 and someone had a *SMiLE* bootleg and played me all the fragments, where I heard all that I'd been hearing about but hadn't actually listened to . . . I got together with Domenic Priore, Darian and Nick [Walusko]. One day we were up at Darian's house from mid-afternoon until late in the evening. We had to order out for pizza because we couldn't stop talking about *SMiLE*. We listened to all the fragments, arguing about what was in or out. Of course, no one can second-guess Brian, but you always hoped that you could put together some sort of a version of it.'

Nick Walusko, *The Brian Wilson Band:* 'In the late seventies, in high school, The Beach Boys were pretty big among my friends . . . In 1984, around the same time I met Darian, I heard there was a bootleg of *SMiLE* in a shop in San Diego. I got a hot tip. Drove down there on my own; it's quite a long haul from L.A.'

Nick was interested because, 'If *Pet Sounds* was a high point in [his] evolution as a composer, I can only imagine what *SMiLE* would have been.'

As Nick told me in 2004, their mutual interest in *SMiLE* 'was a bonding point for Darian and myself.'

Ultimately, Darian and Nick would form their own group (which included drummer Mike D'Amico and Probyn Gregory), the power pop Wondermints, who were a big part of the L.A. indie scene in the 1990s.

CAN'T WAIT TOO LONG

Nelson Bragg, *The Brian Wilson Band:* 'I always felt like [The Wondermints] – this is the music they were born to play. These were the people who were born to elevate Brian Wilson and create this doorway to Brian for the whole world to walk through. It was really those four guys.'

Probyn Gregory worked with Domenic Priore as editor of Priore's *Look! Listen! Vibrate! SMiLE!*, which became the bible for those who knew about *SMiLE*. But perhaps even more importantly, it became the ideal historical introduction for those who would become obsessed with the unreleased album.

Darian, Nick, Probyn, and Nelson would become members of Brian's band, and would be there with him as *Brian Wilson Presents SMiLE* came together.

Unlike his bandmates, it was a DIY tape that's at the centre of Nelson Bragg's *SMiLE* origin story.

Nelson: 'I was never a Beach Boy guy. Not as a child, not as a teenager or in college . . . We'd never had a big record store in my hometown area [near] Gloucester – Rockport, Massachusetts. Never. And then a really great one opened up in the early nineties – Mystery Train Records. And the sales guy became a friend of mine. [One day he said,] "Hey, have you heard this?"

'And it was a bootleg tape, a cassette of *SMiLE*. And he said, "You need to hear this." And I brought it home, and I said [to myself, unenthusiastically], "The Beach, Boys, okay." But I didn't really understand what I was getting into . . . And that was the day that I realized there was a whole different sound The Beach Boys were doing . . . And I went down a rabbit hole after that and *SMiLE* became this mythical thing to me.'

Long before there would even be a Brian Wilson band, four of the musicians who would play *SMILE* with him were already obsessed with it.

A fifth, Jeffrey Foskett, took an even earlier journey to *SMiLE*.

Jeffrey Foskett, *The Brian Wilson Band:* 'I became aware of *SMiLE* quite late in my quest to find out about The Beach Boys. I was a freshman in college, at UC Santa Barbara. It was 1974 – I flipped when I heard *Smiley Smile*. I thought that was so incredible. And my friend, who was a complete Beach Boys fanatic said, "If you think *Smiley Smile* is cool, you should hear the album they were going to make." And through a series of long and involved shopping excursions to . . . all the other bootleg-friendly stores,' Jeff soon heard the snippets of *SMiLE* that had somehow leaked out.

Jeffrey: 'I'm a *Pet Sounds* guy . . . It was such a departure from The Beach Boys that I'd heard; by the time I found out about the legend of *SMiLE*, and all of the surrounding mystery . . . it was really, captivating for me as well, ...[but I] didn't really know about all of the surrounding hoopla with *SMiLE* itself, because I just wasn't much of a reader in those days.'

In one way or another, decades before *Brian Wilson Presents SMiLE* became a reality, five future Brian Wilson band members were deeply in love with the music of *SMiLE*.

As Brian sang on his first solo album. 'The planets are spinning around.'

Slowly but surely, critical mass was beginning to build. Waiting for the master to just nod his head and say, 'Yes. It's time for *SMiLE*.'

★ ★ ★ ★

In 1993, Brian approved the release of over a half-hour of music from the original *SMiLE* sessions for the *Good Vibrations* box set.

David Leaf, *compilation producer:* 'Getting *SMiLE* music on the *Good Vibrations* box set was a great triumph – for Brian, for The Beach Boys, for music lovers, and for us *SMiLE* fanatics. Up until then, Brian and I were just friends. Other than the press kit for his '88 album, this was the first time he and I worked closely together. And it was both terrifying and easy. I went up to his house with the proposed track listing for the box and went over it with him. There was one song he didn't want included. So I crossed it off the list.

'And then, I took a deep breath and broached the subject. I said something like, "Brian, there's this giant hole between the 'Good Vibrations' single and the 'Heroes And Villains' single. As this is a career retrospective, it really should have music from the *SMiLE* sessions." He understood what I meant, was immediately open to the idea of it, asked me which songs I had in mind. I quickly rattled off a bunch of titles. I purposely didn't mention the 'Fire' music. And he said "Yes." It was simple as that.

'In retrospect, I realized that all that I'd done was treat him with the respect he had earned as the man who *created* this music, as opposed to saying, "Here's what *we* think should be done with *your* music." Just talking with him one-on-one – compilation producer to artist – letting him know that it was only my opinion.

'It was straightforward. He'd been told for so long that this music was inappropriate, that it wasn't right for the times or for the band, and he'd accepted that. I just told him why it was important; he said "yes" to everything, and so the box came out with *SMiLE* music. And it went "Gold," in large part, I believe, because it had *SMiLE* music on it.'

Reviewing the box in *Time* magazine, Jay Cocks had this to say:

'It has taken 26 years, but The Beach Boys have finally settled the score with *Sergeant Pepper* . . . The centerpiece of this new, must-have, five-CD 'anniversary collection' of classics and unreleased material is a 30-minute selection from the *SMiLE* sessions: unfinished, incomplete, and glorious. The music is mystic, mad, wild, and gentle, quite unlike anything anyone, including Wilson, had ever tried in pop before. The lyrics were as fleeting as a waking dream . . . This set will put all misconceptions right and demonstrate, lastingly, that Brian and The Beach Boys made luminous music.'

Vindication!

A few years later, I had a long conversation with Brian about creating a version of *SMiLE* that could be performed by a symphony and choir. I went through the familiar (and some unfamiliar) titles with him, asking whether he considered them to be part of *SMiLE*. But the best moment in the conversation was when I told him the goal was for him to hear the music without 'the emotional baggage,' so that this beautiful music could live and breathe on its own. His response was classic Brian. 'Good. I deserve it.'

In 1995, *Orange Crate Art* reunited Brian and Van Dyke Parks in the studio for one of the most beautiful albums of the decade. Brian was the lead singer and the album itself is filled with 'Beach Boys' harmonies. Sung part-by-part by Mr. Wilson as he had done on his '88 solo album.

That same year, the first feature documentary about Brian Wilson was released, and it was inspired by *SMiLE*. The director of *I Just Wasn't Made for These Times* explains.

Don Was: 'In the fall of 1989, I was working with a band who turned me on to bootlegged recordings of *SMILE* sessions. Like a musical burning bush, these tapes awakened me to a higher consciousness in record making.

SMiLE

I was amazed that one, single human could dream up this unprecedented and radically-advanced approach to rock 'n' roll.

'I was really stunned when I met him several months later. Far from the catatonic drug burn-out the tabloids loved to depict, the guy I got to know was lucid and happening.

'How could a talent so great be so misunderstood and underappreciated? The documentary attempts to explain to the non-musician precisely why the phrase "Brian Wilson is a genius" has appeared on the lips of three generations of musicians like holy gospel. This film portrays a man that few people get to meet – deep, sensitive, funny and yes . . . perhaps a bit bizarre.'

Don Was's film succeeded in doing that. And surprisingly, in the film, Brian performed the SMiLE song 'Wonderful.'

In Brian's world, for the SMiLE cult, that was a giant step.

When he was doing interviews to promote the Don Was movie and the *Orange Crate Art* album, Brian was asked why he was now comfortable making music again . . . even singing a song from SMiLE. His short answer spoke volumes.

Brian: 'I have emotional security.'

Meanwhile, unbeknownst to Brian, musicians who had met because of their love for Brian and their fascination with SMiLE, were playing and recording his songs.

At a 1994 Wild Honey benefit concert that was a tribute to Brian, The Wondermints knocked him out with their live performances of his songs, including 'Surf's Up.'

And in a completely different world, in 1981, Jeffrey Foskett began a lengthy stint as a sideman with The Beach Boys. At first filling in for Carl Wilson, he ultimately spent almost a decade touring with the group, singing Brian's compositions. More importantly, when he started performing with Brian, his voice seamlessly combined with, doubled, and sometimes covered Brian; Jeffrey had a sound that would make you wonder if Carl Wilson had been reincarnated.

In 1997-1998, working with producer Joe Thomas, Brian made his second solo album, *Imagination*.

All of these worlds were about to collide.

In 1999, a band was put together to back Brian for a 'let's-see-how-it-goes,' four-city solo tour designed to promote the *Imagination* album. The story of how the band came together is convoluted but significant.

CAN'T WAIT TOO LONG

In L.A., Brian had played a few mini-concerts, usually benefits. Backing him were The Wondermints: Darian, Nick, Probyn, and Mike. All of them were not just well-versed in the legend of SMiLE, but, for them, it was something of musical scripture.

The so-called Chicago contingent Joe Thomas brought in were instrumental, no pun intended, in filling out the sound and giving it a depth that The Wondermints couldn't have done alone. This stellar cast of studio musicians assembled included ace drummer Todd Sucherman, bassist Bob Lizik, Paul Von Mertens on sax and other woodwinds, multi-instrumentalist/singer Scott Bennett, and for background vocals, Taylor Mills. They knew The Beach Boys hits but weren't fanatics. They knew nothing about the legend of SMiLE.

In between these different groups stood Jeffrey Foskett.

When they all came together in Chicago in February 1999, rehearsals were, as Paul Von Mertens recalls, 'kind of tense because there was some, I would say, friction between Joe [Thomas] and some people in the band as far as how to interpret and deliver the music. I think Joe had a vision that was kind of updated, and I might say a little bit slick. And the L.A. guys – Darian and Nick in particular – had a very pure vision of the music and wanted to deliver it as much like the recordings as possible. And so there was some debate about how to play the songs, whether the groove should be updated on 'Caroline, No,' to more of a sort of a smooth jazz kind of thing . . . Aesthetically, the sort of more pure vision of Brian's music prevailed.'

Paul offers a stunning admission.

Paul: 'We didn't know how Brian would perform . . . There were literally discussions of having his vocals on tape in case he couldn't sing. It hadn't been done before, so there were some unknown factors . . . fortunately it worked out [and Brian sang].'

Bob Lizik: 'There were kind of two different camps, and it stayed that way until we all went to dinner together one time . . . and we started forming a bond.'

Paul: 'I really grew to respect them and appreciate them, Darian and Nick. It was mind-blowing how knowledgeable Nick was on so many things, and Darian – what a great ear, and what a great musician. So, it did take a little while, but I grew to really love and respect everybody.'

On the trip to Ann Arbor for the first concert, the band also came together on that tour thanks to a double disaster, one mechanical, the other natural.

Paul: 'There was a blizzard the day before we left . . . the heat broke down [on the bus] . . . It wasn't like a regular tour bus. It was what they call a 'star bus.' And I remember most of the band laying under blankets together in the bed at the back of the bus to stay warm. So, it was an adventure.'

At first, a Brian Wilson concert seemed like a mirage. Was that really his name on the Ann Arbor theatre marquee? Indeed, it was, and the first successful shows led to tours in the East Coast and Japan. It was clear that something special was happening.

Probyn: 'My feeling was that people were really happy to see Brian out there. In October 1999, we did a thing Neil Young does every year called "The Bridge School Benefit." Up in the Bay area. The first year we were there, The Who had the dressing room one or two down. I was there when Pete Townshend got on his knees in front of Brian and said, "Oh my God, I've been wanting to meet you all these years. Your music means so much to me." And that was amazing, seeing these two icons of rock meeting for the first time.'

Scott Bennett didn't grow up a Beach Boys fan, but 'when we did the Bridge School, that was the first time I saw these icons [bowing down] to Brian.' That's when Scott realized, 'The guy I'm playing with is the king of everything. From McCartney on down, people just adore his music and adore him. Neil Young spent the entire after-party seated with Brian, grilling him about *Pet Sounds*.'

There were many moments like that during Brian's first year of touring, and there would be many more to come. And by the end of 1999, The Brian Wilson Band was more than solid, brought together by their mutual respect and their love and admiration for Brian and his music.

Spending time on the road with Brian, the band got to know and understand the person behind the music.

Taylor Mills: 'What's Brian really like? Brian is the sweetest person you'll ever meet. He's very honest. Actually, Brian could be brutally honest, and I love that about him. He's simply like no one else. He's okay with being quiet if you're with him. He's content with silence. You have to be comfortable enough to understand that and be all right with it, because some people are not. Brian can make everyone laugh. He's very funny when he wants to be, and he enjoys catching people off guard.'

Scott: 'The other thing is, in this very pretentious posturing business, he is the least pretentious. He is so unconcerned with cool, that it's cool; it's been so refreshing to be a part of it. And he just doesn't have a bad bone in his body. He gets sort of the label of the most eccentric guy in rock or whatever. If you were a rock star in the sixties, you're not a normal guy. (*Laughs*) I think the difference with Brian is that he's not screwed up in a negative way. He's just still the nicest, sweetest guy.'

Nick Walusko: 'For me, he's quite a gentleman. I mean, both as a gentle man and a gentleman, in the sense that I never once heard him speak ill of anyone or anything . . . He never gets petty, and that's why I'll do anything for him, for a person like that. I think he just wants the world, and people in general, either in his band or in his life, to get along and be harmonious. I think it's very important to Brian. And I think when he senses that it isn't like that, he clams up. He'd just rather be somewhere else but knowing something about his history, you can't blame him . . . So if Brian wants to eat a salad in three gulps and leave the table, I don't take it personally. Because I know, that's the way he is. Eat and run, that's it. But he's a great guy to hang out with, and he's always very soft spoken and really genuine.'

Probyn: 'He's devastatingly honest. If he's at an interview and he doesn't want to talk any more, he'll get up and leave or he'll say, "I don't want to answer that." I mean there's no hidden agenda . . . what you see from Brian, that's really what's going on. He's very honest and direct. He's a very tender soul. Of course, that comes out in his music.

'I think people want him to talk about his art or to talk about what's on his mind and he's a private person. Sometimes, he'll call you over and say "Hey man, can I have a backrub?" . . . Once in a while, I'll go up and just sort of pass the time of day with him when I feel that it's right. But I don't want to invade his space because he's set it up the way he wants it, and I don't want to interfere with that.'

Summarizing, Probyn points out that 'people can take that as enigmatic, in the fact that he's not forthcoming about his art or about what's really on his mind, because either it's private or he doesn't deem it fit to share with the world for whatever reason. That's okay. Again, as they say, "still waters run deep," and I respect people like that.'

The band's sensitivity to Brian as a person would be essential as he began playing live.

Nick: 'He's really trying to explore his own feelings and hopefully they are universal to everybody else ... He always tries to outdo himself.'

Veteran tour manager John Warren, who had worked with The Beach Boys for years, was with Brian in those early touring days. He remembers that, given what they'd seen in the past, people in the business, including the promoters, couldn't believe the quality of Brian's band.

John Warren: 'When we first started, people would be like, "How much of this is on tape?" I would say, "None of it." They're like, "Come on. No vocals?" I said, "Absolutely not. Every one of these people up here is covering the parts." And it blew people away.'

More significant were those who didn't believe Brian would even be there.

John: 'That first year I got promoters calling me, "Is Brian really gonna show up?" [They] were very hesitant, very sceptical. Brian's notorious for not showing up, and I went, "I think he's pretty serious about this."'

As serious as Brian was, he was also incredibly nervous. But when push came to shove, the shows were usually great. Sometimes Brian would have a bad day, but he never backed down.

In 1999, his publicists Ronnie Lippin and Jean Sievers had become Brian's co-managers. The early tours, as Jean recalls, were full of ups and downs.

Jean Sievers: 'Brian freaked out on our way to see the Liberty Bell in Philadelphia and wanted to go to a hospital. He didn't want to do the show. "Okay, we'll just take you to the hospital." And all of a sudden, he did, like, the best show ever. So, there were nights like that. And then, as time went on, he just wanted to tour more and more. Touring became important to him.'

In 1999, Brian and his remarkable band passed every 'exam' with flying colours. In 2000, they would all be further tested: they would play *Pet Sounds* live. Start to finish. With an orchestra. A wildly ambitious endeavour, as Jean Sievers notes, 'Nobody was touring albums back then.'

The band had to learn the album, and Paul Von Mertens had an extra job too.

Paul: 'Van Dyke Parks wrote a suite for orchestra comprised of themes, musical themes from Brian's music, and I was tasked with writing the orchestral accompaniment for the band to play *Pet Sounds* ... That's hallowed ground. There are orchestral elements on *Pet Sounds*. But, really, what's fascinating about it is the way that Brian used orchestral instruments, but kind of had them play like rock musicians. Like the way the timpani parts, the string parts, are conceived are not like traditional classical-style writing.

'So I remember, because I was working with Van Dyke, I was sending my scores to him, and at the beginning, I said, "I don't really need an entire orchestra to do this. What's on the record is kind of like a studio orchestra. It's small groups of musicians augmenting the songs." And I remember Van Dyke said, "My boy, if I were you, I would do what I'm told." So the challenge was to utilize the orchestra without schmaltzing up the music.

'I definitely relied on Darian for input, running ideas by him and figuring out ways that we could incorporate the orchestra without it sounding corny . . . for the most part, I avoided adding musical ideas or textures that were not on the original record. So, the orchestra kind of augmented what was already there. I didn't add sweeping violins or that kind of thing, because we wanted to present the music as much in its original spirit as possible.'

John Warren: 'Darian, a genius – very, very talented, amazing human being. Without him, I don't think a lot of it would have happened. I think he really was sort of like the third base coach [waving] Brian home. It's like, "Let's go." Darian's amazing. The whole band was. Probyn, we used to call him "The Swiss Army Knife." You can hand that guy anything . . . "Here you go, figure out how to play the French horn." He played like six or seven different instruments out there.'

Bob Lizik: 'Musically, it was deep. First, I had such respect for the bass lines. 'I Know There's An Answer.' 'Here Today.' All this stuff is really creative.' And in my head, I'm thinking, "Carol [Kaye] must have come up with this," [or Lyle Ritz or Ray Pohlman]. They must have come up with these parts. And then, in talking with Carol, she said, "No. Brian would say, 'This is what I want.'"'

On short notice, when the band needed a new drummer, thanks to Bob, Jim Hines got the gig.

Jim Hines: 'I am embarrassed to say I did not really know much about *Pet Sounds*. When I sat down to listen to it for the first time, all the way top to bottom, it blew my shit away. And then Bob came over to my house, and we rehearsed it together before that tour, just play along with the tracks.'

Bob Lizik notes the 'times when there's three basses. There's an upright and an electric, and then there's a ticky-tack. And I'm going, "How did he decide this?" And they don't get in the way of each other, which is really unusual because they're playing different things.'

When it came to the drumming, Bob points out 'They are kind of orchestral drum parts. I started realizing how Brian thought. He didn't think in terms of, "Let's put a rhythm section together and play a song." He saw a much bigger picture.'

So learning to play *Pet Sounds* was, for Jim and Bob (nicknamed 'The Tasty Brothers'), 'really hard to do.' Presaging the methodology he would use for *Brian Wilson Presents SMiLE*, Bob remembers, 'Darian sent me [a CD] of just the tracks, so I was able to kind of isolate some of the things. And then, there was like, "Do I play the electric part? But the upright part is more dominant at this section," so it was kind of switching between the two parts. It was, "Man, what did Brian hear?" He heard it all.'

John Warren: 'In band rehearsals, we'd go for days and Brian would just come in, and go through the motions and Foskett or Darian would run the rehearsals. But every once in a while, Brian would turn around and go, "What are you singing? No, it's not supposed to be that. You're sharp. You're flat." It didn't come out often. He wasn't running the show every day, but when he did, you'd hear him turn around and go, "Wait a minute. No, what's that? That's a wrong note." I used to love watching that come out . . . And I thought a lot about [Brian's brother] Carl. It brought back a lot of emotion for Carl. He just would've loved this.'

Jim: 'When I joined the band, Brian impressed me as somebody trying really hard to do something that he had not done for a long time and impressed me as being incredibly empathetic, which I think will surprise a lot of people. He would reach out in his funny little Brian way that he does and say something really sort of meaningful and comforting at a really strange moment when you're not expecting it. Like, "It's gonna be okay." He always seems to know. The man is full of empathy, love, and strength. I think he really understood [that] I was scared to death. I joined that band replacing an incredible drummer [Todd Sucherman]. Brian's like the strongest, strongest human being maybe I've ever seen in my life.'

John: 'The fact that we were doing *Pet Sounds* was like a miracle. That was the first miracle. Not many people get two. We got two. We were all blown away that we were even out there doing that in its entirety. And, with the crew, with Richie Davis [at the audio board]. That thing jelled so magically. And Foskett was the other glue as far as the vocal parts. He was very integral. But that wasn't as much fun to put together as *SMiLE* was, with all the goofy props.'

It wasn't thought of at the time, but the *Pet Sounds* tours (in the US and especially in the UK) were setting the stage for *Brian Wilson Presents SMiLE*.

It really wasn't even ever on the agenda.

Probyn: 'When the band first got together in 1999, we were not allowed to say the words 'Cabin Essence' or 'Heroes And Villains' or 'Surf's Up.' Brian said, "That reminds me of a bad time. I don't want to think about it. So please don't refer to those songs." So, we didn't. Those titles didn't cross our lips.'

In between the US and UK *Pet Sounds* tours, there was a key moment in the resurrection of *SMiLE*: Scott Bennett's Christmas party in 2000.

Scott: 'I said to Brian, "Feel free to tickle the ivories," which, thinking he would never do.' Putting the event in perspective, Scott explains, 'Not three months prior, I said, "We should do 'Heroes And Villains,' maybe 'Cabin Essence.' We should do some of those." And Brian's like, "No. We're never gonna do those songs. Bad vibes."'

Then, as a Christmas present for Eva Easton-Leaf, Brian shocked everybody in Scott's house. He played 'Heroes And Villains.'

Probyn: 'That was the icebreaker; we were overjoyed. I can't remember if I cried and threw my arms around Darian, but spirits were high, let me tell you. That meant a lot that Brian sat down and did that. Just the memory of that now kind of gets to me, 'cause it was so important. And it was important for us.'

Scott: 'When he was finished, David Leaf walked over and said, "Hey, you should do that [at the tribute]."'

And he did.

Three months later, on March 29, 2001, Brian performed 'Heroes And Villains' at *An All-Star Tribute to Brian Wilson* concert at Radio City Music Hall in New York City.

David Leaf: 'As writer/producer of the event, I made sure the program included *SMiLE* music: The Boys Choir of Harlem sang 'Our Prayer,' and Vince Gill, David Crosby, and Jimmy Webb rose to the challenge of bringing 'Surf's Up' to the world.'

Paul Von Mertens: 'When [the tribute's music producer] Phil Ramone [told Vince] 'Surf's Up' was going to be one of the songs, he didn't know the song at all. In fact, he thought it was like 'Surfin' Safari' or something, like a three-minute pop song. And then he heard the record, and he was like, "Oh, shit! I got a lot of work to do." And in short order, while his wife was having a baby, he learned the song. And, of course, you can see from the performance, he just did a stunning job of it.' (Google it.)

Darian: 'When we played 'Heroes And Villains,' it got a great response. Which wasn't a surprise to me. I mean, that really is a tour de force. I was happy that it had such a great reception. But I think Brian was really surprised that it got that kind of response. We have to remember that only a few months earlier, you couldn't even talk about 'Heroes And Villains' with Brian. You bring it up and he says, "I don't wanna talk about it." Or "No comment." Or he'll say, "It's inappropriate."

'But that night we played 'Heroes And Villains' at Radio City Music Hall, we got a standing ovation for that song. I looked over at Brian, and he just had that kind of look, like "Wow. People love this. People actually like this song." (*Laughs*) I think it broke the ice.'

Bob Lizik: 'I remember seeing Paul Shaffer in the audience, just suddenly moved to the edge of his seat, like [he was thinking] "Holy crap." Because that's a big undertaking. I gotta hand it to the guys with all the vocals. They did a phenomenal job. Proud to be part of that.'

Probyn: 'We'd been secretly harbouring our *SMiLE* obsessions, hoping against hope that some of that stuff would see the light of day with this band. I barely remember the actual Radio City performance. I was probably gripped by nerves . . . all I remember was at the end there was tremendous applause, and some people leapt to their feet, realizing the significance of the moment. But I bet a lot of people didn't realize that was the first time that song had been done in recent memory, with Brian being involved.'

Paul: 'That was quite a hill to climb when we started to rehearse it and prepare to perform it live. That was one of those, "Wow, 'never been done'" kind of moments that were really exciting.'

Jeffrey: 'When we started that song at the tribute, it sounds like the record. Brian's voice was not a falsetto voice; it's not a tender voice. It's real. "I've been in this town" – and it sounded just like it did on the record. And the band was really swinging ... It really, really, really knocked the socks off of people. It was just really an incredible moment.'

Bob: 'The reaction of the people that *know* was unbelievable. 'Cause that was all over the internet after that, too ... Vince Gill ... I still listen to that. I listen to 'Surf's Up.' I listen to Vince [doing] 'The Warmth of the Sun.' And the hair on my arm still stands up because he did such a great job on that.'

Probyn: 'The Radio City audience was unbelievable. I saw people in tears at several points during the show. So I know they were definitely giving him the love that night. And I think that might have been the turning point for Brian. Certainly, the preparation for the show helped him get comfortable with it. And seeing the adulation and the utter joy of people hearing this song from him. That was really something.'

A very emotional moment for Probyn.

Probyn: 'That was one of the greatest things I ever did in my life – apart from the premiere of *SMiLE* – being in that house band. That Radio City show was just so chock full of talented people giving great performances, and the audience buying into it. Everyone was so supportive. And of course, it's an iconic venue. Everything about it was just perfect. I loved the Radio City show.'

Paul: 'That probably was the genesis of completing the record. It was like, "There's a couple of amazing songs that we could do if we could have time to rehearse it and buckle down, and if Brian was willing to do it." And it did take some convincing, but that was the genesis of the idea. "Maybe we could do the whole record." "Maybe we could finish the record" was kind of one of those moments where something that seemed impossible was suddenly a possibility, and, then even more incredible that it actually happened.'

The band had done 'Heroes And Villains.' Darian felt that song, 'aside from 'Mrs. O'Leary's Cow,' was one of the heaviest weights, probably associated with some of the worst memories for him. I mean, it was the single that they were pressuring him to put out, and maybe he was a little rushed with it. And it was about that time that it was all starting to kind of fall apart. He was losing his support system. And I think that one being the follow-up single to 'Good Vibrations,' and it not being the smash hit that everybody was expecting ... it's understandable. So, I think he got past a big hurdle there. And [in 2003] that was some of the ammunition I had to go in to present *(laughs)* to Brian that we're gonna actually do this album.'

What had happened? Simply, with the love and encouragement of those who surrounded him, covering him in 'emotional security,' Brian was beginning to embrace his past.

The first tours in 1999 were visitations. The *Pet Sounds* tour in 2000 was a 'Can this really be happening?' moment, and the 2001 Radio City tribute brought *SMiLE* music in front of Brian's eyes and ears. And the world hadn't come to an end.

On tour in 2002, Brian and his band added several *SMiLE* songs to their setlist.

Bob Lizik: 'We did 'Heroes And Villains' and we added 'Surf's Up.' And Brian was back and forth whether or not he wanted to do 'Surf's Up' at times.'

Despite what Brian might have been told in 1967, people did want to hear these songs. They weren't too 'avant-garde.' They weren't too strange. They were just perfect.

But was there going to be another chapter in the *SMiLE* story, one that might have *a happy ending*?

David Leaf (in a 2001 interview with *Open Sky*, when asked about *SMiLE*): 'The only thing that I have to offer on the subject is that there's only one person in the world who knows what *SMiLE* is and hopefully one day he will complete his vision and share that with us. Or I should say, one day he will find a way to share that vision. Whatever that means. I'm not saying it to be oblique – it will be what it will be. And I really am not going to try and guess what *SMiLE* is or should be. I do know this: just the music that's been released from the era, if it were all collected on one record – makes it one of the greatest albums of all time, even in its unfinished state. So, it's not that it's a hyped piece of art. It's just an unrealized, uncompleted work. What there is of it is so incredible as to let you know that it's not hype.'

RAISING THE TITANIC

'To finish a work? To finish a picture? What nonsense!'
Pablo Picasso

'Finish *SMiLE*? You might as well try and raise the Titanic.'
Brian Wilson

VAN DYKE PARKS: 'THERE WAS SOMETHING ABOUT BRIAN'S CHARACTER, his artistic integrity, that appealed to me. And it's the same thing that appealed to me about Van Gogh, what made Van Gogh go was this schizophrenic state of mind. It's there. It's become more of an entertainment and public information. We've all seen *Easy Rider*. And we've ridden beyond it.

'There's much to speak about in theatre that shows artists following their madness in a way. And that takes a willingness to be viewed as mad. Happened to Ravel at the premiere of *Bolero*, when a woman stood up and said, "You're crazy," in the Paris Opera House. And Ravel turned around to a stunned house and said, "You're right. I am crazy."

'So, you have to put that aside if you want to pursue something because there's no shelter in the arts. There's no shelter. You have to be willing to explore with your medium in any way that you can. It takes courage, can't start by wondering what somebody thinks about the fact that you believe in something. You just hope that your powers of expression, infect the participant, your audience, or your mate, in a positive way.'

In May of 1967, Brian Wilson had put the *SMiLE* tapes 'on the shelf.' During the subsequent thirty-six years, *SMiLE* had become the most famous unreleased album in rock history . . . until Brian Wilson decided to finish it in 2004. Live, on stage.

SMiLE

In May of 2003, I accompanied Brian to London when he received the Ivor Novello award for Lifetime Achievement in music. There was more to that trip than just an acceptance speech at the event: the official announcement of the *SMiLE* concerts.

But inside Brian's world, the buzz had preceded it.

Probyn Gregory: 'I was hearing that Melinda was talking to Brian, and saying, "Hey, the fans are wanting this. What do you think?" And Brian was resistant at first. He didn't really want to, even though of course he had already done pieces of it, so the ice was broken in that regard. But not vis-à-vis "the whole enchilada," all of *SMiLE,* or what could be cobbled together of the many, many fragments. I can't remember what the progression was of how it came to be that he said "Yes."'

It seemed more than unlikely, as John Warren remembers: 'I don't think anybody a million years, if you told them, "This is gonna happen," they would have believed it.'

How did it happen?

Glenn Max, *The Royal Festival Hall:* 'I was invited to take over the Contemporary Culture Programme at the Royal Festival Hall, the Southbank Centre, in 2001, where I oversaw the Meltdown Festival and concert programming . . . I was in Los Angeles when Brian did *Pet Sounds* at the Hollywood Bowl. I don't think I ever really understood the vast complexity of it and the richness of it until that night. And Brian's band – the expertise and the confidence and the intimacy with the material that they exude. It was just the most compelling thing I'd ever seen. I went back to London and said, "Why isn't this happening in London?" Because I was well aware that Brian Wilson means much more in the UK than in the US.

'And I went to Neil Warnock [Brian's music agent], made a compelling case, and finally, we confirmed a deal,' and in January 2002, Brian went to Europe and the UK. In London, performing *Pet Sounds* every night . . . in the country that had embraced the record in 1966 . . . was, as Glenn Max recalls, 'Not just a revelation musically. [There wasn't] a dry eye in the house. Everyone you could imagine to turn up was there – McCartney, Elvis Costello, Richard Wright (Pink Floyd), Daniel Miller of Mute Records . . . the range of artists across generations that came to see Brian play *Pet Sounds*. You had a real sense of what an important event this was for London and for the music scene. It was a profoundly unifying moment.'

During those four shows, Glenn saw something else.

Glenn: 'There was something about Brian on stage, especially in those days, when his vulnerability was so palpable and on display. And this sort of support he'd get from the audience is like church. People really gathered around to sort of support this fragile man. His vulnerability and authenticity disarmed the most cynical hearts and discerning ears.'

What could possibly follow that?

Glenn: 'At the end of those *Pet Sounds* shows, there were murmurs between myself and the band. "What are we gonna do next?" Well, there's only one way to top the excitement and success of *Pet Sounds*. But it was very sensitive to even speak of it. But it *was* the only way to do something bigger. The anticipation . . . the enduring mystique of that lost record and the story behind it. I knew *SMiLE*, performed live at the Royal Festival Hall, would be legendary the minute we announced it.'

There were big questions hanging in the air.

Glenn: 'Could it be done? Could you convince Brian to do it? What would this be like for him?'

Neil Warnock, Brian's music agent, points to Glenn Max and the Royal Festival Hall as the key component behind this actually coming to life.

Neil Warnock MBE: 'Festival Hall had a budget to actually bring in something that was, if you will, artistic . . . Somebody like Brian, who is a complete innovator, somebody who had actually created a style of writing and style of music that wasn't anywhere else, was absolutely a real fit for what the Royal Festival Hall wanted to do. Without their funding and without their support it would have been impossible because the finances of putting *SMiLE* together were vast. And it was totally underwritten by the Royal Festival Hall.'

Glenn: 'We basically commissioned *SMiLE*.'

Neil: 'I remember having a conversation with Brian about it. I think he really wanted to do it but was terrified by the enormity of it. Having played Festival Hall [helped]. I think he looked at it as sort of like a home away from home. It felt comfortable to him. He always liked sitting by the side of the stage before he went on. And I think because he did *Pet Sounds* night after night at Festival Hall, [he] felt comfortable. And the way that Festival Hall is set up with the audience that close to you. You feel like you're actually entertaining in somebody's front room – I think [that] gave Brian confidence to actually do it when I'd said, 'Let's go back and do *SMiLE*.'

Glenn: 'I had to justify everything in ticket sales . . . But this was a show I knew would do well, and based on our past success and the mystique of *SMiLE*, we just made a big, brave offer. And it sat there for a long time . . . and we waited and waited until we got a confirmation, which was unbelievable.

'And, of course, I was immediately nervous for Brian because I knew the intense level of work it would require. And then, you just wondered how were they going to do some of this music . . . which is pretty esoteric, let's say, and noise-based, and very avant-garde ideas.'

Looking back, Glenn remembers, 'This isn't something that [Brian's team] even knew would be a success or whether they would be able to do it anywhere else. It wasn't clear in anyone's mind [that] this is gonna be a global tour. It was, "Let's just see if we can get it off once." And so for that reason, the fees had to be pretty extreme. It was definitely new terrain. Could it make any sense for Brian to work this hard, and revisit this music, for what might amount to only a one-off? Would he be able to get through it?'

The day after the Ivor Novello Award ceremony, it was made official.

Jean Sievers: 'I have to give Neil Warnock credit for that. He had talked to Brian and Melinda about it a little bit. But then, Brian was like, "All right, we're gonna do this."'

Ray Lawlor: 'We were in a restaurant in London . . . Brian, you [David Leaf], me, Jean, Neil and a bunch of reporters. It wasn't a big deal press conference. But it was a big deal moment, especially as I'd been waiting to hear *SMiLE* for over thirty-six years.'

Ray describes the scene: 'Brian was standing in the middle of the floor, talking to a crowd of people, talking about his next album, *Gettin' In Over My Head*. Then, he said, "We're gonna finish off the *SMiLE* album." I just remember there was one or more gasps from the crowd that was gathered around him.'

Neil: 'And, of course, once it started going, the momentum and everything else was just enormous, it took on a life of its own and surprised the music world . . . people had to be there to see that show.'

RAISING THE TITANIC

All well and good in England. But would there even be a show? Was Neil Warnock ever worried about the shows actually not happening?

Neil: 'We didn't get all the collywobbles [nervousness]. Jean and Melinda were probably keeping it all away from me. I had great confidence, because his band and the people around him were so supportive and so talented. I didn't imagine that it wasn't going to happen. That band and everybody around him gave him so much confidence to be able to complete the work. So, it was never put to me that there was a likelihood of him not being able to do it.'

Neil was perhaps the only one on the inside who wasn't concerned.

Bob Lizik: 'I found out with the band. We had discussed it prior to the announcement. And I said, "Okay." I didn't realize how hard it was going to be. 'Cause I hadn't heard all the little bits and pieces. I hadn't heard 'Cabin Essence' and 'Wind Chimes. And [it was] like, "How are we gonna pull this off?" I just had no idea.'

Probyn: 'We'd talked about it, The Wondermints guys in particular, and we knew it wasn't impossible. We also knew that it was going to take at least a portion of a dedicated orchestra to do all the strings and the horns. Paul [Von] Mertens and I could only do so much as the only two wind players on stage. And, probably one or both of us, as it turned out, would have to sing vocals at certain key junctures, just to make sure everything was covered, or in some cases doubled when it needed to be doubled.'

What did Brian think about all of this? Well, he wasn't telling me. In the nearly eight months from the announcement to the first performance, we didn't really talk about it. And once we decided to make a documentary, Brian was too on-edge to do a meaningful interview about what was happening. Believe me, I tried. Basically, all he said was, 'I'm nervous as hell.'

But after the first tour was over, the day he got home, he called and said, 'You have to come over tomorrow and do an interview.' I would guess that's the first and maybe only time in the past fifty-plus years that he ever was actually eager to do an interview. Especially one about *SMiLE*. He was so excited about what had happened in London and on the tour, that he was ready to answer any question I might have. So I went back to the announcement of *SMiLE*.

David Leaf: 'Can you remember what you were thinking when you got the award in London and the idea of actually doing it, [doing *SMiLE* live]?'

Brian: 'I know we recorded a lot of the bits and pieces of it, but I never ever thought we'd ever, ever do it on stage like that. It never dawned on me that we ever would.'

David: 'When did you realize it was time to do this?'

Brian: 'When you and Melinda told me that it was about time. You and Melinda convinced me that it was time to go get to work and do it.'

That stunned me. When Brian said that during that interview, it was the first time I knew that I had 'convinced' him. Through the years, I had certainly told him how amazing the music was, that it should be heard. Had even discussed a symphonic *SMiLE* with him. But convinced him?

It happened not because of anything I did musically. It happened just out of loving him. Because all he needed was to be loved. Unconditionally.

Once it was in motion, my wife Eva and I just looked at each other in disbelief and the knowledge that we would have to be in London to cheer him on. Later in the story, I did know that my being there during the rehearsals had encouraged him. But we're not there yet.

On the face of it, the sheer logistics of performing *SMiLE* live were overwhelming. This was a very different challenge than performing *Pet Sounds* start to finish. That's because *SMiLE* didn't exist.

As to Brian's *SMiLE* songwriting partner, when Van Dyke Parks first heard that *SMiLE* was being taken off the shelf, he was concerned for himself and for Brian.

Van Dyke: 'I think that we both feared that the consequences of any further involvement might be as painful as the last ones. But in fact, ultimately that doesn't bother a person whose mind is on the job, whose shoulder [is] at the wheel, whose eye is on the sparrow. That's what we do.'

Reflecting more specifically, Van Dyke explains, 'We just get together, and I hope it happens more often, in more arenas than just music because I love his sense of the absurd, and the kind of way he presents it, and we just kept going that way. There were no conscious decisions to do anything in the process except to make something perfect. Now, there's a Welsh expression – taught to me by a Welsh missionary. What does it mean? "Nothing good where better is possible." And any artist keeps that in mind.'

The press release caused quite a stir, especially among the fans. Van Dyke watched with more than a passing interest.

RAISING THE TITANIC

Van Dyke: 'My first reaction on hearing that Brian was going to open up the can called *SMiLE*, go back and look at the project, and perform in person . . . I thought, "Well, that's incredible. That's a wonderful thing for him to do." And then, I waited. I heard about it in the press, national press. And I thought, "I know he's gonna get around to calling me. He'll need my take on it."'

Did he? Would he? For Van Dyke, 'That was a very long wait.'

After the announcement, for months, Brian didn't want anybody's 'take' on it. It seems that more than anything, he was trying not to think about the work that lay ahead. Because when he did, it wasn't with joy.

Van Dyke was wary, to say the least. 'I think *SMiLE* has, by the force of the music, and by the adequacy of the words, and by the power of the visual images that Frank Holmes put into play, I think it has great potential as an entertainment object. But I'll be damn sure before I do any more work on it that there will be a release . . . I don't like the idea of saying complete or incomplete. I think [those words are] too harsh. For no other reason, I think that because they're pre-emptive blows against my artistic freedom, and if Mr. Wilson might agree with me, I rail against things that suggest losing my artistic freedom or his, in this case, ours. We can do anything we want in a town where nobody really knows nothing, and that's the truth.'

Two or three months passed, as far as I could tell, without any progress. In the mid-summer of 2003, Brian and I were walking up the Third Street Promenade in Santa Monica. Heading back to my apartment from the movies. Out of nowhere, he started talking about the *SMiLE* concerts; he said, 'I can't do this unless you're there with me every day.'

I was taken aback, to say the least. I talked with Brian about my freelance writing jobs and commitments to my production company, which had recently produced a feature documentary on the Bee Gees, a group he loved. I said to Brian, 'The only way I can be there every day is if we're making a documentary.' He said, 'OK.' That night, we talked with Melinda about it. I explained that from my point of view, the film had to tell a story for the 99 percent of the audience who had never heard of *SMiLE*. And then, I set sail into the marketplace to find a network that would finance it. While I did that, the band thought about what this would all mean in 2004.

Darian Sahanaja: 'There's something about an unfinished work of art produced at the height of the artist's most creative period that spans an entire spectrum of opinion. It allows people to project their own "what if" scenarios – a launch pad of dreams. Everyone gets to fill in the gaps and imagine their own perfect version. It's the ideal musical fantasy. Of course, it helps when the music is excellent.'

Probyn Gregory: 'There are moments in *SMiLE* that to me are quintessential, like the zenith of how a certain part of life's sadness can be made manifest in music. I don't know how Brian tapped into that but he certainly has it in spades. I know harmony, I know music. I've analysed the melodies. I've looked at the chord structures. But I can't create the kind of ethos that he made with a body of work – even back with 'In My Room.' Even though that was a simple song, parts of that hinted at this same fragile person trying to express how he can navigate through the world. Parts of that are sad but the main thing is – he's *doing* it. It's a success. He's managed that navigation, made it through the slough of despond. And it might even be because whatever demons were plaguing Brian way back then, this is obviously his way of dealing with it – writing the music and expressing it that way.'

Darian reminds us that 'the *SMiLE*-era music also shines because of musical context. In the same way 'Wouldn't It Be Nice' was an advancement of 'California Girls,' you could hear a further evolution with 'Surf's Up.' Brian was really pushing his creative envelope during this period. But he didn't just sacrifice craftsmanship for the sake of art like so many others did. His was a nice balance. By comparison, you can truly appreciate Picasso's cubism period when you see the natural evolution from his previous works where he clearly had mastered painting realism.

'And we shouldn't forget its context in the pop culture timeline. By 1966, there were only a handful of young composers that were truly pointing the way for a generation. With the youth movement gaining momentum, the music that spoke for them had to evoke freedom. The *SMiLE* music was and still is liberating on many levels, and because of that it continues to inspire creative hearts and minds. Timeless stuff.'

Probyn points to the universality of what Brian expresses.

Probyn: 'Many people have similar things in their lives that he was facing. So to hear someone creating a sonic landscape – it's like saying, "Here's how I dealt with it. Maybe you can relate," and people are, "Yeah. I can relate. That sound – that's how I feel too." It was the height of irony that the unfinished album was called *SMiLE*, because you listen to it and aside from a very few things, like the goofiness of 'Vega-Tables,' most of the music has a streak of world-weary understanding that would not generally evoke a smile.'

Nick Walusko: '*Pet Sounds*, to me, just is more pure rock, pop. And *SMiLE* is definitely much more abstract and symphonic, maybe in a chamber orchestra sense . . . it's pretty surreal. It's getting out there. It's Tin Pan Alley. It's this. It's that. It's all over the place.'

For almost twenty years Darian and Nick and Probyn and so many others had listened to pieces of *SMiLE* on various bootlegs and underground tapes. Even on authorized releases. Now, they were going to play the music they so deeply loved. *With Brian*.

For Nick, it was 'very strange. I would have never believed it. First of all, even if I wasn't involved . . . if I heard he was doing it . . . I'd go see it. But to be involved is like, "No way." I would never have believed it. Even if you told me when we began playing with Brian that we're going to do it, I'd say, for various reasons, it's just not going to ever happen.'

Jean Sievers: 'Darian and Nick and Probyn? Their knowledge of *SMiLE* and their pure love of him, they would have done it for free.'

However, while *SMiLE* fans had been surprised and thrilled by the news, all in disbelief, for Darian, who had once been 'just' a *SMiLE* fan, the man who would become the so-called 'musical secretary' of *Brian Wilson Presents SMiLE*, it all furrowed a forehead.

Darian: 'When the announcement was first made, it was probably a mixture of wariness and excitement. I remember thinking, "How are we going to pull this off? Could it actually be done well?" I just had a lot of scepticism. Probably because of the mystique surrounding it. It was almost too sacred, and I thought, "Why try to do this now?" Given the examples of revisitations of classic territory done by others . . . movie remakes or what not . . . which tend to fall short. There were so many things that could go wrong.'

Nick Walusko, Darian's best friend and musical partner, shared his bandmate's concern.

Nick: 'First of all, I just didn't know if Brian was emotionally ready for it. Because, there was all these legends about what *SMiLE* meant or did to him. And to Van Dyke Parks. And I think coupled with the fact that the *Pet Sounds* tour was such an undertaking. It was a very strange paradox. It was like, "Where do we go?" And the only place to go would be (*laughs*) SMiLE. So, it's just, like, "OK." If he could get over some of those demons, we'll do it.'

Nick points out that by 2003, 'People kind of forgot that we've done some of the songs that would have been on SMiLE.' And these were key songs like 'Surf's Up' and 'Heroes And Villains.' 'But we kept a little bit of a low profile in 2003. Which I think is the least we've played since we've been touring with him. So maybe there is sort of demand building up?'

Regardless of their concerns, perhaps Darian's love for the spiritual nature of the music, that he held it as sacred text, made him sensitive to the challenge.

Darian: 'I think it's even more spiritual than *Pet Sounds*. In many ways it's Brian being about as funny as he can be. Like a walking paradox. Childlike yet at the same time, extremely complex. So much "happy and sad" going on at the same time. A lot of that manifests in a melancholy beauty throughout *Pet Sounds*, but with SMiLE it's like he went even further out in both directions. Inward and outward. Even more childlike and even more complex. And I think that in a lot of ways, that's Brian reaching for the core of his existence.'

Darian smiles as he adds, "'Cause, you know, he's a Gemini. (*Laughs*) He can be way out there, and yet can be so "in" there. And that's what the SMiLE music feels like to me. You have stuff that can sound like nursery rhymes . . . and then others that sound like Stravinsky. And then of course there's an avant-garde element to it . . . a kind of John Cage type approach. But the great thing with Brian is that he never intellectualizes things. It's pure. It's innocent. It's just, "Let's do this." Or, "This is how it should go." It could be some heavy cluster of chords voiced in an unorthodox way and yet he doesn't seem to be aware of any significance that might be perceived. It just "happens."

'And if you look throughout his career, so much of what gives his music depth comes as a result of this. From early on, something like 'The Warmth of the Sun,' taking the basic doo-wop structure, but then without really overthinking it, taking it in a different direction. Because it feels right in the moment.'

Darian is certain Brian's 'not thinking he's doing anything different. He's just going where the music takes him . . . He's not on our level. (*Laughs*) He's on another level.'

RAISING THE TITANIC

Besides the musical and emotional challenges that lay ahead, Darian was also concerned about 'the motivations behind the tour. Because it is a business after all, and I know they [Brian's management team] were wanting to find the best way to get Brian out there in the public eye again, after a nearly a year of non-activity. He's been busy making the *Gettin' In Over My Head* album, and I was concerned that the timing might not be right.'

But the *SMiLE* fan in him won out. The musician who loved Brian had no choice. Darian was riding an emotional and musical seesaw.

Darian: 'At the same time, I love the music. It's so beautiful. And the idea of being able to perform it is a wonderful thing. When it's all about the music, it's perfect . . . a beautiful thing. It's just too bad [looking back], that [for Brian], it's been surrounded and clouded by a lot of adversity in his life. He's got a lot of negative associations with it all. And I didn't really think it would fly. [Just as importantly,] I wasn't sure that we could do this right. And then, as things moved along, and I was able to sit down with Brian,' Darian recalls, 'when it came down to actually doing the work, it became a very, very delicate procedure to approach *SMiLE* with Brian for the first time. As we know.'

Fortunately for the project, Darian is not only extremely talented but also extremely sensitive to *SMiLE*'s heartbreaking past, knew the legends, loved the music that had been released, knew much of the secret history. So he was thrilled at the idea of playing music that meant so much to him, that had actually been so central in inspiring him as he became such an accomplished musician, singer, songwriter, arranger, and producer.

Darian explains how he and Brian (and eventually Van Dyke Parks) worked together to make *Brian Wilson Presents SMiLE* a reality. It's a rare 'behind the curtain' peek of these Wizards of Sound to understand how it happened.

Darian: 'The one thing I had going for myself [with Brian] was that we'd already been working together for five years, and it had been fairly successful. And he's been comfortable with me, and he's confident with the band. I was the representative of the band at that moment.'

It was in September of 2003 when Brian and Darian finally got to work.

'When I started talking to Brian about the music, he really wasn't into it. But then I'd say, "Well, I'm coming over next week at this time," and he'd just look straight at me and say, "Okay."'

When they began, Darian pointed out to Brian, 'Hey, listen, we do 'Good Vibrations.' We do 'Surf's Up.' We do 'Heroes And Villains.'' And [he said to Brian], 'it's about presenting it live. I think it was a good starting point.'

How did the conversation begin? Darian tentatively approached his hero, now boss. 'So, to break the ice, it was all about, "Hey Brian, we're not trying to finish an album here. We're just . . . how do we perform this music in a way that it would flow? How can we present this music so that it's cohesive?" And I think that made him feel a little better.'

Then as Darian, at this point as much musical psychologist as musical secretary, notes, 'Brian could think of it in a modern context, of "how we're going to be performing this music on a stage in front of people." So he can make those kinds of connections. Like "OK. Jimmy's playing this and Bob is playing that. Is Paul going to play the sax there?" It's taking this music into a new context. And that was less scary for him, I think.'

Eternally sensitive to the man, Darian notes that after getting over 'that initial hump, this whole thing has been a series of steps. That was obviously the first big one. And then it was getting Van Dyke involved, and once we got into that, the pieces started coming together. Some of the doubts started to float away.'

And so, Darian began to relax, just a bit. 'Wow. Maybe we can really pull this off. (*Laughs*) It was the first time we'd ever be performing so much [SMiLE] music . . . a good body of Brian's work that has never really been chronicled in an official way. So it's a gamble. I mean, the whole thing is a gamble. In almost a poetic way, if you define art as taking risks, (*laughs*) then this tour is great, great art.'

Darian explains that the challenge he and Brian faced was that, 'In order to present the SMiLE music live, it was finding some sort of flow. Thematically, creative, some sort of approach. And the SMiLE recordings from the sixties were, as we know, fragmented; [we] don't know what Brian would have done with them all. [So] to find some sort of order to all of this, I loaded all the completed [and] nearly completed SMiLE music and [SMiLE] fragments onto my iBook. I put them in a timeline with an audio program. And I brought it over to Brian's.

'And I sat down with Brian and I had them all in a list, and we started listening to different sections, segments. Brian was a little hesitant, as you can imagine. So, I just started putting some pieces that I knew were very musically and thematically similar together. And he would tell me, "Yeah, yeah, that was supposed to go with that. That was supposed to go there." [Or] "No. No. That didn't belong in that. That wasn't a 'Heroes And Villains' type thing." And we just kind of worked in that way for a little while. I was just moving pieces around. [With digital technology] it was really convenient. A convenience that Brian didn't have back in the sixties.'

Darian points out that back in 1966/1967, 'you gotta slap a tape up on the machine, a reel of tape, or acetates, and Brian had to try to remember, how one piece ended and another began. And he didn't have the convenience that we have today. So that was kind of fun, because very quickly, he could audition another piece or another sequence and get an immediate feel from it.'

Brian: 'It was hard to sequence. It really was. Darian Sahanaja and I had a rough time sequencing.'

Darian: 'It was kind of neat. It was almost like he was playing the pieces like it was an instrument. (*Laughs*) And on the [computer] program, the different audio files, the wave forms are different colours, so it has that kind of effect, as well. We just started piecing things along, until he didn't wanna work [anymore]. And he told me he was done for the day.

'I'd come back the next day and do a little more. And then, it became real apparent that musically – I don't know how to say it. The songs started to group.'

A major moment, a dramatic turning point, lay ahead.

Darian: 'At one point, we were listening to a track called 'Do You Like Worms?' And I got to ask Brian probably the ultimate Beach Boys fan's dream question . . . which was, "So Brian, was there anything else to this?" And he kind of looked at me. Typically, Brian will say "No." He'll choose the quick and easy answer. But this time, it was nice, 'cause he was comfortable enough, and we were on a roll. And I had asked him, "Is there anything else to this?" He says, "Yeah, there was some Indian chanting, and there was a melody."

"Do you remember that melody, Brian?" And he goes, "Yeah." So the next part comes around, and he starts singing the melody and humming the melody over it. And I was like, "Wow. (*Laughs*) That's cool." And so I said, "Brian, do you remember any lyrics to this?" And he said, "Yeah, I think Van Dyke had some lyrics to this."'

SMiLE

Darian had something in his back pocket that he hadn't yet told Brian about.

Darian: 'As a matter of fact, I know he has lyrics to this. (*Laughs*) Because, just a few weeks earlier I had visited David Leaf and he had shown me a set of lyrics that Van Dyke Parks had given to Frank Holmes, the original artist for the *SMiLE* artwork. [Anyway], one of the lyrics [Leaf had], one of the sheets was 'Do You Like Worms.' Now I had been familiar with the "Rock, Rock, Roll Plymouth Rock" [lyric], because that was in the recordings. But there were sections without vocals. And so I'm reading this lyric sheet, and I see that "Rock, Rock, Roll" line, but I see all these other lines, before and after. Wow.

'So David was nice enough to share copies of those lyrics in case it would help. And boy did it come in handy. Because when Brian hinted that there were some lyrics to 'Do You Like Worms,' I whipped them out. And he grabbed them out of my hands, and he just starts singing the melody that he had just previously hummed to me, with those lyrics.

'I was just kind of sitting there, stunned. Incredible. We're working on it. We get to the second verse. And he's singing along. And because it was written in Van Dyke's original writing, some of it was hard to read. And we get to one word and Brian gets stuck on it. And he's trying to sing it. He's, like, "Goddamn it. What is that word?" And he says, "Maybe Van Dyke would know." (*Laughs*) He gets up out of his chair, walks over to the phone, picks up the phone and starts dialling. I'm thinking, "Who is he calling?"'

Brian was calling the only person who would know, the person who had been waiting for months for a phone call.

Darian: '"Hi, Van Dyke? This is Brian. You know this song 'Do You Like Worms'?" And he starts asking him about these lyrics. And I could tell that Van Dyke was completely caught off guard.'

Van Dyke: 'Brian called me, first to ask me what an indecipherable word was.'

Darian: 'Van Dyke asked for a copy of the lyrics to be faxed over. And we get an email back from him, and the word is "Indians." So that was nice. The following day I show up at the house, and there's Brian to greet me as he always does at the front door and he says, "Hey Darian, how's it going?" And I say, "Good." And then he just says, "Van Dyke is going to be here in fifteen minutes."'

For a moment, Darian reverted to being just a *SMiLE* fan.

Darian: 'I was, like, "Oh my God." So once again, I was terrified. But at the same time, I thought, "Wow. This is going to be really cool. This is right." I think the fact that Van Dyke hadn't been involved up to that point was unsettling to me. And the fact that he became involved just made everything right. Mr. Parks shows up, I could tell there's a little bit of anxiety with him. He's a little nervous. Of course, I was terrified.

'Van Dyke sits down in a nice wooden chair. I'm on the floor, right next to him. And Brian is pacing nervously behind us. And we start playing some of this *SMiLE* music. And Van Dyke says, "Oh my God, I haven't heard this stuff in thirty-something years." And he starts smiling. And I wasn't really sure what he was smiling about. But I think he was just really, really impressed.'

Van Dyke: 'Darian turned on the assembly that he guessed would work and that he knew would work. And it does work. There were some interstices between these vignettes, this kind of anecdotal music that one hears in "The Project." And I liked all those. I liked the interstices. I like the segues. I thought they were up to the standard of the music that informed them, because most of them had little twisted themes from other sections.

'And so it was neatly tied together. There was music I hadn't heard before, because I left "The Project" because there [were] some difficulties many years ago. But "The Project" continued, with a mind of its own, the way it has today, the very process that brought it up to the present tense.'

Meaning the fall of 2003. Over thirty-six years since his last involvement with *SMiLE*.

Darian: 'He'd forgotten how good the music was. And Brian and I had pieced some of the fragments together. And I did a little bit of chord segues in between, some ideas that Brian had approved. But Brian was there, wanting Van Dyke's approval. Which was really cool. Brian's a real team player. So we're playing through the music and Van Dyke is sitting there with his arms crossed, smiling.'

Van Dyke: 'I was immediately very surprised and pleased about how much life force was in the music. It's still there. And my conclusion was, "It's an old saw, but it can still cut the wood." I thought it was a great thing to hear.'

Darian: 'And I'm nervous. And then a transition would go by and [he would] say, "Good decisions. Good decisions." And I was like, "Phew." And at that point I kind of turned to Van Dyke, and I said, "It's very important to me that the work that you and Brian did [all] those years ago, that I respect the vision you guys had." And he kind of put his hand on my shoulder and he said, "Thank you. It's very, very much appreciated."'

Another genuinely big moment for Darian.

Darian: 'Again, "Phew." And then I just became really, without being a fly on the wall, I was a fly on the (*laughs*) ground.' [Darian was sitting on the floor of the music room.]

Then, it became about reminiscing.

Darian: '"Whoa, I remember when you did that." Or, "What's that sound?" And Brian would say, "What did we do there?" And Van Dyke would say, "Oh, we used a pedal steel, a lap steel, and a vocal." Things like that.

'There were other really great moments. They were so young. [Van Dyke said to Brian,] "You were 24 and I was 23." (*Laughs*) Those kinds of exchanges.

'It was really cool. And there would be an orchestral section that would come up and Van Dyke would say, "I remember this piece. I remember you wanted me to orchestrate this, and I said, 'No, no, no, no, Brian. You do it. You know you could do it.'" Then Van Dyke said that after they cut the track, Brian walked out of the control room and looked at Van Dyke [who said to Brian], "You can do it."

'And it was neat because it seemed really important to Brian that Van Dyke approve of this stuff. Which is always ironic when it comes to Brian. I remember when we did the Radio City tribute show sitting with Brian just as Elton John was about to run through 'God Only Knows.' I asked Brian how he was doing and he says "I'm nervous." I asked him why *he'd* be nervous and he says, "Because Elton John is singing my song."

'A few minutes later I'm over by Elton, setting up the lyrics on his music stand, and he didn't seem very much at ease. So I ask him, "Are you okay? Is everything okay?" And he says, "I'm okay, I'm just a little nervous. The 'master' is sitting over there," as he points over to Brian sitting across the room staring at Elton like this. (*Staring*) The irony being that, if you know Brian, that was simply the look of "I can't believe Elton John is gonna sing my song."

RAISING THE TITANIC

'So, working on *SMiLE* in that room with Van Dyke, I can tell that it was really important [to Brian] that Van Dyke was happy. But the irony is that I know that with Van Dyke, it was most important that Brian would be happy. So there's that beautiful energy going on. And it was work, [but now], it was labour of love.'

Van Dyke: 'So I heard new music. And I heard, a lot of it was vaguely familiar, and, had no [lyrics] attached to it, so I offered to bring in some more words for Brian to hammer into shape, and I'm very happy with them. I think it's gained more cohesion in the process. I think it sounds more cohesive and not quite linear. But a beautiful set of impressions about, America's Manifest Destiny, and still with great kind of a cartoon consciousness, which I think is signature to the piece, small piece of work that was particularly, an American impression.'

Darian: 'And so for the next few days, Van Dyke would show up, they'd bounce ideas around. And I'd be there to kind of be their little musical secretary. I'd take notes down, occasionally I might butt in and convey an idea of how we could do this or maybe that. Small suggestions. And it was just that kind of dynamic. It was really neat . . . The whole Brian and Van Dyke experience was amazing.'

In writing new words for 'Song For Children' and other instrumental pieces, Van Dyke admitted in 2004, 'I've never had a preconception about what *SMiLE* was. I still don't know what it is, but I like it. In doing new work for it, well, it's certainly an out of the body experience by now. It's not as if I had a preconception about what I was doing thirty-six years ago. I certainly didn't. And I respected the fact that the man I was working for didn't either, 'cause that's what made "The Project" valid in my view.'

A reminder: Van Dyke never takes the straight road in storytelling.

Van Dyke: 'Unless you are a Presbyterian, there's no way to predict the future. Beethoven said that. He said, "I have no idea what's going on ahead of me." I said, somebody praised him for some of his ideas. So, the idea of a concept record never occurred to me, absolutely not. I thought the medium for this project *SMiLE* was animation. That's the door I came in through when I first worked in town. My first job was for the 'Bare Necessities' in [Disney's] *Jungle Book*. My first arrangement. It was 1963.

'So, to continue on with [Brian with] that kind of "in excess information" in music, was with its tuneful percussion, with its mallets, with its marimbas and its glockenspiels, and its Spike Jones brouhaha. It just all made sense to me, all made sense, and this had moments of great rhythmic appeal to me.

'[Meaning] when I went back to work on adding a few lyrical informalities, like more of a section, on 'Blue Hawaii.' We'd already gone to Hawaii with the Hawaiian language, the hymn of thanksgiving, "Mahalo lu le." We already had that "thank you" song in there. And I thought it was better that we should just go ahead and start investigating what that was all about. It was the last stop on the move west, one step beyond Horace Greeley, with all of the missionaries to their last position, which was in Hawaii. And that was fun to do and also to introduce those naughty pirates. I really thought it was time that we start picking on pirates.'

Clearly, Van Dyke was engaged.

Van Dyke: 'I brought in a mock melody, that is, a scratch melody with some words, in which Brian Wilson after the fire section says, and I was hoping that he would be in a pin spot [on stage], somehow alone on a stage saying, "Is it hot as hell in here or is it me? It really is a mystery." And just before we go to 'Blue Hawaii,' and something to drink. [Quoting] "I could really use a drop to drink/wish that I were really in the pink." I wanted that to be a Brian Wilson edit, and the colour to represent that, if it ever came to a visual decision, so that we would know that Brian is now consciously wrestling with what it was that was presented to him, of a tormented and a torturous hearing it in his life, and in the American psyche as a matter of fact.'

Darian: 'And Brian was so into it. It was really great. He was just getting off on all of Van Dyke's ideas. Van Dyke would have concepts about pirates, personal triumph. And I [would] think this is interesting, because I think a lot of this is about personal triumph. Brian's and Van Dyke's. The one thing that kept reoccurring with Van Dyke is he kept talking about how relieved he was.'

In our extended 2004 conversation, I asked Van Dyke, 'In the time you spent with Brian in bringing this to completion, were there moments when you had an inner smile and said to yourself, "There's my old friend, He's still in there."?' His answer made *me* smile.

Van Dyke: 'I was pleasantly surprised how Brian plunged in. It's almost, "Which is worse, death, or the fear or death?" Once you get engaged, you lose all those distractions. I misfired on one [new lyric]. He sent me back to the foot of the hill to work on something again. I did that. I think it was just to make it easier for him to croon. But I think it's all terrifically diatonic and what the Trinidadians call do-re-mi music. All the melodies are very reasonable and very, I think, well placed.'

Considering how hurt he and Brian were by *SMiLE*'s non-completion, Van Dyke notes that 'it was so easy to get back to work on this project. Everyone has such a proprietary attitude about it. A lot of people write me letters and email and tell *me* how it should all be sequenced. Well, I have no idea. I haven't listened to it in thirty-six years, and I couldn't care less. What I care about is that the singer be able to deliver his song. That's all that matters to me.

'It's Brian Wilson that matters to me. "The Project" itself, *SMiLE*, to me, is the residue of a real desire, of some things that music can speak to, like, in this case, loyalty, and friendship, and the general humanities, confirmational things. Being able to laugh at what concerns us, to be able to present music on different levels, that can be taken on different levels, with words that can either be relevant or not apply at all.'

Considering his brilliance with words, the beginning of Van Dyke's next comment begins with a surprising statement.

Van Dyke: 'I've never gone beyond the prejudice that nobody listens to words. I certainly don't. I don't. But I think that the words should help clarify melodic intent. As much as Brian was busy in making these sounds, which are replicated faithfully, beautifully [by his band], for the purpose of performance. Great experiments in orchestral timbres and very wonderful, imaginative music.

'I wanted the words to be able to operate on the same level and coming back to them. Those were things undone. It was just taking care of things that had been undone. To me, it was a natural thing to start looking into this project again, to see what was of value. And that beat the prejudices of both Brian and myself, both of us. The last thing either one of us would want to do. I'm 61; I hazard to say how old he is.'

Van Dyke's acceptance of what Brian and Darian had done and then his enthusiastic participation meant so much to everybody.

Darian: 'I didn't really understand it at first. Van Dyke, in his delicate way of speaking, [his] language, he'd use all these words. But mainly implying that he felt a big weight lifted off his shoulder. And I didn't know if it was the same as Brian's, which was this ghost that had haunted them for some thirty-odd years. But I think [Van Dyke] was nervous when he first heard that we were doing SMiLE. You know, this was his baby [too].

'I mean, he had heard about the same time that I had heard that we were going to do SMiLE . . . And imagine being one of the [creators]? And not being involved, and, "Oh boy. What's going to happen with this?" And so I think his sense of relief came from the fact, and he told me later, "It's in good hands." And that made *me* feel really good.'

Darian has thought deeply about all of this.

Darian: 'For Van Dyke . . . I'm sure there was a good amount of guilt, maybe, over the years, of maybe not being there when Brian needed him the most, to help him finish this thing. And then, imagine being the guy that everybody pointed fingers at, saying, "You're responsible for this weird direction that Brian is going in."

'Van Dyke's had to live with that for years and years. He told me that it's been twenty years of people handing him bootleg album covers of SMiLE to sign. He's polite, and he signs them. But he was uncomfortable. And kind of sad about it all. And so, [as with] Brian, this would be a sense of closure for him as well. Which is only a good thing. If they don't have to always feel that it's awkward when somebody brings up the topic of SMiLE.'

Van Dyke: 'It was difficult for both of us to reapproach this personal defeat, and also the desire to try to make something perfect the way Brian used to make his music perfect for the listener. To mollycoddle the listener with beautiful sounds, lay down a bed of beautiful audio, audio experience, and a pleasure to the ear, and so forth. And Brian would do that with his music, and that was very good.

'And we tried to make this an exercise in the same kind of idealism, I mean, as we completed this. "Complete" is a very satisfied word. So I would prefer to think that okay, if it's complete, I can't wait to see [SMiLE] Part Deux . . . after the [London] audience gets any [of their] concern put to rest. And this will do that.'

Darian: 'I imagine it takes a lot of courage. And you know what? Brian – even through rehearsals you could feel that it's something scary. It's not, like, "Yeah, I'm just going to do this. And we're going to do it." You can actually feel how hard this is for him. And if we can pull this off, and he can get through this, I think it's going to be one of the bravest things he's ever done.

'And Van Dyke said it too. I remember after listening to all the music, especially some of the wackier numbers. The stuff that was really adventurous. And Brian, being a little more conservative in his age, he'll say something, like, "Oh, God, I don't know if we should do that. I don't know if people get that. It might freak people out." And Van Dyke will say "No. I would stand up and be brave."

'It's Van Dyke that's always bringing up the word "courage." *Courage* that we're doing this, artistically courageous for Brian to be putting this out there for all to experience. And for us as a band to be courageous enough to not feel like we're doing something, "Oh, isn't this weird. We're hammering on stage. We're making vegetable crunching noises."'

Nick Walusko: 'Oh, it's a risk. But, again, it's strange that Brian, at his age, now wants to take this kind of risk. I think it's pretty commendable. A lot of people want to just rest on their laurels. And these aren't laurels. These are unfinished works that on a commercial level [were] considered a failure. "You want to do a whole album of this kind of stuff? Forget it." So, I don't know. I think artistically, it's definitely pretty risky. But, again, there's a cult, so there's a built-in church there for him to preach to. And, hopefully, the word spreads out.'

Darian: 'I think it's all part of that risk taking that's so important to being an artist. It's this music, it's these tangents, these passion pursuits, that separate Brian Wilson from other artists. Brian's one of the few that creates in a little bubble and yet manages to be accessible to the masses. Somehow, he connects to the masses, even from his little bubble. That's very, very rare. I think Brian really raises the bar for being an artist. Because he takes the greatest risks. And he's suffered (*laughs ruefully*). He's suffered for it, too.'

Nick: 'A lot of the music in *SMiLE* almost comes off like it's lightweight or it's really lilting. And, in today's climate, something like that is probably misinterpreted as being weak. But it's quite the opposite. I think it's pretty ballsy to play. It's "little, jumping gnome-like" music. In certain sections, to lead up to 'Mrs. O'Leary's Cow,' to do something surreal like, 'Vega-Tables'? Who would do that? Who would want to look like you are singing about vegetables? Most people would think, "Oh, this guy is out of his mind." But people are going to dig it. They're going to understand it, the whole elemental suite. They'll get it. Which, I'm glad.'

So many times during the process, Darian was stunned by what he saw Brian do, and felt like he was back in 1966.

Darian: 'There were a few moments when I felt that Brian was clearly tapping back into a previously rendered idea. For example, when he grabbed the lyric sheet out of my hands and started to sing the melody for what was to become 'Roll Plymouth Rock.' It was so immediate that I couldn't help but feel that it was always there. But Brian doesn't necessarily verbalize his intentions. He never comes off as calculating, and so it did blur that line between old and new.

'Van Dyke, handling things on the lyrical end, seemed more in tune with the conceptual flow and imagery. That's how things like "rock, rock, roll" from 'On A Holiday' were incorporated.'

For Darian, a *SMiLE* devotee for over twenty years, 'It wasn't so much about working with Brian, but watching the dynamic between Brian and Van Dyke. It was so fascinating to see two people who, on the surface, were so different, work so well together on a creative level. It became so obvious to me why they were drawn to each other back in the day. They kind of got off on each other's energy. So, in a way, they weren't that much different from one another at all. That blew me away.'

And in assembling *Brian Wilson Presents SMiLE*, all that mattered was whether the ideas, new *or* old, worked.

Paul Von Mertens wasn't steeped in *SMiLE* lore.

Paul: 'Mostly I read about it and talked to Nick and Probyn and Darian about it . . . But it wasn't until the decision was made to go ahead and actually begin work on those songs . . . And Darian worked with Van Dyke and Brian to complete a vision for those songs, a song order. [Then] Darian began roughing out demos of the songs . . . sending them to me and to the rest of the band. So that's when I started writing the string and horn parts for it.'

Darian: 'Whether they were original 1960s ideas or not, whatever felt natural to completing the big picture was the priority. Brian and Van Dyke were on a creative roll.'

If one were in the room – or watching 'Darian-cam,' the videos he made of the sessions with him and Brian and with him, Brian, and Van Dyke – one would see how Brian came alive during their work together.

It was wonderful. One would see Brian's enthusiasm as he and Darian worked on the second act, nailing down the transitions. Or the delight Brian expressed when he heard original *SMiLE* tapes.

One would observe the writing process for the third movement, as they're filling in the gaps with Van Dyke's new lyrics. And Brian's joy at learning the new parts. At seeing how the new pieces so closely complement the original material, and how important it is to all of them that they do fit in seamlessly.

There are moments of family life, when Brian uses colourful language in front of his daughter, and she gasps, 'Remember what Mama said!' 'What?' 'Not to say that word!' 'Oh, okay. All right. I won't.' It's all so very sweet and normal.

As to shedding light on the history of *SMiLE*, some of the mythic elements of the project remained mysterious throughout the process.

Darian: 'Brian never ever referred to any of the pieces as being part of some "Elemental" concept, and whenever I did bring up the concept, he didn't seem to react to it with any enthusiasm. I brought it up again while Van Dyke was around and didn't get a clear reaction from him either. My gut feeling is that it was one of many subplots and underlying themes being tossed around back in the day. It does however tie in nicely with the concepts of western expansion, Manifest Destiny, birth and rebirth, and so I'm sure they would respect a listener's interpretation.'

As to the ultimate three-suite structure, nobody knows whether that was ever considered in 1966.

Darian: 'Neither Brian or Van Dyke have ever talked about it . . . I think as we were listening to the sequence, as the music started being grouped together in themes, we had the Americana, the American Gothic, 'Home on the Range,' industrial, historical themes. There was that group. And the 'Wonderful,' 'Child Is Father Of The Man,' 'Surf's Up' . . . [that] was musically . . . I want to say, musically similar, but at the same time, lyrically, thematically, it had to do with the cycle of life.'

Darian describes how they were 'just linking themes. If there's a song like 'Wonderful' and 'Child Is Father Of The Man,' and there's a segment in the middle [without lyrics], it'll remind them, "Oh, yeah, maybe there was supposed to be something there." And whatever [new] ideas they had, they feel good.'

'And then you had 'Mrs. O'Leary's Cow,' and you had 'Vega-Tables.'

And [because historically] at one point they had the idea of having an Elements suite, we [put those] with air and water and earth and fire. There was a song called 'I'm In Great Shape' that talked about "fresh clean air around my head, morning stumble out of bed. Eggs 'n' grits, and lickety split, look at me jump, I'm in the great shape of the agriculture."

'Van Dyke said, "Agriculture. Part of one with the earth." And it's the shape of the earth, body, soul. And so that all seemed to be a certain theme. And so, once we had those themes, I don't know what it was, but it seemed to have sparked some of the original ideas that were there . . . it seemed like they just sort of picked up where they left off.'

'When Van Dyke would bring something up,' Darian would say, '"Wow. Where did that come from?" He said, "It was always there." (*Laughs*) Van Dyke says, "It's just been there." He'll use words like, "It's inevitable that this stuff be presented in this way."

'Half the time I don't know what he's talking about. But it sounds good to me. He'll say things, like, "You've just come out of the hell of fire, and we have to find a way of baptizing yourself." And then he'll say, "This is the baptism. This is where Brian, it's important that Brian talks about how he's going to stand up and walk away from hell." And hence there's these [new] lyrics.'

Nick: 'One thing I've got to add about 'Fire.' I didn't realize until playing this live [in rehearsal] that the drums represent water putting out fire, which fuzz guitars and the bass and all that are sort of the rumbling fire in the distance. And that the drums or the cymbals, actually, are the final thing that put it out. And I'm not going to say a word or get on the internet, but I'm just going to be curious to see if anyone gets it. Any other musician out there that, either our friends or just people that, who are into *SMiLE*, which I know a lot of the famous British musicians, they are totally Brian devotees. I'm curious to see if anyone says anything about that.'

There were countless discoveries like that along the way. Darian's description of the process is, as he told it to me before the world premiere in London, is the key to understanding why *Brian Wilson Presents SMiLE* is the legitimate completion of the work that Brian and Van Dyke had begun in 1966. Work suspended in 1967. The collaboration rekindled in 2003. And finished with the enthusiastic participation of both creators.

RAISING THE TITANIC

Unlike either Van Dyke or Darian, when asked about the project, Brian's answers are short, to the point and often surprising.

Brian: 'When Darian and Van Dyke came over, I knew we were into something pretty special . . . the process was Van Dyke would come up with some lyrical ideas, and I would come up with music for it. So, between Darian and my music, and Van Dyke's lyrics, we finished it.'

Beginning with 'Our Prayer,' Brian explains, 'It's a way to soften up the audience . . . leave them with a soft feeling, and boom, right into 'Heroes And Villains.''

A project begun when he was 24 is finally completed when he's 61. What did that mean to him? Did Brian ever think he would finish *SMiLE*? 'No, I never ever dreamed that we would finish *SMiLE*, ever.'

As always, Brian sums it all up more succinctly. As to how the project might have been completed in 1967 versus 2003, Brian is clear. '*This is how I feel about this music now.*'

In mid-December of 2003, with the world premiere of *Brian Wilson Presents SMiLE* only two months away, Darian remembers, 'It got to the point where they had so many ideas about whether something should be expanded upon or left alone. Just these decisions. And it was getting close to the holidays. And I knew that we were going to have to pick up with the band [after the first of the year] and start rehearsing. And I had to start getting the vocals arrangements transcribed. We were running out of time. (*Laughs*) Which was really funny, ironic. It was like, "Who'd have thought that it would ever come down to the thought of 'Can these guys finish already?'" (*Laughs*) We got the final approval, maybe a week before Christmas. And then the real work began.'

By the 'real work,' Darian meant getting the music to the band so they could start to learn their vocal and instrumental parts for over forty-five minutes of music.

Bob Lizik: 'As he'd done with *Pet Sounds*, Darian sent a lot of the tracks without the vocals, so I could learn the bass parts. I worked at home, God, for at least two or three weeks, before we went out to the West Coast to rehearse . . . I'd call Darian, "Is this right, or is this right?" Is it this note or that note. And then there's one where the major seventh is playing in the bass against the chord. I'm going, "Is that right?" He goes, "Yeah, that's right."'

Before the Christmas holidays, the West Coast-based members of the band convened to hear the three-movement assembly that Brian, Van Dyke and Darian had been working on. Had just finished.

Probyn Gregory: 'The first time I heard it through I was struck with the same kind of melancholy as *Pet Sounds*.'

Jeffrey Foskett: 'We showed up at Scott's . . . a beautiful day, a really crisp winter day. And I was really, really, really excited because [when] I had heard the first CD of *SMiLE* [music] that was given to me [months ago], and I thought to myself, I'll be completely honest, I can see clearly why Brian didn't want this album released. And then having heard that, and then going in to hear what Brian, and Van Dyke, and Darian had ultimately come up with, in order, proper segues written, bits and pieces remembered from their own minds, fabricating new things . . . hearing it in its new form, the three parts, was so unbelievably great.

'It was just beautiful. It made sense. It was a complete piece of music. And just absolutely mind-boggling how intelligent the music is. You can use all the adjectives you want. Sophisticated . . . Brian is a conduit, you know. And God sends his music down, and Brian's one of the conduits that he uses to present it to us. He clearly has said that many times. And I think it's such a beautiful thing that he does that. And as David Leaf pointed out to me, the name of the album is *SMiLE*. And the music is supposed to make you smile. And this record really does.'

Nick Walusko: 'I can't think of a better person than Darian to, I won't say, direct, because I don't know if he is directing . . . but someone who understands it. I will defer as far as, like, how this part should be played or how that should go. He, Brian, and Van Dyke had obviously deconstructed and then rearranged things, and reconstructed, and we didn't say a word. Darian was the main man.

'Because I know he really loves the music intimately, has gone over all the stuff with a fine-tooth comb and really understands, I think, beyond just him being an uber fan of the stuff. I think he really, really appreciates the music. And, hence, when he played it for us at Scott's – when we all had a little pow-wow and a listening party – "This is going to be what we're going to do." He sang a lot of the parts that didn't have lead vocals yet.

'Darian just popped in the CD and we're listening to it. I was blown away. I really liked it, and people were already getting ideas. "Probyn, you're going to play that part; I'm going to play this part." And the one thing that's remarkable about all the musicians is that everyone's pretty much playing what they want to play. It's not like anyone's like, "Oh, gee whiz, I wish I could play that." Or, "You get all the fun parts." Everyone gets to do what they wanna do.

'We had to iron out a lot, but I think everybody is really gung-ho to get the parts right. There's a lot of work to be done. And I was just like, "Wow, can't wait to hear this stuff." And then all the harmonies and lyrics in things that never had lyrics. Because that's the first time I ever heard any of that stuff.

"So then I said to Darian, "Man, what was it like? You were getting this from those guys." So, it's a thrill and it's still kind of fresh. I mean, it's only been since December that a lot of this stuff was sprung on us.'

Other than Brian, perhaps nobody felt more pressure than a new member of the band, as Nelson Bragg told me.

Nelson: 'I saw your [tribute] show at Radio City Music Hall in 2001. I visualized myself in that band. I said, "I've got to get into that band." I don't know how. I don't know why. I just [felt] . . . "That's my people." I knew half the band personally. But I felt like, "God, I really . . . need to be in that band. I've gotta be in that band." So it was something that I thought about.'

Then, in mid-November 2003, he got a call from Darian to join the band. He almost jumped through the phone to say "yes." And shortly after, he was in *SMiLE* nirvana.

Nelson: 'Darian asked me to go to his house, and he was gonna play for me *SMiLE*. And he had finished the missing pieces – personally recorded missing pieces that he learned about from Van Dyke and Brian. So, he had in his possession the first finished version of *SMiLE* in history. But it was him, in his voice and playing that filled in the parts that had not been filled in. And that was a really significant thing.

'And I was sitting there just freaking out, listening to it. I just couldn't believe how beautiful it was. So I was listening to the finished *SMiLE* – the finished *SMiLE!* – the absolute first-time-ever finished *SMiLE* at Darian's house. And then he gave me a copy on CD.'

There was one more big hurdle for Nelson.

Nelson: 'Darian filled me in on the band, people, his perspective. He brought me to Brian's house. When Brian met me, that was the final "yes." I came in, [briefly] met him. He said, "You gonna come out with us?" "Yes. Thank you." "Good. See you later." I talked to Foskett, and he gave me his perspective about things . . . But the first time I met some members of the group was at the vocal rehearsals at Brian's.'

All of the band members had gotten custom-made CDs from Darian, with the tracks on one channel and just their vocal parts on the other. They assiduously learned them and showed up at Brian's house on January 12, 2004, for the first day of vocal rehearsals.

Scott Bennett: 'Because of Darian's leg work, and everybody in the band doing their homework, the first day we opened our mouths, it sounded pretty dang good.'

Nelson was, perhaps, even more diligent than the others. After all, this was not just a big break but his dream come to life.

Nelson: 'It was like, "I'm going to show up, and I will be perfect." Which is what happened. I was as perfect as that could possibly be. I knew this was it.'

Nelson felt like he was on trial that first day of vocal rehearsals, but in truth, it was Brian and *Brian Wilson Presents SMiLE* that was being tested.

Jeffrey: 'We walked into Brian's house on the first day of rehearsal for vocal rehearsals, the band came in just absolutely ready. Everyone knew their parts. We were ready to sing. I thought it sounded phenomenal. I thought our leader couldn't have been less interested in what was going on. And I thought, "Boy, if this is going to be an uphill battle, we're really going to have a struggle on our hands."'

Probyn: 'Brian really didn't seem like he was very involved. He didn't seem like he wanted to be there at all. And in fact, that was my main worry, that he didn't want to do it at all, and that it would sort of hurt him to be playing this stuff again.'

Director of Photography James Mathers, who would shoot the entire *Beautiful Dreamer* documentary, recalls how quiet Brian was on that first day.

James: 'We were the first ones there, [to] set up the gear . . . And Brian came in, and he was just totally quiet. . . . it wasn't that big a room . . . It was almost like he was in a trance . . . I'm not a psychiatrist. But when there's something that comes up that's really stressful, like finishing up something you hadn't done for decades, that gonna be pretty scary.'

Jean Sievers: 'I think Melinda had a lot of confidence in it. Or she wouldn't have allowed it to happen. But then, we lost him one day in rehearsals.'

On the first day of rehearsals, Brian seemed to be almost completely disconnected. Then it got worse. Much worse. On the second day of vocal rehearsals, around 2 p.m., Brian left the music room saying, 'I gotta go.'

And then he disappeared. For over three hours, we didn't know where he was. Finally, we learned that his fear had become so overwhelming that he had walked out of the house and driven himself to the emergency room.

Probyn Gregory: 'I know that Brian was resistant to the idea. But he faced his demon or whatever parts of the equation that the demon represented, and he did take the bull by the horns, and did sing, and did finally get on board. So, I have to give him major props. If I put myself in his shoes, I might have held out longer and said, "I'm not gonna come to this. I'm gonna go and sit in my car and pretend it's not happening."'

As the newcomer, Nelson Bragg 'didn't understand what level of problems that Brian was experiencing . . . I figured that could be it. But as it turns out, he was just freaking out.'

Brian came back the next day and slowly started to participate.

Nelson: 'I think everyone – myself included – we were really hoping that this was going to happen . . . And that, combined with, "I really need to sing really, really well, blend in perfectly." I didn't want anyone to think, "Okay, we have to deal with a new guy." I just want to be invisible as possible. But at the same time, I was worried that maybe it wouldn't happen, because Brian was having such a tough time.'

Darian: 'The first week of vocal rehearsals, poor Brian. That was really rough. I really felt bad. He just seemed incredibly nervous. He would just pretty much sit there . . . I think it was important that he sit there and hear the work . . . when he's hearing the music, it can only be good for him. And he didn't do much that first week. I'm sure that your cameras caught that. (*Laughs*) But I think slowly, it's just like anything else. He gets familiar with stuff, and he realizes it's nothing to be scared of. And it's been a slow process.'

Probyn: 'It took him a little while to get up to speed. And he doesn't really like to rehearse in general. (*Laughs*) So no big secret about Brian.'

Darian: 'I was happy one day. He didn't sing, [but] he's looking around; he's listening to the harmonies. It's like, "Wow. He's absorbing it. He's absorbing the music." He's not actually going through the motions of rehearsing, but mentally, it's part of the process . . . But when he kind of opens his eyes really wide and as we're singing, he's looking around the room to see who's singing what [part]. I think that's a sign of engaging . . .

'He's like a basic creature? Like the plains of the Serengeti, it's about, (*laughs*) it's about food. Survival. He's a survivor. But with Brian, music, fortunately, music is one of those basic needs. And it's good when he responds to that. 'Cause when I can see that he's responding and engaging with the music, it means that it's really reaching the guts with him.'

And then, there's a small breakthrough, where he starts singing and asks Darian to double him vocally.

Darian: 'Oh, my gosh, yes. Yes! That was great. It's wonderful to see him so comfortable with the music that he can improvise and have fun with some of the lyrics. And once again, it's proof that he's become less scared of this music and what it represents – the bad memories. It's so inspirational. I think we all get off when he's getting off. We really feed off of that.'

Nick: 'When Brian started to sing, I felt at ease. I knew that it wasn't just so much that this was his stamp of approval. It's that now he's participating in all this, and that's what we need. We couldn't have Brian just sit there and watch us do it and have somebody else substitute for his vocals. He had to do it.

'And in a weird way and I know you hear this cliché all the time, but this is therapy for him, too. On some level it really is, beyond just it being music. He has to get over this somehow. And it's good that he does. There could have been, in some dimension, Brian Wilson didn't get over it. But in this one, hopefully he will. I think he's made incredible strides in that.'

In 1966, Brian constantly articulated what this music meant to journalists. To anybody who would listen. But in January of 2004, weeks before the world premiere, he didn't want to talk about it at all. We spent an afternoon in a studio taping an interview for *Beautiful Dreamer*. None of Brian's terse answers made it into the film. He was too scared to talk about *SMiLE*.

After London, after the first successful shows, he would talk.

RAISING THE TITANIC

Brian: 'I was scared [during vocal rehearsals] because I knew we were into something pretty heavy, and it scared me a little bit. Have to admit, I was a little frightened of *SMiLE*, but I got over it. The second day we were there – you were there the whole time, right? Soon as I talked to you about it, as soon as I got the feel for Jeff [Foskett], I knew we were into something very, very, very special. And I was very, very nervous about it. Very nervous.'

The two weeks of vocal rehearsals had begun terribly but had gotten progressively better. There were even moments of pure Brian levity, like the day he arrived late after having his prostate exam.

Darian: 'And he says, "You shouldn't be scared. It's easy. Five minutes. You just pull down your pants, and the doctor puts a glove on and sticks his finger up your ass, *(laughs)* wiggles it around a little, and that's it. Done."'

Nick: 'He demystifies these things, turned it into almost like a "Catskill Mountains" joke. You're expecting the punch line? That *was* the punch line. He just tells you what happened.'

Funny, deadpan moments. Difficult ones too. Among many stumbling blocks, Brian consistently refused to sing 'Wind Chimes' during rehearsal.

Darian: 'There's his present fear of doing anything that's difficult. He'll choose the path of least resistance. If you say to him, we're going to do *SMiLE*, I think aside from bad memories, he's also thinking, "Oh my God. That's difficult music. It's complex." And maybe 'Wind Chimes' falls under that. Maybe he just thought it was something that was a lot of work, there's a lot of high notes. It could be anything. I really have no idea.'

Brian, like an all-knowing, all-seeing, sometimes silent Buddha at rehearsals, never explains why. He just sits passively. Or joins in. But by the end of two weeks of vocal rehearsals, the sounds in Brian's music room, which now include Brian singing, are beautiful. *Brian Wilson Presents SMiLE* is coming alive.

Then, the entire band began work at Center Staging, a large rehearsal facility near the Burbank Airport. One of the first pieces they tackled was 'Mrs. O'Leary's Cow.'

Darian: 'We were just doing a run-through of it and getting the tempos, getting the sounds. And trying to describe the vibe and the feeling. And so we start into it. I said, "Okay, ready? This is it." And I actually was thinking, "Wow. This is kind of historic." I don't know that 'Fire' has ever been performed. So, Jimmy counts it off, and we start jamming, you know? And like, seven, eight bars into it. Bam! The power goes down.'

Nick: 'All the sound, everything went out. We're like, "Good thing Brian is not here." . . . Things happen, but it never had happened [before], but as soon as we started played 'Fire,' it happens.'

Darian: 'That was spooky. And all I kept thinking was, "Thank God Brian's not here." That would have flipped him out.'

Bob Lizik: "'Cause he would have just said, "We're done."'

Perhaps. Everybody in the band wondered and worried what was going to happen when he did show up.

Darian: 'The first few band rehearsals, we'd see him come in, sit down on the sofa for about maybe five minutes and then leave. And we'd all look at each other and be like, "Oh, boy." But we just kept working. And then the next day, he'd come in and maybe stay a little longer. Okay.

'And then, Day Four, he'd come in and that's when I noticed him starting to make small breakthroughs. He might look at one of the players. He might look at Probyn while Probyn was playing a part, and you could see he's mesmerized by the sounds. And then something else would happen on the other side. Maybe Paul might play a sax part, and he'd turn his head, and he'd look over at Paul.

'And it was at that point where I thought, "Wow. I think he's starting to hear this music as it's breathing and living and alive," as opposed to this thing that's been sitting on the shelf, maybe getting stale. It was here, and it was hitting him emotionally in a new and different way. I felt him making those connections. And I would say that was the breakthrough.

'It would be more of those, sort of staring at different members of the band, and it was very gradual. By the fifth day . . . and we did do a lot of rehearsing for this which was great for us . . . he was very, very comfortable. I remember his body language being almost looking forward to hearing certain parts being played. It felt to me as if he was saying, "Wow. This could really happen! I really like the way the band sounds!"'

Paul: 'The rehearsals in L.A. were intense, probably as hard as I've ever worked on anything in my life. And we felt very well prepared. And I know to a person in the band, we all thought it was amazing. We also didn't know how people would react. We really didn't know what we had. It was like, "This is so cool." But who knows? I mean, "Is it going to fly?" Or "Is it going to flop?"

'Because there was so much weight to it that there was some trepidation about doing those first shows, and it was a triumph to see somebody get their life back. [For Brian] to return to something that everybody said was a failure and a mistake and to retrieve it and get the acclaim and appreciation that it deserves is just a once-in-a-lifetime experience for me. It was really amazing.'

Bob: 'I remember going to rehearsal, and there were times I thought, "It's not going to happen. How are we gonna do this?" And it started to come together. After a while you're hearing the vocals for 'Wind Chimes' and you go, "Wow! Hope we can pull this off live, in front of an audience."'

Nelson: 'The one thing that was really weird was that I was a percussionist and singer [for *SMiLE*]. I'd spent my life playing drums; that was my instrument. And this was like, "Wow! I'm changing instruments." So, I think the pressure was off, because I was playing percussion, something that in many ways was much easier than playing drums . . . I was wrong on many fronts. Because the kind of complicated percussion that I had to do and the complicated vocals I had to do at the same time turned out to be really, really difficult. But I just knew that if I practiced every day for hours, I'll learn it. It's just a matter of working.'

But as enthusiastic as Nelson was, there was one key singer who just wasn't ready to work and practice.

Bob: 'Brian didn't seem really excited about it for quite a while. I think we were pretty well into it before he finally started to accept it.'

Paul: 'There was a lot of emotion in that regard, because I was not sure if Brian could see it through, or if he could do it. At that point we had done some touring and performing for a few years, and Brian was kind of hit and miss at times. But he always came through, it seemed, when it really counted. Even before an important show, like the British Music Awards. He did not sound good at the sound check and camera rehearsal, to the point where I was afraid. I was like, "Okay, it's over. This is gonna be a disaster." And when the cameras rolled, he delivered a great performance.

'So during the *SMiLE* rehearsals, I think we were all hoping that Brian would rise to the occasion and we were trying to remain, first of all, focused on the music, and making sure that we delivered the music in the best way possible to support him and also to be as encouraging as possible to Brian, because it seemed like he needed emotional support.'

Darian: 'After we'd done a bunch of instrumental rehearsals, I remember moving on to the next stage, where we started introducing all the background vocals. I think that's when Brian really started to get excited and wanting to participate. He wanted to be involved. 'Cause, there's nothing like human voices for Brian. He just really loves hearing harmony.

'And I do remember when we started singing along with the band is when he was – I don't know that he would have said, "Oh, let me sing with you guys," but it was really like, "Hey, Brian, are you into singing now?" And he was like, "Sure!" Because he knew it was there, and he wanted to be part of it, wanted to participate. So, at that point during the rehearsals, things were looking up.

'I think, by the end of rehearsals, I felt we were very, very well-rehearsed and very prepared. I was confident as a band that we knew our stuff. We knew all the moves. But with Brian, you just never know. You just never know.'

James Mathers, *Director of Photography:* 'The music was the key to get him going. He'd sort of be a zombie, and then sit down [at the] piano and start playing. And once he started playing with the band . . . He might not verbalize too much but he would communicate through the music.'

Paul: 'It was emotional for me, too, because we were on the cusp of something that I felt was really important, and I wasn't sure how it was going to turn out.'

Nelson: 'There was a day when – and it's in the [*Beautiful Dreamer*] documentary – where he saw a *Playboy* magazine, and he was just in a good mood. It was kind of like his mood denoted his participation. I don't think it ever was about ability or memory. He knew what to do, always did. It's just, he didn't want to do it. So, if his mood was up, then his brain would go. "Oh, I can sing this." And so it was kind of like that day. His mood was really up, and then it was like, all of a sudden, he was just singing everything, sort of enjoying himself.

'So his mood was much more important than his participation per se. Because I learned that how he was feeling mentally, and the mood he was in, denoted how much he would sing and participate. So, if he was in a good mood, even if he didn't sing much, we were still happy. We're like, "Great." More important than anything was "How was he feeling? Was he smiling? Was he laughing? Was he up?" – It was like, "Oh, he's into this." It was one day that that happened.'

David Leaf: 'One day, I brought the original *Pet Sounds*-era lyrics to 'Good Vibrations' to rehearsal. I walked over to Brian at his keyboard holding it, told him what I had, and he snatched it out of my hand before I could even finish the sentence. I guess if Darian was the *SMiLE* police for the project, making sure of the integrity of the arrangements, then I was the human archive who helped a few times with lyrics. Which was very rewarding.'

Jim Hines: 'I was astounded at how well it came together so quickly. But I was getting a sense of how terrifying this was for him. "Was it gonna work?" In every moment of every day, it was like, "Is he gonna do this? Is he gonna do it?" We've got to get him to do it because this is so awesome. So, for me, it was just, "God. I hope he can do it." I was very concerned.'

As for the band, Jim remembers that playing the music was 'really fun. We were having a blast.'

Scott Bennett notes that 'Brian's stuff is so brilliantly arranged.' He hyperbolically adds, 'I'm amazed at how many times he's the only guy in the room who knows what's going on.'

John Warren, *tour manager:* 'My fondest memories when we were first putting *SMiLE* together. Brian's got a list. "Okay? I need a saw, a hammer, an anvil. And go buy me ten power drills." So we send the runner and, of course, the runner comes back with cordless [drills]. Brian goes, "No, no, no, no. It's gotta plug in." . . . We sat there, Brian [auditioning] with the power drills, (*motions with hand drilling*) "Nope. Nope. That's the one. Get five of those." We went through power drills. We went through saws.'

Jeffrey Foskett has an observation and memory that may be the most revelatory of all.

Jeffrey: 'Brian is one of the most spiritual people that I know. Brian doesn't talk about God, Christ, Judaism, Buddhism, whatever. He is very spiritual, he is very God-like, and he's very God-loving. And he gives glory to God and he honours God when he says, "I am God's conduit and God gave me this music. I want to share it with these people." How much more spiritual would you like to be? And we actually prayed today, on the way to rehearsal from the vocal lesson. He had some things bugging him, and I suggested that we say a prayer. And it was really beautiful and he was very thankful. [Later on, he] said, "Thanks a lot for doing that this morning; that really helped me out." I think he's just really a normal guy – a normal cat that would like to be anything but "the great Brian Wilson." He wants to be Brian Douglas Wilson.'

Unlike any concert Brian and his band had ever played, the challenge facing the band of doing three extended pieces was extraordinary.

Darian: 'It's just started happening within maybe the last few days where I feel like the band is not thinking too much about the music, about what they're playing and what positions they need to be in and where their hands are at. We're actually starting to feel the music. And that's important because this is what this music's all about . . . We're at a stage where we're getting past the logistics . . . to really achieve the feeling.'

As to playing over forty-five minutes of music without charts, Probyn admits that 'I know the music so well, but it's just a matter of, "What part do I play or sing now?" So I go, "Okay, I start out on the fifth of the chord, and then I go up a major seventh but remember to micro tune that a little flat," and so forth. So, it has been a bit of a challenge, but a fun challenge, and one that I gladly accepted, because as I say, the music is so dear to me that how could I not love every minute of working on it?'

Nick: 'I want to dig more into the music, and discover more ways of playing it fluidly, rather than just saying, "I think this is how it goes." There's amp settings. There's all the minutiae of what it is that creates a certain sound in combination with other people's sounds, and I think everyone is very responsible for taking their time being meticulous about these things. Darian's keyboards from song to song completely change. Some sound darker, some sound brighter, some sound more out of tune, but that's what it demands. And we could have done it where he plays one keyboard. I have one guitar, one sound. They are still the same songs, but we want to go that extra mile for Brian. And for the music. And I think Brian's definitely in league with that right now for sure.'

RAISING THE TITANIC

But the band, as versatile as it is, couldn't cover all of the instrumental parts. Probyn explains some of the endless challenges the band faced.

Probyn: 'The band talked about the logistics of, "How much of this can we do ourselves, and who will we need to play these strings and horns?" Darian got a hold of some multi-track breakdowns where we were able to hear, without the vocals, some of the original tracking sessions. And things like 'Fire,' we just shook our heads and went, "Okay, for starters there were three bass players. Do we have three bass players in the band? No. How can we cover this? How can we make that sound?"' And then we heard there was a chord of three flutes playing. We have Paul [Von] Mertens and no one else plays flute in the band.

'So how many extra players are we going to need? Listening to things like 'The Old Master Painter' and other things where there were strings, we figured we could get away with two violins, viola, and two cellos. Bass would have been nice, but that was beyond the budget.

'We wanted to have two multi-wind players because there's a place for two clarinets in one of the tunes, 'Holiday.' So, we're pretty sure we need the two extra wind players and Paul [Von] Mertens. We actually weren't able to get those, but my trumpet with a cup mute is in the ballpark, so I'm pretending to be one of the multi-winds. And then there were some brass parts that I couldn't cover, as a single player on French horn and trumpet. I could have played some valve trombone, but some of these were calling for bass trombone or even tuba. So, we thought we could get away with two lower brass players.

'A few of us then had a meeting at The Sportsmen's Lodge [the band's L.A. hotel] where we ran through all the songs and talked about how many total string and wind players, at the bare minimum, we could get away with and still do justice to the music. We figured it was eight people.

'The orchestrations by Paul, he'd been very careful so that people had a few beats to change from flute to clarinet. Or from trumpet to French horn for me, or to some of the other instruments I had to play. Before the orchestra came in, I had been used to playing other parts in songs that now were different, because there was a whole new Paul orchestration, such as 'Surf's Up.' There were a lot of songs where I played different parts.'

Darian: 'I was one of the strong, heavier lobbyists for getting a real string section. Real strings and extra players. Which challenged the budget.'

Paul recalls that 'the idea of using contracted musicians at each show was floated. Hire the players locally. Save a lot of money on hotel and travel and all that. But Darian knew the Stockholm Strings, and he was very much an advocate for them.'

So the most exciting addition to Brian's band for the upcoming concerts in London is that they'll be joined by an eight-piece string and horn group, the Stockholm Strings 'n' Horns.

Darian: 'It was real important to me that whoever we have that they not be 'pickup' players . . . for the same reasons that we're playing this music, not having to read, I would love it if by the end or [even] the middle of the tour, these players are just playing the music and not even having to think about the notes. Or read the notes. That's what we need for this music, to be presented with the feeling. There's a lot of spontaneity in this music. It's kind of whimsical. It's almost like organized chaos. (*Laughs*) And it should feel like that. And I think that that's where the band is at this point.'

Probyn: 'Now we had a real team aboard, so we could actually cover nuances. Paul did a lot of the arranging or distillation, hearing what had been done during the *SMiLE* era and then writing out the string parts. Or in some cases, there was new transition material which was created, between Brian and Van Dyke (and Paul and Darian to a certain extent).'

To give a sense of the complications the band faced in performing *SMiLE* live – what the band had conquered thus far in touring with Brian – Nick points out that 'when Brian recorded the songs for *Pet Sounds* and *SMiLE*, he had the studio musicians playing the tracks and The Beach Boys sang the backups. They didn't play the parts. And now we gotta do both. *Live.* So, that's the challenge. And to pull it off every night and do it hopefully excellent every night? Because it's one of these things where we have to realize that first of all, it's never [all] been heard. Except for the [few] songs we've played. But we have to match those segues and other sections so they feel like [to the audience] we're as familiar with them as we are with those [other] songs. And it's a lot of sounds going on. A lot of little disparate [musical] elements that just come in and out.'

'That's why,' Nick thinks, 'People [will] have to come back and hear it all again, like the bottle blowing or something like that. And how many people [are there] going, out of Brian's ilk, at his age, and attempting to do something like this? I think if McCartney took *Sgt. Pepper* and just did it [start to finish]. Obviously, there were other composers on *Sgt. Pepper*. But that'd be one thing. But *SMiLE* wasn't a success per se. So Brian has to deal with that aspect . . . I've heard someone say that there is definitely a cult behind *SMiLE*. So there's going to be a lot of devotees that are going to be pretty happy to hear this, one way or the other.'

Getting very specific, Nick picks out a favourite part to play:

Nick: 'I love to play the fuzz baritone guitar in 'Cabin Essence.' Just like these quarter note, pounding sounds. And then I'm singing a new part in there that is barely audible, but it's part of [a] cacophony of voices. The whole "truck driving man do what you can" part. And I think that's pretty exciting for me. I think my favourite moment, though, has to be when Jeff and I do this part right after 'Child Is Father [Of] The Man'. It's just guitars, and it's been just like this quiet moment until everything comes back in. That's [been] another real high point [in rehearsals] for me.'

For weeks, rehearsals had been closed. How would this music play for a music journalist? Randy Lewis, a pop music writer for the *Los Angeles Times* for nearly forty years, remembers.

Randy: 'I've been a Beach Boys fan pretty much all my life, and I knew the place that *SMiLE* held in it . . . what it represented. I wangled an invitation to be a "fly on the wall" at one of those rehearsals . . . When I arrived, there were a handful of people in the space – maybe ten, no more than a dozen. Brian was seated at his keyboard and surrounded by his band, which I had seen and truly admired since he had returned to touring in 1999. I love the band's respect and authority they brought to all the music, to all the sounds Brian had heard in his head and put on The Beach Boys' records.

'I sat down on a little couch facing the group; there was one person seated next to me. They counted it off and did the entire work from top to bottom. I was just speechless – extremely privileged and also gobsmacked at how stunningly beautiful it was, how much fun and how intricate the music was . . . how beautifully executed it was, how the band played it . . . the interplay between Brian's music and Van Dyke's lyrics was just extraordinary.

'It really did elevate his music – pop music – to a whole different place. This was the beginning of my journey with *Brian Wilson Presents SMiLE*. At the end of that run-through, I asked Brian how it felt for him, and he said, "This feels so good – so good I can't believe it."

'I conducted other interviews to put together an overview story to try to place this in context. This was one of the most mythologized projects in all of pop music history. One of the interesting things about this to me was that it wasn't just another example of empty speculation. What music might Buddy Holly have made if he hadn't died? What about Jimi Hendrix? What about Jim Morrison?

'*SMiLE* had been worked on for [months] in various recording studios, just never assembled into final form. Hendrix had heard a little bit of it and called it "a psychedelic barbershop quartet." Having heard it at long last, I felt it truly, fully justified all the early excitement that people had about it.'

'Interviews with Brian can be challenging – and my sense is he consents to them because he recognizes they are necessary. But all he really wants to do is make music.

'I asked him what it was that allowed him to come back to *SMiLE*, because for so long he couldn't bear to hear anybody talk about it or mention songs like 'Heroes And Villains.' He just said, "I have emotional security."

'That stemmed from his stabilizing marriage to Melinda, as well as the care he was getting from a team of physical and mental health professionals who were helping him better manage all this post-traumatic stress and depression he had suffered through so much of his life.

'In this interview he told me, *"It is the best work I've ever done."*'

Brian explained to Randy that he wasn't trying to merely reconstruct something that he had done almost four decades earlier, but 'how I feel about the music now.' When I asked if he felt satisfied at how everything sounded that day, he said, 'I think it's perfect.'

In talking to Jeffrey Foskett about his impressions of it, Jeffrey told Randy, 'It's so far beyond what I imagined it could be.'

Randy: 'I liked the way [Jeff] framed it when he added, "The way I see it is that The Beach Boys' first ten albums made them stars, *Pet Sounds* made them great, and *SMiLE* made Brian Wilson a legend." Jeff also told me, "I just hope that in completing this, it gives him peace and lets him put this behind him after all these years."'

RAISING THE TITANIC

As Jeffrey would later add, 'an interesting transformation from a nineteen-year-old kid renting instruments to becoming a legend in a matter of five years.'

Randy was one of the few 'outsiders' allowed into rehearsals, but he was working on a story. In the months and weeks leading up to the world premiere, curiosity was intense. Fans were desperate for every nugget of information. Nobody outside the room knew what was happening.

Paul Von Mertens: 'We took a day off to play an event in Edmonton. The bathrooms for our use were accessible to the public. While I was washing my hands the person I was with – a friend who I knew well – asked me how the music was coming together. I knew better than to go into detail, but I did say Brian, Darian, and Van Dyke had come up with a running order that was kind of a continuous suite in three sections.

'The next day Melinda called and said, "Paul, please don't talk about SMiLE. Someone in one of the bathroom stalls overheard you and is blabbing about it on the fans' message boards!"'

A tiny hiccup.

For *Beautiful Dreamer*, we videotaped the band rehearsals every day, and there was so much to absorb, so much we'd never heard before. As there was no stage, one really didn't know where to look. But it was thrilling to hear SMiLE getting ever closer to being realized.

Perhaps nobody would be happier than a man who came to just one rehearsal, only a few days before the band would be heading to London.

Van Dyke: 'The only thing I was thinking about . . . on the way to the rehearsal, my first concern was that I not distract the process at all, not distract Brian Wilson or the group. Or have any opinions. Because I think an absence of an opinion is a very good thing, very healthy way to look at any work. Develop an opinion. That's good. But I throw out the Napoleonic code when it comes to music, and there isn't much music, as long as it's very smart or very well intended, that I don't just love.'

Van Dyke continued: 'I'm a goat. I eat anything. I love all kinds of music. And I was ready for this kind of music. And I was ready to resign [myself] to the fact that I was totally unnecessary. I was just happy to see it, happy for it to [exist] . . . face the facts. There's nothing I could do about it.'

What did he think?

Van Dyke: 'I was, to tell you the truth, astonished. But quite frankly because I hang around with musicians all the time. I'm surrounded by talent. I was satisfied with it, and I realized that I was satisfied with it. That's what happened at the first rehearsal I saw.'

Paul: 'I remember Van Dyke giving a little speech, a little pep talk, when we concluded rehearsals, and it was like, wrapping up, and it's like, "Okay, we'll see you at the airport tomorrow." And Van Dyke stood up and said something to the effect of, "You all sound fantastic. It's beautiful."'

And then, for American emphasis, Van Dyke added, 'You're gonna show those "tea bags"!'

For Van Dyke, that day wasn't 'just another brick in the wall. This is a keystone. It's an important stone to put into place . . . I feel that it creates a self-ensured, self-supporting, free-standing structure. I think it's fine. But I "never say never." . . . I'm in the race to the end.'

A week before the world premiere, I sat down with band members for my final pre-show interviews. Given the months of work, how did Darian feel about where the band was . . . and how did he think Brian was feeling?

Darian: 'I tend to be reserved in my thinking. (*Laughs*) I've had most success in not having too high expectations of things. 'Cause if you don't have high expectations, you're less likely to be disappointed. (*Laughs*) So, I came into this thinking not to expect so much from this band in such little time.

'But . . . if I could step outside of myself for a moment, and I do have to do this every now and, and then, just imagine what it's like to just hear a group of musicians playing this music. It's pretty remarkable. The parts are there . . . The real work here is stringing it all together. Trying to find that cohesion that we were talking about earlier. And I think we're in a good place right now. The wild card, of course, is Brian. I think he's still maybe a little nervous about doing this stuff. Understandably so.

'But again, I think that if we can get it back to the music, if we're playing as a band, and he's hearing these chords and these notes, these sounds, all coming together, and it's beautiful to him, then hopefully, it's back to what's most important to him. What's real; what's honest.

Something that won't betray him. And, hopefully, that's what we'll achieve in this tour.'

Nick: 'Definitely anxious. Definitely excited. And I think England is a good place to start because I think they get it. Not to say the Americans don't, but I think it's a good place to start the buzz and have it just spread out everywhere throughout Europe as well. But I know the UK . . . most of the musical publications vote him number one artist of all time.'

Probyn: 'I'm excited. I'm mostly excited to see the reactions of the people. I know what this music means to me, and I know there's a lot of people out in the world that have a similar feeling about this body of work. I'm so honoured to be part of this team. And to be part of bringing this [to the concert stage]. I mean, this is really the holy grail for a whole bunch of people. No one ever thought they would see this and certainly the new interstitial stuff that nobody has ever heard that is of the quality of the old material, that's going to really be amazing.

'So, I'm not nervous about it. I know that we can do it. I'm hoping that we can catch the vibe and send the vibe out although it may not even really be necessary for some people who are coming halfway to us with their expectant vibe, meeting us halfway. I'm looking forward to doing it mostly because I think there's a lot of people out there that are going to really feel deeply about this and I'm looking forward to being part of helping that happen.'

As for Brian, when the band watches him in these final moments before *SMiLE*'s day of reckoning, what do they think?

Nick: 'He definitely is always a guy that wants to be accepted. Who doesn't? But I think he's really not sure. And he's kind of got a short-term emotional memory loss of, "Wow, do people like me? I can't remember." And then gets in front of an audience, and they like him again.'

Probyn: 'I think Brian is always concerned about what people think. I don't know that he's scared about it, about the reaction. I think he knows people are going to like it, based on the fact that we've done four years of successful touring where he's gotten almost nothing but rave reviews at every stop. But it's hard to know what Brian's thinking. He's a very private person. We can only guess what he's scared about. I'm hoping that he has rid himself of the weight of '67 or whatever demons came from that time. I'm hoping they have been shed but they may not have been.'

We were all worried, but it's hard for anybody who isn't close to Brian to understand how prone he is to ups and downs. In the summer of 2003, he wasn't in 'a good place' regarding the idea of doing *SMiLE,* and it might have vanished then. But he had soldiered on and as 'the finish line' was in sight, Brian's determination to do it had won out.

Probyn: 'He's great under pressure. I have to say he's been a trouper on stage. Like when the chips are down and it's time to dive in and do a good show, or, like, we've done a bad first half and we huddle at the intermission and say, "God, we have to pull this one out. We're in New York, we gotta give it to them." Brian's there and he'll do it. I have every confidence that he will do that here. It's a little hard to tell what he's feeling, but I think he's gonna do great.'

As London approached, as the end of rehearsals neared, one person with decades of experience on the road was confident it would work.

John Warren: 'Just watching that come together. You knew it would run. It would tingle your spine every day . . . that just adds to the electricity of it and then the wonderfulness of it all and the miracle.'

When playing the music of *SMiLE* had first been discussed, Jeffrey Foskett thought, '"How in the world are we going to perform this?" And then after Van Dyke and Brian and Darian got together and made some sense out of it, I thought, "I can't wait to perform this. This is going to be astonishing." And today, the second to the last day of rehearsals, *I* was astonished, for the first time. Because I wasn't really working; I was really enjoying it. It was very fun for me today.'

Days before the premiere, while nobody could read Brian's mind, the early 'bad' days of vocal rehearsals were now in the rear-view mirror, and as full band rehearsals continued, the music of *SMiLE* became central to Brian's day.

Darian: 'I have to say these last few days, it's been like [Brian comes to rehearsal excited], "We're going to do *SMiLE*? All right." And that makes me feel great . . . I think it's a good thing for two reasons. One is the obvious one, that I think this will bring some sort of closure to him. It's one less thing for him to fear.

'And the second thing is that a friend of mine told me the other day, "If Brian Wilson's ever going to do *SMiLE* or if *SMiLE* is ever going to be presented in any official way, this is the time. Because all the right people are in place." And I thought about that. He's right. It may not be perfect, but it's pretty darn close. And that made me feel good . . . Considering Brian's life and all the scenarios and environments he's been in, this is a pretty good one. And I think because of that, there'll be enough integrity there that this music can be presented in a good way.'

Nick: 'Today I saw Brian having fun. I haven't seen that in a long, long time. Definitely not in these last three weeks, but even way before this, I've not seen him just goof off like that. [So] I can't wait. I think we still need to get a few bugs out. And it's just mainly connecting some points. For me, I can't wait to hear, even at rehearsal, what our little mini-orchestra is going to sound like. 'Cause there's a lot of sections that will bring us to another level and Brian too. It all builds to something.'

As to how the world premiere concert will go, Darian remains unsure.

Darian: 'I have no idea. I really don't. I have to say. I'm a little nervous because we've never performed music the way we're going to. We're talking eighteen minutes. Fifteen minutes straight. I know that a lot of what Brian enjoys in live shows is feeling the love from the audience. And in the past, we'd play a song, three minutes, "Yay," big applause. Next song, two minutes, "Yay," big applause. This time we're not going to have that. It's going to be long stretches. And I don't know how that's going to affect him. I don't know if he's going to feel satisfaction. But I'm sure that he'll be happy to have it under his belt. It's ridding your house of the haunting. It's exorcising certain demons.'

Jeffrey Foskett, having played with The Beach Boys and Brian, had a unique perspective of what was going to happen.

Jeffrey: 'Knowing what I know about Brian, and knowing what I now know about *SMiLE* . . . I have a pretty good idea on what some of his anxiety towards performing this music might be, starting with this was an album that was completely shut down by a record label, by his partners. And I'm excluding Van Dyke, his songwriting partner in that. But his performing partners. I believe his dad didn't want it to be released. Obviously, the record label wanted a different type of music than he was delivering to them. And, in 1966, maybe rightfully so. But he certainly was a harbinger of everything . . . at the forefront of everything. And you can see that with *Pet Sounds*, and [as] they trusted him with *Pet Sounds*, they should have trusted him with *SMiLE* as well.

'Would the public had been ready for it? They weren't ready for *Pet Sounds*. They probably wouldn't have been ready for *SMiLE*. As he proved himself with *Pet Sounds*, the album, and 'Good Vibrations,' the single.

'All of the people that doubted him, be it his partners or the label, or whomever, should have trusted him with the *SMiLE* project. And unfortunately, I don't think that trust was ever brought forth. And the album was shelved.

'So I think those fears translate thirty-plus years later into all of those things that were told to him then are still inside of him. And all of those things bounce around in his psyche from time to time. And every time he may feel good about performing this, a notion might come back to him that tells him that it's not going to be successful. I think after we perform it on opening night at Royal Festival Hall, all of those [fears] should be allayed. I'm really very hopeful that's what happens.'

Probyn: 'I think it takes a lot of courage, especially for someone like Brian, who was already a fragile person, more fragile than most people realize. They say he's enigmatic. Most people don't know the daily battles that he has to go through just to be at steady state let alone to play music and to perform and to send it out into the audience. That takes a lot. And I have great respect for Brian. It's like me trying to lift a thousand-pound weight. Yet he's doing it. And he's very good at it, and I can see that with *SMiLE* in particular.

'That's why I never thought it would be played, because we know how he's felt in the past about doing this material. He didn't want to. He said that it made him feel bad. It reminded him of a bad time. He didn't wanna go there. He didn't want to remember those feelings. We can only hope he's gotten over most of it. It takes a lot of courage to get over that and to pull through and just perform this music and to say, "Yes it's done and here, I'll give you *SMiLE*."'

Darian: 'As a musician I'm excited, because it's always exciting to play great music. I remember that when we played *Pet Sounds*, the cool thing about playing *Pet Sounds* was, it's never been done, right? So it was kind of neat, felt almost like we were an indie band playing *Pet Sounds*. It had that feeling of doing some cool interesting songs with interesting sounds that kind of are not that common in live shows. How often do you hear a bass harmonica and a theremin, those kind of instruments? So that part of me is really excited. Because I think we're going to [do] one better than that. Or maybe ten better than that with *SMiLE*, with all of the different stuff going on on-stage. And I'm nervous. I'm nervous for Brian. I have to say, I'm nervous for Brian.'

Darian's love for Brian shines through.

Darian: 'I hope in the best possible, in an ideal world, we'll finish the first show, and he'll feel the love, and he'll see, "This wasn't all that bad." And then, even better, "Wow, people actually like this. Some people actually love this." And that's so silly. Isn't that silly? Brian Wilson, before every show, he's nervous, and you'll ask him, "Brian, why are you so nervous?" "I'm scared." "Why are you scared? What are you scared of?" "Rejection." "Brian, there are four thousand people here. They bought tickets to see you because they love your music." "I know. I know. I know. I'm just scared." What do you say? The only thing we can do is play the music. And play it with a lot of love and a lot of feeling. And hopefully it helps him overcome those fears.'

Given that for twenty years, Darian's relationship with *SMiLE* was as a fan, has he been able to step back and enjoy the miracle of what's happening?

Darian: 'It's hard. I've been so close to this project, and it's been a working process that, I almost . . . gosh, I don't want to be so bold as to say that it almost feels like one of my own. When I think deeply about *SMiLE* in its legend and mystique, how it was made, how it may have been the album to have changed the course of music history, it's overwhelming. It's almost too scary to think about. Which is why it's better that I just be the musician (*laughs*) and just play the music, and let the history unfold (*laughs*) around me. It's just important to me that the music be conveyed and expressed in a very focused manner. Hopefully with the original intent that Brian and Van Dyke had. And I think if we can stick to that, then we'll just let history be made, and (*laughs*) hopefully it'll be good history.'

Darian offers one last thought.

Darian: 'I hope for Brian and Van Dyke Parks' sake that this is a great success. Because I love those guys, and they deserve all of the adoration that this music deserves. Let's hope [the tour] is a good one. Let's hope that we're flying home [in three weeks] on that plane and thinking, "Yeah. We did it!"'

Probyn: 'To be strong and to go out there and be ebullient and say, "Here's my art. Love it." That's one thing. But to publicly be sensitive and tender in a real way, the way that Brian is, the way I've seen him do it, that's something else, just about the *ne plus ultra*. I can't imagine a more valuable asset, musically. I think one of the hallmarks of a great musician is to be able to be passionate and tender and honest and open and do that in front of people and let them see that, let them feel it. And I think that takes art and courage. I think Brian has both.'

In conclusion, Probyn adds: 'I'm very fortunate and I'm quite honoured to be part of the whole project. I think it's beyond great that this is being made public finally. I remember I took out an ad in the back of the *L.A. Reader* paper over twenty years ago [circa 1983], a little personals ad that said something along the order of, "SMiLE is the greatest album you never heard. Please, Capitol, take the fragments, release it. Do something. And the rest of you, go and find it and check it out. SMiLE." That was my little megaphone in the back of the paper. So, the only other thing that I wanted to say is give a little praise for Domenic Priore, for making the book *Look! Listen! Vibrate! SMiLE!* Domenic, you have something to do with this [premiere] too.'

The band was ready. Was Brian? This lightly-edited sequence from *Beautiful Dreamer* gives us insight into the emotions of the last moments.

Danny Hutton: 'Just probably a week before he left [for London], he just started phoning every night and sometimes he'd phone four or five times a day to say, "I'm feeling scared."'

Brian Wilson: 'I'm nervous as hell, yeah. I am . . . I'm nervous about just doing the show. Just, about doing this show.'

Melinda Wilson: 'I actually got really nervous before we left to go on tour. I really felt that emotionally, he was going backwards, and yet at the same time, when I would say to him, "Okay, do you not want to do this?" "No, I'm gonna do it. I'm gonna do it. I have to do it."'

DREAMS DO COME TRUE

'An artist never really finishes his work; he merely abandons it.'
Paul Valery

'It is through art, and through art only, that we can realize our perfection; through art and art only that we can shield ourselves from the sordid perils of actual existence.'
Oscar Wilde

'Creativity takes courage.'
Henri Matisse

'A man of genius makes no mistakes; his errors are volitional and are the portals of discovery.'
James Joyce

'The essence of all art is to have pleasure in giving pleasure.'
Mikhail Baryshnikov

'Never in a million years did I think I would play *SMiLE* live.'
Brian Wilson

AND YET, THERE WAS A DATE CERTAIN. THE WORLD PREMIERE OF *BRIAN Wilson Presents SMiLE* was scheduled for February 20, 2004, at the Royal Festival Hall in London.

The clock was ticking. The last pieces were falling into place.

The day before the first show, there was a full run-through with the Stockholm Strings 'n' Horns. Their *only* rehearsal with The Brian Wilson Band.

SMiLE

Paul Von Mertens: 'For *SMiLE*, some of those orchestrations existed . . . had been recorded. It was a matter of transcribing them. Other orchestral elements we added to *SMiLE* . . . and there were a few things on *SMiLE* where I had a clear idea, like something that I was hearing in my head that wasn't on the [original] recording, and I would check in with Brian on those things. We [had] used some L.A. players for the rehearsals, so that we could hear it and make any adjustments to the parts. The Stockholm Strings had the music ahead of time.'

Anna Dager, *cello:* 'When I found out about the project from Darian, I realized this was going to be something really special and historical, to get to perform this lost masterpiece with Brian for the very first time live.'

Van Dyke: 'Their coming into the rehearsal situation was a matter of concern to me. Because I wanted them to be, once again, uncreative. I wanted them to simply nail down what Brian had written down, which now appears only, in some audio references from some tapes that were stolen. So, I wanted the strings and horns to be accurate. I wanted them not to elaborate further than the original parts that I could remember by heart. And their performance *is* faithful. Great ideas. Really great ideas.'

Paul: 'On 'Surf's Up,' I added a string quartet on the "dove nested towers" section of that song because I was feeling it. I talked to Brian about it, and he said, "Do what you feel." So [our] *SMiLE* is a combination of existing orchestration that was either duplicated or somewhat augmented. Some things that I came up with on my own and got the okay to include them.'

Malin-My Wall, *violin:* 'I think I was too young to appreciate what a great honour this was. It was hard to grasp the depth of his music. We were just kids at that time.'

Viktor Sand, *flute, clarinet, saxophone:* 'I fairly quickly understood that I had the chance to be part of something spectacular, something I won't experience every day, every year. We understand this is a big thing. We might not understand how big; we understand that it's massive, but we're just too young for this too. But let's just go with this ride and take this chance and do whatever we can. Let's just bring our spirit into this whole thing.'

Paul: 'They're superb musicians. Working with them, too, was one of the great joys and one of the great experiences that I've had with

Brian, because they were such good musicians, and so enthusiastic, so full of love for the music. And they clearly had a real bond of friendship between them. And the band immediately embraced them, and they felt welcomed. It was a very special relationship.'

Van Dyke: 'I can tell you that I think that brilliant chamber music is a wonderful medium. It happens to be my favourite music. And to hear the strings and horns come in, to be included, showed what a chamber sensibility there is in most of this music. And that it is not just a miasma. That those are particular notes. And they are played a certain way. And my greatest concern about them was that the strings and horns were as economical as intended when Brian wrote those strings . . . so beautifully. He wrote [those] one night to surprise me. When I told him I didn't have time to go get the strings copied, let alone written.'

Bob Lizik: 'We knew they were coming. We didn't know how that was gonna be. And they were great. I can't say enough how great that was. They were such a huge part of it because they didn't just play it. They became it. They were involved in every aspect of it, pulling out the vegetables during 'Vega-Tables', bringing the fire helmets out and pretending to put a fire out with the hose. They brought some life to that, too. And it gave us life.'

Anna Dager, *cello:* 'It was so exciting; you could feel the nerve in Royal Festival Hall, and we were very thrilled to do the premiere and we were also really well-prepared for the evening after the many rehearsals [in Sweden]. So it was very nice to be able to go on stage and play the music and do it focused and with great joy. The whole group and Brian [were] well-prepared for the premiere so that helped to get through with the nervous feelings and we could enjoy playing the piece and also bring joy to the audience and good vibes to support Brian too.'

Bob Lizik: 'At the time we did *SMiLE*, I was 55, and all the other guys were coming into that age, too, and here's a bunch of 20-year-old kids . . . We got to enjoy this whole thing as a very large group of people, and to be thankful for it every time, and just have fun. It was great!'

As showtime approached, nerves grew ragged. One backstage eyewitness was Jerry Weiss. Jerry had met Brian in 1994, become a close friend, and would often volunteer to accompany Brian on tour supplying him with large doses of 'emotional security.' On February 20, 2004, Brian needed just that.

Jerry Weiss, *personal assistant:* 'When we got to London, we had dinner every night together, you and Ray, Melinda, our wives, a few other people. I didn't get a sense of his being that nervous. Joking and funny and eating and talking and everything else. Even at rehearsal, he was the Brian that I knew. However, when we got to Royal Festival Fall, he was unbelievably nervous.

'He looked at the stage and around the hall. And he went out to the empty audience seating area and sat by himself absorbing the energy, history, feelings, and emotions. When we went to his dressing room, he knew this thing was real – he's gonna walk out on that very stage, with that band, in that place – that's when it hit him like a brick. And then he became a basket case of nerves. He was holding it together but scared shitless.

'He usually dealt with his nerves in two ways. Conversation and physical relaxation. Sincere conversation really helped but there were very few people he wanted to talk with at that moment. He tried to relax by ordering a massage and a masseuse came in. After the masseuse left, he asked me to dig my elbow in up and down next to his spine. Wow. Two hours before he went on stage, I could feel the lumps of tension in that man's back.'

Bob: 'None of us knew if he was gonna do it. We all thought the same thing, "Is he?" Because he had given some indication that he's still scared to do this. We all felt the same way. We were all wondering if he's going to walk on stage. I think we were all kinda tight-butted, unsure at that time. Here we are, the first time we're playing in front of a live audience this incredible piece of music. And, okay, maybe Brian will be fine, and we won't. One of us is going to make a big mistake . . . So it was a scary time.'

Taylor Mills: 'Oh my God, Brian is so brave to do this, and to allow us to be a part of it because there are a lot of judgmental people out there, and everyone's going to have their own opinions about what it should be. We're just there to perform it, but it's Brian and Van Dyke's baby, and we're just going to do what we do.'

Jerry: 'The night of the premiere, he wanted me in his dressing room. Then he wanted my wife, Lois, to come in. Then he wanted Melinda, then you. At different times. And then the band guys would come in and come out. And then, he really wanted to be left alone. So I sat in a chair outside of his dressing room and made sure that he wasn't bothered. A lot of people wanted a piece of him that night, all with good intentions. They just wanted to see if they could help.

'I remember him saying, "Jerry, I think I'm gonna throw up." And I said, "Because you're that nervous, right?" He said, "Yeah." I said, "Brian, this is my prediction." I said, "First of all, you have every reason to be nervous. This is taking you right back to 1967." And I took him by the hand, and he clasped his other hand over mine. And I said, "Brian, look at me. After the first note, your nerves will go away. I promise."

'He said, "Why are you so sure about that?" I said, "Because back in 1999, I said the same thing. And did they?" He said, "Yeah." I said, "Trust me. It's gonna happen." And he thanked me. He knew I was sincere. I told him his nervousness was real and justified. And it's miraculous that he's here. It's miraculous this whole thing is happening. And I'm so glad to be by his side for it. And he's gonna have a great time. And I said, "Brian, after the show, we're gonna have dinner. I'll buy you the biggest steak there is in London." That's how that night went.'

Jeffrey Foskett: 'It's 2004. If I'm Brian Wilson, I'm thinking, "I shelved this project thirty-seven years ago, because my closest associates, my business partners, my record label, my family, told me that I and the music was going to fail. Why would I want to bring this back to life now? I mean, gee, it would really take a miracle to do this." So personally, I'm really grateful that Brian has the people around him that encouraged him to do this. Because I'm hearing the end result. And it is really phenomenal.'

Paul Von Mertens: 'Maybe a half-hour before showtime, I was standing in the wings with Brian, and we were kind of peering out at the audience, and he said, "Wow, there's a lot of people there." And I said, "Yeah, it's sold out. Actually, all six nights are sold out and people have come from all over to see the show." And he said, "How much for tickets, like a hundred dollars?" And I said, "I think some people paid a lot more than a hundred dollars for these tickets." And he was silent for a moment. And then he looks at me and goes, "We've got to do a fucking good show."'

Just before they took the stage, Nelson recalls 'talking to the tour manager, Ky Cabot, and he's like, "Nelson, I don't even know if you understand tonight and how important this show is, what a big deal it is. This is one of the hottest tickets in the history of London . . . one of the most exciting, most anticipated shows in the history of London.'"

Ky, who worked with John Warren on a number of Brian Wilson tours, remembers the moments before the show.

Ky: 'I'll never forget Brian sitting on a chair just off stage right, the opening night of *SMiLE*. He was quite clearly nervous about it. But the cast of folks around him were all incredibly supportive. It was one of the few times I've seen a group of people truly 'all in' for the benefit of someone else; everybody was really there for him. People were committed – truly committed to Brian and the project. Darian was obviously a huge part of leading everyone, keeping them on point and focused on what the real mission was . . . I just gave Brian a pat on the shoulder and said something like, "It's going to be amazing." Not tremendous words of wisdom, but, like everyone else, I was really supportive of what he was trying to do.'

Nelson: 'Being in The Brian Wilson Band was a two-job gig. One is to play and sing the music right and be a good person to be around. And then the other one is supporting this guy and helping this guy who's got a lot of problems. And so, getting job number one [done] was almost a given. It was just like, "Just do that. Get it out of the way." That would be one hundred percent of anybody else's band's job. [In this band], that was like fifty or sixty percent of the job.

'It felt like the other forty percent was making this guy happy, taking care of him, and worrying about whether he was gonna actually do something. So we had the luxury of not worrying about whether we could play and sing this music, this very complicated music at this very high-end, high profile gig at Royal Festival Hall on this magical evening. All of that excitement, I don't think we got to have. We didn't get to feel any of that, because all of our attention and energy was towards, "Is he gonna do this? Is the lead singer gonna show up? Is he gonna be okay?" Even after all the rehearsals we'd had for a month, and all the build-up, we were never completely comfortable that it was going to really happen.'

Minutes before performing *Brian Wilson Presents SMiLE* for the first time, Brian sat quietly, thinking. Nobody approached him.

Jim Hines: 'All I knew was that it was gonna be the biggest live event I'd ever done in my life. And I was well aware of how important this was gonna be. And hoping Brian could hold it together and get out there and do it. I knew he could. I remember Brian. In that chair offstage, half-hour before the show . . . until that moment I was still questioning whether he was actually even going through with it, because I heard he might. He might not.'

Taylor Mills: 'I was always more concerned about Brian and how he was feeling. I felt like we had worked hard and knew our parts, and we were ready to go. But we never knew if he was ready or confident, and so I was always a bit excited and a touch nervous for him. We always were very aware about how he was feeling.'

SMiLE was performed after intermission, after Brian and the band had done a terrific 'unplugged' opening set and more. The audience loved it, but that's not why they were really there.

Nelson: 'Just all of the emotions of everything else, so much bigger than the actual job. And then, when you think about what the job was, which is playing percussion and singing SMiLE, which is really, really complicated. I was dangling off a cliff with a smile on my face. The whole situation was surreal. It was everything I dreamed of since I was a kid, since I started playing music. And everyone was feeling it.'

What did somebody who was there when Brian put it on the shelf think? What was Carl's wife's reaction when she heard that he was going to finish SMiLE and play it live?

Annie Wilson-Karges: 'Amazed. All these years. The power of completion. It's so huge. The risk-taking involved.'

Was Annie surprised that he had the courage left?

Annie: 'Brian always surprises me. He really does. I'm surprised, not surprised. That's how it feels.'

Did Annie think it was a good idea?

Annie: 'I think completion's always a good idea.'

When asked in 2004, what did Annie think it means to Brian to confront all of this?

Annie: 'I think it's just a great healing. I think it's an inner healing. I think it'll continue. It's a wave of healing for him this time. It's definitely well-deserved.'

And David Anderle? Other than Van Dyke, he was perhaps closest to Brian during the SMiLE-era. Here's what he said in *Beautiful Dreamer*.

David: 'The longest gestation in history. The guy gets pregnant in 1966 and he has the baby in 2004. That alone is worth the price of admission.'

David said that with a smile and a laugh. But he had more serious things to say about the trauma that this might cause.

David: 'I mostly thought the fact that he couldn't pull it off. I thought the weight of it, and then just starting to do it would conjure up all these memories and there's never been anything that has had the kind of expectation that this [has] . . . So what a weight to carry around. And to deal with. So that was a concern to me. But it's Brian.'

From his old friend's point of view, what did it take to even attempt this?

David: 'Oh, it takes a lot of courage. Takes a huge amount of courage to do that. Amazing.'

Jeffrey Foskett: 'I think he has every right to be afraid that this doesn't live up to the legend. People haven't heard this yet. On February 20, there won't be anything to be afraid of. I've never been more ready to perform anything in my life. I have never been more well-rehearsed. Seventy-five days ago, I didn't even know some of this music existed. With *Pet Sounds*, I had twenty-five years to learn it. And a number of years to play most of the songs on stage at different times. With *SMiLE*, it has just grown on me immensely and intensely, to the point that I am so ready to perform this. It's beyond description. I mean, it is awesome. It was an awesome undertaking, and it's going to be awesome to perform it to the public.'

As for Brian, he was getting ready to meet his destiny – all the myths and legends – head on, and take the stage and present the *SMiLE* music to the world for the first time.

His creative partner on the project was in London; he had a lot to say about what he was about to witness.

Van Dyke: 'The life force of this process is a living one. It's a contemporary experience. It is one man dealing with his own musical history. To me, that's the unknown in this. And it just takes a lot of moxie, a lot of courage, for Brian Wilson, to be willing to do this at this time in his life. And that's priceless. The man's wrestled with his own ghosts. It's serio-tragic and comedic at the same time. And like any good or fulfilling emotional experience in my book. Just not knowing whether to laugh or cry. It's what it's all about. It's what makes it priceless.

'But the real unknown element here that makes it exciting before show time is not knowing how they will possess it. And if that same woman who stood up to Ravel is still somewhere lurking in London, ready to say at the end of the performance, "You're mad." I have no doubt that Brian Wilson, who is very quick with the truth, will say, "You're right.'"

In 2004, a time when in popular music, rhythm was ruling over melody, SMiLE is intensely melodic.

Van Dyke: 'I think the timing of this project is entirely inappropriate. And it should be. To me, it's a dividend. It's a mitzvah. It's something from heaven. For this thing to come into the present tense . . . its musical possibilities that really are [not] rhythm-dominated and without melody. I think it's a great thing to see such power of melody be presented here. And to see how it will sell. I think it will do well. I think people are eager for melody. And so, I think that the timing of the performance of this work is probably very good. Because we were approaching just as polarized a situation now as we had then [in the 1960s]. The severity, the tectonics between the left and the right in politics and between the developed and the undeveloped world are just as great as they were then.

'There is a lot of friction which suggests that maybe it's time for a little sense of celebration. And this is what this stuff does. It celebrates and confirms what I think [are the] unique qualities [that] American popular musical idioms have to offer. It's a whole bunch of stuff in a small place that speaks to a very common American experience. I don't know how American culture is selling these days, in England or Afghanistan. But I think it's worth a gamble by taking the step, putting it forward and seeing if the world is more interested and curious about this kind of display than even The Beach Boys themselves were in 1967.'

Looking back, Van Dyke explains how far they've come: 'Here is a man – Brian was 23 when I met him . . . he had a very high degree of self-confidence, fluidity in social situations in the studio. And that was because it was like a chamber sensibility. So, all players are working to serve the same will. And that's basically, the dynamic you get. But the performance, that's what makes it exciting. So much can go wrong. They will never know what hit us.

'There are hard notes both vocally and instrumentally, doing some weird things. Some things as mysterious as the Bulgarians, the Eastern European music with the dissonances, unprepared suspensions, and so forth. All kinds of interesting, good things. That can only come from a mind that has been thoroughly schooled in barbershop and American low church hymnology, and all those wonderful things that Brian Wilson was really interested in . . . no snob when it came to bringing a horn player or a string player into the equation after he had come into music as a real rock and roller. I think he is in the Hall of Fame. Yes, he is.'

Most interestingly, on the verge of its world premiere in concert, Van Dyke is one who always believed that *SMiLE* should have been a performance piece.

Van Dyke: 'It's nice to see Brian sitting there as it looks like what the anthropologists call a nonparticipant observer. That's what that's called, where you step into a scene without putting another footprint on it. And this is, basically, Brian sees his work come to life with these musicians around him. And he can play all the parts. He can do all the stuff. And Brian was always investigating the most fundamental conundrums of sound recording. So now he has a chance to go back and hear how that translates to the stage.'

How will the audience respond?

Van Dyke: 'I have no idea how it's gonna snap, crackle, or pop. But I know it will have a different potential. It's imaginative music. Recently, I saw *The Last Man Standing* from Spike Jones . . . And this doesn't matter to anybody who isn't maybe 61. I can remember Spike Jones in 1948. I can remember his recording of 'Cocktails For Two'. Performance will be different. But it will also, I think, fascinate him [Brian], how it comes together to satisfy a person who has a real feel to the recording itself.

'So, to me, the thing about anticipating the concert . . . that's really exciting. Because – I feel, to me, like Bette [Davis] just said [in *All About Eve*], "Fasten your seatbelts. It's going to be a bumpy night." That's the way I feel. I think it will be a bumpy ride. I think there will be many people who approve of the situation, knowing what the merits of the performance represent. There will be other people who will be distracted by the niceties of art. And that's fine too. But I think not to know how it's going to go is terrifically exciting and can't be anymore insulting than it has been for the last thirty-eight years.'

Van Dyke, of course, can never resist a good line: 'My mother always told me, speak British, think Yiddish. The British are so receptive to individuality.'

But then he gets serious again.

Van Dyke: 'The kid in him is still very much there. Very much alive. I can see it when he does this material . . . through the performance, Brian Wilson's performance of his own songs, which I think, is not a dastardly deed when you come to think of it. I think it's a wonderful moment which he's earned. And I'm looking forward to it. But with absolute uncertainty and excitement bordering on fear. Because I know any insult that might come to the process is not only irrelevant, it's redundant. I keep thinking that there can be no more downside to this, to this risk of getting out there. Getting up on the high-wire without the net. Which is what he will be doing.'

This conversation with Van Dyke took place just before the world premiere. What did he want to have happen?

Van Dyke: 'I think that it's important to perform this piece so that it can be analysed on its own merits. But I think that it will be favourable the whole way around. Certainly, cathartic for me because the other shoe will have dropped. And any further attempts to demonize the effort will be passé. Because the project is without malice, and I think that it will be startling to hear it and to deal with it.

'What really interests me about the performance of SMiLE is that Brian Wilson will have done SMiLE. He will have done it for himself. For his own pleasure. To hear it. And see how it works, in a real direct, interactive way, and not just through the web of piratical forces that are out there, that have determined how the project should end. It won't end. It will find its proper dynamic. My feeling is that what Brian is doing now, putting it in performance, and what the words still do is, allow for and invite an opportunity for a new audience that has no preconceptions or proprietary interest . . . They are the ones that interest me. And that is the dynamic that I think we will see come out of this.'

Van Dyke reaches one final conclusion.

Van Dyke: 'There's a question [that] does hang in the air now, before these London performances that are finally coming in the late winter of 2004. What would it do in performance? I just have no idea. I have no idea how that will affect anybody at all.'

The promise of SMiLE had always been that it was something new. Something that couldn't be defined or put in a box. And that's why Glenn Max had been so eager to bring it to the Royal Festival Hall. Before the show began, Glenn would go onstage and make an introduction.

Glenn: 'On that opening night, I turned to Brian. I remember saying, "Oh, man, I'm always so nervous when I go out there," and he just looked at me with terror in his eyes, and said, "I'm scared as hell."

'I was like, "Oh, shit." He was scared. He would sit on the side of the stage concentrating or trying to calm himself, and then everyone would gather, and there'd be a little prayer circle type of situation where they'd all support each other, and the band would go on stage. I'd always hang with Brian right until he went on stage and then I'd go to my seat. But I'd always be right there with him. [For] the support.'

Darian: 'I just remember during the break. "Okay, here we go." Brian didn't say a word.'

As the band took the stage, Darian remembers thinking that when Brian came out, 'This could be history in the making. We're performing the *SMiLE* music for the first time.'

Brian: 'I was about two inches away from not going on that stage. I was, really . . . I went on stage, but I really didn't want to. I really didn't. I was afraid I was gonna get nervous and blow it, you know (*bleep*) up, excuse me, mess up.'

Brian told me that long after the London premiere. I didn't talk with Brian just before he went onstage. Nobody would do that. But afterwards, he was eager to talk.

David Leaf: 'What was going through your soul just before going out to do it for the first time in London?'

Brian: 'I was going through conniptions. I was going through the worst anxiety I've ever been through in my life. So anxious, the anxiety, that I had to really try hard not to be scared. 'Cause I knew we were into something. I knew that. I wasn't positive of what we were into, but I knew we were into something very special and very *meant to be*.'

David: 'Were you scared of how the audience was going to receive it?'

Brian: 'I was. I was scared the audiences would think it was too far out music, too far out. And I said to myself, "But how could they think it's too far out if it's that good of music?" But I wrestled with it. I wrestled back and forth. Wrestled with it. Finally, I came to the conclusion that, "Yeah, it's gonna be successful."'

I was there in London to support Brian as a friend but also to finish my documentary, *Beautiful Dreamer*. How will the film end? In triumph? Or disaster? We've got an experienced team shooting the concert itself, but I also have my *cinéma vérité* camera crew. Where do I want them?

I asked our Director of Photography, James Mathers, to be behind the band during the concert so we can see the audience's reaction when (again, if) Brian comes out. But that would come after he follows Brian up the steps. I told James, 'I think It's going to be like *Dead Man Walking*.' I knew that Brian would be terrified in those final moments.

James Mathers: 'I remember you telling me that. That was part of my mission to follow him up on stage.'

David Leaf: 'At that moment, I remember thinking, despite lots of previous director credits, that was the first time I could see the scene I wanted in the film. But that wasn't as important as what was to come. Either way, I'm surprised (and relieved) that instead of a slow, scared walk, Brian walked up the stairs deliberately, with purpose. As soon as I saw him reach the top of the stairs, walking onto the stage, I ran to my seat, to join Eva. Yes, I'm making a film, but I'm a fan first, and this is a moment we've dreamed about since . . . forever.'

So, with over two thousand other believers who had come to witness a miracle, we saw Brian Wilson at centre stage; *Brian Wilson Presents SMiLE* was about to be performed live, for the very first time.

What was the band thinking at that moment?

Paul: 'I just remember there was a huge response when he came out, and the excitement in the air was palpable. And to be honest, I think I was so kind of high on the whole experience, that I was just riding a wave. I don't really have specific memories of thinking about things.'

Bob: 'We better not screw this up. Seriously. I mean, we better not fall on our faces, because this is really important. Any number of things could have happened. I could have broken a string. Jim could have knocked over a cymbal. We could have completely blanked on something, like, "Oh my God! I forgot that. This follows that, and this follows that." But, yeah, I was scared that I don't screw this up. It's important . . . This can be done by the Chicago Symphony and the Chicago Choir. There's meaning to it. It's musically brilliant. And vocally, it's a great piece of music.'

Brian: 'I was so scared, because I didn't know what to expect. And I was almost ready to vomit, throw up, I was so scared. But when we first started, after we hit our first note, I relaxed.'

And during the show?

Darian recalls exchanging glances with Nick 'quite a few times. Same with Probyn. I'd look over – and these are two guys that I'd known for, at that point, twenty years – and just thinking, "Wow, we got together, we know each other and met each other based on our mutual love for Brian's music." And with Nick, within the first five minutes of us meeting each other, he was telling me how he had driven a hundred miles to get a *SMiLE* bootleg at a record store in San Diego . . . it was surreal in a lot of ways.'

Jim Hines: 'It looked like I was working hard. It always felt like flying. And once we started playing, it was just that bed of wonderful harmonic stuff. *SMiLE* was like flying on a beautiful fall, sunny, crisp morning, with big puffy clouds and sky.'

Scott: 'Every soul that's on stage is coming together as one, and they're giving of themselves their full emotional being, to create something beautiful, and every member of the band, and Brian, rose to the challenge to make it great. And that was an incredible feeling.'

Jim: 'It was immediately after 'Our Prayer.' And I knew Brian had it. And I knew we had his back, and that was our goal. We all just wanted to have his back . . . I was happy for him.'

Bob: 'I looked at Jim, and we're like, "Okay, this is happening." But there's still a lot more to come. It was a scary night, until it was over.'

Probyn: 'Mostly I was very nervous again. Because I had to do a lot of things in *SMiLE*. I had to play guitar, trumpet, French horn, banjo, a little melodica (when it was the two harmonicas for 'Cabin Essence'). I had to rattle pieces of sheet metal. I had to remember it all. And I was not looking at music. We had memorized this stuff. I was not able to really remove myself so much.'

Nelson: 'Once the show started, you go into performance mode, and your brain is very locked into a function, and that's the function of playing and singing correctly, perfectly. And time goes by. So, all the concern about Brian went away. We were there. He showed up. He sang . . . So there was a relief. There was a little bit of a relief that was sort of peeking its head through the daunting task of singing and playing music.'

Anna: 'I felt nervous, but "happy nervous" . . . People really could feel, hear, and see the good energy on stage so it felt really great and fun right away and it was just positive feelings afterwards. The focus and the fun and the privilege to play with such good musicians totally outshined the nervousness. I felt very proud over the Swedish ensemble that I got together for the performance since it all turned out very well.'

Nelson: 'It was after the first movement, the applause that erupted was a life-changing moment for me. It was the most thrilling moment of my life as a musician. There is nothing that has touched that before or since. The thrill of hearing that audience was so exciting, and the sound of them screaming as loud as they could, and applauding . . . It was the most deafening, loud, exciting applause ovation I've ever heard.

'This was the first time that I heard anything like that in my life. And it was incredible. And it was the most defining sound of incredible joy that I'd ever heard. And it was because these people got to see this and hear this thing that they've been talking about their whole life. For the first time. And that first movement, and the end of the first movement, gave them a chance to say, "Oh, my God, this is it. Brian's okay. Brian is okay."'

Darian had expressed concern that unlike every other concert Brian had played, there wouldn't be applause every two or three minutes, after each song. How did that affect Brian?

Brian: 'I wondered that, myself. But then after the [movements] were over and I got such an applause, then I knew they liked it. But during the performance, I didn't know. There was no way to know if they liked it or not.'

James Mathers was on stage, shooting the audience: 'They were hungry for him, and they enjoyed it so much . . . he couldn't get a friendlier audience. I don't think I've ever seen one. They were in awe and appreciation.'

Darian: 'The first performance was very technical . . . a lot of choreography. And we rehearsed it, so it was like what would hopefully happen if you're an athlete at the Olympics. You've got that moment. You've practiced and practiced and run over your routine over and over. You just hope to nail it, get a high score on that when it matters.

'Even for Brian, it was just about getting through it. "Can I do this? Can I make it all the way through?" And it was at the second show, for me personally, that he was a lot more comfortable, and now he could feel it more than he did the first show. The second show was like, he had reached the peak of the mountain, and now he was looking down into the valley, as were we. The second show was just much more emotionally satisfying.'

What did Brian think of that first ever performance of *Brian Wilson Presents SMiLE?*

SMiLE

Brian: 'Actually, I was kind of anticipating the response from the audience. I was proud that they liked 'Surf's Up' so much. They loved 'Surf's Up' and 'Heroes And Villains.' Those two they particularly liked the most, and I was very proud of those two songs.'

David Leaf: 'When you were playing *SMiLE*, did you step out of yourself, or were you so into it that you weren't even thinking?'

Brian: 'I was so into it that I couldn't even think. I was so on top of, the moment that we were performing it, that I had no bad thoughts about it. You know what I mean? All my bad thoughts disappeared.'

David: 'What was the best moment of that first night for you?'

Brian: 'The best moment was when we did (*singing*) "Not far from blue Hawaii," [in] the third movement. The third movement was my favourite.'

And in a forty-six-minute blissful blink of an eye, it was over.

Brian: 'And then I got a ten-minute standing ovation, which made it all worth it.'

Paul: 'I do remember the ovation at the end of *SMiLE* that went on for a long, long time. And I saw Brian just standing there, taking it all in. He seemed a little unsure of what to do but also relieved that we had completed it. It was clearly successful. And all of that weight was lifted by the applause and by the audience reaction.'

Bob: 'A deep breath afterwards, and you saw it yourself with Brian. Finally. I think it was a big, big weight off his shoulders when it finally got done and was accepted the way it was. It looked like he changed when that was over. He suddenly was . . . He was more happy. He was more engaging with the band . . . He'd just wanna hang. He was having fun.'

Probyn: 'When it was over, there was this intense wave of relief. I don't think I was the only one in the band that felt that way. The audience reacted – they had obviously gotten it – and we'd done it justice, I think. Maybe not perfect, but we'd done it justice. And Brian, more importantly, Brian had done it. He'd gotten through the show with flying colours, sang everything great as far as I remember . . . there was no backing down. 'Don't Back Down,' as The Beach Boys sang. He'd done it and we got through it, and it was a triumph. It was a success. And then of course there was the night after that and the night after that.'

Jerry Weiss: 'He went up there and faced the music and faced the crowd. After the show, he thanked me profusely and said, "You're right. I felt that I got this thing."'

Many of us saw what looked like demons leave his body.

Darian: 'I don't know whether it was the first or second show, that was the night I saw him . . . Brian stepped back, and he was beaming. Just, this glow, twinkle in his eye, and I just felt like, "All right, all right, they're [the demons] floating away."'

Nelson: 'I remember it vividly. It was a very specific moment, like a couple of seconds, and in *Beautiful Dreamer*, I'm in the shot in the back, applauding and smiling when the moment happened. He accepts the fact that he's not going to shut everyone up [from applauding]. But there was a heave of his chest, and there was his eyes closed for a minute, and there was sort of a shuffle – I can't really describe the way he stepped, but it was really a moment where it really, truly, truly felt like it was a physical manifestation of a relief and a release of great pain. It just kind of lifted out of his body, and then he flashed the OK sign to the audience. It was a palpable, actual thing that I saw. Some of the other guys in the band saw the same thing.'

There was no stopping the ovation.

Nelson: 'Brian gets nervous at the beginning of things. Then when he's in it, he's, "Okay, now all I have to do is my job. Got it." But now it's over. He's done it. He's thinking about leaving – "I gotta get out of this theatre and go back to my hotel." Even after the first performance of *SMiLE*. That's probably what he was thinking. "I gotta get something to eat." But I think that he gave himself permission to feel something. That's what I think. He let himself feel something, like, "Instead of running like I always do, I'm gonna enjoy it." And that joy was this manifestation . . . joy and that feeling of acceptance, "I'm allowed to feel this. I'm allowed to let this go." That's really what it felt like. And yes, it almost seemed visual. It almost seemed like a visual thing.'

Nelson recalls, 'It was amazing. I was kind of walking off stage going, "I think I'm gonna like this gig." This is way, way more than music. This job is way, way more than what the job description was given to me.'

Neil Warnock MBE: 'I'm totally emotional about it because for Brian, it seemed like a completion of a piece of work that needed to be seen in such a respectful way, and it was being seen in a respectful way. There'd been so much snide commentary, in my opinion, about *SMiLE* and the "stop started-ness" of it and Brian's mental condition at the time. And to actually see it on stage, I think my emotion was mainly pride. Pride in what Brian had achieved. And it was an emotional charge, it really was. And I felt that. How could you not feel that through the whole of the audience? It was just overwhelming.'

During that seemingly endless ovation, Brian brought Van Dyke on stage so they could take a beautiful bow together. If *that* didn't bring tears to your eyes, you didn't belong in the building.

David Leaf: 'When you finished *SMiLE* for the first time, what were you feeling?'

Brian: 'I was feeling relieved that we got we got our feet wet, involved in it. I was very relieved . . . that proved that we can do all three sets together.'

David: 'When you're doing *SMiLE*, is it hard not getting feedback between each song?'

Brian: 'For the first few concerts in London, I felt that way. But then after we got three or four concerts, I started to relax with it. I wasn't as worried. I wasn't thinking, "Oh, I wonder if this is going over good or not." We had to wait for the end of each movement to see what they thought.'

David: 'When the third movement was over, how did all the applause make you feel?'

Brian: 'Proud of course, proud, and then it made me feel like I had accomplished something that I never thought I could accomplish. Do that to people and not knowing what they're gonna think until after, after it was done . . . [The second night] I remember how the applause wouldn't stop. And I blew it by saying, "Please stop." I should've let them go on for twenty minutes. You know what I mean? And let them just carry on and carry on, but I was getting so tired of being applauded that I had to stop it.'

David: 'It was like we could see the bad vibes leaving your body. Were we imagining that . . . or was that real? Did you feel that at all?'

Brian: 'That was for real. I felt the peace.'

In an April 2005 interview, Brian explained to me, 'I had auditory hallucinations for years and years, and they've gone down to a minimum now. They're not gone. But they're down to a minimum.'

David: 'What about the demons of *SMiLE*? Was that something that dogged you all these years?'

Brian: 'No, actually, I dismissed *SMiLE* from my mind a long time ago.'

David: 'Knowing how great that music is, was it hard to dismiss it?'

Brian: 'No. It wasn't hard at all. I dismissed it as far as listening to it . . . The album *SMiLE* would come up in my mind a lot, but I didn't really think about the music.'

David: 'How did playing *SMiLE* live help to chase the demons away?'

Brian: 'It helped to chase them away because it was such a powerful piece of music, that I think the auditory hallucinations were very proud of it and I think it really got to them, psyched them out.'

David: 'It wasn't the fans' overwhelming reaction of the audiences or the great reviews that did that?'

Brian: 'No, it didn't chase the demons away. No, it didn't. The actual performance of *SMiLE* did.'

Not answers or admissions I expected.

★　★　★　★

I asked Brian, 'If somebody had just listened to *SMiLE* for the first time, what would you like them to feel?'

Brian: 'I would like them to feel like they've experienced something unique, they've never heard before . . . a new and exciting adventure in music.'

After the show, our camera caught a few fans outside the Royal Festival Hall. Here are their off-the-cuff reactions:

'Fantastic!' 'Sonic tour de force.' 'The best I ever experienced.'

'Absolutely mind-blowing. I'm floating.' 'A genius.' 'Brilliant.'

'A miracle.' 'Absolutely superb. 'The pieces of the puzzle have been put together at last.'

'I went through a hundred descriptions and each one disappeared and the next one was inadequate. Never seen anything like that in my life. Moved to tears.'

'The warmest, the best. Just wonderful.'

'Totally mesmerizing. It was magic. He should be so proud of himself.'

'An incredible triumph of the will for him to come back and play these songs that should have been played thirty-five years ago.'

SMiLE

'What I got was more hip, more happening, more today than I was expecting.'

'Everything was a surprise. I'm still trembling from it all.'

'I've waited thirty years for this. Exceeded all expectations.'

'Out of this world. Finally, he unleashes the mystery. Worth being born for that.'

'So intense. Moments when I had to shut my eyes and let the sound be and do what it wanted to do. Fill you up. Sensory overload.'

'If this album had come out in early '67 as it should have been, it would have blown *Sgt. Pepper* clean out the water. Absolutely. Without a shadow of a doubt.'

'*Sgt.* who?'

'This is my first trip to London, and as I was walking through the Tate galleries and seeing the timeless art on the walls, tonight was the same thing. A beautiful piece of art.'

'I think that I've been busted open, to be honest. It was the reason I got into The Beach Boys twenty-five years ago, this mystical trip that was called *SMiLE*. And I'm feeling some kind of closure. I feel like it's been validated, everything I've ever thought would happen has happened tonight and for that, I'm very grateful.'

Our other camera crew went backstage and grabbed immediate reactions from everybody involved as well as many long-time friends of Brian's who were there, relieved, but enthusiastically celebrating.

John Warren: 'I never thought it would happen. I never thought that I would see the music the way it was originally meant to be performed. For, in all the years that I was with The Beach Boys, it was never performed properly, and now it is. It's very cool. I think it's a triumph for everybody – mostly for Brian, but also for the fans, and for all of us who put all the years into it, and the effort and the sweat, and the crew. It's cool.'

Taylor Mills: 'It was awesome. It was so much fun.'

Jeffrey Foskett: 'I gotta tell you, my friend, I'm stoked. What a great crowd. What a great audience. What a great show. I love London. I love performing here. What can I say?'

Nelson Bragg: '*SMiLE* baby, *SMiLE!* We did it! We've done *SMiLE*. It's very exciting. It's very thrilling. I'm completely delirious right now; actually. I'm not of sound mind.'

Probyn Gregory: 'It's amazing. It's the first run-through of the whole thing. The audience dug it more than I thought. We missed the entrance of a song; they were so loud. It was amazing.'

Darian Sahanaja: 'We did it. We did it! I'm so proud and relieved, and I think we did good. I was concerned for Brian that the audience wouldn't be that into it, but, whew, we didn't expect that. That was great. Like, I think they would have stood for minutes, if we didn't start new music.'

Probyn: 'I thought it was great.'

Darian and Probyn together:

Probyn: 'Oh, God. What a relief!'

Darian: 'Yeah, it was awesome.'

Probyn: 'Thank you, Brian and Van Dyke, beautiful music. And Darian.'

Darian: 'And the band . . .'

Nick Walusko: 'I loved it, man; it was really good today. For a first try, I think, we scored pretty good. Brian was conducting more than he ever has. That's a really good thing, too. He was having fun, people wearing fire hats. What more do you want?'

Jim Hines: 'It went just like I thought it was going to go – painlessly, smoothly, easily. It flowed out . . . it was terrific. I had so much fun. I'm happy for Brian. Can't wait to do it tomorrow. It was just a really, really emotional experience for me. I'm tingling.'

Bob Lizik: 'It's a big weight off our shoulders because you don't know. I mean, we knew while we were doing it, rehearsing it, that it was really special for us. But you never know how everybody else is going to appreciate it, because everyone's got their own vision of what it should be. I thought that the response from the crowd was overwhelming. In between songs I was thinking, "How cool is this, man?" It's probably the greatest moment of my [musical] life. This was real, this was a real moment of my life. I couldn't be happier.'

Paul Von Mertens: 'I was struck by the variety of Brian's music, like the tremendous range of it is incredible. Like, when you hear it in two hours, to go from some of America's favourite pop songs to *SMiLE* and everything in between, I was just really struck by that, more than ever. I was very happy with the way *SMiLE* came off. I felt like the audience was totally with it, like hanging on every note. And I was hanging on every note. It was just a blast. I feel tired, and it's also exhilarating. I don't think I've ever been this well-prepared for any new performance of a piece, so it was nice to be able to walk on stage and feel like, "We know this. We totally know it." So that was thrilling. And I want to play it again, right now!'

Scott Bennett: 'It was very emotional. The high point for me was Van Dyke and Brian together onstage . . . What a journey, and what an arrival. And I think it's going to be even better tomorrow. I was very pleased. I thought Brian sang very beautifully. Very happy.'

Van Dyke: 'I just can't believe that these people put this thing together so carefully and with such a sense of respect for these "rusty old goods that still cut the wood." It's all over but the shouting, and my verdict is "innocent until proven guilty." And this was a very powerful concert . . . I have a tendency to laugh at funerals and cry at weddings. So, I'm not sure if my emotions are of any significance, but I'm very relieved and deeply touched, and totally incredulous."

David Leaf: 'Happiness for Brian, relief for all of us that it was everything we dreamed it would be and more. I think we need it more today. We really need harmony, and this music is just full of his harmonic love. I only wish that Brian would have stayed there longer and taken the ovation, because I think they might have clapped 'til tomorrow. I can't wait to see it again tomorrow.'

Sylvie Simmons, *UK journalist:* 'I'm still trying to come down from it. It was so completely mind-blowing. It was very odd being in the audience because everybody was [mouth agape in wonder] like this. They were all holding their breath. In fact, at some point, I thought everybody was going to turn blue in my row, because you just didn't want to miss anything.

'There was so much going on in there. But it was incredible, it was kind of Aaron Copeland meets circus music – everything just thrown in there. It was absolutely stunning stuff. What I found interesting is that Brian looked less nervous than when he played the *Pet Sounds* tour, which I also reviewed for *Mojo*. He was doing a lot more hand movements, and he was looking around nervously. But he was spot on. He was in there. He was brilliant. Stunned. Happy. Full of joy.

'I think it was on par with the legend. It's one of the things people keep asking. Would this album mean anything if there hadn't been a tragic story of Brian? I think the tragic story just makes good stories. The music is incredible. It is amazing when you think about when he made it, and how he made it, with little bits of sticky paper in a studio . . . still mind-blowing. This was majorly psychedelic. It was Brian Wilson, an incredible, mind-blowing composer, who should be up there with Copeland and Barnum & Bailey.'

Debbie Keil-Leavitt, *forever friend:* 'The first few pieces, I realized at some point, that I wasn't breathing, and all of a sudden, I heard through my head the James Joyce comment that, "When there's a perfect piece of art, it arrests the person experiencing it." And then, all of a sudden, I started to cry and cried through the rest of it. I must have been holding my breath for thirty-seven years. Those of us who heard pieces of this. Those of you who have been waiting for this, this is what you're waiting for, folks. It's the best thing I've ever heard in my life, the best day of my life.'

Mark Linett, *recording engineer for Brian Wilson Presents SMiLE:* 'How close I came to crying towards the end of the third set. It's just amazing. I'm just so happy for Brian. Having heard so much of the original music and to hear it finally presented. A dream come true for me. A dream come true for everybody. And certainly, it must have been a dream come true for him.'

Wayne Johnson, *friend:* 'I'm speechless. It was unbelievable. I couldn't have imagined it to be any better. It was well worth the wait. I came out from Los Angeles. I'd have gone to the moon to see that. It was just a dream come true. Never thought he'd finish *SMiLE* after all these years. I never thought it would happen.'

Richard Waltzer, *producer, Beautiful Dreamer:* 'I was thinking that what I read in *Crawdaddy* magazine in 1966 was right. They talked about this album that Brian and Van Dyke were working on. It was the most anticipated album for my generation, and I'm glad I was around to hear it. It's magnificent. It's like a dream coming true that you don't even dare to dream. That seemed like the one impossibility in the pop music world, that *SMiLE* would ever exist, and that Brian would be performing it in London is extraordinary.'

Ray Lawlor: 'It's like the thirty-seven years never happened. It's as fresh today as it would have been thirty-seven years ago. It's contemporary, ahead of its time, still way out of its time. It's phenomenal. I think the audience response shows that – the actual explosion after each one of the movements. Now, he's done the two greatest records in rock 'n' roll. I couldn't be happier. I want to hear it again, and then I want to hear it again. I think everybody else will feel the same way. It's irresistible, and quite simply, the best thing he's ever done.'

Tom Bagdonas: 'I can't even come up with adjectives for how I felt. Thirty-seven plus years. Totally blown away. It all makes sense. It all flows. He's a genius. We knew it. Now to me, this is closure – for the fans, for Brian. It's a great event. The Super Bowl. The World Series. The World Cup. It's everything. I flew from New York to get here. I would have walked across the Atlantic to hear this show. It was mind-blowing.'

His brother agreed.

John Bagdonas: 'I made the plans for this trip six months ago. Unfortunately, two weeks ago, I was diagnosed with bone marrow cancer. You never saw anybody go get things set up for treatment as quickly as I did. I told the doctors there is no way I'm missing this concert. I'm going to start treatment when I get back next Thursday. They [the doctors] all accommodated me for this very night. I'm just so happy. I've never been so happy in my life. I speak to Probyn Gregory regularly, and we talked about it and said, "This music is healing." After the concert, this might sound weird, I said to him, "Probyn, I might have lost half that tumour tonight."' (Author's Note: John lived *sixteen* more years.)

Randy Lewis, *Los Angeles Times:* 'I think it all makes sense. It is just a fabulous piece of music that gets richer the more I hear it. I did get to hear a couple of the run-throughs at rehearsal, and so this is now the fourth time I've heard it from beginning to end, and it just opens up more every time. Elation. It's a very remarkable thing to see the path that Brian's taken to get to this spot. When I first saw him back onstage at the end of the nineties, when he started doing shows again, I was happy for him. But it wasn't always a fabulous musical experience. And it's gotten to the point tonight where it's a transcendent musical experience . . . I think it's just virtually unprecedented. It hit me as I was working on a story that Mozart was born, lived his entire life, and died in less time than it took this work to come to fruition. It's just phenomenal.'

After the backstage celebration, a few of us got into the elevator to leave. Camera still rolling.

Brian: 'I was thinking about the concert, believe it or not. Did you like it?'

DREAMS DO COME TRUE

David: 'What did you like?'
Brian: 'Heroes And Villains.'
David: 'Are you relieved?'
Brian: 'Yeah.'
David: 'Happy?'
Brian: 'Yeah. I feel good in my heart. I feel good. I have a good feeling in my soul.'
David: 'Did you ever doubt it?'
Brian: 'Nah. It finally came true, our dream, our *SMiLE* dream. (*Laughs*) It came true!'

In the interview I did with Brian when he returned from the first tour, it was during the second show that he knew that it worked.

Brian: 'The first movement on the second night, I rested my case. I knew we were into something. I knew we could do it. We proved to each other that we can do it. We proved it, and it was proven. As soon as we started the second night, as soon as the first note of, "I've been in this town so long, I'm back in the city" – as soon as we did 'Heroes And Villains,' I knew we were home free. I knew we were home free.'

★ ★ ★ ★

Ky Cabot: 'I just remember overwhelming enthusiasm and joy. People were truly excited about something that had been shelved for so long finally coming to fruition. The way people embraced it was remarkable. It was unquestionably a high point for me in my career working with musicians.'

Malin-My Wall: 'I was very excited on the opening night! I really loved the songs and the way they were combined into this piece of art. These beautiful interludes that combined the songs and thus making the whole journey of *SMiLE*. After the show, everything was madness. I never in my wildest dream could have imagined to see so many celebrities at the same time. It felt like, "Everybody was there."'

Viktor Sand: 'The idea of the artist comes to life, and it meets the audience with the light, with the sound, with the reactions with them. When everybody goes in the same direction that you know, no one goes untouched from that. You have to have both. Everything is just a whole. And when that just meets the audience, then it powers up. And I think that's what you feel.'

Brian's music agent, Neil Warnock MBE, recalls that world premiere week became 'a zoo. Everybody wanted to be there. Every industry person you could think of. Everybody wanted to meet Brian. David Gilmour, [Sir] Paul McCartney, Roger Daltrey. Unbelievable. So many genuine long-term fans of Brian's music. It was just an extraordinary situation of people coming out and actually being reverential. And almost, it did have that feel of being in church, if you will, going to the church of Brian Wilson . . . he is a musical God . . . Quite frankly, I don't believe that the Royal Festival Hall has had another season like that from an artist, do that number of shows. I think it was unique and hasn't been repeated.'

On the fourth night at the Royal Festival Hall, before the show, there was a surprise and very special backstage guest.

Jerry Weiss: 'Brian's nervousness decreased with each show, except on the fourth night when he heard that Sir Paul McCartney was coming. It made him a bit more anxious and a bit more nervous, just to know that his idol is coming to see him. There's a knock on the dressing room door, and there's Paul McCartney with his ukulele. And he came in, and he sat next to Brian. I walked out; shut the door. I heard them talking. I heard them laughing.'

David Leaf: 'He was playing ukulele for you. What was he playing?'

Brian: 'I don't know what he was playing, but he was playing something cute. Because he's such a cute guy, you know what I mean? So he was playing something pretty cute. I knew that. I knew he was up to being cute.'

For Brian, for everybody in the Royal Festival Hall, Sir Paul McCartney's presence was a big deal.

Brian: 'A good friend to have. His being there meant he liked me, he supported me . . . a good person to hang with . . . we're the only two who can understand each other musically . . . It's like medicine for my soul.'

For Brian's band, it was a once in a lifetime moment. Before every show, Brian and his band join hands in a circle. It's a moment for reflection, for encouragement, for bonding.

Darian told Sir Paul they were going to 'Circle Up,' and as Darian recalls, 'Paul said, "I don't want to get in your way." And I said, "No. You should join us."'

Brian: 'And he goes, "Okay." And the whole time he's holding my hand, just moving my hand up and down. I think he wanted to let me know that he liked me, 'cause he kept going like this to my hand. We were holding hands, and everybody else was feeling his hand was going like this. So, he was proud to be with me. He was happy to be with me.'

Nelson Bragg: 'The whole thing was just so surreal. Most of us are saying things like, having Paul and Brian together in the circle, [. . .] what a big deal that is.'

Brian: 'I was so thrilled that he was right next to me.'

Taylor Mills: 'Paul just adores him, loves him. And Brian digs him too.'

Darian: 'He was holding Brian's hand . . . Just to have him there, two of the greatest songwriters of all time.'

Paul Von Mertens: 'He happily joined the circle before the show, and I don't even remember what he said, but he said something encouraging and positive about it. I know it meant a lot to Brian, too, that he was there.'

Nelson: 'And then when it comes to Paul. He goes, "Dear Lord," and all of a sudden, everyone's eyes closed. All of a sudden, we're in prayer mode.'

Paul Von Mertens: 'He got right in there and asked God to help us do what needed to be done. And it's just so cool that he gets the music, and that he's into it. That he really digs it. Coming from him, that's a supreme compliment.'

Nelson: 'It was just incredible. I'm there praying with Paul McCartney.'

Taylor: 'It felt like I was floating a foot off the ground. There are no words for how excited we all were that he was there, in our pre-show circle. Brian was excited that he was there with us supporting him.'

Scott: 'An out of body experience. Couldn't tell you what was said or what was going on, other than "There's a Beatle in my circle."'

Nelson: Then, the show happened. And we're seeing him watch us. Now we've done it three times already. So nerves are not as bad. We're okay. I can enjoy the fact that I'm playing a show for [Sir] Paul McCartney and [Sir] George Martin. I can enjoy that, get into that. I know the music well enough so I can let that emotion come into me. It was incredible. It was so thrilling!'

Ky Cabot: 'Being able to look out in the audience and see Paul

McCartney on his feet, just absolutely over the moon at what he was witnessing really drove home what a monumental achievement this was.'

Scott: 'He was so happy to see it come to life, and to see Brian be going from strength to strength like he did. Paul, more than just about anybody, really respects Brian's composing abilities . . . I think Brian's music moves Paul on levels more than just about anybody. And so, the support from him is always lovely to see, so cool to be around.'

After the show, Sir Paul had a surprise for everybody.

Darian: 'The Stockholm Strings 'n' Horns were always the first to exit the stage, and I would follow directly after them. So, I was behind the line of Swedes exiting the side of the stage, and there was something blocking the way. And it was sort of dark, this little corridor, and I just remember seeing each one of them, because they were still in the light, each one of them walking off and then turning their head and going (*gasps*) and shaking a hand. And one by one they did that. It was like, "What's going on?" Until I got there myself, and it was Paul. He waited there to shake everyone's hands as they left the stage, and it was beautiful. It was a nice, nice moment. And then of course, as I get backstage, every one of the Swedes is on their cell phones, calling their parents. Saying something in Swedish, "Paul McCartney!" It was so adorable.'

Nelson Bragg: 'It was astonishing. It was like this beautiful, sentimental, lovely, sweet thing that he did for us. I was the last . . . so I got to see it happen seventeen times before me, and then I was the eighteenth. My left hand went on his shoulder; my right hand gripped his hand. I looked at him. He said, "Great job. Congratulations on your incredible night. You'll never forget this. Take it from me. You'll never forget this." And I said, "I'm never gonna forget all of this. Thank you. Thank you so much for being so generous with your time." . . . That was my time with Paul McCartney.'

Taylor: 'I remember I was the only one to get a kiss on the cheek and I thought, "I'm not going to wash that off for a bit."'

Paul Von Mertens: 'I'm not often starstruck, but he just seemed to be on another plane to me, on another level. And he was very kind to Brian, and to everybody, really. He was open and present. Many people are jockeying for his attention. And he's used to being the centre of attention. And he's very graceful about it. And he doesn't shy away from the crowd.

DREAMS DO COME TRUE

But there's also a certain amount of space that is just understood. And I felt extremely grateful and happy that he was there.'

Nelson: 'One of the most thrilling nights of my life. I called my twin sister from a pay phone from the Marriott County Hall, and said, "I just met Paul McCartney! I just hung out with him." It was so exciting. I had to call [her], regardless of what time it was. It was incredible. And you'll hear this from everybody else you talk to, that that was one of the most thrilling moments of my life, that he was there and looking at us and talking to us and telling you how excited he was and congratulations on getting this done.'

Paul had come back at intermission to offer encouragement before SMiLE, and he and Brian spoke again, after the show.

Brian: 'Paul was so blown out by SMiLE, he came backstage after SMiLE was done. He told me he had tears in his eyes half the time, that he was crying, he was sighing, he was dying for the music. He loved it more than anything he's ever heard in his life.'

After SMiLE was finished, he was on his feet for the extended standing ovation. With our backstage camera rolling, he was most enthusiastic when I asked for a post-show comment.

Sir Paul McCartney: 'Brian Wilson. SMiLE: Excellent! The man is my hero. I love him. I weep when I hear his band, I hear him sing. I love him. Post-show comment! YES! Good-bye!'

In fact, Sir Paul was so impressed by what he saw and heard, he had his band come to see the next concert. Right after they had seen it, our camera caught up with two of Sir Paul's band members.

Abe Laboriel Jr., *drummer:* 'Absolute religious experience. It was truly like going to church and seeing the history of music all condensed into one. And the reason why we play. It was just overwhelming. It truly was. I'm kind of speechless and excited. After seeing that music, that had been hidden for so long, to see it finally in the light. To see the influence that it's had. Amazing. It's going to be really exciting to see what happens with this.'

Brian Ray, *lead guitar:* 'My mind is officially blown. One more time, Brian Wilson just took my heart out. He has a way of reaching inside you and showing you your heart. And then putting it back in and going, "It's okay."'

Glenn Max remembers that UK musicians, including 'Gruff Rhys

(Super Furry Animals), Jason Spaceman (Spiritualized), Kevin Shields (My Bloody Valentine), [and] Richard James (Aphex Twin) came to the shows . . . artists who were part of the indie label revolution in the UK and the US. Those artists were coming more than once. Elvis Costello was there. Richard Wright. Jeff Beck.'

Glenn has one final, most significant recollection of this time.

Glenn: 'The last night of SMiLE . . . I took the time to go in [to Brian's dressing room] when I knew Brian would be alone to chat with him and I said, "Brian, you know it's been amazing to watch you, from the first time I met you, when you were so nervous and fragile, to this person I see at the end of SMiLE, who is confident and makes jokes on stage and looks like he's pretty happy to be up there with his band doing this. This is almost not the same person I first met when you first came to the Royal Festival Hall." And in the most lucid way he said, "This has been the most cathartic experience of my life. To be able to do this has just been incredible for me."

'I'm just blown away and almost to tears. And I said, "That I could have had anything to do with your catharsis is just the greatest thing in my life."

'And we chatted. We did a little small talk after that, and as I left the room, he said, "I love your ass," in that sort of way, like I hear him speak to some of his old buddies. When he gets around his old friends, he's a pretty relaxed guy. He's that guy who goes out for a steak and drives his Cadillac. In his private life there's a more relaxed Brian who jokes around and stuff, but you don't see that too [often].

'But by the end he was more comfortable in his skin than any one of us, I think, would have ever imagined . . . a beautiful, beautiful thing . . . a whole bunch of other people who knew Brian. They could all see what was happening.'

Right after the final show in London, I had a chance to talk with Darian.

Darian: 'I'm stunned at the reaction. This is beyond all of our expectations. I'm so happy for Brian and Van Dyke. Brian has really embraced this, come out of his shell.' For a moment, Darian gets choked up. 'I'm speechless. It's quite touching.'

Looking back on the week, Darian recalls that after the first show, 'Brian is like, "The sky hasn't fallen; the world is still here. It hasn't ended. And I made it through." . . . Van Dyke was weeping and kissing all of our faces. But the second night, *that* was the night. That ovation went on and on and on. And the look on Brian's face. I've seen it once before when Ronnie Spector was singing in his ear. He knows it's good for him, but he can't believe it's happening. He just had that look. The look in his eyes. I can almost see the demons just floating away. Since then, it's just been, "Yeah, this is some cool stuff. Kinda wacky." He's digging it, and we're just right there with him. The world should be hearing this. It's beautiful and it's a shame that it's been hidden for thirty-seven years. If [London's] reaction is any indication, the time is now.'

During the next-to-last concert in London, Brian said, 'I'm not scared.'

Darian: 'You know what that's all about. He has been scared. And then tonight, he said, "I'm smiling. I'm *really* smiling."'

'During the past five years,' Darian explains, 'we've seen him force a smile because he knows he should be smiling.' But, as Darian enthuses, 'he was smiling because he really felt like smiling. Then, he was celebrating that. The fact he felt like smiling. And that was really nice . . . Every single night has been a highlight, some sort of revelation. It's a real blessing and an honour to be playing this music. It's beautiful. And I'm happy. I'm really happy.'

Just after I spoke with Darian, I was interviewed.

David Leaf: 'The whole week here was an unreal dream come true. Never could have imagined that it would happen, and now that it's happening, I'm just so happy for Brian, so happy for people who love music. I'm happy for myself, too. Long time I've been waiting for this music to escape into the world. And Brian gave it to the world this week, brought a lot of joy to others, and he's really made himself happy with the music.'

How did he change from the first night to the last?

David: 'The first night he was wondering how people would receive it. By the second night, he knew that what he was doing was right. When he took the ovation on the second night, it really took him back to when he made this music, and you could see almost the ghosts leaving, the demons flying away. And suddenly, he was Brian Wilson, a great artist no longer haunted by the failed, incompletion of *SMiLE*, but Brian Wilson, a great artist triumphing with the presentation of *SMiLE* to the world.'

Talk about the night when Paul McCartney came?

David: 'When Brian and [Sir] Paul get together, the only two people in the world who have done the same things, who know how hard it is to do what they do ... the respect and love they have for each other is enormous. Whenever Brian is in Paul's presence, he stands a little straighter, he sings [and] performs a little better because he feels the love from Paul, and he wants to return it the way he knows best which is in the music. Paul is like if you were in the hospital with pneumonia and they give you an IV drip of penicillin, you would get better. And when Paul's around Brian, Brian gets better.'

How good is this band?

David: 'They are the best band in the world. They are multi-talented instrumentalists, and nobody other than them knows how hard it is to sing these complex harmonies at the same time they're playing all those instruments.

'They're great people. They love Brian. They love the music. They did this with integrity, love and feeling and passion. And they brought it to life for the world. And best of all, they brought it to life for Brian.'

★   ★   ★   ★

My first post-London interview with Brian began with a perfect example of his sense of humour.

Brian: 'I'll give you twenty minutes of my time. My time is precious. I charge $200,000 a minute.'

David: 'Let me write you a check. Do you take cash? $200,000 a minute?'

Brian: 'No, I was just kidding. I'm just joking around.'

David: 'When the last [London] shows were over, do you remember how you felt?'

Brian: 'I knew that we had it down pat. I knew that we had our little regime down pat. So, I was obviously relieved as we took off in the bus. I look back upon the whole show as, "That's the past. We got that." Now we go on to the future.'

David: 'Tell me about the tour of England. You really had a good time.'

Brian: 'Every single night it got, we got better and better, until the very last night which was way beyond life. It was, like, bigger than life experience.'

David: 'What about it got better?'

DREAMS DO COME TRUE

Brian: 'The way we felt about each other playing together, the way we related to each other, the way we felt about the audiences, our love for the work of SMiLE, our appreciation for Van Dyke's lyrics, and his and my music. All that took into effect.'

David: 'Talk to me about the music of SMiLE. How do you feel about where SMiLE stands in what you've done?'

Brian: 'Except for 'Good Vibrations' and 'California Girls,' which, of course, were our two great records, SMiLE kicked butt on anything we'd ever tried. It was far and away the greatest piece of music that we've ever written. Even 'California Girls' [doesn't] hold a candle to SMiLE.'

David: 'Talk about Pet Sounds versus SMiLE?'

Brian: 'People loved Pet Sounds. But if you were to put it on a scale to one to ten, I'd give Pet Sounds a four and SMiLE a ten. That's how much I'd rate it.' [In subsequent interviews, he would give Pet Sounds a seven.]

David: 'What is it about SMiLE that you think outrates Pet Sounds?'

Brian: 'There's more to it. There's more exploration into a completely different music bag. More exploring, more adventurous, more rock opera-ish . . . it's a rock opera.'

David: 'Can you compare the SMiLE from 1967 to the SMiLE we heard on stage in 2004?'

Brian: 'No, because it was hardly ever finished. It was in an unfinished work of art, which we knew. We had something; but we junked it. All these interviews about, "What about the SMiLE tapes, Brian? What do you want to do with the SMiLE tapes?" We junked it. That was the whole thing, until Van Dyke and Darian came over. We started working on it. We finished up all the songs, we sequenced them all together, which was a plus for us.'

David: 'Tell me how you feel now that the tour is over.'

Brian: 'If you want to believe this or not, I'm so sorry that the tour is over. The last week of the tour was so good. It was magic. The audiences were magic. SMiLE was magic. The guys all played their parts really well, and I hated to see it come to an end. I really do – the first time in my history of my whole career that I've ever wanted to go right back on the road again. Never ever have I ever wanted to do that.'

David: 'What is it about playing SMiLE that's getting to you?'

Brian: 'Well, Van Dyke and I have made some music that was fairly ahead of its time, and it was ahead of its time, and it will continue to be ahead of its time. I call it a rock opera. I don't know if I'm right or not. Am I right? I call it a rock opera.'

David: 'What are you feeling when you're playing it?'

Brian: 'I'm feeling proud. I'm feeling emotional. I'm feeling creative. I'm feeling thankful that I can be there to do it. Stuff like that.'

David: 'What are you getting from the audience?'

Brian: 'We're getting support, appreciation, and love from the audience, mostly love, and then support and appreciation.'

David: 'How do you feel now that you've finished it?'

Brian: 'Obviously, David, proud, proud of course, and a little bit scared because it's, like, heavy duty stuff, you know?'

David: 'Do you really think *SMiLE* is that much better than *Pet Sounds?*'

Brian: 'Absolutely. Yeah, I think it's *way better* than *Pet Sounds*. *Pet Sounds* doesn't hold a candle to it.'

David: 'What are your favourite songs in *SMiLE*?'

Brian: 'My favourite songs in *SMiLE*, "Waving From The Ocean Liners" ['Roll Plymouth Rock'], 'Wonderful,' 'Cabin Essence,' 'Wind Chimes' – those are favourites.'

David: 'Did you ever imagine you'd be on stage hearing the music?'

Brian: 'How could I have, David? How could I have imagined? How could I have imagined? I couldn't.'

David: 'When you heard it recreated, what were you thinking?'

Brian: 'I don't know. I can't answer that question.'

David: 'You were really into it.'

Brian: 'I was going overboard almost. I was, like, way out of my bounds. I'm thinking, "Oh, my God. What is this? What is this 'Fire' tape?" It brought back a lot of memories.'

David: 'How did you feel when you looked up and saw that the string and horn players had fire helmets on?'

Brian: 'I was laughing my head off. I started laughing. I said, "Oh, my God, that's what we did in the sixties. They did a repeat of the sixties in 2004."'

David: 'Did that make you laugh when they started passing out vegetables?'

Brian: 'It sure did. It sure made me laugh.'

David: 'Talk about the joy you feel.'

DREAMS DO COME TRUE

Brian: 'I'm so proud of SMiLE. I'm so happy I can cry. And I've never been more happy with a concert idea than I was with SMiLE. So obviously I'm gonna be very, almost choked up over it.'

David: 'Can you put into words what it means to you to have finished this and have people love it?'

Brian: 'I don't know if they love it, I don't know if people love, but they sure like it. I mean, love, you mean, really love it? Probably so, yeah, probably so.'

David: 'How does it make you feel? SMiLE is always brought up in interviews.'

Brian: 'Yeah, but I had no idea what it was gonna turn out to be later on when Van Dyke and Darian and I got together. We created the whole SMiLE thing. It was all sequenced together. Believe it or not, it sounds like one big rock opera. It really does.'

David: 'You're going to record SMiLE.'

Brian: 'We're gonna get together and rehearse about the 12th of April. We're gonna rehearse for two or three days at a rehearsal hall. Then, we're gonna go into the studio and record it one piece at a time, one movement at a time. It's gonna take us three or four days to get it. I think.'

David: 'How do you think the record will be different from the live experience?'

Brian: 'I think it's not gonna be any better. I don't think it'll be any better. It'll just be on tape, that's all. It won't be any different. 'Cause we [already] perform it as good as it can be performed.'

David: 'Is it [going to be] a challenge getting it on tape?'

Brian: 'It's gonna be an exercise that we have to do to get it on tape. I feel this way. If we can go in there and do half as good as we did on stage, we're miles ahead. We're miles ahead.'

David: 'Are you excited about getting back on tour?'

Brian: 'Absolutely. I can't wait. I can't wait to [do] the second tour, 'cause I think it's gonna be an even better with SMiLE II.'

David: 'Do you think you'll change it?'

Brian: 'Oh, no. No. Not one note. Not one word. We're not gonna change it.'

David: 'You were writing a song about how you felt coming off the tour?'

Brian: 'I'm trying to, yeah. I'm trying to get a song written.'
David: 'Do you have anything you can play at this point?'
Brian: 'No, nothing.'
David: 'What's the feeling that you're trying to get into the music?'
Brian: 'I'm trying to get a sentimental thing off my chest.'
David: 'What emotions do you want to express?'
Brian: 'The idea that I'm proud that we could've done that.'
David: 'Do you have a melody?'
Brian: 'No. No.'
David: 'Are you going through *SMiLE* withdrawal?'
Brian: 'A little bit, yeah.'
David: 'How are you gonna deal with your *SMiLE* withdrawal?'
Brian: 'Gonna take it one day at a time, and it'll slowly fade away.'
David: 'Are you gonna sit at the piano and play the *SMiLE* songs?'
Brian: 'Yeah.'
David: 'Which one do you think you'll play?'
Brian: 'Wonderful.'
David: 'This was a dream come true, wasn't it?'
Brian: 'It's the great *SMiLE* dream. It came true. (*Laughs*) It's a dream come true.'

Watching the interview were Brian and Melinda's two oldest daughters, Daria (age 7) and Delanie (age 6). What can't be completely communicated in a book is how much fun the girls and Brian had during the interview. He played songs for them to dance to ('Heroes And Villains' and 'Vega-Tables'). And they shyly answered my questions about how they liked *SMiLE*, their favourite vegetables, and how they felt bringing flowers up on stage the night of the world premiere. A very sweet moment.

I WAS THERE: MY FELLOW 'BRIANISTAS' LOOK BACK

SCOTT BENNETT: 'IT WAS AN ABSOLUTE, ONCE-IN-A-LIFETIME LIVE EXPERIENCE. And if you were there – and this is why it's important you talk to some of the fans because I was on stage, and it was magical, of course, in a different way for me. But grown men were crying. It was transformative. And it was really, obviously, we've told it in *Beautiful Dreamer*, but more than the music, it was just this triumph of the human spirit, this triumph of art. It should be an inspiration to anybody who's afraid to throw down the gauntlet in the name of what they want to do artistically. Maybe you've got to wait thirty-seven years to do it, but hopefully not. And hopefully you don't have roadblocks along the way. But it was a really beautiful, beautiful moment.'

How beautiful? Let's hear from those who were there.

It may have been the late, great Bob Hanes who came up with the phrase that we were 'Brianistas.' Bob was something of a *SMiLE* and Brian Wilson guru.

Being at the Royal Festival Hall for the first shows in 2004 was indeed like a pilgrimage. We'd dreamed about this moment. But what would it be? What could it be? We were all there to see if *SMiLE* was just a myth, more chimera than masterpiece, to find out if our passion for *SMiLE* was well-placed. Here are a few memories from fans who were at the world premiere week in London . . . from a 2024 perspective.

(*Author's Note:* To include as many as possible, these have been edited.)

Paul Trimble: 'I'll never forget the nervous anticipation during the interval that night in the Royal Festival Hall as we prepared to witness *SMiLE* for the first time. The quiet tension built as everyone filed in to take their seats again, silent nods were exchanged as friends moved past and as the lights went down it was almost possible to feel the good vibes being directed *towards* the stage.

'The angelic harmonies of 'Our Prayer' filled the auditorium and I tried to scribble notes while still savouring the music. Murmurs went around the hall as familiar segments of music blended into each other, and unheard lyrics were added as the music flowed – it was mesmerizing, transcendent. The music faded to a close as tears ran openly – we had witnessed something very, very special. Brian had triumphed and history had been made, a moment in time. The sword had been pulled from the stone.'

Paul Jones: 'The music made during the *SMiLE* era touches me more deeply than anything I've ever heard. It feels as though Brian captured my DNA and recorded it on tape. I was lucky enough to be at the Royal Festival Hall for the premiere of *BWPS* (and in fact I attended all the London shows, wanting to soak up every moment). I could not believe what I was seeing and hearing. Never in my wildest dreams did I ever believe that I would be a few feet away from Brian Wilson as he sang, "Over and over the crow cries, uncover the cornfields." When Van Dyke appeared on stage at the end of the show, and Brian instinctively pulled him in for a bear hug, the tears flowed. And when I got home, I tried to tell my family what I had just experienced, but I was still so stunned that I could barely speak. I will never forget that night.'

Joel Dunster: 'The thought it would be premiered at a live performance on my doorstep in London was simply beyond my wildest dreams . . . this was like finding El Dorado! I was lucky enough to be at every one of those February shows at the Royal Festival Hall. Twenty years on feels like yesterday as I recall my intense excitement and expectation on that opening night. Yet there was also a slight nervousness. Would *SMiLE* live up to the myth? Might it all prove too much for Brian? Clearly not . . . Wow, those triumphant concerts were simply addictive!'

John Porteous: 'Hearing *SMiLE* played live night after night – yes, I went to most UK shows – it all made sense . . . Backstage at the London premiere read like a who's who of Brian Wilson fan, friends, and family . . . From those first days of snippets to the finished show I spent a fortune . . . as so many did. Do I regret it? Of course not . . . it's the masterpiece that is called *SMiLE*.'

I WAS THERE: MY FELLOW 'BRIANISTAS' LOOK BACK

Pat Panuska (AKA Bluebird): 'I saw SMiLE every night in London, Row Three, Stage Right. After every show there was the usual backstage party in the venue lounge with fans and band members. Van Dyke Parks was at the parties and one night Scott Bennett played the piano and Van Dyke and I danced, including a waltz. During the opening night party in London, Scott grabbed my bag and hand and walked me down the hall telling me that a friend was asking to see me. He took my hand and knocked on the door. Jeffrey Foskett opened the door and thanked Scott. A familiar voice called me by my name and offered me a seat on the arm of his oversized chair. It was Brian Wilson! He asked me if I thought the show was a hit, which it was. He asked me why I was crying a few times so I told him I was amazed by what l was hearing. Did I think other people felt the same way? He asked me a few more questions and then what he could do to make SMiLE better! I told him to get his buns into a studio and record it. He laughed and hugged me, saying they have a good studio booked.'

Tom Bagdonas: 'My brother John and I followed the SMiLE saga through the pages of *Crawdaddy* magazine . . .

'When Brian's SMiLE performances at Royal Festival Hall were announced John and I knew where we would be on February 20th . . . Three weeks before the show my brother was diagnosed with a blood cancer called multiple myeloma. His doctors at Sloan Kettering wanted to start treatment immediately but John told them it will have to wait until he returned from London.

'John felt a bit weak but his excitement for the concert put his ills in the rearview mirror. After a thirty-seven-year wait, we were able to experience together the greatest concert performance of our lifetime . . . John started his treatments at Sloan and responded so positively that he survived his cancer for another sixteen years . . . I am comforted by thousands of memories of how we shared our musical passion together.'

Mike Grant: 'February 20, 2004, "a Birthday to remember."

'At this point, as a Beach Boys/Brian Wilson Fan for forty years, I was filled with excitement with the anticipation of something very special happening on this day. The first ever performance of the legendary SMiLE Album. Would it work "Live"? Would I be disappointed? Answers: Yes and No!

'The concert was a triumph for Brian Wilson and his fantastic band, hearing those opening lines in 'Do You Like Worms' ('Roll Plymouth Rock') for the first time, I was blown away, "Waving from the ocean liners" and "Once upon the Sandwich Isles." The three separate sections worked brilliantly. Closing with 'Good Vibrations' with original lyrics was a nice surprise and fitting.

'A word of praise to Darian Sahanaja for his great involvement.

'I went home a very happy man following my best ever Birthday Present!'

Susan Lang: 'At the intermission, the excitement built, and the trepidation turned to fear. What if? What if??? What if he couldn't – wouldn't – do it? What if he took the stage and then walked right off again, ultimately unable to perform what he'd been practicing for months . . . what had haunted him for years? What if he just couldn't? But he did, and it was glorious and soul-stirring. The set whizzed by; like everyone else, I just sat there slack-jawed.

'And then it was over. Ten-minute standing ovation that felt much longer. Brian had conquered his biggest fear, and I had been there to see it.

'It's still hard to believe.'

Harvey Williams: 'To describe the 2004 Brian Wilson *SMiLE* shows at the Royal Festival Hall as mere "rock 'n' roll gigs" does them quite a disservice . . . The shows were without question the most uplifting, life-affirming concerts I've ever seen. To watch a man perform this beautiful, haunting music, accompanied by the most sympathetic backing musicians, while also facing and conquering his demons – all in front of a live audience! – was indeed a dream come true.'

Wayne Johnson: 'Usually when something is overhyped for years and years, it's a let-down. This was the opposite. He exceeded all our expectations. It was certainly a magical moment.'

Michael Whitewood: 'The *SMiLE* shows weren't gigs in the traditional sense – they were more like attending a Sufi ceremony or an esoteric Tibetan Buddhist ritual that opened a gateway to another realm for two hours. The *BWPS* concerts at the RHF were the most profoundly spiritual experiences of my life and I'm so glad I got to experience the shows with my late father, Clive Patrick Whitewood, who introduced me to the music of Brian and Beach Boys when he took me to the UK premiere of *An American Band* at London's Dominion Theatre back in 1985.

I WAS THERE: MY FELLOW 'BRIANISTAS' LOOK BACK

'My Dad lost his long and courageous battle against cancer in 2021. We talked about The Beach Boys' music every day and I miss talking with him.

'God bless you, Dad. Thank you Brian and VDP. And to Darian – there are legions of fans across the planet who will forever be in your debt.'

Mandy Miles: 'SMiLE. Without a doubt the absolutely perfect title for this masterpiece. After *Pet Sounds*, I never thought I'd ever hear anything to top it . . . I was full of excitement and expectation as the day drew near . . .

'From that very first note, something magical happened, this explosion of warmth reached out into the auditorium, embracing us all, the angelic sounds filled our hearts with joy. I was taking in every note, word, image I could, I didn't want to forget a thing, it was a breath of life for me. It took away any stress and strains I had been carrying, everyone was *Smiling*, some were crying. Brian was really reaching out and touching our hearts. Never had I felt so much from music and probably never will again.'

John Manning: 'I sensed a collective awareness that, despite the preparation, anticipation, publicity and excitement, it might not happen . . . That it happened at all, that it was an incredible success, still seems as miraculous as the music itself proved to be.'

Dorian Mead: 'I was as nervous as hell before taking my seat in the RFH auditorium on that opening night of the tour. Trepidation as to how *SMiLE* would translate into a live production . . . but the band smashed it, Brian could feel the emotional arms of the audience holding him through the journey, and when the closing chords came, I had tears on my cheeks.

'As one, we all stood and clapped and cheered our hearts out.

'That mythical album that has caused so much angst and torment was finally delivered and all the stronger for the lengthy gestation and now laid down with the technology that Brian so needed in the sixties.

'*SMiLE*. I still do, every time I listen to that masterpiece.'

Daniel McGeever: 'I find it impossible to summarise my feelings about the music and the event. I separate the RFH *SMiLE* shows from all other gigs and musical events I've ever witnessed. It was so much more than a "gig." It felt like the unveiling of one of the world's greatest musical mysteries. Even hours before the concert I just had to go to the venue, to be there in the freezing cold, to believe it was actually true – it was happening. I was intensely nervous – for Brian and also in other ways I cannot explain.

'To hear this now-completed work, all the bits I knew so well intertwined with all the new links and sections and lyrics, was like a forty-five-minute thrill ride. I've never felt anything like it or had my breath taken away so many times. And I've never witnessed an ovation like it either.

'It was and remains a triumph of the human spirit and an unparalleled achievement in pop music.'

Andy O'Brien: 'The way it was sequenced gave an uplifting counter to every melancholy introspection . . . It might sound precious, but SMiLE had an effect on my personality. I wanted the intense joy of that experience to last forever. Being mean, losing my temper and stuff like that felt like I was harshing my own SMiLE buzz. I think I'm a bit nicer since that night.'

Jacqui Dove and Brian Barry: 'We both turned up at London's Royal Festival Hall on that cold February night, worrying about how the night would actually go . . . Second half started, the cold from outside was replaced with wonderful 'Our Prayer's chills up our spines. The rest of SMiLE followed, with magical stardust falling around our ears. An ovation like no other followed. With SMiLE ringing in our ears, and joyful tears on our faces, we left the venue, with love that's still there twenty years later. How lucky we both were. Yes, Brian Wilson had made it happen.'

James Green: 'I live in upstate New York and went to London with friends to see the second night's performance of BWPS. As I was leaving a reporter from National Public Radio asked what I thought of the concert. My friend looked at me, turned to the reporter and said, "He's speechless right now," something I am not typically accused of.'

Jacopo Benci: 'That night remains the most extraordinary concert I've ever experienced. I can only compare it to Scriabin's 'Prometheus, the Poem of Fire,' which took a century to be performed with the composer's coloured light score at Yale University in 2010. Yet, that's an event I've only seen on YouTube. Witnessing SMiLE live was an unparalleled privilege, truly a highlight in my life.'

Patrick Humphries: 'Sonically stunning, and frankly just to be in the same room was enough . . . I was there the night Brian Wilson performed SMiLE . . .'

I WAS THERE: MY FELLOW 'BRIANISTAS' LOOK BACK

Vincenzo Lembo: 'My brother Peter and I were lucky to attend every one of Brian Wilson's *SMILE* concerts at the Royal Festival Hall in London in 2004 . . . Great memories.'

Angela Jones: 'Nothing prepared me for the complete album. It was bewildering in its complexity and in its paradoxical simplicity. It was like a multi-dimensional jigsaw puzzle of sound. The audience was rapt. The applause went on for about ten minutes. I remember seeing men and women crying. Then "Aloha nui means goodbye" and it segued into 'Good Vibrations' and the audience went wild. After the show was over, we had to talk and share it. Total strangers from different continents.'

Liz Jones: 'The last night of the run of shows was the most precious moment of my life. Each movement a ballet. Probyn put down the French horn during 'Surf's Up' and as it swung, moved on to the next instrument. Around me were friends from all walks of life, all parts of the world, all bound by our love of the music, all feeling the same magic. Watching Brian in his spotlight halo now confident and happy – now, the success was assured, all the wishes over all the years brought to the pinnacle.'

Val Johnson-Howe: 'Taking our seats for that very first night in the Royal Festival Hall, faces beaming, waving to so many others . . . Concern *almost* outweighed love, but Brian, the Band, and the joy that night brought, solidly remain in our hearts, rest of our lives.'

John Etherington: '*SMiLE* was one of the greatest experiences of my life. I cautiously bought one £50 ticket, then additional tickets for twelve more shows. When questioned by a reporter as to what I thought of *SMiLE*, I said, "It's a miracle in one word!" . . . The universe itself seemed to be aligned with *SMiLE*, since on the opening night, a Crescent Moon (symbolizing new beginnings) appeared in the heavens close to Venus (the planet of *SMiLE*s), visibly forming a *SMiLE* in the sky. I have many treasured memories of *SMiLE*.'

David Slater: 'I'd booked tickets for my wife and kids for later in the week and at the last minute scored a ticket for the first night of *SMiLE*. End seat on the back row of the balcony but for me - the best seat in the house . . . My dream came true when I met Brian on the first night of *SMiLE*.'

Malcolm C. Searles: 'To say it was magnificent would not do it justice. Moving, beautiful, awe-inspiring, jaw-dropping – just some of the words that spring to mind, but even they cannot fully converse what this work means to so many.'

Markus Aberg: '"It was twenty years ago today . . ." I was there and thought it was amazing!'

Michael Fredrich: 'What I remember most vividly about the day of the premiere is that I met many people in real life who I only knew from the internet.'

Kim Lange, Denmark: 'In the first set Brian's voice was rather weak and he seemed nervous. Almost miraculously this changed completely when he presented *SMiLE*, and the show was a stunning triumph with Brian in full control . . . *SMiLE* is his masterwork.'

Franz Stradner (father): 'I came out of Royal Festival Hall, still stunned after attending *SMiLE*'s world premiere. I stepped down the stairway when a man held a microphone in my face. I later realized that this was David Leaf. He asked me where I came from. "I came from Austria," I answered. "Was it worth coming?" "Absolutely!"'

Franz's children, Dennis and Maria Stradner: 'Our generation-spanning fascination for Brian Wilson's music culminated in visiting the world premiere of *SMiLE* at the Royal Festival Hall on February 20, 2004. At that time, we became aware that we're witnessing a milestone not only for pop but for music in general. No matter whether you are a boomer, Gen X, Y, or Z, Brian Wilson's music is classical in the sense of its timeless beauty. Bach, Beethoven, Brahms, Brian!'

Lucy Hall: 'The biggest memory for me of the opening night of *SMiLE* was the change in Brian. I have a photo of Darian giving him a pep talk; the part Darian has played in all this cannot be underestimated. At the beginning, Brian looked terrified. By the end, you could visibly see the change in him: his posture, his face – everything about him oozed confidence. It felt as though all those years of doubt were swept away in just a few hours. I felt blessed to be there to witness it. It was truly a joy to behold!'

Justin Paton: 'Before: Curious. During: Very attentive and tickled. After: Inspired to get on with my own music and keen to listen back to my MiniDisc recording of the concert.'

Mark London: 'Having been there from the beginning – from Brian agreeing to do it, to designing (with Frank Holmes) the first public announcement to the world ("Brian Wilson presents SMiLE – Coming soon to a face near you!"), to rehearsals, creating the tour merchandise, and finally boarding the plane with Brian and Melinda – nothing could prepare me for the emotional impact of witnessing that opening night performance. It was, in the truest sense, a spiritual experience.'

Mark Linett: 'As you might imagine, my memories *of Brian Wilson Presents SMiLE* are somewhat unique. I recall attending the rehearsals in L.A. (and recording some) before we travelled to London for the recording of the premiere concerts at RFH. Sitting in the recording truck and witnessing Brian's triumph was a simply amazing moment, and the shows were so good that I ended up staying on after the two scheduled recording dates to capture the rest of the shows in London. Then a few months later I engineered the recording of *Brian Wilson Presents SMiLE* in Los Angeles, the live DVD and the shows at Carnegie Hall. It was quite a year, and hard to believe that it happened twenty years ago.

'To have helped Brian finally achieve his vision for *SMiLE* after so long is one of the proudest moments of my career, and I hope more people will get to hear and appreciate the music in the future.'

At the Royal Festival Hall shows, it was something of a ritual for Brian and Melinda's two daughters, Daria (right) and Delanie, to bring Brian flowers at the end of *Brian Wilson Presents SMiLE*. Here they are on February 27, 2004, the final night of World Premiere Week.

On *The Charlie Rose Show* in 2005, Brian said: 'It brought joy to me. I'm so proud... I was so nervous to do that doggone *SMiLE* show in London that I almost had to go to the bathroom and [throw up]... I have an eighteen-piece orchestra, including strings and horns, and I'm telling you, Charlie... They're the best. They are the best that I've ever worked with.'

THE CRITICS CHIME IN

HOW DID THE PEOPLE WHO GET PAID TO OFFER OPINIONS BASED, NOT ON emotion, but on critical analysis, react to the world premiere?

There were a couple of naysayers, but, except for those few 'spoil sports,' the reviews for the London premiere of *Brian Wilson Presents SMiLE* were overwhelmingly positive. Superlatives galore.

London's *The Independent* headline read: 'This is the most ambitious exploration of the boundaries of pop.'

Rolling Stone: 'Beach Boy unveils a lost masterpiece.'

The *Telegraph* called it 'A tangled, glorious symphony.'

Richard Williams' five-star review in *The Guardian* began: 'So how good, finally, is *SMiLE*, the great lost song cycle that Brian Wilson kept the world waiting 37 years to hear? The only possible answer, after Friday night's world premiere in London, is that it is better than anyone dared hope. Multiple spontaneous ovations were the reward for the former Beach Boy and his musicians, whose pristine performance breathed life into a 45-minute work previously known only through various shattered and dispersed fragments . . . Even the familiar sections – including 'Heroes And Villains,' 'Surf's Up' and 'Cabin Essence' – sounded utterly refreshed.

"Our Prayer' provided a lustrous a cappella prelude, but it was the astonishing variety of instrumental texture that constantly took the ear. Banjos, calliopes, Swanee whistles, tack pianos, fruity trombones, a cackling trumpet and a Polynesian ukulele made it seem like the grandest of American symphonies, with Wilson the natural heir to Charles Ives.'

★ ★ ★ ★

The London correspondent for *Billboard.com*, the music industry's bible, described the 'intricate, challenging and yet warmly familiar, full of tempo

THE CRITICS CHIME IN

shifts, snippets of vintage romantic melodies and banks of harmonies and instrumentation that rolled and roared as unpredictably as a mighty wave.'

Giving it five stars, the *Financial Times* headlined, '"Teenage Symphony to God" comes to life . . . Full "*SMiLE*" on his lips at last.'

The Australian reported that 'the sell-out audience greeted the performance with tearful reverence and repeated standing ovations.'

BBC News Online: 'A triumphant Brian Wilson has performed his great "lost" masterpiece for the first time.'

CNN.com: 'It brought the house down.'

The Press Association reported that 'grown men wept.'

In his 'first night' review, Keith Shadwick found it to be 'an overwhelming performance . . . a huge panorama that can only be compared to Bach in the way the intricacies interwove in wondrous counterpoint, spinning a web that embraced an entire vision.'

In *The Observer*, the article began, 'It was the Holy Grail of rock music . . . the scribbled notes of this reviewer contains umpteen exclamation points . . . *SMiLE* was revealed a majestic work, full of warmth and playfulness.'

London's *Sunday Express* headline ended with, 'SMILE BRIAN, WE ALL LOVE IT.'

Joe Muggs in *The Daily Telegraph*: 'The music was truly electric, and the music echoed everything from Philip Glass to Kurt Weill to Chuck Berry . . . Leonard Bernstein said Brian Wilson was one of the greatest composers of the 20th Century: he was not wrong.'

NME.com exclaimed, 'It's rare that you can honestly say you were present at a moment of genuine historic significance. And it's rarer still that the reality of these occasions measures up to the hype . . . *SMiLE* is sensational: about 45 minutes of the most head-spinningly odd and beautiful music you're ever likely to hear . . . it's an astonishing show, made even more so that this staggeringly ornate music was designed for the studio, not the concert hall.'

What was Brian's reaction to critics saying that this was one of the greatest concerts they'd ever seen?

Brian: 'I was proud, David. I was very proud, and I was very, very amazed that someone could say that about me. Very proud. Oh, [my mind] was totally blown, yeah . . . I couldn't believe it. They were pumping my ego. They were actually pumping my ego up!'

SMiLE

Randy Lewis was sent from Los Angeles to cover the event. His article was titled 'Mona Lisa *SMiLE*.' The sub headline was, 'Brian Wilson's lovely and long-anticipated work is a masterpiece of Americana.'

Looking back on it twenty years later, Lewis had this to say:

'I wrote a story for the *Los Angeles Times* and it appeared on the front page – not of the entertainment section, but of the main news section of the whole paper. It was placed in a spot called Column One, which is reserved for some of the most resonant stories, those with the most wide-ranging appeal or that have the broadest news and cultural impact. So, I was incredibly pleased that the editors recognized how important this work was and the significance of Brian coming back to it all these years later.

'We published it on February 20, 2004 – the same day Brian and the band were to give the world premiere performance at the Royal Festival Hall in London.

'I had also persuaded my editors to send me over to cover that extraordinary performance, taking note of a rather fascinatingly diverse audience: a lot of them were grey- and silver-haired patrons. A lot of the others were younger and looked like they were ready to see My Bloody Valentine or one of the other *au courant* pop acts that would play the Meltdown Festival in London.

'I wandered around before the performance asking audience members what their history with *SMiLE* was, their connection and affection for The Beach Boys and Brian Wilson. I'll never forget one guy who said – and he practically had tears in his eyes – he said, "I've waited *my whole life* for this."

'It was certainly one of the most emotional musical evenings I've ever experienced. The band and Brian delivered it beautifully, and you couldn't have asked for more. Brian sang some of the best he'd sung since he returned to the concert stage. I remember one David Leaf turning to me at the end of the performance and saying, "This is beyond all expectations."

'In an interview that fall with Van Dyke Parks, perhaps speaking as much for himself as for Brian, he said, "Something like this doesn't happen to many people often, where you do something like this in your youth, you give it up for dead and then it hits you again with all of its emotive force after a long period of time."

THE CRITICS CHIME IN

'I'll never forget those performances and *SMiLE* to this day remains to me a masterpiece of American music – not merely "pop music" or "rock music." I pull it out and listen to it regularly. Something that touched me so deeply about *SMiLE*, and that still does, was the vernacular that Van Dyke and Brian brought to it, this sort of exploration of all that came out of the American frontier and the Old West, a lot of it which was underpinning to the cultural revolution of the 1960s.'

In their June 2004 story of the '100 Greatest Gigs Ever', Q magazine put the *SMiLE* world premiere at number 5 just behind Coldplay, Oasis, Nirvana, and Radiohead at number one. The Beatles rooftop concert was number seven. L.A. music critic Chris Morris would put *SMiLE* at number one in his year-end 'Best of', writing, 'I listened to the former Beach Boys' opus countless times and saw it performed twice, and never tired of it… Melodious, complex, rousing stuff.' *Rolling Stone* would list the *Brian Wilson Presents SMiLE* album as number four in their 2004 year-end poll.

THE ALBUM & THE DOCUMENTARY

IN 1966-1967, BRIAN AND VAN DYKE HAD SPENT APPROXIMATELY NINE months writing and then recording *SMiLE*. By the time The Brian Wilson Band went into the studio in Spring, 2004, having rehearsed and played the music for several months, getting it on tape went amazingly fast.

Darian: 'There was conversation of whether we should go in and record it live, just basically capturing the performance and putting that out as a record. And I don't remember if it was in talking to Brian or if it was just a band discussion about being able to get certain parts to segue correctly, and certain sounds, and then it just turned into, "No. Let's do this in the studio and really try to capture the vibe of the movements, the message, the concepts of each movement."

'But we were prepared. We had played it live. The only difference is that we had to – well, I had to – lay out how we were going to record certain segments.'

Paul: 'We played in the studio the way we played live, but without singing, with very little overdubbing of instruments. It was just, 'Set up, play, hit record, and start playing.' I think we did the whole thing in a few days, maybe two or three days of doing the basic tracks, and a few instrumental overdubs, a very few.'

Probyn: 'Sunset Sound, famous place, had a particular reverb chamber that we were interested in using, that I heard had been untouched since the sixties. One of the trombone players – I think it was Staffan [Findin] – the part called for a sousaphone, and he didn't have one. I did. I couldn't play it very well, but I owned one. So I brought it down to the studio, and he played it.

THE ALBUM & THE DOCUMENTARY

'I remember that in the recording of *SMiLE*, we were in pretty tight quarters, especially at Sunset Sound. And there was one transition where a piano part needed to be played. I was physically closer to where that was – my set-up with the guitars and the horns and all. I was just a hop, skip, and a jump, ten feet away, less. So when the time came, I went over and briefly played a piano part on *SMiLE*, on the recording. It was one of the interstitial bits which we didn't do live; I'm not sure why it wasn't being done.

'On stage, we had more room than we did in that studio. There were baffles and microphone cords where they wouldn't have been in the live show. It was so complicated; there were so many moving parts. Even my own moving parts were hard to keep track of, let alone, "Okay, here's where the strings and horns take over. And then you have to do such-and-such. And remember your vocal part! And you swap with Nick on something." It was filled with things like that.'

Bob: 'It was great! It was so much fun. Because we knew all the stuff. And so now we're getting a chance to hear everything individually, and I had a chance to play ticky-tack bass on some of the stuff that needed [it]. I don't think Nicky was able to do it live because he was playing guitar. Nick was like, "No, you play it." So, I got a chance to do that.'

Nelson: 'We knew it cold. So instrumentally speaking, recording *SMiLE* was just mowing the lawn. Just do the parts, play the parts, lean on the notes. Give it as much gusto and emotion as you can. But we know this music really well. And we were at Sunset Sound. Recording it was probably easier than doing it live because we could do maybe an extra take if Brian let you. Brian was so engaged. and I was happy to see it.'

David Leaf: 'My main memory is how quickly it was done. And on a personal note, Brian invited me to come out into the studio during 'Barnyard,' and asked me to make an animal noise. My sheep sounded more like a goat, but I'm a ham, so I loved every moment of it.'

Probyn: 'I remember that it was a really joyous time. We loved working with the Stockholm Strings 'n' Horns.'

Malin-My Wall: 'Musically, the thing I remember most of the recording was the clarity, engagement, presence, vision, and determination of Brian in how he wanted everything to be . . . a side of him I didn't see on stage, where he seemed less comfortable in a way.'

Anna Dager: 'One of the greatest days for me was when we got to record 'Good Vibrations' since the cellos are really distinctive in that song, so me and Markus Sandlund had a really good time that day. And I remember Brian was in a good mood too that day and enjoyed being in the studio with us.'

Viktor Sand: 'When we recorded it, we scaled a lot of things down from the actual live act . . . I remember when we were in the studio with Paul and all of a sudden there was this voice in our ears talking to us, giving us instructions, and it took me a while to understand that it was actually Brian . . . he knew exactly what he wanted. I had hardly heard him speak, only sing on stage. And then it was like, "Okay, guys, we're gonna do it from Bar 38. We're gonna do this. Come on, let's do this. Let's do this now, and we're gonna go to Bar 42. Then I'm gonna stop, and I'm gonna hit the next section. You ready? Hey? Here we go! Come on, come on, guys, 1, 2 . . ."

'And sometimes, you're just fortunate to be in these very special situations . . . .and at that moment I realized that he was in his very special moment that was beautiful. That's something also that I carried to this day that, "Wow! I got to sit in that room and I got to hear *him* instruct us and me what to do, and it was just like he was the fish *in* the water."'

Nelson: 'It was thrilling. There was one time when me and Darian and Scott were all in there playing on the same marimba all at once, 'cause there were three marimba parts. There's a photo of Brian with us, with our mallets.'

Darian: 'We had already been performing a version of ['Heroes And Villains'] that incorporated the "Cantina" section, and so Brian wanted to go with that structure for the recording. It was more about how we were going to get in and out of it. This is where having all the pieces easily accessible on my laptop was extremely helpful. Modular assembly.'

Probyn: 'I was in a state of constant "mind-blowedness." There was not really "normal." The new normal was that I was in heaven. I was walking on clouds, going to those sessions. This was one of the greatest things that I had ever done in my life. First, we performed it; now we're recording it for posterity.'

Bob: 'We just had a ball. It was a piece of cake to record it because we all knew what we were doing. It was just like second nature. I remember Nelson came up with all these great little toys and parts that he assumed were on the original one. I'm sure they were. I think he did his research and got things right. And so, it was hearing all this stuff that you couldn't always hear on stage . . . And then, to hear vocal parts that I hadn't heard before.'

And maybe best of all, Bob recalls 'Brian being in charge . . . it was nice to see him in charge . . . nice to hear that.'

Probyn: 'I was bringing everything I had. This was an emotional high point for me, being part of this. Some of the songs . . . like 'Wonderful' is such an amazing song, it's hard to even perform that without some part of you floating in the ether.'

Nelson: 'And it was really this exciting thing where you see each individual part of everything [that] was captured [in *Beautiful Dreamer*]. Which is such a big deal to me because it really showed the people behind the music. It was really like, "This is what we're doing. This is how we're doing this."

'But then, when it came to the vocals, that took two weeks over at [*Brian Wilson Presents SMiLE* recording engineer] Mark Linett's place. That was different. That was harder because you're looking for a take where everyone's in tune at once. Because we were singing around the microphone . . . So we had to just all really stand on our toes and sing the best we can to get those magic takes.'

Probyn: 'I did worry a little bit about what the other Beach Boys would think. We, The Brian Wilson Band, are not The Beach Boys. We didn't earn our stripes the way they did, coming all those years from the early sixties with the band. And we don't sound like them either, vocally. We do okay, but it's not The Beach Boys. And I didn't want to ruffle Mike, Al, or Bruce's feathers. Of course, Carl and Dennis were gone by then.'

Jerry Weiss: 'Brian was nervous about the recording . . . On many levels. It was exhausting for him mentally. He couldn't move at the end of a recording session. He was just exhausted. With the talk-back and everything else, running out to the guys and showing them, "Do this. Do that. You're playing flat here. You're playing sharp here. Let's put that over here and put the strings over here."

'Certain tracks, he got wide-eyed and showed a great amount of interest in, more than others. And those were the difficult things for him in a lot of ways. He was glad when the 'Surf's Up' track was done . . . . And so, through it all, by the end of the last day and session he was spent. But he was thrilled. Elated!'

Nelson: 'And then the thing that was the hardest was Darian producing Brian's lead vocals. I don't even know how long that took. But that was a three-step tier of the creation of the recording, and of course, Darian, mixing it with Mark. I throw that in with producing Brian's vocals as the same sessions. Same room, same place happening, right after the other.'

Darian: 'And Brian was so into it. He was so into it. To this day, I don't recall him being more excited recording any of our albums. He just really wanted to be there to observe or be part of or produce any part, any section we were working on. He wanted to be there. It was great.'

Nelson: 'The thrill of hearing that recording for the first time. I'll never forget it. No one in this band will ever forget it. Darian got speakers shipped across the ocean. I think it was Holland. We were given a particular time, a little hotel room where we all can go. We're all gonna listen to the final mix of *Brian Wilson Presents SMiLE*. And Darian had the speakers set up to his laptop. And it was like this really big deal. And some of us cried at certain moments. Darian had done such an incredible, magnificent job. It was absolutely stunning.

'The main reason was because he captured the vibe sonically of each song as it was recorded by The Beach Boys themselves. So, while it was a modern recording that we were hearing, Darian made sure that what we were doing did not stray too far from the sonic spaces that The Beach Boys' [*SMiLE*] recordings had. Which means that the reverbs were all matched . . . each particular song and section. And that was just so insightful of him. So when you heard *Brian Wilson Presents SMiLE*, the first time, you were not alienated by it. It was close, that's what was so shocking. It was so close . . . And the second big deal was Brian's singing . . . I don't know how he did it. I don't know how Darian did it, but he produced Brian's vocals the best that Brian could possibly do. The best you can possibly do. That was really a great credit to Darian for the production of that record.'

Probyn: 'Most people I've known musically, known for years, they didn't think that *SMiLE* was necessarily a fait accompli. It was not necessarily guaranteed to have been done. But they said, "If there's anyone that deserves to be part of that team to do that music, it's you." People often cite just The Wondermints in general as a subset of The Brian Wilson Band as being the balloon that buoyed Brian up so that he was

THE ALBUM & THE DOCUMENTARY

able to do that. And I don't think we could take credit for that. I mean, for starters there is the rest of the actual full band, but it's mostly Brian's deal. Sure, we did our bit to support Brian. But most of that, I think, came from him, from inside. I can't take responsibility for that. I just was as supportive as I could be, and it was up to Brian to take the ball and run and get over the end line with it.'

★ ★ ★ ★

After the album was done, I talked with Brian about it.

David Leaf: 'Did the confidence from how well the music was received in concert inspire you to want to go into the studio?'

Brian: 'It did. In fact, my band kept saying to me, "Brian, we gotta record this." And my wife, Melinda, would say, "You gotta record this. It'll be a great album." So we recorded it. And we took our time. We didn't rush through it. We took our time, and, eventually, it was done.'

David: 'What was the significance of recording it at Sunset Sound?'

Brian: 'Some of the early, original *SMiLE* sessions were done there. That's why we went back there, to get the vibration of it. To get the vibe.'

David: 'Were you chasing away old ghosts?'

Brian: 'I was trying to. Couldn't successfully do it, but I was trying to. My favourite part was doing the instruments. The instrumentation. That was my favourite part. Then I liked the leads. Then I liked the background voices. In that order.'

David: 'What was your favourite part of the tracking sessions?'

Brian: 'Actually, the drums. We worked real hard to get the drums to sound pretty good. The drums were the best. The guitars and pianos and keyboards were also much superior to anything we'd ever done. Nelson Bragg blew my mind. He is so versatile. He can play any kind of percussion.'

The second day at Sunset was a difficult one for Brian.

Brian: 'I had especially a lot of demons and auditory hallucinations that day. More than usual.'

David: 'The original vocals were written with Beach Boys voices in mind. Does recording them now with your band present any special challenges?'

Brian: 'No, I knew that my band could do it better than The Beach

Boys. My band is a superior band. Period. Very superior people. Very superior. They're able to sing, not only on key, but they're able to sing very sweetly and very sensitively, which makes them a unique bunch of singers. They follow directions very well when I direct them and produce them. They're very sensitive to my leadership.'

Mark Linett, Brian's long-time engineer (and recording engineer for the album) remembered the day when he handed Brian the CD of *Brian Wilson Presents SMiLE*.

Mark: 'I swear you could see something change in him. And he's been different ever since.'

Darian was there to witness that miraculous moment, and his special memory is the coda to this section.

Darian: 'I watched as Brian was handed the CD. He grasped it tightly but tenderly, close to his chest and said, "I'm going to hold this dear to my heart." And Brian was trembling. I'd never seen him like that. Because he was trembling with joy. And all the fear of *SMiLE* was gone.'

★ ★ ★ ★

For David Bither, President of Nonesuch Records, the label that released *Brian Wilson Presents SMiLE,* it was an emotional experience just to be involved. Like so many others, he had been chasing the *SMiLE* dream for a long time.

David had flown to London to see one of the Royal Festival Hall concerts. This is what he told me right after the show.

David: 'I've been waiting to see this for a long time, but I never thought I would. As I just said to Brian, I don't have the words to tell you . . . The love that I felt in this, the fact that he was doing this. I think this music is some of most sophisticated, complex pop music . . . or music, forget the pop part of it, that's been written in the last century. The fact that this happened is monumental, and this music is monumental. And God bless him. I know that it was a long road to get here, but it was more than an honour to be in the audience tonight.'

While in London, David met with Melinda and made his case as to why his label would be the right home for it.

David: 'I sat down with Melinda at the hotel where they were staying and explained how much Brian's music and *SMiLE* meant to me, my understanding of its significance and my passion for it. We also talked

THE ALBUM & THE DOCUMENTARY

about Nonesuch's place in the worldwide Warner Music group where at different times in his career, both with The Beach Boys and solo, Brian had worked.'

The concert, as Bither recalled in 2023, was 'incredibly emotional. Even to this day it's hard not to get choked up thinking about it because of everything it represented. You felt it. You saw it in Brian's face. You saw it in the band who were so crucial in their support. You saw it when Van Dyke got up on stage with him afterwards. They were free, at last.'

A few months later, David Bither had another unimaginable moment.

David: 'I will never forget the day the finished mixes arrived, closing the door to my office and looking at the tape thinking, "I'm holding *SMiLE*."

'It was mind-blowing because [I'd been] dreaming about it for so long. I was one of those [DIY] uberfans who had sequenced *SMiLE* on cassette for years. Suddenly, there it was, finished by Brian with a group of musicians who were so understanding and supportive and able to realize this music.

'So there it was. I played it. It was very emotional. And I was dumbfounded at how good it was. I didn't think "Wow! It's almost like a carbon copy." It wasn't. It had its own integrity. Brian's voice was obviously different all those years later.'

As to the album, 'There were ways it was organized that validated the educated guesses we had all made over the years . . . but there were other elements that surprised me. There were sections and transitions where I thought, "Where did this come from?" It felt like Brian and Van Dyke had both come back to it with a spirit of resolve: "We can do this. We can make this happen." So, as I heard the music, I was so thrilled. So moved. So grateful to be a part of it.'

As to comparisons with the original *SMiLE* sessions, Bither notes, 'You can argue forever whether the original sessions from back in the day are better than these recordings. I don't care. They're both great. They both speak to the ambition and the realization, *finally*, of that ambition. While no one can ever replace Carl and Dennis and everybody who took part in those original sessions, the joy and the triumph of this as it was finally realized has its own weight, that to me is undeniable.'

Besides all of the hard work of actually selling the record, David Bither had one very special opportunity to celebrate.

SMiLE

David: 'The night it was released, Brian hosted a dinner at one of his favourite places in Los Angeles. There were about twenty of us there, sitting around a big table. I was sitting next to Van Dyke. Maybe you were on the other side of me. And Brian got up at one point to thank everybody, the people nearest and dearest to him, all those years later, for making the day possible that *SMiLE* was released. I felt so privileged to be sitting in that room. It was something I'll never forget, sitting with Brian the night *SMiLE* finally was released.'

The night before Brian hosted that dinner in L.A., one of his best friends was in New York, about to do what had once been unthinkable – go into a record store and buy *SMiLE*.

Ray Lawlor: 'In '67, the first time I went to buy *SMiLE*, I took a bus to Record World. Needless to say, they didn't have it. In 2004, we knew that *SMiLE* was being released on September 28. I already had the Nonesuch promo disc, so this wasn't about hearing *SMiLE*. I just wanted the feeling of walking into a store and buying it. I found out that Tower Records in Greenwich Village would be open at midnight. Release day, I drove into the city. Ironically, the car I was driving was Brian's Corvette that I'd bought from him a year earlier. It still had the California tags.

'I got to the store at 11:50 p.m. I watched them unpacking boxes. There was a line of people around the block. I called Brian to tell him. He said, "You're kidding me. No way. I can't believe it." I said, "You better believe it." It was thrilling. I bought twenty copies. *Mission Accomplished!*'

David Leaf: 'Looking back at all that transpired – and listening to the music in 2024 – here's my two cents: It's inconceivable that the indescribably beautiful and otherworldly melodies and ethereal, magical harmonies of *Brian Wilson Presents SMiLE* came from one very special mind – Brian Wilson's. Given all the songs and lyrics and pieces that were written in 1966-67, and the new material Brian, Van Dyke, and Darian worked on in 2003, it must be noted that the way it was assembled into a three-movement rock opera was absolutely brilliant. I'm so proud that I had a small role in making it happen. Greatest thing I've ever done in my life.'

Backed by a robust marketing and public relations campaign, *Brian Wilson Presents SMiLE* was released by Nonesuch Records on September 28, 2004; as with the live concerts, the critics were almost universal in their acclaim for the recording.

THE ALBUM & THE DOCUMENTARY

If you've never heard *Brian Wilson Presents SMiLE*, you could stream it now. Before you read what the critics had to say.

Rolling Stone: 'A Triumph ★★★★★.'

Newsweek: 'Wilson's Masterpiece.'

The New York Times: 'Likely the most coherent long-form composition in rock.'

The Independent, London: '★★★★★A serious contender for the greatest album ever made.'

USA Today: 'Brian Wilson's fabled opus delivers on its original promise of beauty, sophistication and audacity . . . glorious.'

The Detroit Free Press: 'An original, idiosyncratic and unabashedly American song cycle . . . it may be the most unimaginable comeback in pop history.'

The Village Voice: 'It just might become the album of the year.'

The San Francisco Chronicle: 'Rating: Wild Applause. It's unlikely that a more vigorous, rhapsodic record will be released all year.'

The Philadelphia Enquirer: 'A timeless natural wonder – a sound as majestic as a mountain, resounding for the ages.'

The Chicago Tribune: 'A uniquely spiritual vision of Americana.'

The Boston Globe: 'Brilliantly complex . . . SMiLE brims with the master tunesmith's inimitable melodies, youthful melancholy, ardent reach.'

The Washington Post: 'Thank you, Brian Wilson. Thank you and thank you again.'

SMiLE

Randy Lewis, *Los Angeles Times:* 'Listening to Wilson's resurrected and newly recorded version of *SMiLE*, it's as easy to understand why the other Beach Boys balked at putting it out 37 years ago as it is to lament the Pacific Ocean-sized missed opportunity. It's difficult not to imagine that *Sgt. Pepper* wouldn't have sounded nearly as revolutionary – conceptually or structurally – had it appeared months after *SMiLE* as originally scheduled.'

'Some purists may pine for the voices of the late Carl Wilson and the estranged Mike Love, who played key roles in the original recordings. But the real genius of *'SMiLE'* isn't who sang what, but it's ingeniousness as a composition.'

In the *Brian Wilson Presents SMiLE* CD, my liner notes ended with these thoughts:

'I was fortunate enough to visit the studio for a number of days during the making of this album, and I can't even begin to describe how surreal an experience it was to watch as this legendary music was finally being recorded for all to hear ... I was very aware of the history I was witnessing. Still, even having seen it, it seems impossible to write, "This is *SMiLE*."

'*Does SMiLE really exist?*

'For those who have waited for this moment forever, it never seemed possible that Brian would summon the sheer audacity it would take to finish and record this album. For decades, asking him about *SMiLE* would evoke stony silence or Brian would say, "It's inappropriate music." And yet, here it is.

'The wait is over. So, on behalf of all of us who have been dreaming of this moment, "Thank you, Brian." Thank you for being so brave, for casting aside your demons and confronting the music that has been a giant question mark for all of these years. And thank you for finishing it so brilliantly.

'For those who don't know the entire drama, you might rightly ask, "Is this *SMiLE* thing really such a big deal?" A fair question, and a lengthy retelling of the history and mystery of the original *SMiLE* era might convince you that *SMiLE* matters. Or it might not.

'Cast all those questions aside; the best thing we can do is listen to this music without the burden of history. Just as Brian did when he composed *SMiLE* over thirty-seven years ago, rejoice in the glory of the music itself.

THE ALBUM & THE DOCUMENTARY

'And remember, just as it was back in 1966, Brian's goal is simple. This music was created by him not to cause pressure, but to ease it. He believed then and still believes in the spiritual power of laughter. Very simply, Brian wrote this music to make us SMiLE. Eternally.'

That's how my liner notes ended.

Writing the notes had been a wonderful break from the incredibly difficult work of cutting down the footage we had shot – extensive interviews with almost everybody involved, countless days of rehearsals, run-throughs, recording sessions and concerts – and make a coherent documentary about what had just happened, a film that would touch those who knew nothing about Brian Wilson or SMiLE.

John Scheinfeld: 'This was David's dream project and as we had a production company, I was there to support him as best as I could during what would be a wildly productive and inspiring ride.'

For well over a decade, beginning with *The Unknown Marx Brothers*, John and I wrote, directed, and produced dozens of pop culture retrospectives and music documentaries. For *Beautiful Dreamer*, I asked Richard Waltzer, an experienced film executive who shared my passion for SMiLE, to join the team. He brought the project to Showtime and after our pitch, they were in.

David Leaf: 'During rehearsals Richard and I watched joyfully (and incredulously) as the music came together in early 2004.'

Richard Waltzer: 'Those [few] of us who had [now] heard SMiLE completed knew how great it was, but there was still the uncertainty about the responses from the public and the critics. I recall Van Dyke resisting the adulation, insisting that "we not get ahead of ourselves." Still, it was hard not to feel a sense of great anticipation for the artists whose work was about to be revealed.

'The mood in the lobby of the Royal Festival Hall was truly electric. Many of the concertgoers had literally flown in from all over the world to be present at the momentous event. My task on the first night was to interview this eclectic group of pilgrims. While some were old enough to have experienced the disappointment of SMiLE's initial shelving in 1967, there were many others who clearly knew about the music from a historical viewpoint.

'After the [triumphant] premiere, the remainder of the shows in London were, in some ways, more enjoyable as the unknown factors of the performance and response were eliminated. Each night, Brian and the band would relax in the hotel lobby in an air of celebration.

'For those who had anticipated the "Next Big Thing" back in 1967, it now exists for everyone, and we can all celebrate a completed, fulfilling journey in the search for lost time.'

For six weeks, James Mathers and his team had obsessively documented how *Brian Wilson Presents SMiLE* was put together by he and his band. I had interviewed everybody who would sit in front of our camera and talk about Brian and *SMiLE*. We had taped the world premiere concerts. We now knew how the story ended. Making it work as a film was a completely different trip.

★　★　★　★

Peter S. Lynch II: 'Helping to craft *Beautiful Dreamer* was one of the most difficult projects I've ever edited. David was very passionate about telling the *whole* story and getting its complicated history right. It was also my first feature-length film, so I wanted to get it right too. Just the sheer volume of footage that had been shot – there were so many great moments that were left on the cutting room floor. David's first "paper cut" [for a two-hour film] was ridiculously long. Like six hours. He was just too close to the material. John and I had to politely tell him to cut it down. A lot. But we got there.

'Maybe my favourite moment of the project was the first time we screened a cut for Brian. We were close to "locking picture," having a finished film that we were all happy with. It had been a long haul. This was a small, intimate preview screening with a very short guestlist: myself, David, John, producer Richard Waltzer, and the guests of honour, Brian and Melinda. I remember our team being extremely tense before they arrived. David was palpably nervous. To briefly paint a picture: it was a windowless edit bay with cheap linoleum title floors situated in, basically, a giant walk-in storage closet (ah, the glitz and glamour of documentary filmmaking!). David was hoping and praying that we had succeeded in telling the story of *SMiLE* – that we had done Brian, his journey and, most importantly, the music, proud.

'Brian and Melinda arrived casually and introductions were made. When Brian came into the edit bay the first thing he noticed, which caught him

THE ALBUM & THE DOCUMENTARY

pleasantly by surprise, was a photograph of his [youthful] self, peering up out of his old backyard swimming pool. It just happened to be up on the monitors, by chance, not by design. We'd been tweaking the edit right up to the last minute and that's just where my cursor was parked in the AVID timeline. Anyway, Brian exclaimed, "Hey, that's me!" almost in awe of his younger self. Brian definitely got a kick out of it, and then humbly took a seat in the back corner of the room, as far out of the way as possible.

'Then, everyone else disappeared out of the room for a few moments, and I found myself sitting alone with BRIAN WILSON behind me. I was young, 26, relatively green in the business, shy as can be, and this was probably my first encounter with a celebrity, certainly with a celebrity of Brian's stature and legendary pop star status. I was mortified, tongue-tied, and definitely starting to sweat uncomfortably under the collar. Some people don't get weird around famous folks. I'm not one of those people.

'After some brief, awkward small talk about the project, Brian got around to asking me if I liked the music. And there it was – subtle, but unmistakable in the cadence of his voice: the still-lingering trauma of *SMiLE* and a slight apprehension as to how it would be received by listeners. Now, this was well after he'd blown the roof off Royal Festival Hall with the concert performances, but before the album was released. And I knew *he knew* it was great. I'd seen all the footage of him recording the album – in command, confident, knowing what he wanted, having a ball, cheering on his musician collaborators, and absolutely relishing the music-making. There could be no doubt in his mind as to the quality.

'Yet I sensed this child-like longing for the work to be received the way he had intended it. Of course, I told him genuinely and without hesitation, "It's great!" And then I was saved by everyone returning from wherever they'd run off to and we proceeded with the screening. Perhaps an older, wiser, less shy version of myself would have expanded, "It's one of the most exuberant expressions of pure musical joy I've ever heard." And, "Thank you for finishing it."'

Richard Waltzer: 'As post-production came to a close, there were just two instances where I wished we included a few clips from the interviews that were cut. Both showed the incredible emotional response to *SMiLE*'s 1960's demise.

'Durrie Parks, Van Dyke's first wife, wept when she recalled the disappointment of Brian abandoning the project. It would have catapulted her then-husband into the hierarchy of pop's songwriters and showcased his immense talent to a huge audience. The other was from Tom Nolan, the accomplished author and journalist, who movingly told of his efforts to try to piece together, from *Smiley Smile* and subsequent Beach Boys' albums, what would have likely been the song line-up to SMiLE. He too cried when recalling his attempt to re-create what would have been a landmark album from his youth.'

One last observation about how different the real Brian Wilson is from what one sees splashed across the media.

John Scheinfeld: 'Much has been written and said about Brian Wilson over the past six decades . . . that he often appears distant, lost, unengaged, not forthcoming in interviews, and that his memory is fuzzy, a casualty of mental illness and drug abuse. However, what I witnessed was clear and present proof that there is so much more to Brian.

'What's the old cliché? "Believe only half of what you see and nothing you hear?" Good advice for anyone trying to figure out Brian Wilson. When it comes to this musical genius, anything is possible. And after what I witnessed, there was nothing else to do but SMiLE.'

★   ★   ★   ★

When I interviewed Brian about the documentary for a promotional disc, even though I knew he was happy with it, I was nervous all over again.

David: 'What feeling did you get from seeing the movie the first time?'

Brian: 'The first feeling I got was I was very proud to see myself in action, of course. I was very proud of the other guys . . . I was proud of you for making it. My favourite part of the movie is when I played 'Beautiful Dreamer' at the start of the movie.'

David: 'Why is that your favourite part?'

Brian: 'Because it's my favourite song (*laughs*).'

David: 'That was something you told me in private . . . Does it bother you that something you told me in private gets put into a movie like that?'

Brian: 'Not at all. I thought you were very creative and very appropriate by having me do that in the movie. I thought it was very appropriate.'

David: 'Were there parts of the movie that were hard to watch?'

THE ALBUM & THE DOCUMENTARY

Brian: 'To tell you the truth, some of the stuff, watching myself was a little rough for me . . . seeing myself at sixty-two years old was a little rough for me to see.'

David: 'Was it tough to sit through the part where *SMiLE* was coming apart in 1967?'

Brian: 'It wasn't tough to sit through. It brought back a lot of memories, of course, when we were taking drugs, and Van Dyke and I were in action, and stuff like that. But it was in the bag, though. It was in the bag.'

One more comment from Brian about the film.

Brian: 'I was in awe of Danny and Van Dyke and David Anderle and all those great people. I was in awe. They're all great people. So, I was a little bit scared to see where they were coming from, but I was okay. I was in awe of their verbal skills. I thought what they said was very accurate and true and very creative.'

★ ★ ★ ★

The late-September release of the album was followed by the October 2004 premiere on Showtime (and eventually the BBC) of my film, *Beautiful Dreamer: Brian Wilson & The Story of SMiLE*. The reviews for the film were very positive.

A few weeks later, we had the sheer joy of seeing Brian and the band perform *SMiLE* at Disney Hall in Los Angeles. With the enormous critical and commercial success of the *SMiLE* album, 2004 ended with nothing but smiles.

There was a frown ahead. But that wasn't even a cloud on the horizon. At least, not yet.

SMiLE ON TOUR

UNTIL 1999, BRIAN WILSON HAD BEEN A RELUCTANT STAGE PERFORMER. For him, the anticipation of his first solo concerts must have felt like waiting in the dentist's office to have a tooth pulled. But with each show, he became more comfortable on stage. (Listen to *Live at the Roxy*).

The *SMiLE* tours were in a different league. He revelled in playing and hearing *Brian Wilson Presents SMiLE* live.

Here are a few memories of those who were behind the scenes with him, some professionals, some just friends, making sure that everything would go well, supplying Brian with large doses of 'emotional security.'

Jean Sievers*, Brian's manager:* 'The *SMiLE* tour was just one of the first times where people were like freaking the fuck out that they were seeing this piece of music. Because it had such lore to it. It was so special, and so there wasn't anything ever like it before. And I don't think there's been anything like it since. It was completely unique. To take an album that had caused so much pain and destruction. And the rift between The Beach Boys and Brian and Van Dyke, and Brian's illness taking hold during that time. And people were just rooting for him.

'People really wanted him to be happy, and they wanted to hear this music. They wanted people to know how ahead of the curve he was way back when, and he's still ahead of the curve. The concerts were filled with young people. It wasn't like the people that go to Beach Boys concerts. Were there older people there? Yes, of course, but it was filled with like the hippest of hip and the coolest of cool. And it just really brought him back to a place that he deserved to be. He was the hip guy back in the sixties. When nobody wanted him to be the hip guy. They wanted him to churn out hits . . . Had he been allowed to, he would have been like the Jay Z or Dre of those times.'

SMiLE ON TOUR

Jean's favourite part of the tour? 'Every single show. People wanted it to be great for him, not just for themselves. And they just saw how absolutely bizarre and unique this project was. And what I really love, which I'm sure pissed off some of The Beach Boys, but I loved how when we did 'Good Vibrations' during those shows, people got to see 'Good Vibrations' in a totally different form, right? Which I thought was really cool.'

Paul Von Mertens: 'The tour was like taking care of a baby: joy and excitement but always alert and focused on what's needed at any moment.'

Bob Lizik: 'Every other gig after [the premiere] was just like, "This is amazing." We were all flying pretty high. With the exception of Carnegie Hall. Because we get to Carnegie Hall and found out there's going to be a live broadcast at our first show in Carnegie Hall. It's like, "Oh, great." But that went well too. Of course, the New York audience [and] there's a ton of New York musicians out there that we all respect.'

Paul: 'No particular show stands out in my mind, because the entire tour, I was so focused on delivering the performances, that where we were and who we were with was peripheral to doing the job. I don't remember doing any sightseeing or any partying or hanging out or anything like that. I just remember the work of preparing for each show. Traveling, sound check, basically making the gig, getting to the gig was a lot of work.

'Every show was — I wouldn't say the same, in a way — but every show was an effort to deliver this gem. And to be honest, I wasn't thinking about anything else, except, "Do we have what we need? Is everybody here? How are the monitors?" That's what I remember. I don't remember meeting any famous people. I'm sure we met famous people all over the place. I don't remember hanging out very much at all. But I remember being on stage with the Stockholm Strings doing soundcheck and all the work of presenting the music.'

Jean: 'It was insane. I've worked big tours. Like Prince's twelve sold-out nights at the Staple Center. But this was different. It was just different. There's always some critic there to tear you down or everybody's got an opinion. But people really wanted this to work for Brian, and it was really nice to see . . . It cost a hell of a lot of money to put on the road . . . 'cause there was a lot of people [on-stage] and a lot of production involved, for not a big budget. But it wasn't ever really about the money, it was about giving this man some peace with this project that had been haunting him for so long.'

Nelson Bragg: 'Nothing will beat the six shows at Royal Festival Hall. Nothing. I will say the Hollywood Bowl show was close. That was amazing. It was the hometown crowd, and everyone we knew and loved in our hometown – my adopted hometown – was there. Really exciting. And the two nights at Disney Hall . . . In many ways was even a bigger deal than the Hollywood Bowl, because we were playing in this new, amazing concert hall that had just been finished. So we were excited about playing there for the first time. And so those were really special shows.

'Two nights at Carnegie Hall. I'm going to say that that rivals Royal Festival for sure, because of the mythic status of that room. When you play Carnegie Hall, you've done something in your life that is right.

'And then to get to be able to do it twice and then be on NPR [National Public Radio] and get to listen to it on Thanksgiving. It was surreal. I had arrived as a musician. Japan was exciting. Sydney Opera House, incredibly prestigious two nights there. Very big deal.'

Bob: 'Pretty much after any of the shows there would be meet-and-greet afterwards. At the time in London, and in England, at least, there was always people after the show coming backstage. Roger Daltrey, people from different bands that came in. They were all amazed that it was done. All the shows were just kind of like, "This is amazing, and we're kicking ass, and this is great." It was a great period for Brian. He seemed more creative at the time, too. Remember him playing a lot of piano in the dressing room beforehand, and he just seemed really happy.'

Nelson: 'The other guys in the band had been with Brian for five years, so they were used to the fans, but I wasn't. I was still the new guy. [The fans] were appreciative: "You're contributing a lot to this show, and your energy and musicianship really comes off the stage. And we feel that." And that was something I got from people a lot throughout my time with Brian.

'It made me really feel like I'd really made the right choice to be a musician. Not that an audience is gonna tell me that, but it was nice for fans to ask for autographs. I was signing autographs all the time. People were stopping me on the street in Ireland, in London. They saw the show or were going to see the show, knew me by my name because they'd read things or heard things. It was amazing. My sister and my brother-in-law came to Dublin. And people stopped me on the street and asked for my autograph right in front of them. My sister started crying. She couldn't believe it.'

Scott Bennett: 'I just remember that, as a band, we were all really close during that time. We knew that we were doing something really special. We knew Brian was in a really cool place, where he was just more in the room. Of course, it's Brian. Some nights, maybe not.'

The musicians were out front. They felt the love from audiences every night, met fans after every show. But what about the people backstage?

Ky Cabot: 'The show was "quiet time" that I could work, uninterrupted. But I would try to make a point of going out and watching the show. And I just remember watching the majority of that show. And being just overwhelmed at how cohesive the band was, just how locked in they were . . . for all intents and purposes they were sidemen to Brian, but they didn't function that way at all. They really felt that they were part of something, and it came across. Virtually every night I tried to make time to go out and watch. It really was magical for me, and I never got sick of it.'

One of the reasons *Brian Wilson Presents SMiLE* was such a great concert experience was that *the sound* was so good. Richie Davis is the reason for that.

Richie Davis, *senior audio engineer:* 'Probably one of the best experiences of my career. We had nine vocal mics up there. It was a wall of vocals. That, to me, was what the Brian thing was all about – the vocals. But this was even more. It was personal; it was emotional. We *had* to get this right. I felt as if we got the vocals right, the rest of it will follow. I knew every single vocal part, and who was singing what part when. With those voices combined with the intricate musical arrangements, I kind of felt like a conductor of an orchestra. It was amazing.

'What was most difficult for me were all the small bits and pieces of music that each band member would play. Every day at sound check, we would work on some part that Darian or Brian felt wasn't right and we wouldn't quit until it was right. That was an everyday thing.

'The key to Royal Festival Hall or anywhere else isn't just about mixing the show. It is about bringing the show to life, connecting the audience with the entertainers through a great auditory experience. People talk about Carnegie Hall and other places as, "Oh, they're tough rooms, not great-sounding rooms." Sure, but I spend extra time evaluating the room: the size, the shape, the staging, the pitch of the roof, the seating, all the peripherals that impact the sound of a live show to ensure those rooms sound as good as they possibly can and will deliver on the experience. There's a lot that goes into it but if you sing it and you play it, I can mix it wherever you are.'

The 2004-2005 SMiLE tour included ninety-one shows in fifty-eight cities in fourteen countries. Three continents (Europe, North America and Australia). The UK, Japan, and New Zealand. During that trek, nobody spent more time alone with Brian on the tour than his friend, Jerry Weiss, for years his volunteer personal assistant. Jerry tells us about what it was like to be on the road with Brian.

Jerry Weiss: 'We shared an amazing number of deep conversations about life and about God. Sometimes about music . . . what did surprise me is how engaging he is, how introspective he could be, how funny he could be, how sincere he can be, and just a wonderful, warm human being, who had a lot of things to share – and very few people to share them with. He knew when people were flattering him and were insincere. That was my experience. The most important thing I learned was Brian doesn't like talking about himself. At all. And anybody who's ever interviewed him, that's clearly obvious. With one exception, and that's the author of this book.

'The most surprising thing I learned about him? Life itself. Humour, exercise, and food. With Brian, food and music are a close one and two. We had a great time together, even if it was just eating a burger while watching sports on TV. And the other surprise to me is he is an average guy who liked the simple things in life. Whether we were in a two-bedroom suite or one small room in a Holiday Inn, it was all the same to him. Which was engaging.

'On the road, there's a lot on the man's plate. It was draining at times. We were walking three miles a day. I got him into walking a couple years before that, and he was in great shape physically, great shape mentally. One evening after dinner we had a conversation about our lives. Brian talked about how God came into his life as a little boy and what God means to him today. During that conversation, I mentioned how I walked down a path nearly every day along a river in Valley Forge National Park and how it made me feel. Brian said after the tour he wanted to come to my house, visit, and take that walk.

'The next morning around six a.m., Brian came out of his room in his robe and sat down at the keyboard and played these same seven beautiful chords over and over and over again. I buried my head in a newspaper, drinking coffee as he kept playing these chords. I didn't want to disturb what he was doing because I was witnessing him composing right in front of my eyes and ears. After several minutes he asked me how I felt hearing these chords. I said, "They make me feel very spiritual." He said "Me too. Can you help me out and give me a few words?"

'I said, "Keep playing them," and counted 1, 2, 3, 4, 5, 6, 7. And thought about our conversation the night before and said, 'Walking Down the Path of Life.' He leaped up and yelled, "Go grab a pencil and paper right now!"'

And with Jerry's lyrics, they wrote that song.

Jerry: 'He was boundless in his energy and his determination and his enthusiasm for what he was doing. The *SMiLE* concerts were going great. Unbelievable reviews and mesmerizing performances. But part of him was already by it, on to his next idea, a rock and roll record with new songs and a few covers he had always wanted to arrange and record.'

Nonesuch Record's clever UK teaser ad for the September 2004 release of the *Brian Wilson Presents SMiLE* album.

THE 'BRIANISTAS' ...
PART TWO

NOT EVERYBODY COULD BE IN LONDON FOR WORLD PREMIERE WEEK; HERE are brief memories from a few dozen fans around the world about their experience seeing *Brian Wilson Presents SMiLE* live.

Stuart Piper: 'Brian's my all-time hero in music . . . I live only a few miles from Bournemouth and I can't stress how utterly surreal it felt hopping on a local bus to go and see him . . . I remember thinking perhaps this was how folk used to approach going to see a Mozart premiere in Salzburg back in the day, when, as here, nobody had heard the finished article beforehand!

'It was stunning – I still can't listen to 'Surf's Up' without getting a flashback set of goosebumps remembering the orchestral intro into it. I shed a tear or two, soppy old sod that I am . . . the sheer sense of immense expectation being matched and then surpassed that night remains spine-tingling every time I think about it.'

gxios: 'I was at the Bristol show – first one outside of London. Travelled from the US to be there . . . My 19-year-old nephew (and ride) was knocked out by the show, exclaiming, "I was born in the wrong decade."'

Mike McLouglin: 'I went to the Manchester concert with a friend who was only a casual fan and he and I were both blown away . . . a massive success and an emotional event from a personal point of view as I never thought this would occur as a long-time Beach Boys FAN since 1969 (age 13). The Liverpool gig was even more electric . . . of course, Liverpool audiences are known for our "Celtic" enthusiasm!!'

David Lowen: 'My wife and I travelled to Liverpool to see Brian's *SMiLE* show. I was never as excited. I brought a pen and paper with me

THE 'BRIANISTAS' ... PART TWO

to record the order of songs played. It formed the basis for playlists on my iPod before the release of Brian's *SMiLE* album ... An incredible evening.'

Lou Nemes: 'My [girlfriend said] to me, "This doesn't sound like his usual songs." I replied, "You are seeing musical history being made!" He goes through *SMiLE* ... I left feeling like Brian finally brought his music to another level. I was floating on air. Truly a moment I will never forget!'

Jurgen Verhoeven: 'It's always exciting to see your idol live for the first time ... There was so much going on musically and visually when they played *SMiLE*. I know I did miss some little parts. It was hard to follow those top musicians. My eyes and ears went from left to right and back, again and again. It was so overwhelming ... I was so happy after the show. I saw and heard the legend Brian and the legendary *SMiLE*.'

René Steenbergen: '*BWPS* to me was a true rollercoaster of emotions. It was so touching to see Brian, after all that he's been through, embraced by the love of the band, getting that *SMiLE* burden off his shoulder. I'd never expected to witness *SMiLE* in its full glory. And it was kind of funny that the definitive *SMiLE* turned out totally different than almost forty years of bootleg versions. *BWPS* to me is almost a religious experience.'

Priscilla Smits: 'I had no idea what to expect, but during the concert I couldn't believe what was happening, I was overwhelmed ... I can't describe how I felt after the show but I can describe how it feels now ... I feel so much pride, still emotional, the concert no one would ever believe would happen. It's very special to me, the thought "I was there!!!"'

Gerard Hubert: 'When they announced *SMiLE* being played at the mythical Paris Olympia, French music aficionados wanted to attend the event; so the March 14, 2004 concert sold out ... a great concert.'

Don Giller: 'I was one of many who didn't attend the London premiere ... Someone who did captured the event on [their] cell phone and within hours, uploaded the contents onto a secret site. The sound quality wasn't as important as the mere fact that I could hear this. Finally hearing the correct architecture that early morning was, in a word, breathtaking.'

Giggens: 'The air felt different that night. There really was a communal glow from the audience, like we were all sharing this same vibration, all putting out this energy because we knew we were witnessing a once in a lifetime experience. It was the album that wasn't, the time that was erased, the memories deeply repressed. Yet, hear it was in every shimmering, harmonious, transcendent note . . . If Brian intended for us all to leave the theatre that night with the album's name plastered on our faces, he succeeded in his mission. Long live Brian and his incredible body of work! The rest of the music world might catch up someday.'

Phil Rotella: 'Excited, filled with anticipation for months leading up to the first show in the UK. First show I attended was the Nov. 3 show at the Disney Concert Hall . . . during intermission meeting friends and seeing many familiar faces throughout the venue. Finally settled back into our seats, the band nailing the SMiLE set in all of its brilliance.'

Tony Soprano: 'What always struck me most, besides the great music and of course the wonderful band, was that it was easy to talk with people there about what SMiLE meant to Brian, the impact it had on his life and of course the impact it had on all of our lives . . . I'll never forget it.'

Quentin Collier: 'I instantly bought four tickets as I knew I had to share this experience with some "non-believers" . . . The second half began with 'Our Prayer' and we were transported . . . Sublime . . . A night I'll never forget.'

Shawn Franklin: 'I was over the moon when I learned Brian would be touring SMiLE. This was before the material was recorded as an album. We would all finally hear the finished version of the lost, unfinished masterpiece by the creator.'

David Chase Lopes: 'It was like listening to the final takes from the original recording. The music moved across and through the theatre into my soul. A unique moment of union between music and humanity. We were at one.'

Brad Rosenberger: 'Twenty years on, it is now hard to imagine what a world without SMiLE was like.'

Gary Haggerty: 'Disney Hall . . . absolutely the "can not miss" concert of the year . . . Sometimes, some things are worth the wait, and SMiLE was one of those times.'

Steve Abramson: 'Waiting in anticipation for decades . . . And my waiting was rewarded in 2004 . . . it was the culmination of all that I had hoped for.'

David R. Beckey: 'Favourites were 'Wind Chimes,' 'Wonderful,' and

THE 'BRIANISTAS' ... PART TWO

of course, 'Surf's Up.' ... At one point later in the show Brian asked the light man to put a spotlight on his wife, Melinda, so he could tell her he loved her. It brought the show to a momentary stop, it was so sweet! ... one of the best concerts ever!'

John Barone: 'Midway through the concert my wife turned to me and asked, "Where can we see this again?" ... The *SMiLE* shows are definitely the best concerts I've ever seen in my entire life.'

Barry Soltz: 'Can dreams come true? It was the early seventies when I first heard about *SMiLE* ... Nothing, however, could prepare me for seeing Brian and his Orchestra live preforming *SMiLE* at Carnegie Hall in NYC! ... I was spellbound ... Dare I say it? It was like a spiritual experience. The love from the stage and audience was overwhelming. God is love. Brian was given this God-given gift of music and he shared it with everyone that night. Never could I have imagined witnessing a concert like this! Beyond my wildest dreams.'

Glenn Greenberg: 'By 2004 I had amassed a sizable collection of *SMiLE* bootlegs and tried to piece them together into a cohesive whole. It became an obsession, much to my wife's annoyance. Eventually I came to accept that a completed *SMiLE* was just a fantasy. But on October 12, 2004, at Carnegie Hall, with Van Dyke Parks himself in attendance and receiving a wave of applause, I watched that fantasy become a reality – and one of my very favorite musical works.'

Tommy Burton: 'What a memory! ... breathtaking and stunning. Bravo!'

Greg Boone: 'It was powerfully emotional to witness. As a fan of The Beach Boys for many years, this was the dark and painful part of the history that had tried to destroy Brian and his creativity, so getting to witness his performance was this brilliant moment of light as he finally conquered all of the demons associated with this incredibly beautiful music. I actually cried as the first chorus of voices began to sing 'Our Prayer.' It was as though their incantation lifted this terrible dark cloud away from Brian. It was a triumphant moment that I felt honoured to have witnessed! It was a magical day for me and remains one of the great musical experiences of my life.'

Perry Cox: 'So happy I was there to soak that all up.'

Greg Mazzeo: 'I can't recall ever having such anticipation for another event – and Brian and The Brian Wilson Band delivered in a big way!

From the first breaths of 'Our Prayer' to the last note of 'Good Vibrations,' I was in a trance-like state. Transcended to Brian's world of harmony and musical imagination. I was helpless but to linger on every note in an attempt to savour each moment . . . It was surreal to be immersed in the live performance of this legendary album, and to experience it with so many enthusiastic and passionate fellow fans was the gift of a lifetime. Twenty years on it still feels like just yesterday. I'm grateful to have been present for this moment in music's history!'

Carey Schalber: 'The mood at the concert was very electric and exciting. The concert itself was magical and hypnotic. It was like watching abstract art come to life in music. I've been to many concerts but *SMiLE* was unlike any other . . . When the show was over, everyone there was buzzing . . . we all just witnessed a rare musical historic event.'

Louise Heifetz (aka Joy Germain): 'Brian's performances of *SMiLE* evoked happiness, whimsy, a blissful state of harmony and peace, and enlightened energy . . . Brian's music continues to fill me with joy every day for which I am eternally grateful.'

John Paris: 'How do you describe witnessing an event you had dreamed of for over thirty years? I was crying through at least half of it . . . The greatest concert of my life, and I've seen many.'

Billy Onder: 'My friends and I brought toy fire helmets for 'Mrs. O'Leary's Cow' and vegetables for 'Vega-Tables.' Even tossed him a carrot up onstage during the song! Someone must have enjoyed our enthusiasm because we got invited backstage to meet Brian after the show.'

Tom Thieme: 'Having followed his story since 1966 in *Hit Parader*, hearing 'Surf's Up' on the Leonard Bernstein TV special, spending decades reading about and scavenging for recordings of *SMiLE* outtakes, it was a dream come true to witness him finally get to celebrate the fruition of his own beautiful dream.'

John Tilden: 'I cried several times while hearing songs like 'Surf's Up,' 'Wonderful,' and even 'Vega-Tables' performed by Brian and the band. I grew up with the bootlegs and what-ifs – to hear it live and a "complete thing" was a gift.'

Terry Aycock: 'I convinced my wife she needed to see the concert. She did not grasp my "devotion" to Brian's music so I thought this would help with her understanding . . . As we are walking back out to the car, my wife turns to me and says, "I think I get it now. You cannot listen

THE 'BRIANISTAS' . . . PART TWO

to his music without feeling joyful and happy! So I get your fanaticism now!" Made the experience that much more delightful and meaningful.'

Matt Coffey: 'I wish everyone knew of his music. If they did, they would know his soul.'

Bobby Salerno: 'What impressed us the most was Brian's obvious renewed enthusiasm while performing these wonderful compositions. This combined with his wholehearted appreciation of the ovation he received from attendees . . . What does it mean to me now? *SMiLE* is an example of how to never give up on your dreams as in many cases time does have the ability to turn your dreams into your reality regardless of what others may think.'

Curt Lambert: 'I had heard about it for years . . . And so I gobbled up a ticket to see Brian Wilson perform *SMiLE* in its entirety at the Disney Hall. I cried. I smiled. My heart "hung ten" with joy. It was magic, it was music, it was legend. And I . . . heard Brian Wilson perform it live. *SMiLE*.'

Kevin Bourinot: 'I grabbed my closest friends . . . It was the greatest moment for me. Like seeing God in person. Amen.'

Sean Courtney: 'A mind-blowing show, hearing *SMiLE* live, just a few miles from where the famous [Chicago] fire started . . . The next day, I turned 30. I can't imagine a more monumental way I could have ended my twenties.'

Mark Dillon: 'As I sat in the second row at Toronto's Massey Hall and Brian's band leapt into the "Who Ran the Iron Horse" section of 'Cabin Essence,' I could feel the house shake. I looked up to the ceiling of the cathedral-like venue, closed my eyes and thought, "This is THE moment!" It was the realization of a dream I'd had through years of obsessing over *SMiLE*. I could not believe Brian had completed the album and was in front of me singing it live!'

Marty Dansack: 'It was transformative – amazing concert. What a great night. I was privileged to be there.'

Josh Hutson: 'I was moved to tears on multiple occasions. Seeing Brian immersed in the blue stage lights with his eyes closed taking in the band singing 'Our Prayer' was the most moving live concert experience I've ever witnessed . . . I'm so thankful to have been alive in that time to witness it all.'

Jon Kanis: 'Despite the decades of speculation and anticipation, nothing could have prepared me for the emotional roller coaster ride of hearing *SMiLE* reproduced by the man himself along with the support of his remarkable band . . . It's nothing short of miraculous how Brian managed to transcend his personal demons in order to present his masterpiece to the world . . . I get goosebumps every time I think about this mystical, magical evening. Thanks, guys, for changing the course of musical history!'

Lucy Denning: 'I remember going to see *Brian Wilson Presents SMiLE* in Chicago with my sister. She and I spent the evening going to dinner and then we went to the concert. We had fun. It was me and her. She was dying of cancer, and I will never forget that night. It was one of her good days. She then died in January 2006.'

Garry Jay: '*SMiLE* was the Holy Grail for me.'

Mike Malone: 'It's been a journey and a labour of love that began with Derek Taylor's pre-release rhapsodic comments re: 'Good Vibrations' in *Hit Parader*. I remember where I was when I first heard it. I was hooked.'

Robert Flory: 'On that October night in 2004, with my best friend of over forty years Mike Parsons, I sat down in the Verizon Theater in Houston anxiously waiting to hear this historic work of music performed. I realized that while it was a high point in my life as a fan of Brian Wilson's music, it was much more. It was also the culmination of over thirty years of a long-travelled road as a Beach Boys fan. The ups and downs that I (and other fans) rode with this group regarding *SMiLE* had brought me to this moment. While not the "crazy" Brian fan that I am, my friend knew the history of this project because of his near encyclopaedic knowledge of all sixties music. Its importance did not escape either of us.

'I revelled in that satisfaction as his symphony soared around the theatre on that magical night. To be honest, of all the recollections I have about seeing *SMiLE* performed live, the joy and satisfaction I felt of seeing Brian happy realizing his dream of completing this piece of art, is the only lasting memory worth relating.'

Lawrence (The Professor) Lavery: 'MOMENTOUS!.. My sister Annika and I – we witnessed a modern-day Mozart perform a new form of music . . . I'd call it an avant-garde classical! It brought me to tears and also a *SMiLE* to my dial!'

Jeff Celentano: 'The thought of experiencing *SMiLE* as a live concert

THE 'BRIANISTAS' ... PART TWO

was almost incomprehensible. The *SMiLE* music always held a very special place in my heart. I studied every musical arrangement, memorized every vocal harmony and now, we'd finally get to hear how it was all supposed to come together from the composer himself. Needless to say, it was one of the most significant and moving musical moments I've ever experienced (before or since). Not only did Brian fulfil a promise to his long-time fans, we all collectively felt the weight lift from our hero and we knew then that Brian truly was back. In that moment, the artist and the fans were literally in perfect harmony in a way none of us had ever quite experienced.

'For that reason, the *SMiLE* music means even more to me today than it did before.'

GRAMMYS, LAWSUITS, AND BOX SETS

ACTUALLY, THERE WERE TWO GRAMMYS BUT ONLY ONE LAWSUIT AND BOX SET.

In 2005, Brian won his first Grammy for 'Best Rock Instrumental,' noteworthy and ironic that the most innovative arranger of vocal harmonies of the rock era won for a very disharmonious instrumental, 'Mrs. O'Leary's Cow.' And it does actually have vocals. Shhh. Don't tell the Recording Academy.

Jean Sievers: 'He doesn't care about awards. But he's fiercely competitive. I think he's happy that he got a Grammy for a rock instrumental. And *SMiLE* bought him another Grammy for the box set, and rightly so. He's happy. But it doesn't affect him. He's "take it or leave it."'

The success of the worldwide tour and the Nonesuch album, the incredible press garnered, and the prestigious television shows Brian was on (Google Charlie Rose + Brian and David Leaf) gives you a sense as to how much positive mainstream media attention Brian was getting.

The Charlie Rose program is worth watching for Brian's stark honesty.

Brian Wilson: 'It took all the way until 2004 for the world to catch up with *SMiLE* . . . The world was finally ready for something as great as *SMiLE*.'

Indeed, it was. But nearly twenty-one months of *SMiLE* success was met with this headline on November 4 in *Billboard* magazine: 'Mike Love Sues Brian Wilson Over *SMiLE*'.

The article stated: 'Love filed the lawsuit in Los Angeles federal court yesterday (Nov. 3) accusing Wilson of promoting his 2004 album, *SMiLE*, in a manner that 'shamelessly misappropriated Mike Love's songs, likeness, and The Beach Boys trademark, as well as the *SMiLE* album itself.'

GRAMMYS, LAWSUITS, AND BOX SETS

You can read the entire *Billboard* story online. What it doesn't mention was that also named in the lawsuit were Brian's wife and Brian's managers. And me.

I won't go into the details of the lawsuit, other than Love lost in the lower court. Online, you can read that the appellate court judge denied his appeal, in part writing: 'The central issue before us is whether American claims for relief can be asserted on the basis of conduct that only occurred in Great Britain. The defendants think not. Love wishes they all could be California torts.'

I think it's also worth mentioning that The Beach Boys could have performed the songs of *SMiLE* in concert at any time, but in the thirty years prior to this lawsuit, they rarely did. Perhaps they felt the music still wasn't right for their audience.

In this joyous and celebratory book, I won't waste any more space.

★ ★ ★ ★

The Beach Boys SMiLE Sessions box set was released in 2011. Without the success of *Brian Wilson Presents SMiLE*, it's hard to know if this would have or could have happened.

It should have, because now you can hear the master at work on his masterpiece. Hear the brilliance of every piece. Hear how in control of his art Brian was.

Compilation producers Alan Boyd, Mark Linett, and Dennis Wolfe, plus *SMiLE* historian Domenic Priore and the prolific Howie Edelson (as a consultant), all made sure this package could be as great as possible, the ultimate *SMiLE* fan's dream.

It was greeted with deserving praise, and it won the Grammy Award for Best Historical Album; as the producer of the original sessions that were compiled on the box, Brian won his second Grammy.

It is worthy of every accolade. It's a spectacular collection, especially the big box, which not only includes a *SMiLE* sequence (patterned after 2004's *Brian Wilson Presents SMiLE*), hours of outtakes from the original sessions, but also a handsome book filled with vintage pictures, Frank Holmes's illustrations, a timeline, sessionography, historical essays, and commentary from each of 'the boys.' Given that Mike Love has rarely spoken at length about *SMiLE*, his clever essay is worth reading. Bruce's is especially terrific.

A few comments from the promotional campaign for the box set:

Bruce Johnston: 'It's like a time capsule coming back to earth from the stars. And now we get to listen to it. We're part of it, but I feel like a fan only. I listen to it and I go, "Wow, somebody dreamed that up?"'

Alan Jardine: 'It's just a magical experience.'

Brian: 'When I hear the [original] *SMiLE* tapes, I almost cry. It's great music . . . I'm honoured to hear it.'

With this collection, the world can now hear how amazing Brian's original composing, arranging, and producing work was. We can revel in Van Dyke Parks's dazzling lyrics, as sung by Brian and The Beach Boys with all of the beauty of their harmonic ecstasy. All in pristine sound.

It's genuinely wonderful to delight in The Beach Boys' astonishing vocals. The tone and tenor of their blend is unmatchable. The songs and song fragments are remarkable. The alternative versions make me shake my head in wonder.

I can hear the purity and youth in Brian's voice, a sound that had changed by 2004. I mourn that lost vibration. More than that, I mourn the incalculable loss.

So, in that sense, I find listening to *The Beach Boys SMiLE Sessions* difficult, upsetting. Because of what happened back in 1967, what happened in Brian's artistic and personal life since. But that's just me.

Given what *SMiLE* means to Darian Sahanaja, given the 'deep dive' he had spent listening to the sessions in 2003, was there anything on the box that would have changed *Brian Wilson Presents SMiLE*. His answer? A simple 'No.'

But the collection added a surprising new wrinkle to the *SMiLE* conversation. Because Disc 1 basically follows Brian's 2004 *BWPS* presentation, the debate became, 'Which version of *SMiLE* do you prefer, Brian's or The Beach Boys?'

For me, it was such an odd question. The human drama, the impossible dream, the building up of expectations and the artist's triumph – that all happened in 2004.

The 2011 collection is exceptionally well done. But it is a luminous artifact. From another century. Released about forty-four years too late.

So, for me, the answer was simple. I prefer the 2004 version that was done with love and passion and pure devotion to the artist. With a dedicated band that brought the music of *SMiLE* back to life.

GRAMMYS, LAWSUITS, AND BOX SETS

That said, *The Beach Boys SMiLE Sessions* are 'better' in the sense that it's Brian's original work in the studio with the best musicians in town. It has the vocal instrument he created, The Beach Boys, and their incomparable, inimitable vocal blend. Brian at his absolute peak.

In the outtakes – including the so-called 'pieces' – one can hear not only the artistic genius, but the challenge Brian faced in assembling all of this music for release. And again, applaud how he, Darian, and Van Dyke did that so adeptly and successfully in 2003, how the new music and Van Dyke's new lyrics seamlessly worked.

Hearing it all, one can only wonder again, why didn't it come out? Why wasn't *everybody* cheering Brian on?

In 1967, *SMiLE* could have transformed the music world in a positive way. Releasing the sessions in 2011 was something the fans wanted. It's a wonderful collection. But it doesn't change history. Instead, it re-affirms the tragedy of 1967 and the importance of what happened in 2004.

One last note: As with *The Pet Sounds Sessions* box set, The Beach Boys' name is on the *SMiLE* sessions because that's what the contracts demand. That's what the marketers need. But like 1997's *The Pet Sounds Sessions*, they are, in almost every sense of the word, Brian Wilson's *SMiLE* sessions. He composed, arranged, and produced almost every note.

In his essay in the box set book, Brian wrote that he shelved *SMiLE* because '*SMiLE* was killing me . . . truly, my creative heart was broken . . . it just about choked me to death.'

From the point of view of music history, what else, besides *SMiLE*, did we miss in those thirty-seven years until his heart was healed?

What masterpieces . . . small and large . . . might have emerged if Brian Wilson had finished *SMiLE* in 1967? We got quite a few – 'Diamond Head' and 'Time to Get Alone' and 'Breakaway' and 'This Whole World' and ''Til I Die' and 'Still I Dream of It.' 'Melt Away.' The *Friends* album. And more. We all have our favourites.

But there were so many years of heartbreak and heartache and torture and wasted energy all in service to a 'Brand' that had reached its apex with 'Good Vibrations.'

What would Brian have composed had he not had to devote so much of his energy to his personal survival . . . and The Beach Boys' survival too?

SMiLE

So that's why I can't completely celebrate this box set.

After his brother Carl passed away in 1998, Brian and *his* band began to tour, playing his music live the way he had originally envisioned it. Entire albums, both old (*Pet Sounds*), and brand new (*That Lucky Old Sun*). His magnificent, 'full-circle' record – *Brian Wilson Reimagines Gershwin*. Van Dyke's *Orange Crate Art*.

And, of course, *Brian Wilson Presents SMiLE*.

It's said that from simple acts of courage, great things happen.

There was nothing simple about Brian Wilson presenting *SMiLE*. But it was the most courageous act I've ever had the privilege to witness. And the greatest.

This book honours what Brian Wilson created with Van Dyke Parks in 1966 and presented to the world in 2004 and how that music still resonates today. And will forever.

Van Dyke Parks and Brian Wilson after the world premiere of *Brian Wilson Presents SMiLE*, the Royal Festival Hall, London, February 20, 2004. Celebrating a moment of long delayed triumph.

REPORTS FROM HERE, THERE, AND EVERYWHERE

IN THE 'AUTHOR'S NOTE,' I WROTE THAT MY GOAL WAS FOR THIS BOOK TO include as many different voices as possible. This section is for people I felt had a lot to say, who needed their own space. In this mini-anthology of new *SMiLE* essays, they'll have their turn.

Why did I choose them?

Tom Nolan's 1971 two-part story in *Rolling Stone* was the inspiration for my life with Brian. As he actually was there during the *SMiLE* era, he begins this section. And his piece delights with personal and eyewitness detail.

For additional insight into Brian's approach to composing, arranging, and producing skills, 'School's in Session' is for you.

Prolific rock writer and author Harvey Kubernik follows. He knows everybody associated with Brian's life and the *SMiLE* story, can contextualize their role, has frequently interviewed Brian and talked with all 'the players,' including Debbie Keil-Leavitt, who was not only a true friend of Brian's in the 1970s but also an important figure in mine: her roommate, Eva, became my wife. In Debbie's essay, she writes about their moment together right after the world premiere of *Brian Wilson Presents SMiLE*.

My old orange-juice drinking pal, music journalist and musician Gary Pig Gold, is up next; he's another music lover who has followed Brian, The Beach Boys, and the story of *SMiLE* for a half century. We're then graced with a heartfelt piece from veteran music journalist and author Sylvie Simmons. She should write a book about Brian. One who has, Brian Wilson biographer Peter Carlin, weighs in on *SMiLE*, followed by two musicians for whom Brian was a profound influence: High Llamas mastermind Sean O'Hagan, and David Scott, he of the great Scottish band The Pearlfishers (and a university professor), and a dear friend who was at the world premiere. Mr. Scott's piece is filled with remarkable musical analysis.

Also at the Royal Festival Hall that first night was Andrew G. Doe, *the* British Beach Boys historian and creator of an important Beach Boys/Brian Wilson website. Of course, no book on *SMiLE* would be complete without hearing from Domenic Priore who *Mojo* magazine called 'the world's foremost *SMiLE*-ologist.'

In the penultimate piece, music professor and scholar Dr. Daniel Harrison gives us informed insight on the classical nature of *SMiLE*.

That's followed with contemporary memories from Brian's band and friends when I asked them to look back and tell me what it means, twenty years later, to have been part of *Brian Wilson Presents SMiLE*.

And finally, a personal memoir from by far the youngest of our essayists. She wasn't even born when the original *SMiLE* sessions took place, but Charlotte Martin's relationship to Brian Wilson's music and the story of *SMiLE* is – as Brian wrote in "Til I Die' – as 'deep as the ocean.' For five years, she's thought, almost compulsively, about Brian and what he's had to overcome, as he's gotten past "Til I Die' and come back to 'Surf's Up.' And as you'll read, this water analogy isn't used carelessly.

INSPIRATION
by Tom Nolan

I drew the boy away from his audience. He pulled back from my touch, but he came along and sat down with me on a cracked leather couch. Some of the younger boys had put an overplayed record on a player. Two of them began to dance together to the raucous self-parodying song. 'Surfin' ain't no sin,' was the refrain.

— Ross Macdonald, The Far Side of the Dollar, 1965

IF YOU GREW UP IN SOUTHERN CALIFORNIA IN THE 1960s, YOU'D HAVE HAD to make a special effort not to be exposed to The Beach Boys several times a week. Their hit singles were in constant play on the AM stations (KFWB, KHJ) we listened to. The Boys performed at the Hollywood Bowl. They were sometime guests on KFWB's Sunday night *Teen Talk* radio show with deejay B. Mitchell Reed. Their Capitol LPs were on prominent display at Clyde Wallichs' Music City at the corner of Sunset and Vine, the biggest (and priciest) record shop in white L.A., just a couple blocks from the Capitol Records tower, home of The Beach Boys label, owned by Clyde Wallichs' brother Glenn.

Living in L.A., we were used to seeing celebrities out in public. At the private school I attended, Hollywood Professional, several well-known young people were our classmates: Ryan O'Neal, Peggy Lipton, Brenda Lee, Mouseketeer Cubby O'Brien. We took them in stride.

But it was a whole other matter when Beach Boy Carl Wilson joined our student body in 1964. His first morning at school was unlike anything ever seen there. An awestruck crowd of teens surrounded him in the hall as he tried to make his way to class. He was the calm and quiet centre of a big soft cloud of welcoming admirers. Other Beach Boys-affiliated students would also join our ranks, someone in the hall said: David Marks, an original BB who'd left the band after their first four LPs (replaced by Al Jardine) and two sisters, Marilyn and Diane Rovell, who with their cousin Ginger Blake, recorded on Capitol as the Honeys (produced by Beach Boys leader Brian Wilson) and were heard doing the cheerleaders' chants on the Boys' recent single 'Be True to Your School' ('Push 'em back, push 'em back, waaaay – back!'). Now our school, in a sense, was The Beach Boys' school. The Beach Boys! How great was that?

The reserved and unassuming Carl immediately became a revered presence at HPS. Our auditorium assembly house band, the Renegades – with Eddie Medora and Marty di Giovanni – would gather around him on the sidewalk after school to talk shop. 'Who plays that great guitar solo on 'Fun, Fun, Fun' – oh, is that you? That's so cool!' Carl caused our HPS band to be signed by Tower, a Capitol subsidiary, where, as the Sun Rays, they were produced by the Wilsons' father Murry. Years later, Carl would say he'd done all this to keep his meddlesome dad (recently fired by the Boys) out of The Beach Boys' hair.

There was still plenty of room on the charts then for Beach Boys-style discs celebrating sunshine, new cars, and carefree hedonism. But the times and the sounds were changing. Forces of the British Invasion had captured large sections of the Billboard 100, and folk-rock had opened up a second front. The Beatles came to America in February of '64, when 'Fun, Fun, Fun' was number three; in August, they played the Hollywood Bowl. (Two HPS seniors, Peggy Lipton and Mirandi Babitz [younger sister of Eve], met the English visitors that week at a party in the Hollywood Hills and formed significant friendships – Peggy with Paul, Mirandi with Ringo.)

Carl Wilson's older brother Brian, The Beach Boys' leader, chief writer, co-vocalist, arranging maestro and wizard producer, was at first flabbergasted by the success of this English group, his Capitol labelmates in the States. He soon claimed kinship with them, though, and knew he needed to up his musical game. In '65, after an emotional breakdown during an airplane flight, he quit touring with the Boys to concentrate on writing and recording.

In the summer of '65, The Beach Boys put out 'California Girls,' an impressively conceived anthem to sun-kissed pulchritude co-written by

INSPIRATION

Brian and his cousin Mike Love, which went to number three on the charts. (The Beatles' 'Help' was number one; number two was Bob Dylan's 'Like a Rolling Stone.')

In early 1966, Brian began recording a new album, *Pet Sounds*, which he largely co-wrote with lyricist Tony Asher, a London-born ad copywriter and the son of early screen star Laura La Plante. The album featured orchestral instruments – brass, strings, reeds – all scored by Wilson. A great departure instrumentally and thematically from the Boys' previous recordings, *Pet Sounds* was harmonically adventurous, its lyrics melancholy and bittersweet.

This Beach Boys' response to The Beatles' ascendancy was approached with a seriousness that approached the spiritual: 'My brother Carl,' Brian would say to me, 'thinks The Beatles are an act of God.' The two brothers prayed together before they began work on *Pet Sounds*, he'd reveal – prayed that they would make as good an album as The Beatles' recent *Rubber Soul*. But *Pet Sounds* was met with consternation at Capitol Records; the label gave the LP minimal promotion upon its May 1966 American release. In England, by contrast, it was a smash.

Popular music was changing at a remarkable rate on both sides of the Atlantic. Moods and styles shifted month to month. New artists asserted themselves each week. I wanted to be a part of this scene, as a paid observer if not a performer. After HPS, I became a writer for *West*, the new *L.A. Times* Sunday magazine. I was 18 and Brian Wilson was 24 when I met him on assignment one afternoon in August 1966 at his in-laws' house in West Hollywood. Also present was his wife of two years, Marilyn Rovell. The Beach Boys' coolly charismatic publicist Derek Taylor was there, too: The Beatles' ex-associate responsible for an ongoing 'Brian Wilson is a genius' press campaign. ('I'm not a genius,' Brian would say. 'I'm just a hardworking guy.' When the brilliant PR man died in 1997, Brian would add: 'It was Derek Taylor who was the genius.')

There was no pretension about Brian when I met him in the Rovells' dining room. He wore white jeans and a tee-shirt with big blue stripes, and on the table was a neat pile of tuna-fish sandwiches.

For the last several years, he'd been a Prince of Pop in L.A., writing more songs than his own group could handle, doling out extra hit tunes munificently to Jan and Dean or The Hondells. The pop wunderkind spoke with much enthusiasm of The Beach Boys' own in-production 45, to which he was still adding finishing touches; he was in the final production stages of The Beach Boys' twenty-fourth single in five years, 'Good Vibrations.'

With a taskmaster's relish, he spoke of how he would soon get 'the guys' into a booth together and crank up their harmonic focus and intensity to the sticking-point. 'It's gonna be a monster,' he told me. 'It's a song about a guy who picks up, you know, good vibrations from a girl. Of course, it's still sticking pretty close to that same "boy-girl" thing, you know, but with a difference. And it's a start; it's definitely a start.'

Toward what? In which direction did he think pop music – his brand of pop – was heading?

'Spiritual,' he said without pause. 'White spirituals, I think that's what we're going to have. Songs of faith. Anyhow, that's the direction I wanna go; I'm very religious. Not in the sense of church, going to church; but like, the essence of all religion. Yeah.' He liked that. 'The essence of all religion.'

What prompted this drastic change in artistic direction for the co-author of 'Fun, Fun, Fun ('Til Your Daddy Takes the T-Bird Away)'? As you've already read, as he told me, it was LSD. Brian: 'I consider it a very religious experience.'

If consummate devotion to a task is equivalent to religious dedication, Brian Wilson was looking spiritual a few days later, at Hollywood's Western Studio, recording instrumental parts for a track to be called 'Look (Song For Children)', one of the cuts for the next Beach Boys album (working title, *Dumb Angel*). Several session players were assembled, along with engineers and technicians, Marilyn Rovell Wilson, and, at the centre of everything, uber-maestro Brian Douglas Wilson: throwing cues, calling takes, correcting nuances, rallying troops: 'Okay please, one more.'

Among the musicians were jazz guitarists Barney Kessel and Herb Ellis, one of whom called out to Brian that a four-bar vamp in his chart was from 'Twelfth Street Rag': 'You can't use that; that's copyright material.' 'That's all right,' Brian said, with a look of mild annoyance, 'I'll pay for it.' He gave Barney a stern look. 'You know I don't steal.'

During Take 20's playback, he placed a chair beneath a wall speaker, stood on it, cupped his one good ear and placed it right up next to the woofer-webbing to make sure everything he wanted to hear in the mix was audible. An engineer asked Marilyn if she thought her husband would

INSPIRATION

be satisfied with this one? 'No,' she said. 'When he gets home, he won't be satisfied. He's never satisfied.'

Wilson was content, at least, with 'Good Vibrations,' released as a single on October 10, 1966, and becoming as huge a hit as its producer had predicted: The Beach Boys' first number one million-seller. Meanwhile, work continued on the album *Dumb Angel*, soon renamed *SMiLE*. The LP was touted in Capitol's in-house magazine as a Christmas 1966 release (in retrospect, a wildly unrealistic promise).

In the wake of 'Good Vibrations' and *Pet Sounds*, advance interest in the new album was fast building. But many problems were developing around its production. Later, I learned one of them came into Brian's life through my *West* magazine piece.

Brian told associates he thought he was being followed by someone: he recognized the same car showing up all the time at his destinations. His pals downplayed the notion, one of them told me: 'We said he was just being paranoid, but it turned out to be true! [His father] Murry had hired a private detective to tail Brian, after your story quoted him saying he'd taken LSD. Murry wanted the detective to find out if Brian was still buying or taking drugs.'

Murry and Brian had battled throughout Brian's childhood. The friction hadn't ceased after Brian's early success. If anything, the chief Beach Boy's rise magnified the tensions inherent in a family plagued by ego contests, power struggles, and the clash of wills.

Carl recalled to me (in 1971) how, when they were teens living at home, Brian rigged up a speaker that let him broadcast out his car window; and how he parked in the driveway near his parents' bedroom window early one evening when he thought Murry and Audree were engaged in physical intimacy. In his best bullhorn basso, Brian barked: 'All right, you in there! This is the police! We know what you're doing! Cut it out! Come out of there, right now!'

High jinks? Teen spirit taken a bit too far? But what awful words and deeds was Brian trying to get back at, from the parent who'd insulted and abused him through many toxic years (but had also taught him to play boogie-woogie piano, and wept in happiness at the harmonies sung by his three young sons) and who'd made a pest of himself for years during The Beach Boys' recording sessions until at last his own sons forced him to leave?

Once Brian became his own Murry-less producer, he was free to take some gripes out through his art. 'I'm bugged at my old man,' he'd write and sing in a 1965 track of the same name, 'and he doesn't even know where it's at.'

Weirder warps than Murry Wilson's espionage were being woven into the *SMiLE* weave in late 1966. One revolved around the November recording at Hollywood's Gold Star studios of a number called 'Fire' (later, 'Mrs. O'Leary's Cow'), an off-centre, atonal boogie-woogie Walpurgisnacht featuring loopy slide-whistle sirens, a runaway carnival organ, and wordless moaning vocal riffs – part of a suite called 'The Elements.' Listening to it induced a weird vertigo: like getting seasick in a plunging elevator. Brian had the fifteen assembled musicians (including three bass, four flutes, and a string sextet) wear red fire helmets, to put them in a fiery mood; and smoke from a bucket of smouldering wood enhanced the atmosphere.

Subsequently, Dennis brought to Brian's attention that there'd been a serious fire at a nearby building a day after their 'Fire' session. 'Dennis had a map,' said a witness to the event, 'on which he'd drawn a line connecting Gold Star to this neighboring structure. "Look," he said, "they're in a straight line." Well – any two points you connect are in a straight line!'

But Brian was spooked. Dennis all but convinced him the conceptual 'Fire' they'd summoned at Gold Star had caused the actual one at this other edifice. Already nervous about the 'witchy' nature of the session he'd conducted, Brian decided this 'magic fire music' should never be released. 'I don't have to do a big scary fire like that,' he told writer Jules Siegel, a journalist embedded with The Beach Boys on assignment from the *Saturday Evening Post*. 'I can do a candle and it's still a fire.' (But might not even a candle be enough to melt the waxen wings of an unbalanced Icarus?)

Even as Brian's insecurity, anxiety and paranoia increased, the outside world's interest in the music he was creating in a couple of Hollywood recording studios was growing exponentially. In December, a CBS production crew came to L.A. to film segments for a Leonard Bernstein special on artistically ambitious modern American pop music. As one of their prime subjects, Brian was filmed in solo performance, playing piano and singing 'Surf's Up,' one of the extraordinary songs he and *SMiLE* lyricist

INSPIRATION

Van Dyke Parks (then 23) had written: unique compositions spun out of blue sky and old earth, recurring visions and intricate rhythms, American myth and European gloom. Here pop song met art song. Perhaps nothing like this had been heard before on AM or FM, in the States or the UK. And it seemed not at all like *Pet Sounds*; it was a new conception.

But more weeks passed. 1966 became '67. Brian had felt daunted by The Beatles' February single 'Strawberry Fields Forever' and worried the English group had already surpassed whatever he could achieve with *SMiLE*. Was that yet another flaming bale of hay thrown into Brian's path, convincing him to abandon his *SMiLE* dream? A dream-become-a-hydra-headed tar-baby of a nightmare?

When Mike Love, Brian's cousin and (until *Pet Sounds*) long-time lyricist, insisted Van Dyke Parks explain the words to 'Cabin Essence,' *SMiLE*'s co-creator, a young man grounded in history and aesthetics and with highly individualized ways of expressing himself, decided he'd had enough of this increasingly problematic and contentious project. His lyrics all written, he took his leave of the Wilson clan. Brian gave him a pricey foreign sedan as a farewell present. 'Brian was very generous,' he'd say.

I asked Jules Sigel, circa 1969, why he thought Brian couldn't, wouldn't, didn't choose to finish *SMiLE*. He paused a while, then said: 'I think he was afraid that if he put it out, somebody would kill him.'

'Sometime in the spring of '67,' Brian Wilson would recollect, 'I just told everybody that we weren't going to finish *SMiLE*.'

I woke on the morning of July 24, 1967, and turned on the radio, which was tuned to KHJ. It was the top of the hour and deejay Sam Riddle said he had a fine surprise for us: the new Beach Boys single being heard for the first time – 'Heroes And Villains.' Best single heard since 'Good Vibrations.' Was this a sign that *SMiLE*, said to be abandoned, had been resurrected? Finished at last? Soon in stores?

Not quite. Instead of *SMiLE*, there was *Smiley Smile*: a brief LP with minimal production elements and an intimate feel, full of invention and whimsy and shifts of aural textures. It sounded handmade, homemade - like songs emanating from a canyon cabin. Laurel Canyon? Edgy charm. Wit balanced on a rubber-knife's edge. Even 'Good Vibrations' (included) surrendered to the shaggy-dog mystique.

So this is the way that *SMiLE* ends: not with a bang but a whisper.

SMiLE

Was this some sort of joke? In 1967, *Smiley Smile* seemed to many *SMiLE*-awaiters a great disappointment, even a mean prank.

And then – turn around little one, and you're 56 – in 2004, when no one ever expected any such thing, a merciful zeitgeist (with a little help from its *Friends*) delivered *Brian Wilson Presents SMiLE*: not a recreation per se, nor a brand-new creation, but a transcendental deconstruction reconstructed by the gentlest and least intrusive of near-non-collaborators. With Brian aboard, it toured the world. Critics liked it. Patrons loved it. And the notorious 'Fire' music won a Grammy award.

Flash-forward seven years ('57!' '58!' '59!' '60!'): Capitol puts out a handsome box, *The Beach Boys SMiLE Sessions,* holding a goodly assemblage of those legendary, long-abandoned, never-heard, original working tapes for universal delectation, learned discussion, comparison, and, most of all, enjoyment.

And on the very last page of the *TBBSS* booklet, at the tail end of the many thanks and credits, are these lines, tying up what surely must be the very final loose *SMiLE* end left and fit to be tied: "Look (Song for Children)' contains music from 'Twelfth Street Rag.' Music by Euday L. Bowman (Public Domain).'

So there, Barney Kessel.

(Copyright 2024 by Tom Nolan)
Tom Nolan is the author of *Ross Macdonald: A Biography* and *Three Chords for Beauty's Sake: The Life of Artie Shaw.*

SCHOOL'S IN SESSION

IF YOU'RE INTERESTED IN WHY BRIAN'S MUSIC IS SO SPECIAL, IN LEARNING about the recording techniques that Brian used during the *SMiLE* era, this piece is for you. Brian understood recording technique in ways that astounded Brian's closest friends, collaborators, his band, and those he influenced.

Van Dyke: 'Brian was aware of proportion, but he was also trying to make his music accessible. And he did that by saturating the tape with sound . . . There is this thing called kinematic viscosity. And you take tape or film through a gate at a certain speed. And it's the medium itself that determines how fast you can do that . . . And Brian knew about that. You could see it in his work. He would take the needle and he knew what his working area was. And in the sounds that he got, it was in the relationship between the sounds.'

This is important as it relates to Brian's one-of-a-kind ability in the studio.

Van Dyke: 'He would premix some tracks, say, two or three tracks, not adjacent tracks to get, because you couldn't use the adjacent tracks. We were working with three-track. And if you wanted to have twelve different re-recordings, you had to continue to commit sound to tape and premix the tape.'

David Anderle: 'You had to do what we called "ping-ponging." So you'd have to record one thing on one track, then you'd mix that, and then you'd move it over to another track. Do another recording – back and forth, to build the sound. I never saw anyone do that like Brian. He just knew what he wanted to hear, and he just went for it, and he'd be mixing with every recording. He was a total music machine.'

Van Dyke: 'This *SMiLE* thing came from his interest in studio procedure. "What was going on in the studio. How can we do that?" Let's see – play the mallets half as fast, twice as well. If I reduce the tape speed by half, I can play them up an octave, and I'll get a decent roll. That's something you find out if you're somebody like Brian Wilson or Les Paul. You find it out by yourself. Studio technique.'

Danny Hutton: 'I have four tracks and I have eight tracks. I can bounce things. I can layer things. I can stack things up. And all of a sudden, the studio becomes one of the instruments that you're playing.'

Van Dyke: 'And what Brian would do was take a radical approach to compression of sound . . . to limit the amount, the decibel excursion, so it wouldn't be too loud or too soft. It took a lot more thought, and it was a lot more hazardous to premix these tracks. What Brian was doing was really working in a high-risk way with sound. And it's fair to say that he did it by saturating the tape. Saturating it on the bottom end. Saturating at the top. "Stretching the ends," is what it's called. It's not for anything but to make the listening experience more gratifying.'

What Danny Hutton saw in the studio was something we can all hear today. Genius. Or 'ingenious', as Brian preferred. Who wants the pressure of being called 'a genius?' Not Brian.

In the tracking sessions, as Danny Hutton explains, 'He went in there trying to get emotion out of [classically-trained musicians]. I think a lot of them were shocked, 'cause they were just used to playing the notes correctly and he'd go in and say, "No. I want you to lean on the note more. Make it sound like crying." "When you're shaking a tambourine, make it sound like jewelry," or "tinkling or like wind chimes, wind . . . soft, like warm breeze . . . slowly going through the wind chimes." So, he talked in a different way to them.

'What was fascinating, not only would he get a great sound but the ability, with the lack of tracks in those days, to get a great sound. And then go to a completely different studio, different sized room, and record pieces. And then be able to seamlessly put them together. And have it flow. Just amazing.

'In those days, if you wanted a little section of a record [to have] silence, you couldn't just put it in. [Back] then you had to physically snip tape. You couldn't just snip in a piece of blank tape. You'd have to record, "Everybody be quiet," record the ambiance of the room, the silence of the room. And then put that in. It was that sensitive. And he

SCHOOL'S IN SESSION

had the ability to go from one studio to the other, and [the] wonderful, technical skill to do that.'

Fortunately, Brian's twenty-first century band was filled with musicians for whom *SMiLE* was their holy grail. Probyn Gregory explains how innovative this music is.

Probyn: 'The only other person I know that has this kind of inventiveness with alternate bass notes is Johann Sebastian Bach. He used to put all sorts of things in the root notes of chords, unheard of at that time. And it wasn't really done much subsequently. Of course, there are modern avant-garde composers that do that, but someone that was as popular as Brian Wilson was in popular music, it just wasn't done. In the mid-sixties, nobody was doing that.'

Asked to explain this to a non-musician, Probyn had to be more than a bit technical, but it's worth it because it gives you a sense of why the A-list, jazz-based studio musicians were amazed by what Brian was doing in the mid-1960s.

Probyn: 'One of Brian's tricks was to put a major seventh in the bass. A major seventh is a note one half step away from the octave. As an example, let's say you have a root note, C. And the natural octave is also C. The next note down from C in the major scale is B. When you play those two notes together alone, B and C, it is harsh – they rub. It sounds like something's wrong when they're playing together. Although if you add the other notes of the chord, it evens out and sounds good, C E G B. But imagine if you took it one step further, and put that major seventh (B) down an octave, in the root of the chord instead of C.

'Now you have B C E G. It's a disturbing sound with the two close notes rubbing against each other way down there. I remember the first time I heard that in 'Holidays.' I said, "They're playing the wrong bass note. The studio musicians must be not reading it right, they're playing the wrong note." But then, the more you hear it, it works. It works! They have the major seventh, thrown down into the bass, against a C chord, having a B in the bottom. It's calculated to unsettle the listener, and to create a new colour. And Brian's really great at that. And a lot of songs he has thirds or fifths or dominant sevenths in the bass. But the major seventh, I don't think even J.S. Bach ever did that. (*Laughs*)'

Nick Walusko elaborates and contextualizes it. 'Brian was doing very advanced music, for his age, at a time where he had to obviously cloak it in the surf and fun and car thing. But those things are deceptively simple.'

Sir Elton John: 'Brian just threw away the rulebook . . . For a keyboard player like myself, he changed the goalposts when it came to writing songs. He was one of the first to move the root note of the chord to the third or the fifth of the bass, and if you're a songwriter or a keyboard player, that was revolutionary.'

Phew. 'School's Out.'

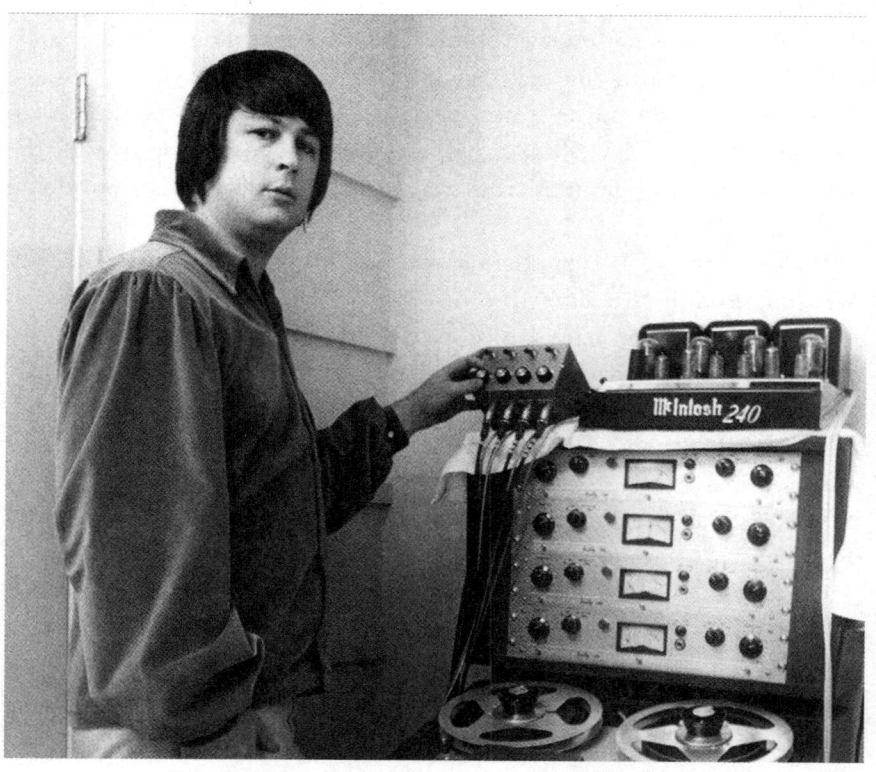

Brian, in 1966, in his home studio on Laurel Way in Beverly Hills. Audio experimentation had begun in earnest.

HONOUR THE INCARNATION

by Harvey Kubernik

I FIRST READ ABOUT *SMILE* IN THE *KRLA BEAT*, A WEEKLY MUSIC PERIODICAL published in Southern California. As a teenager, I was confused. Why would The Beach Boys record Charlie Chaplin's song 'Smile,' from his 1936 movie *Modern Times?*

I would soon learn that was the name of an album. I kept reading about it being recorded at various studios including Gold Star, United Western, RCA, Columbia, and Sunset Sound, and I remember waiting for many months for it to arrive at Wallichs Music City in Hollywood.

As school started at Fairfax High in September 1967, I purchased a copy of *Smiley Smile*. At the time, I knew nothing of the machinations of the original *SMiLE* Brian Wilson was carrying around in his head.

My mother worked at Columbia Studios in Gower Gulch, and from 1965-1968 was based at Raybert Productions, producers of *The Monkees* television series. She helped type the weekly TV scripts for two seasons. After school, I would spend hours after school on the lot or navigating Sunset Blvd.

I recall in 1966, mulling around the nearby Moulin Rouge venue (later to be known as The Hullabaloo Club, The Kaleidoscope and The Aquarius Theater). Brian was inside with The Beach Boys teaching them the intricate vocal parts of 'Good Vibrations' so they could perform it live on tour. In 2007, Brian told me in a lunch interview that he flew to Michigan in '66 to see 'Good Vibrations' performed live for the first time.

'I wanted it to be done right. I knew it could work on stage. I never thought, "*How* is this gonna work live, in front of an audience?" I just remember saying, "That's fantastic." Ten-minute standing ovation. What was it like? I was proud as hell. I took a bow. I knew the group could perform the material on stage. When it went to number one, it did give me some confidence [to] write in sections.'

Before the London premiere of *Brian Wilson Presents SMiLE*, I was invited to a Burbank rehearsal stage to watch Brian and his band do their curated *SMiLE* repertoire.

I knew there would be a sense of relief for Brian that some of his 1966 *SMiLE* vision was going to be seen and devoured by an audience in England that was fully aware of the saga of *SMiLE*. He was smiling.

In the fall of 2004, when the tour came back to L.A., *I* got to devour the Brian Wilson-centric *SMiLE* concert at Disney Hall. I had feared that *SMiLE* would be something which would happen posthumously for Brian and that classical orchestras were going to start performing sections and selections from *SMiLE*. I realized for Brian that it was a joyous and liberating feeling for *SMiLE* to finally be heard in a live setting, then to have his recording hit the highest chart position of a new Wilson-produced album since *Pet Sounds*.

Over lunch at his favourite neighbourhood deli, I asked him about the songs he and Van Dyke Parks wrote in 1966. Brian: 'I always knew the songs were strong enough. 'Heroes And Villains,' 'Surf's Up.' Like on 'Heroes And 'Villains,' and 'God Only Knows . . .' There weren't songs on the radio with God in the title. Then, there were no songs with 'Villains' on the radio.'

Brian reiterated: 'The songs kept sticking with me. I knew they would be heard one day. I don't think about where I was when I wrote them . . . I did not write it for any specific one of the guys. I wrote it for myself.'

Do *I* still have a sense of dread about *SMiLE*? Yeah, because I wonder where pop music would have gone if *SMiLE* was issued a handful of months before The Beatles' *Sgt. Pepper's Lonely Hearts Club Band*.

As for *SMiLE,* it's filled with revealing and complicated stories of America. Nothing is more regional than a composition by Brian Wilson and Van Dyke Parks recorded in Hollywood on Sunset Boulevard or Vine Street with instrumental tracks supplied by Local 47 Hollywood Musicians Union members.

HONOUR THE INCARNATION

You get elements of the movie *Shane,* the Old West, plus the omnipresent influence of the beach. A words and music examination of the toil about our sacred soil.

What a sense of accomplishment it must have been for Brian and his band to perform *SMiLE* the way he wanted it presented.

However, I admit *SMiLE* to me will always have a murky and misguided history. But, as Ram Dass reinforced to me, 'Honour the incarnation.'

Acknowledging that instruction, I quote this letter from poet/deejay, Dr. James Cushing, a retired Professor of English and Literature at Cal Poly San Luis Obispo. Cushing discussed the connection of *SMiLE* and Hart Crane's *The Bridge*.

'I think *SMiLE* and *The Bridge* are both brave art-essays on the subconscious, poetic meaning of the contradictions of American history and the American character.'

(Harvey Kubernik is the author of twenty books on music and pop culture, including 2009's *Canyon of Dreams: The Magic and the Music of Laurel Canyon* and 2014's *Turn Up the Radio! Rock, Pop and Roll in Los Angeles 1956-1972*. As industry commentator Bob Lefsetz, said, 'Harvey is a music history savant . . . dedicated his entire life to rock and roll, and his memory is extraordinary. Harvey experienced it all first-hand.')

THE NIGHT OF THE WORLD PREMIERE

by Debbie Keil-Leavitt

'SEE DEBBIE, YOU *CAN* LOVE SOMEONE ENOUGH.' EVA AND I WERE IN THE lobby of the Marriott County Hall with a bottle of Taittinger sitting between us. What we had just witnessed was the breathtaking first performance of *Brian Wilson Presents SMiLE* at Royal Festival Hall.

Eva was Eva Easton-Leaf, my roommate for five years before she and the author of this book connected. She had a way with 'one-liners,' and that was the best line of the whole event.

When asked to write this remembrance, that was the first thing that came to mind about *SMiLE*, looking back twenty years later from the perspective of my 'advanced years.'

We knew that this wonderful work would be treasured as long as humans can listen, but we also experienced nearly everyone we saw at the performances brought to tears. We were taken on a hero's journey through Brian's glorious music and Van Dyke Parks' sublime lyrics, and yet this was a mythic journey unfolding inside an actual 'live' resurrection myth.

When *SMiLE* was shelved, I didn't dare to dream that it would actually be finished someday, let alone in 2004. In the past, I was honestly too afraid to even mention *SMiLE* to Brian. While I avoided the subject, little did I know how much this unfinished work haunted him until that performance.

It took immense courage on the part of Brian and Van to face that ancient wound and generously share this healing with everyone who

THE NIGHT OF THE WORLD PREMIERE

listens. As amazing as Brian's band was that night, it took a lot more than their remarkable versatility and talent to make this happen. They loved Brian and the music enough to help bring this much-anticipated work of art to the public. It was impeccable.

His family and friends loved him enough to support him through his experience. His fellow musicians and fans also surrounded him with the love needed for Brian to visibly transform while performing. At that point, life, art and myth came together to create the rare achievement of the sublime through art – nothing less than transformation through the power of love.

These many years later, I am simply, profoundly grateful for what happened, that I got to witness it. And to see that yes, we *can* love someone enough.

(Debbie Keil-Levitt worked for The Beach Boys for a year, and she and Brian were close friends throughout the 1970s. After a long career in management, Debbie became a private pilot and volunteered her technical writing skills to assist aviation safety groups in honour of her mother and father, Gerry and Harold Keil, who worked for TWA. She moved back to her hometown of Kansas City with her husband, Prof. Harvey Leavitt. She continues her lifelong study of the stars and the history of humanity's relationship with them through storytelling, archetypes, and mythology.)

THE *SMiLE* THAT YOU SEND OUT

by Gary Pig Gold

AS A PROUDLY SELF-CONFESSED MUSIC OBSESSIVE STRUGGLING THROUGH not only high school, but the very early Seventies in those Toronto suburbs, there had been intriguing clues sprinkled along the way: The absolute thrill rediscovering 'Heroes And Villains' as it opened Side 2 of the first Beach Boys album I ever owned (a typically quickie Capitol compilation called *Good Vibrations*). Then, soon afterwards, the cinematic-and-*then*-some sweep of the final five minutes from *Sunflower*, the title track of the band's *next* LP [*Surf's Up*], then last but certainly not least the Boys' 'Prayer' and even more so 'Cabin Essence,' which I can hear filling my pre-dawn headphones now just as it did in '74 via that enticingly packaged *Wild Honey* and *20/20* two-fer.

But! It was two extended volumes of reading that mattered – a full reprint of Tom Nolan's landmark 1971 *Rolling Stone* study I uncovered in a Beach Boys songbook, followed several years later by David Leaf's one and still only *California Myth* – which not only began to put all those pieces of the *SMiLE* saga scattered across the above-mentioned long-players into some sort of context, but fully burst open not just my ears, but my *mind* to the magic, musical and otherwise, of what was, and remains, Brian Wilson.

Farther down this path was the burgeoning underground tape trading community of the 1980s. That, then a thorough scouring of Greenwich Village, ahem, specialty shops helped to slowly but ever surely stitch together this sonic puzzle, culminating with Domenic Priore's expert

THE SMiLE THAT YOU SEND OUT

SMiLE reconstruction as broadcast over the WFMU New Jersey air circa 1996. *Then*, as things became 'official' with actual box sets, literary studies, and the inevitable websites focused upon those critical months of Brian's, folks as diverse as Peter Buck and Linda Ronstadt were suddenly rhapsodizing over one particular hour of music and madness which never *quite* made it out of 1966/67 intact. Wasn't it no less than Todd Rundgren who once suggested loading each fragment into the nearest CD-ROM and having us all compile our own *SMiLE*'s? Maybe he was on to something . . . though Darian Sahanaja got there first (thank heavens).

Now, those more pragmatic chart-watchers amongst us persist in debating whether, if released as scheduled, Capitol could indeed have been sure to sell a million T-2580s in a pure pop marketplace totally dominated by Monkees. Even if it *did* come hot upon the heels of the band's recent good, good, good global number one. And/or if the Boys' tragic non-appearance at Monterey that summer sealed, at least for a few decades, their fate as, quote unquote, surfing Doris Days. But what can *not* be questioned whatsoever is that the *sounds* of *SMiLE*, unlike the vast majority of said era's most notables, seem far from haplessly trapped in vintage DayGlo amber; to wit, despite a half-century's hoopla we hear even *Pepper*'s each and every groove continuing to scream one big loud '1967.'

On *much* the other hand entirely, Brian Wilson's finest creations remain as timely as they are timeless.

Examples? It still warms my soul to recall the tearful standing ovation awarded Van Dyke Parks as he rose, introduced by Brian, from his seat at the 2004 Carnegie Hall *SMiLE* recital. Two old soldiers in heartfelt recognition and appreciation with this particular battle of theirs, against all odds, finally and indisputably won. And it still raises a grin to recall, following his intimate gathering at NYC's 92nd Street Y, Lindsey Buckingham ravenously insisting I tell him all about the big new *SMiLE Sessions* box I'd just that afternoon received from Amazon . . . much to the chagrin of his publicist who was trying in vain to get their post-show meet 'n' greet back onto track and on to some others waiting in line.

After all is said and sung however, most reaffirming and gratifying to *me* is the too true knowledge that, after seeking out or perhaps simply stumbling upon it, somewhere someway out there today, and I'm sure over countless days to come, someone brand new is breaking into a *SMiLE* for the first time and forever falling deep under its spell. Completely.

So won't you excuse me now as I join them, once again, to close my eyes and lean back, listening deeply too.

(Gary Pig Gold turned his lifelong love of music, Beach Boys and otherwise, into Canada's first-ever self-published fanzine *The Pig Paper*, before launching his own career as a songwriter, arranger, performer, and producer.)

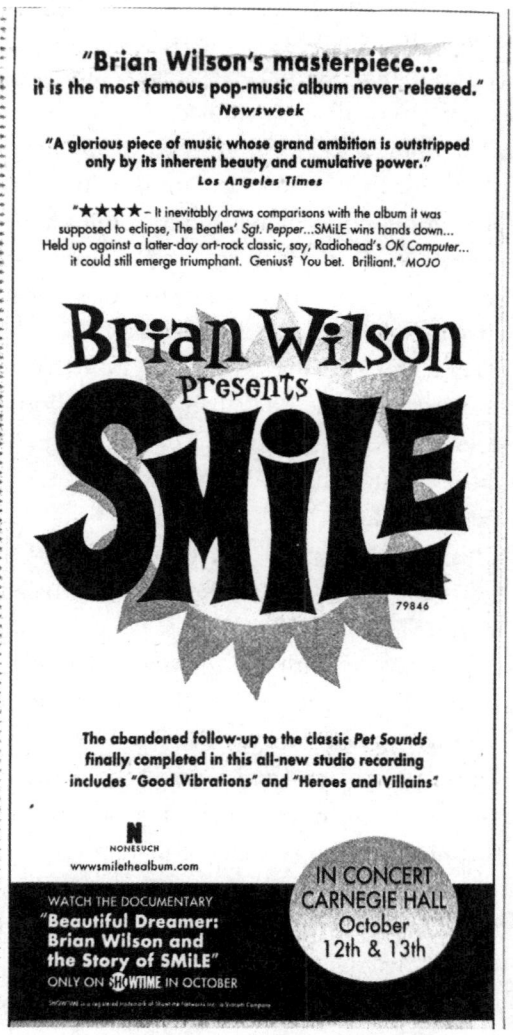

The record company went all out to sell this record. Just one of the Nonesuch ads for *Brian Wilson Presents SMiLE* in *The New York Times*.

HALLELUJAH!

by Sylvie Simmons

WE WERE TALKING ON THE PHONE NOT LONG AGO, DAVID LEAF AND I, about the night in February 2004 when Brian Wilson's *SMiLE* had its premiere at the Royal Festival Hall in London. How the place was packed to the gills. The churchlike silence that fell with the opening notes of *SMiLE*. The feeling that this was something special, sacred even. Then, when it was over, that delirious ten-minute standing ovation, everybody on their feet, big-name fans included. It seemed like no-one in the room was ready to leave, so there they stood, many with tears in their eyes.

Backstage after the show, the first person I ran into was Van Dyke Parks. Brian's lyricist, arranger, and friend was smiling and crying at the same time. I can't recall his exact words when we hugged but the look on his face said everything. Brian, on the other hand, was grinning from ear to ear. 'What do you think of my album?' he asked me, 'What do you think of it?' I told him it was glorious. It was.

I didn't remind him that the last time we spoke about *SMiLE* his mood couldn't have been more different. A couple of months earlier I'd been interviewing him in his house in L.A for a feature on *SMiLE* for *Mojo* magazine. With each question I asked he became darker and more and more agitated. Not only didn't he want to talk about *SMiLE*, he seemed to deny having anything to do with it. Around halfway through my questioning Brian got up, shook my hand, and said goodbye. He walked out of his front door into his car and made his getaway. And now here he was, in my hometown, happy and proud, entirely owning *SMiLE*.

Darian Sahanaja, the member of Brian's remarkable band who'd worked closely with him on the project, witnessed that transformation himself.

At the end of the London show, during the ovation, he looked over at Brian who sat impassively at the front of the stage. 'I saw,' he said, 'what was almost like the weight just floating away from his body.' In the wings Brian grabbed his arm and declared, 'Darian, we *did* it. We *did* it!' Certainly did.

SMiLE – such a simple title for an album of such sweeping complexity. Such an incongruous title given its nightmarish effect on the man who created it. As I write this, two decades after the show and more than five decades since the album's origins, I've been thinking about what it was that made *SMiLE* such an enduring obsession for so many. There's been no shortage of lost albums, or lost artists, since the Sixties, so how did this one come to be the Lost Ark of pop/rock? Though to be accurate, it wasn't lost. It was shattered, like Brian was. The pieces were stored on tapes in the archives or in parts of Brian's memory where for a long time he was unwilling or unable to go.

I came up with some answers, as rock writers do, but I erased them all, because there is no simple answer. It depends on many factors: your age, your provenance, your interest in music and cultural history, where you fit on the scale of Beach Boys fandom between casual and superfan, and what your expectations were, given the brilliance of the last album Brian wrote alone with the band on tour, quite how much of a masterpiece Brian's 'teenage symphony to God' was likely to be.

I was a Beach Boys fan since the Sixties, a young child listening to the radio and singing along with their sunny singles under a dark grey London sky. But my musical obsession, being British, was The Beatles. I had no idea then, having never read a music magazine let alone written for one, that Brian was obsessed with The Beatles too. And The Beatles with Brian. In retrospect it makes sense they would become fellow-travellers – and competitors. They had a lot in common, both inspired by black American music with additional ingredients of their own. In The Beach Boys' case, Gershwin, doo-wop, jazz harmony, plus Chuck Berry; in The Beatles,' Chuck Berry, black girl-group harmonies, and British music hall.

More importantly, neither was content in staying musically in one place. I grew up with The Beatles, literally. As their music matured, experimented, and expanded, so did I. I entered my teens with The Beatles as my instruction manual and bible. I still liked those Beach Boys singles, but it was the *Pet Sounds* album that knocked me over. It astounded me when I found out later that it wasn't an enormous hit in the US, because in the UK it was a very big success. Brian never forgot that and debuted *SMiLE* in the UK in large part because he loved the Royal Festival Hall and British audiences. And British audiences loved him.

Brian – you know the story – had decided to stop touring and stay at home working on their next album alone in the studio. Like *Pet Sounds*, *SMiLE* – essentially a Brian Wilson solo album to be sung by The Beach Boys and bear the group name – was to be more than a collection of new songs. *SMiLE* would be a story, a symphony, an audio painting, stretching not just the parameters of what could be done in a recording studio in the Sixties, but of what a pop album could and should be. There's no argument that *Pet Sounds* raised the bar for my beloved Beatles; they responded with *Sgt. Pepper's Lonely Hearts Club Band*.

These were important albums. They changed things. They made pop and rock music important, an art form. There was more than a little Gershwin and Bernstein in some of the *SMiLE* songs we did get to hear – 'Surf's Up,' 'Good Vibrations' (with a *Theremin!* You can imagine the look on Lennon and McCartney's face). If Brian's teenage symphony had come out intact in the Sixties, who knows what it would have done for the art of pop music.

All I can say is that what I heard at Royal Festival Hall was sweeping, sophisticated, overwhelmingly beautiful.

A week or two ago [in 2023], I asked Brian how he felt now about Brian Wilson's *SMiLE* and what effect if any it had on him. 'It was very emotional,' he replied. 'I had shelved the album for so many years. It was a relief to get it done and bring it to the world. I was so proud,' he said. 'Proud of everyone involved. It really changed my life a lot.'

(Sylvie Simmons, a rock writer since 1977, has authored a half dozen books including a classic biography of Lou Reed. As a singer-songwriter, she's released two albums.)

IT'LL KNOCK YOUR SOCKS OFF

by Peter Carlin

FOR YEARS, DECADES, WHAT SEEMED LIKE A LIFETIME, THE STORY OF BRIAN Wilson and The Beach Boys was as much about the music you couldn't hear as it was about the music they had actually released. What made this particularly extraordinary was how large their extant catalogue is. From 'I Get Around' to 'Help Me, Rhonda' to *Pet Sounds* to 'Good Vibrations,' to 'Sail On, Sailor' and onwards, Brian and his bandmates have released dozens of the rock era's most beloved and influential records. But for nearly forty years the keystone of Brian and The Beach Boys' career was the one album nobody had heard: *SMiLE*.

I first heard about it in 1976. I was thirteen years old, one of the new generation of fans drawn to The Beach Boys by the smash 1974 repackage *Endless Summer*. My interest expanded with the follow-up collection *Spirit of America* in 1975, and that sent me back to the record store. I came home with *Pet Sounds* and heard something like magic. When the publicity surrounding Brian's return from self-imposed exile introduced me to the record that was meant to follow *Pet Sounds*, the abandoned psychedelic album *SMiLE*, I was transfixed. Only a handful of people had heard the music during its production, and all described it as a masterpiece. Beautiful, innovative, the work of a genius whose new work was powerful enough to alter the course of popular music. Then something had gone wrong, and the album was abandoned. Brian continued writing and recording with The Beach Boys, but never with the same ambition he'd brought to his earlier work. And nobody seemed to know why.

IT'LL KNOCK YOUR SOCKS OFF

All we knew for sure about *SMiLE* was what we could read about it. And that the few pieces of the album that emerged on other albums – 'Cabin Essence,' 'Our Prayer,' 'Heroes And Villains,' and then 'Surf's Up' – all co-written with Van Dyke Parks – were just as mysterious and beautiful as the whole album was said to be. What seemed clear was that Brian had been on to something very special in 1966 and 1967. But his artistic vision was overwhelmed by his emotional vulnerability. In the silence that followed a legend began to grow.

It's easy to romanticize a record that doesn't exist. Take everything you love about the artist's other work, multiply it by your dreamiest dreams and subtract absolutely nothing since an album that only lives in your imagination is always perfect. And for some fans the lost *SMiLE* felt even more resonant. It came to symbolize everything fragile that could be lost to a cruel and uncaring world. Brian either refused to discuss the lost album, or said he'd never liked it in the first place. 'That was inappropriate music,' he said at one point. It was hard to know what made him think that, and easier to imagine how bitter his disappointment had to be. But if Brian wanted only to forget *SMiLE*, the world wouldn't allow it.

Years went by. Decades. The 20th century gave way to the 21st. The Beach Boys persisted, mostly without Brian, whose occasional comebacks rarely approached the artistic ambition that had gripped him in the mid-1960s. His personal life veered repeatedly toward catastrophe until the early 1990s, when he finally achieved a level of stability he hadn't known for thirty years. He joined with his old *SMiLE* partner Van Dyke Parks for the justly celebrated *Orange Crate Art* album in the mid-1990s, but his memories of their original collaboration remained dark.

The first time I interviewed him, around the release of his *Imagination* solo album in 1998, Brian sighed impatiently when I asked about his much-celebrated unreleased album. 'That was just a bunch of short pieces that didn't amount to anything,' he grumbled. I must have looked stricken by that; a moment later Brian smiled. 'But I guess we did it pretty good,' he said with an amiable shrug.

A few more years passed. Brian's tours began, then ramped up to include full performances of *Pet Sounds*. Brian took a tentative step into his deep end by performing 'Heroes And Villains' at Radio City Music Hall in 2001, then added the song, along with *SMiLE*'s opening vignette, 'Our Prayer' to his concert setlist that summer. Dragging the haunted old songs into the light seemed to have a transformative effect on their creator. In 2003 came unexpected news: Brian's next tour would include most, if not all, of the other songs that had been meant for *SMiLE*. Then came the shocker. Instead of performing a few selections from the unfinished album, Brian had decided to get back to work with Parks and complete the album they had set out to make in 1966. Which is exactly what they did. The premiere performance was set for London a few months hence. And then, nearly forty years later, *SMiLE* existed.

It felt like magic. And what felt even more magical for me was that *SMiLE*'s rebirth coincided with my work on *Catch a Wave*, a biography of Brian I had started imagining the day I first met him in 1998. Having the opportunity to write about an artist I had admired since I was a boy and to spend time with him just as his greatest work was finally come to fruition, was an extraordinary privilege. Twenty years later it still feels like a dream.

No moment was dreamier than the evening in 2004 when the *SMiLE* tour came to Portland, Oregon, where I was living at the time. The Arlene Schnitzer Concert Hall was sold out, and the first half of the show, during which Brian and his band played a rich array of favourites from his Beach Boys and solo albums, had been a huge success. I was sitting near the stage with my family, and when the intermission came, I took my son Teddy, then seven years old, backstage. We wound up in the band's dressing room, where the sweet musicians Darian Sahanaja and Probyn Gregory came running up to stuff cookies in the boy's pockets. He was still giggling when Brian came over to say hello.

He's a big guy, a few inches above six feet, so he kneeled in front of my son and took his little hand in his own. 'What do you think so far?' he asked. Teddy, stupefied to be speaking to the star of the show, wasn't sure what to say. 'It's pretty good!' Brian nodded thoughtfully. 'Pretty good, huh? Okay.' Then he leaned in closer and said something I never imagined I'd hear Brian Wilson say to anyone, let alone to my own son. Words I'd been wishing to hear since I was nearly that young, first reading about the legendary album that nobody would ever hear.

'Wait'll you hear *SMiLE*. It'll knock your socks off.'

(Journalist Peter Carlin is the author of biographies of such rock heroes as Bruce Springsteen, Paul Simon, Paul McCartney, and Brian Wilson.)

'CABIN ESSENCE' COMES ALIVE!

by Sean O'Hagan

WHEN PLANS FOR THE LIVE PERFORMANCE OF *SMILE* EMERGED, I WAS excited but not surprised.

The Wondermints plus Paul Von Mertens and Jeff Foskett (and the rest of the band) were a brilliant and empathetic musical force. We knew from their presentation of *Pet Sounds* in 2002 that they had an intimate understanding of how this fragile and indefinable music needed to be performed.

It's fair to say that presenting *SMiLE* would be a tough task. Compared to *Pet Sounds*, *SMiLE* is virtually intangible and capturing its essence could almost be like catching summer rain. But it was handled with passion, delicacy, and joy. It was perfect. A truly elevating experience.

After the show, I recalled a winter afternoon in a dark west London flat in 1983, listening to cassettes of *SMiLE* – the sound barely there in these tenth-generation [bootlegs] – and holding my breath in awe. I was experiencing a near-religious encounter. A sliding-door moment for me: history and art made in the past but shaping my future.

I needed to contextualize that memory with the *SMiLE* performance in 2004. I decided that for me a circle had been completed in the most beautiful way. I left the theatre a happier person.

Encountering Brian Wilson's songwriting and production was the defining moment of change in my life. For his musical acolytes, like me, discovering Brian's unique approach to composition and sound-gathering opened the world of musical and artistic possibility. While as a composer, I have tried to explore a Universe of music, it could not have happened without a foundation in Brian's world of composition, especially *SMiLE*.

Sean O'Hagan, The High Llamas

Key figures in bringing *SMiLE* to life: (Top Row, L-R) Paul Von Mertens, who not only played a plethora of instruments, but wrote out the orchestrations for and conducted the Stockholm Strings 'n' Horns; Nick Walusko (doing his Pirate rap) was Darian's brilliant musical partner and best friend for over thirty years; Probyn Gregory exhibited amazing musical versatility, and his passion for *SMiLE* and Brian Wilson's music knows no bounds. (Middle Row, L-R) Jeffrey 'The CEO of Falsetto' Foskett; the enthusiastic, ecstatic, and energetically effective percussionist, Nelson Bragg; and the remarkably gifted Scott Bennett. (Bottom Row, L-R): The beautiful tones of Taylor Mills; the sartorial splendor and precise bass of Bob Lizik; and the perfect and joyous beat of Jim Hines.

'THE OLD MASTER PAINTER'

by David Scott

ALL OF US BRIAN WILSON PILGRIMS MADE OUR OWN JOURNEY TO whatever seat we occupied at the Royal Festival Hall, London, on the night of February 20, 2004.

Mine started with the first album I ever bought with my own money: The Beach Boys' *Pet Sounds*. People don't believe me when I tell them it was my first; I mean, would you? But it's true. I'd read about it in a book called *The Rock Primer* by John Collis, an early and outstanding example of those 'here are 100 albums you need to own' books.

It piqued my interest because I'd already fallen in love with another album by The Beach Boys, called *SMiLE*. Or, I should say more accurately, bits of an album I now know was called *SMiLE*. During the summer of 1978 my dad played *The Beach Boys 20 Golden Greats* cassette non-stop in his car as we drove around the mostly rainy west coast of Scotland. Every tune; every intricate vocal arrangement; every unexpected, heart-stopping production dynamic was revelatory to me, a then-fourteen-year-old kid, skipping games at school to sneak into music rooms to teach myself piano and (whisper it) write songs.

The main objects of my obsession were two tracks: 'Good Vibrations' and 'Heroes And Villains.' It was 1978, twelve years removed from their birth, but they still seemed so far beyond anything that had been created in the interim; gorgeous, hilarious, knock-you-over entertaining, and white-knuckle scary. Later, when EMI reissued The Beach Boys' 1960s singles en masse I enjoyed the boisterous 'Wild Honey' but was entirely spellbound by its B-side, the *Smiley Smile* version of 'Wind Chimes' which – whatever the timeframe of its recording or its remove from the *SMiLE* sessions per se – felt recognisably of a piece with 'Good Vibrations' and 'Heroes And Villains.'

I started working at Falkirk Library in 1980, a grand old Andrew Carnegie-funded building in a Scottish borough town with an iron spiral staircase running from its basement up through four floors. The job description stated I was to 'hide round shelves in the main library reading the books; or alternatively pretend to sort out racks of vinyl in the record library while checking out the credits on cool 1960s albums.' Or words to that effect, anyway.

In those vinyl racks it was possible to encounter scratched copies of the *Smiley Smile*, *20/20* and *Surf's Up* albums; and the Brian Wilson/Van Dyke Parks *SMiLE* treasure scattered throughout seemed as mysterious, cyclical, ancient and pioneering as the ribbon of iron that connected one level to another in that Victorian library. It's easy to project what we later come to know upon an original moment of discovery, and writing at forty-odd years' remove doesn't help. But my experience of listening to those snippets of the *SMiLE* music is not something I've ever been able to shake.

By 1988 I was four years into my own music career: one that occasionally promised but more often creaked and groaned, usually under the weight of whatever the music industry was feeling at that moment and what sonic fashion I imagined I needed to chase. An ongoing obsession with *Pet Sounds* notwithstanding, I'd otherwise lost any connection with The Beach Boys 'story.' Too many terrible records in horrible sleeves. Too many damp squibs about summer. Cheerleaders.

But in Woolworths' Falkirk store one Saturday I was stunned to see a cassette copy of an album – a solo album – by Brian Wilson. In a gorgeous sleeve. Out of left field. It's no exaggeration to say the beautiful, fully realised art music contained therein put me on a creative path I've stayed on ever since, and concurrently sent me headlong back into the *story* not least – via 'Rio Grande' – the by-now legendary *SMiLE* story.

That meant obsessively making cassette versions of 'what could have been' out of the existing cuts scattered across various albums (fellow pilgrims will nod sagely), alongside what could be gleaned from cassette bootlegs (ditto) and – in my own songwriting for my group The Pearlfishers – adopting some of that modular, sketch-booking approach to run simple ideas through many prisms (musicians will nod sagely).

By the late nineties it meant putting together a show called *Smiles & Good Vibes* with my friend Duglas T. Stewart and many other Scottish musicians in which we learned and performed pieces like 'Cabin Essence,' 'Heroes And Villains,' 'Wind Chimes,' and even the 'Fire' music, and later still developing a Brian Wilson tribute album called *Caroline Now!* (Marina Records, 2000). Both of these endeavours were supplemented by interviews with Brian Wilson himself.

The sum total of all of this for me was one of the most profound musical educations it is possible to experience. To pull apart even one of Brian Wilson's 'simplest' songs is to realise a level of complexity, most specifically harmonic complexity, that underpins some of the most memorable, most emotional musical statements of the time. Techniques of repetition, variations on a theme, playful harmonic juxtaposition (Daniel Harrison memorably describes an audacious early example of this in the song 'The Warmth of the Sun' in his essay 'After Sundown,' 1997) and multi-dimensional dynamics.

When I was attending the Glasgow School of Art in 1984, a tutor called John Cunningham once brought in a Sausage Supper (non-Scottish readers: look it up) and told us to draw it. Use a graphite stick, he said. Now an oil pastel. Take a photograph of it. Have a piece of sausage. Draw it like a cartoon. Now like a Picasso cubist painting. Have a chip (non-Scottish readers – a french fry). Do a line drawing in nail varnish. Now do a drawing of the drawing.

In Brian Wilson's music – most evidently in the *SMiLE* music – that same meditative, incantatory, dare I say obsessive process is brought to bear in developing musical ideas that are multi-layered and always surprising but nevertheless retain a core identity that supports, and in some cases suggests, the lyrical concept. Those music ideas were, and remain, clearly distinct from the pop – or what was starting to be thought of as rock – music of the day.

Among some early *SMiLE* bootlegs there lurked a piece that was not from *SMiLE* at all. It was in fact a Gershwin composition, performed by Miles Davis and arranged by Gil Evans, called 'Here Come De Honey Man' taken from *Porgy & Bess*. Many listeners – myself included – were only too happy to accept this famous recording, lushly textured with horns and rich in melodic ostinato, as a *SMiLE* relic.

Why? Perhaps because something that sets *SMiLE* apart – and marks it out as so revolutionary in the context of *pop* music – is its symphonic nature. That Gershwin classic sat happily alongside 'Surf's Up,' where instruments are utilised outside the pop norms of the day: where guitar lines act both as harmony markers and staccato rhythm, where glockenspiels multiply that rhythm and sound like, well, 'like jewelry'; and where a distinct second movement suddenly opens to a glorious vocal chorale.

In 'Cabin Essence,' two distinct and equally beautiful melodies – the top-line vocal and a darkly-coloured plucked banjo – coexist on parallel trainlines before diverging into a widescreen cello, choral, and anvil clatter; while the melody Wilson invented for 'Wonderful' – recalling German high-art songs or lieder – elegantly moves in opposition to the left hand of a harpsichord. In Don Was's documentary, *Brian Wilson: I Just Wasn't Made for These Times*, Danny Hutton tells a story about Brian spending several hours on a late, probably lubricated, L.A. night teaching Iggy Pop and Alice Cooper the song 'Shortenin' Bread.' Pausing for comedic effect, Danny adds . . . 'Parts!' The story is funny, the punchline enlightening.

Wilson's influences – Gershwin himself, the complex jazz harmony of The Four Freshmen, perhaps even how he was hearing George Martin adorn recordings by The Beatles – explain some of it; but there is an ambition in the *SMiLE* music that seems born of the composer's drive to push music beyond the physical space and connect with the spiritual; to channel 'God's voice.'

When I first started connecting the *SMiLE* songs with each other via *Smiley Smile*, *20/20* et al. that core musical ambition was matched inch for inch by the lyrical approach. What were these songs about? Who was the speaker? From the Andrew Carnegie Library in Falkirk in 1980, it felt far away not just because of its clear roots in American experience, but ancient too. Old world. Bygone. I imagined my grandfather, Jimmy Scott, leaving New Jersey as a five-year-old boy to come and live in Scotland in the early 1900s, moving back and forth between new and old worlds.

It taught me as a composer that you could write about history, or nationhood, or falling asleep, or eating vegetables. That you could be mysterious in one verse then playful, humorous, or just plain raucous in

'THE OLD MASTER PAINTER'

the next. But also, and bear with me here, that there is a kind of magic even in the credits on a record. Jimmy Webb talked — actually kind of complained — about being the songwriter who spills his lifeblood only to be relegated to a short label credit in the song 'Parenthesis.' But to this beholder the credit on Beach Boys' records (Wilson/Parks) held a key: almost like a cipher; a sign that one was about to enter a space where new things would be said and discovered.

New things were indeed said and discovered at the Royal Festival Hall, London on 20.02.04 where I saw the opening two nights of *SMiLE*, the first sat together with David and Eva Leaf who'd had such a key role in supporting its realisation. David later told me I'd spent most of the show sitting forward in my seat with my hand over my mouth intently staring at the stage; in truth I was so invested by that time not just in the un-believable music, but in the *story*, that I felt kind of bamboozled that it had actually come to this. And, more, as an artist myself I very well understood what it takes to give blood, and the risk to heart and soul that accompany it.

It's hard to overstate the heart-stopping bit of theatre that was the emergence of that huge SMiLE sign, rising up right after the opening 'Our Prayer' and the sense of victory, perseverance, and pilgrimage that accompanied it. (Wilson/Parks) had brought forth additional layers of wow in the ways that well-known sections were woven together, entirely new elements added — Van Dyke Parks' punning pirate rap delivered with aplomb by Nicky Wonder in 'On a Holiday', the elegiac 'Song For Children' — and the clearing back of layers of dust accumulated over thirty-odd years to grasp original melodies and lyrics out of the air for 'Roll Plymouth Rock.' 'Waving from the ocean liners . . .'

Brian Wilson himself was in something of a late-period vocal prime and - by now a seasoned solo live performer — was able to command the front of the stage with his trademark goofy/odd/beautiful charisma. As a performer, I know that when you have the goods in your back pocket to deliver across an hour-and-a-half show you spend at least a bit of the time like the cat that had the milk; just waiting till the audience hears the next knock-out moment.

Of course, *SMiLE* is another level entirely and I saw the confidence, the knowledge of how special the music was, growing in Brian and those amazing performers, so that when he finally implored the audience to stop applauding at the end of the show, and then just accepted it with a weary sigh, it was just one more piece of stunning theatre. This time a moment of salvation and rebirth.

On the afternoon of the second day, I was invited by David Leaf to sit with a handful of other people in the empty hall while Brian Wilson and his band played *SMiLE* for what David explained was 'coverage.' I'm guessing some of the musicians were still tired and emotional from the previous night's triumph, but they persevered, stopping for breath and camera resets now and then. Brian himself, staring motionless into the dark middle distance, kept doing something unexpected: he sang 'The Old Master Painter' over and over again, which up till then I only knew as the cello instrumental from the first *SMiLE* movement:

> *The old master painter from the faraway hills*
> *Painted the violets and the daffodils . . .*

At the time it felt like a fun glimpse into the source of one corner of *SMiLE*: an unexpected early Easter Egg just for me and the half-dozen other folks scattered through the hall. But go look at the lyrics of that 1949 Smith/Gillespie song and perhaps you'll recognise another part of the legend of Brian Wilson's great artistry: the notion that God, in whatever form you recognise, speaks to us through colour, through poetry and through music.

(David Scott is Head of Arts & Media at The University of the West of Scotland, BBC Radio Scotland presenter, and lead composer and performer of The Pearlfishers.)

A *SMiLE* RETURNED

by Andrew G. Doe

THE WORLD PREMIERE OF *BRIAN WILSON PRESENTS SMILE* IN LONDON, February 20, 2004, represented the triumphant culmination of Brian's often troubled and conflicted thirty-seven-year relationship with the music he created then shelved when at the height of his fame and powers. That it was such a triumph was never guaranteed: indeed, there were those who, right up to Brian taking his place behind his keyboard for the second, *Brian Wilson Presents SMiLE* part of the show, seriously considered he wouldn't make it.

I was one of them, for I knew what this music meant to him, and how heavily it had weighed on his shoulders for almost four decades . . . but he did, and he didn't merely make it through the performance, he triumphed - he made it through the fire (literally) and took us all along for the ride. It was a defining moment in my BB/BW fandom, celebrating this incredible event with so many friends from all corners of the globe, who came by plane, train, boat, car, even foot. But they came, from the Americas, from Europe, from Asia, from Australasia, and even from South Africa, and they came in droves. At previous Beach Boys or Brian Wilson shows I routinely knew a handful of fans in every third row or so. That night in the Royal Festival Hall, I knew everyone in the first ten rows (and for good measure, most of those on stage, for these were no longer Brian's band but rather our friends).

Which brings me to another point, that the London *BWPS* residency of February 2004 was, simply, the biggest fan gathering the BB/BW cosmos has ever seen. London for those seven days was Briansville, and the twin epicenters were the RFH and the County Hall Premier Inn where post-show gatherings lasted until the very small hours. Daytime it was unusual to *not* see someone wearing a *SMiLE* t-shirt walking around the adjacent streets of Westminster. Truly, it was a magical time, one with the very best soundtrack of all and one of the highlights of my life: I doubt I'll experience the like again.

The music? It was at once as comfortably satisfying as we'd dared hope and as utterly surprising as could be imagined. There was a moment during the exquisite second movement when at one of the transitions you could almost hear everyone thinking 'So that's how it goes.' To see Van Dyke sharing the seemingly endless standing ovation at the end with Brian would have moved the stoniest of hearts but, of course, we were all in floods by then anyway. This was more than mere music. This was an affirmation of the spirit of one man over decades of adversity, and he was sharing it with us.

There's more: to my mind, *BWPS* meant one more thing for Brian – it lifted the weight of the past from his shoulders and ushered in a burst of renewed creativity with the elegiac *That Lucky Old Sun* and *Brian Wilson Reimagines Gershwin*. I truly think that had he not finally laid *SMiLE* to rest, neither of those would have come to pass, and for this I am eternally grateful, for I consider *TLOS* to be Brian's very best truly solo work. *BWPS*, in my view, stands outside his solo canon: it's that special, and to this day, I ration my listening so as not to dilute the magic.

One final observation: later in the run I asked one of the band if there had been a Plan B for that first night if Brian hadn't showed after the interval. Of course, was the reply: 'We'd just start playing and wait for him to come out.' But, I persisted, suppose he hadn't? 'Ah, well,' they said, 'then we'd just carry on anyway and we knew you'd all understand.' I'm still not sure if I was being strung a line. Thankfully, we never found out.

(Beach Boys historian Andrew G. Doe has been seriously following the group since summer 1975. His website, www.bellagio10452.com, is the result of years of gathering the most specific and important factual information about the group's career. Compiled with the invaluable assistance of several leading Beach Boys researchers, it's widely regarded as the single most important Beach Boys resource on the 'net.)

DIY . . . THE SMiLE POT BOILS IN LOS ANGELES, 1980S (AND BEYOND)

by Domenic Priore

BY THIS POINT IN THE BOOK, YOU'VE READ A LOT ABOUT THEM; TWO KEY players in the *Brian Wilson Presents SMiLE* story, kindred spirits I found at a record swap meet. In fact, I'd found a couple of rare LPs that I could talk to. Those guys were called Darian Sahanaja and Nick Walusko.

This was 1984, in the daytime, at a club on Pico Boulevard in West L.A. called The Music Machine. I was behind the counter working for record dealer Chris Peake; Darian came to the table wearing a home-made psychedelic t-shirt of The Byrds; he'd used the *Preflyte* album cover images to illuminate it. Nick had on the kind of Beach Boys tour baseball jersey you'd see Dennis Wilson wear (in other words, not one of the tacky ones). It was obvious from the get-go, the three of us would hit it off.

Soon after we had connected, on my first visit to Darian's family home, he, his brand-new music partner Nick (they'd just met a few months earlier) and I formed a bond. The three of us were all sitting on the floor, Nick with his guitar and Darian behind a nice-sounding, but clearly home studio electric keyboard, the portable kind that had just become popular around that time.

The first song they played for me was the *Pet Sounds* cut, 'That's Not Me,' and it was really well done. Quickly, they jumped into 'I Know There's An Answer' and blew me away again. I stopped them after that and said, 'Do you realize, these are songs that even The Beach Boys would never attempt live?' They said, confidently, 'Sure.' That had been the whole point of doing those.

It was then, on that first day, that I said to Darian and Nick, 'You guys should be The Beach Boys' actual band.' I wasn't kidding, because what I'd seen from the legendary group on stage in the late seventies was 'good' but tired. Darian expressed to me that he'd never gone to see The Beach Boys in concert, because he felt it would ruin what was most important about the greatness of the band to him, that their show could not do the music justice. Of course, at that first meeting, there was no way any of us could have imagined what would happen twenty years later in London.

I was also fascinated that Darian, who was younger than Nick and I, was so well-versed on some of the more interesting music that had come from the sixties that you didn't really hear too much about (and were well before his time) like the Merry-Go-Round and one of his other primary favourites, The Zombies (who Darian would ultimately tour with).

Darian and Nick were slowly on their way to becoming part of the larger Alternative music scene in America, a phrase popularized by the Sam Goody record chain, not in irony, but ironically, nonetheless.

By the 1990s, DIY was the mode o' day for so many creative people who had exited mainstream culture, rejecting both the extremely narrow and ultimately, conservative kind of new music Classic Rock radio stations had to offer or the 'bought' morass being screened on MTV during the eighties. Soon, this would be deemed 'Generation X' by the literary world, and that new reality would dovetail into a revival of politically motivated protest with the World Trade Organization demonstrations in Seattle. More recent demonstrations such as 'Occupy Wall Street' and 'Black Lives Matter' (peopled primarily by Gen X, Millennials and Gen Z) were repercussions of what had begun in the nineties, all of which had been inspired by what had happened on the streets during the 1960s.

DIY ... Doing It Yourself ... seemed to be the only option for me to be able to even *think* of doing a book on *SMiLE* during the late eighties. When I told people my plans, the response was: 'You're doing a book ... on an album ... that was never released?' People joked, as if you were crazy. As an escape valve, Darian, Nick and I instead revelled in the tape-trading community that had begun to flourish in the netherworld of Beach Boys fandom mid-decade.

Through a very tumbled series of circumstances, I gained access to

DIY... THE SMiLE POT BOILS IN LOS ANGELES, 1980S (AND BEYOND)

some very rare tapes from the *SMiLE* sessions. The record dealer I'd been working for, Chris Peake, put me in touch with former sixties wunderkind record producer Curt Boettcher (Sagittarius, The Millennium) who simultaneously was supplying tapes to the good people in England at *Beach Boys Stomp*.

This fanzine-and-convention oriented group of Britons discovered Brian with *Pet Sounds* back in the sixties; after the closing of their annual gatherings, they would have *SMiLE* listening sessions, underground tapes that only several people had. We were amazed by the existence of such a thing but were fortunate to be connected to their source. A small tape-trading network developed that included Bob Hanes in Eugene, Oregon, a UK fan, and just a few others. Darian, Nick, Probyn, and I listened to all of these tapes, endlessly obsessed with trying to piece together this 1966 masterpiece. There was a lot to work with: these 'found' tapes and actual released *SMiLE* gems by The Beach Boys. Along with the legendary and supposedly 'lost' 'Fire' section of 'The Elements,' I remember what a big deal it was hearing Brian Wilson's 1966 voice on 'Wonderful' for the first time. That may have been the biggest reveal.

Almost from the moment we met, Darian, Nick, Probyn, and I had many conversations about how the possible formation of *SMiLE* as a concept album from these tapes could happen. These weren't arguments, but deeply felt discussions. There was a lot of conjecture as to how the album should be sequenced. Mostly it was me leading the way. As musicians, they were more into the technical sections of the music; I had to find the answer.

Most importantly, we felt with the passion of youth that leaving *SMiLE* in the can was a huge waste, but how do we, virtual kids from the then-unfashionable and unfathomable East Side of Los Angeles, go about changing this debacle of great repression?

We believed in the music. We would do anything.

All along, Darian and Nick had been developing their own music, and as they gained confidence, made recordings (solo and with each other), and their own band was born. Initially (as it was the early eighties), they imagined they could just be a duo with tapes behind them on stage, but I would emphasize that nothing could make it with an audience without a bass player and especially a drummer. With the addition of these players – including Probyn - they became The Wondermints, among the most popular of the L.A. indie bands to emerge on the Los Feliz/Silver Lake/ Echo Park Alt-rock scene that had escaped from the Pay-to-Play hell that was L.A.'s West Side.

My *SMiLE* obsession continued with the fanzine *Dumb Angel Gazette*, and for me, one of the important discoveries was finding Tom Nolan's original article 'The Frenzied Frontier of Pop Music' in *The Los Angeles Times' West* Sunday magazine supplement. Here, Nolan may have been first in intelligently analysing the early psychedelic music scene that was breaking on Sunset Strip in 1966, prior to what happened later in San Francisco.

In putting my book together, I had help from everybody. Even David Leaf got into the act, setting me up with a guy who was then the man, outside of the group, with the greatest collection of Beach Boys items we will probably ever see, Peter Reum. Peter had been given access to the 'industrial waste' of Beach Boys items at Capitol Records in Hollywood, which would have otherwise gotten thrown away during the 1970s. Through Peter, the world would get to see Brian Wilson's handwritten list of song titles that would appear on the back cover of the *SMiLE* album art mock-up from 1966 . . . as well as the album art itself.

We were in on all of these discoveries: the music, of course, was paramount to Darian, Nick and Probyn. We were able to read all of the original 1966 interviews with Brian Wilson about *SMiLE* that had appeared in publications out of London, New York and Los Angeles – stories from '66, during a time when he regularly spoke in the music press with detail about *SMiLE*. The readers were looking forward to the actual release.

I had already been consumed by these thoughts, but now, we were getting first-hand information from the Brian Wilson of 1966 on paper, speaking loud, clear, and lucid – and very confident in his coming follow-up to *Pet Sounds*. We even had loads of *SMiLE* session tapes featuring studio chatter where we could hear Brian Wilson himself as he gave direction to musicians. For me, THOSE TWO THINGS let on exactly where different pieces of music would go in the album-length tapestry.

Entering the DIY world was my biggest leap of *SMiLE* faith. The independently published *Look! Listen! Vibrate! SMiLE!* (edited by Probyn!) resonated with said Generation X audience: it was because of them that I was able to go beyond the projected 2,000 I was forewarned would be the max I could expect to sell of a Beach Boys-related fanzine. Once it was picked up by Last Gasp as publisher, total sales wound up being

DIY... THE SMiLE POT BOILS IN LOS ANGELES, 1980S (AND BEYOND)

40,000, and as David Leaf reminds me, helped build a growing *SMiLE* faction that had nothing to do with The Beach Boys.

Leaf supported the work, welcomed me into the world of more traditional believers and through him, I managed to double-fact-check my information with the crucial direction of a planned two-sided 'Heroes And Villains' single with original Western Recorders engineer, Chuck Britz. For good measure, I had a couple of long talks with Stephen J. Desper, who began working as a Beach Boys engineer in 1966 when Brother Records was formed.

So, with the secretly provided tapes, conversations with the original *SMiLE* engineers and archivists, and all the 1966 articles featuring Brian, Darian, Nick, Probyn, and I had as much information as possible.

In 1988, for me, there were two big Brian Wilson events: the release time of *Brian Wilson*, the man's debut solo album on Sire Records and my first book, *Look! Listen! Vibrate! SMiLE!*. There were still a couple of nuts to crack.

An even greater interest in *SMiLE* was by now being stirred up by bootlegs coming from all corners of the globe. All of this, of course, was a process that created an even greater market for *SMiLE* within the Alt-Rock audience of the nineties. The timing, in the wake of *Look! Listen! Vibrate! SMiLE!*, was rather fortunate, if not symbiotic.

At the Wild Honey benefit show in 1994, The Wondermints, for me, came full circle from that time in their living room in 1984, centring their three-song set with 'That's Not Me.' The 'Mints performed a soulful, spirited version of 'Surf's Up' (sung by Probyn Gregory). Backstage, listening, a stunned Brian Wilson turned to the old friends he was running around with that night ... including KROQ's Rodney Bingenheimer ... and told him, 'If I'd have had these guys back in 1966, I could have toured *SMiLE*.' Finally, a sense of validation. From this, Rodney took Brian over to meet The Wondermints. In a few years, they would become the musical heart of Brian Wilson's band for over twenty years, touring *Pet Sounds* numerous times, and having the nerve to follow that up with ... *SMiLE*.

Of course, as you've read, none of this happened overnight. This is where the final two nuts to crack, broke open.

In preparing the *SMiLE* concert to be played in London with Brian, Darian Sahanaja became what I consider to be the Executive Editor of the project, working directly with Wilson. Darian would be working with

SMiLE

Brian on the project, using all the knowledge he, Nick and I studied together during the eighties. Thinking and talking, making educated guesses as to what could be the right sequence of *SMiLE*. Darian had absorbed all the research as it was going into *Look! Listen! Vibrate! SMiLE*.

As you've already read, in 2003, Darian and Brian and Van Dyke, worked together to make sense of all the pieces. It was done on intuition, but I am sure that deep down, all those years of our talking about *SMiLE*, listening and thinking and guessing about how it could fit together had an impact, must have had some influence.

One of the big surprises in this process concerned 'Surf's Up.' Because it had closed the *Surf's Up* album, and because it seemed to be in profundity something akin to The Beatles' own 'A Day in the Life,' I'd always assumed 'Surf's Up' to be the closer for *SMiLE*. But as Darian and Brian pieced together the second movement, 'Surf's Up' closed that segment, part of the larger 'life suite' in the middle of the album, beginning with both 'Wonderful' and 'Child Is Father Of The Man' (of course! DUH!). For Darian, there were many 'aha' moments that he experienced working with Brian and Van Dyke that made the three-segment sequence that they created feel natural, as if that was what had been intended all along. In creating this performance piece, the sequence became very much like the one we had been discussing for years.

Finally, the creative mastermind collaborators, 'the old master painters' who came up with *SMiLE* put their heart into re-creating the music and meanings behind this incredible piece of work, music dreamed up in a time just before The Beatles would be recording their landmark single, 'Strawberry Fields Forever' b/w 'Penny Lane' and The Rolling Stones were riding high with 'Paint it Black' and 'Ruby Tuesday.' The effervescent feel of the sixties, at its most unique in the timeline of history, now belonged also to The Beach Boys' nascent masterpiece as well, something that had never made it, as Icarus flew too close to the sun. Perhaps only Syd Barrett of The Pink Floyd rode as buoyantly during the times he was making 'See Emily Play' and 'Lucifer Sam,' or perhaps Andy Warhol's Exploding Plastic Inevitable featuring The Velvet Underground and Nico could approach aurally, aesthetically or, in a revolutionary sense, some kind of peak experience previously unknown in a musical sense. The deal was now done.

To be in London for the debut of *SMiLE* was indeed surreal. Though the record was to have debuted when Carnaby Street was at its colourful

DIY... THE SMiLE POT BOILS IN LOS ANGELES, 1980S (AND BEYOND)

climax, with bob-headed Sasoon kiss curls, exotic Yardley eyeliner design and swingin' mini-skirts roaming its streets, the Royal Festival Hall nevertheless was filled with just the kind of *sounds* that could have lifted the soles of those Capezio-wearing feet.

To see Londoners who had been around since *Pet Sounds* made its huge impact in England, something many American Beach Boy fans of the sixties had no concept of, was staggering. These were the people who had literally bought into all that *teaser campaign* pre-publicity about *SMiLE*, had been excited by Tracy Thomas' news bits in *New Musical Express* as well as Derek Taylor's brilliant in-house insights to the whole *SMiLE* thing as it was being made; these were the people who had been waiting for *SMiLE* in frustration ever since (TV's) *Ready! Steady! GO!* shot its final episode in December 1966.

That night before the concert, my partner Becky Ebenkamp and I also got to go around to some of the nightclubs of London during this 'job,' visiting legendary '50s, '60s venue The 100 Club for a Mod show starring Sharon Tandy (around twenty-five of the younger members of the *SMiLE* crew from Los Angeles were in attendance) as well as Saturday night's *Blow Up* club at The Metro for our Britpop dancing pleasure. During the daytime Becky and I enjoyed an afternoon roaming around the shops of Camden Lock with *Mojo* magazine writer Sylvie Simmons. It was a wonderful moment for us all.

What was natural, but still caught me: walking through the avenues and taverns of London with a semi-removed sense of reality, was being someplace, and hearing on the radio or other sound delivery systems, television, news feed, what have you, that Brian Wilson was in town, and he was going to be debuting *SMiLE*, 'the most famous unheard record in Pop' (according to *The Daily Mail*). This was news, all over the city, it was ubiquitous, and the average Joe on the street was able to talk about it and was hearing about it. It was positive and exciting to stroll around the former land of The Kinks, The Who, The Creation, and other Gods of Mod, and have The Beach Boys ... sorry, Brian Wilson's *SMiLE* ... streaming through the consciousness of the streets in those few days we were in town ... marvellous. I even heard somewhere or other that *I* was in town (on the radio and in print) and was glad to know it was actually true ... this was something in the media I could prove! Man, when I say surreal, I do mean, surreal.

SMiLE

We were brought to London as staffers for the production of a forthcoming documentary by David Leaf, *Beautiful Dreamer: Brian Wilson and the Story of SMiLE*. Most of my work was being done back in Los Angeles, though we were in London to shoot the concert, backstage festivities and fan reaction. I made a cameo in the film as 'the guy who came out from L.A.,' in a medley of voices who'd come to London from as far as Tokyo to hear Brian Wilson perform *SMiLE* for the first time in public.

The concert itself allowed Becky and me to experience the audio glory of a staggered, wood-panelled room such as Royal Festival Hall, and our friends Darian, Nick, Probyn (and the rest of the extended band) delivering every sound that had been envisioned on tape by Brian for *SMiLE* during 1966. It might very well have been the best pure audio experience I've heard in a concert setting, but that can also be attributed to Brian's original arrangements as to the musicians who were able to carry them forward in this resonant, wooden room.

We got to sit alongside Van Dyke Parks, and watch his reactions, as well as meet so many of the long-time British fans who had nestled toward this moment for so many years that it might have seemed impossible for this to have ever happened, like some kind of enchanted fairy tale.

The sense of release in the room was like nothing I'd ever experienced in a live music setting, and how could it be? Music journalists drooled, comparing *SMiLE* to the hanging gardens of Babylon or the comeback of King Lear (the latter was *The London Evening Standard*). Who else had such a wild masterpiece 'in the can,' going back to such a truly heady time in music history, that dawn of a new day that led to The Monterey Pop Festival and its East Coast copycat two years later, The Woodstock Music and Arts Fair. Yes, those festivals that you all might still be attending to this day, with all the latest valid or otherwise bands making headway in the here and now, this was all spawned by the music created during the mid-sixties. *Brian Wilson Presents SMiLE* in 2004 was giving you a huge, new dose of it in the here and now.

(In addition to Domenic Priore's classic books, such as *Riot on Sunset Strip*, his landmark publications on *SMiLE* are his first book, *Look! Listen! Vibrate! SMiLE!* and his 2005 book on the subject, *SMiLE: The Story of Brian Wilson's Lost Masterpiece*.)

A SACRED ORATORIO

by Dr. Daniel Harrison

IN THE HISTORY OF MUSIC, THE 1960S MARK A DECISIVE AND ENDURING shift in the valuation of popular music among cultural elites. As recently as the previous decade, serious music that wasn't clearly classical was a niche market compared to that for the light entertainments heard on the radio, not to mention the pesky but lucrative Rock & Roll of the teenage segment.

By the time *SMiLE* was conceived, Rock & Roll had been transformed into Rock thanks to ongoing imports of newly finished material from the UK (the so-called British Invasion). It was no longer a faddish kids' music but an international phenomenon with apparently lasting commercial and even artistic potential. The adults in the industry, having lost touch with emerging cultural trends, had little choice but to turn artistic decisions over to the younger generation – though grudgingly and with suspicion. Those with money, vision, and support were thus able to make serious attempts to elevate pop music into the same space as classical.

Of the several ways to elevate – from adding symphonic support to staging operatic scenes to mixing in classical tunes – the way attempted in *SMiLE* is unique on several counts.

For one, to a degree the passing of years has only made clearer, *SMiLE* is a genre of sacred music, suffused with non-conventional spirituality and lightness of being. 'Our Prayer' makes this clear, but one has only to recall the amount of pure, repetitive chanting throughout the album to appreciate the appeal to a meditative state.

SMiLE

The brilliant merging of repetitive chant with more recognizable song structures in 'Cabin Essence' is an outstanding example. But there are several others where a song surprisingly breaks out into a chant. No other industry hitmaker tied artistic ambition with spiritual enlightenment to the degree Brian Wilson did in *SMiLE*.

For another, Van Dyke Parks's lyrics for the project were uniquely literate and pretentious for the time. Always beautiful and evocative, they remain mysterious and indirect. On their face, setting them using 'off the shelf' structures like verse/chorus would be nearly impossible. To be sure, while simple strophic repetition worked for 'Wonderful' (which has a recognizable story structure), Brian had much more writing to do for 'Surf's Up,' reflecting its complicated structure as he read it. The result is a multi-sectional masterpiece which showcases Parks's very complicated lyrics in sometimes lush, sometimes spare arrangements. The invitation to listen more deeply is irresistible.

Finally, and of a piece with its unusually frank spiritual and literary aspirations, *SMiLE* resisted being made into a conventional LP. Many partial tracks were recorded with placeholder titles as Brian explored different soundscapes and instrumentations, which he called 'feels.' Many of these are the basis for repetitive chants mentioned above. Some were designed as transitions that wove together elements from different songs. All were able to be tried out in different orders to judge the overall effect.

This painstaking process of composition, arrangement, and production was completely at odds with commercial interests. Thus, the immense pressure to package this material into recognizable album tracks contributed to its demise.

When revived in the early 2000s, the outlines of a nearly hour-long concept became clear, with a hierarchy of material ranging from long, multi-part songs to shorter (but still surprisingly substantial) entr'actes. Too much for a single album in 1967 yet not enough for a double, *SMiLE* ultimately premiered as a live event, unconstrained by the limitations of yesteryear and thus able to be appreciated for its aspirations.

Simply put, *SMiLE* is an oratorio – a large-scale choral work on sacred or historical themes. Part of it can make a recognizable pop-music album, but taken all together, *SMiLE* is very poorly served by that vehicle. In 1967, a pop-music oratorio was unthinkable and thus unmarketable (though *Godspell* premiered by the end of the decade), and so *SMiLE*

A SACRED ORATORIO

had no way to find its audience. It took nearly forty years for that to happen, thanks to the efforts of those who kept faith in its concept and promise.

(Dr. Daniel Harrison was a professor at two of the most prestigious music schools in the world, the Eastman School of Music at the University of Rochester and the Department of Music at Yale University. You can see him in the Don Was documentary, *I Just Wasn't Made for These Times*.)

As a youngster living in Princeton, New Jersey, Van Dyke once was part of the American Boychoir, singing Christmas carols in the neighborhood which included Albert Einstein, who joined the caroling group with his violin. Of that encounter, Van Dyke remarked, 'I've been in the presence of genius.' As for Mr. Wilson, the Mississippi-born Van Dyke calls Brian 'a real ingenious Yankee.'

TWENTY YEARS LATER: LOOKING BACK AT 2004

PROBYN GREGORY: 'THAT FIRST NIGHT OF *SMILE* AT THE ROYAL FESTIVAL HALL in 2004 remains the high point of my musical career. I don't think that will ever be eclipsed. To be part of a team that was helping Brian expunge those demons, to actually perform the great abandoned *SMiLE*, in front of an adoring audience – couldn't have been better in London . . . I think a couple of times I was able to float above myself and watch us playing . . . I was elated beyond imagining.'

Darian: '[If Nick were still here], I know he would just look at me and go, "Dude, can you believe we did this? Can you believe we were part of that?" I'd look at him and say, "Yeah, I can't even believe that. You and me, we met based on the love of this music, and we were so much a part of the revival." I think he would be incredibly proud of that fact. I think he would say that too, that he's very proud of being part of it.'

Scott Bennett: 'It was more than the music. It was an event. It was something that permeated people's hearts and souls and has lasted. To see Brian Wilson gather up the courage to do that record. You were there. You remember. He was nauseous before the debut. He could barely get up there. But then, when we did it, I saw a change in the man. And I think that led to his confidence to do *That Lucky Old Sun*. He was invigorated by finally getting the ghost of *SMiLE* off of his back.

'But the people that came, they knew they were experiencing absolutely a once-in-a-lifetime moment. And twenty years later, it's as powerful, I think, to all these people and myself and the band as it was then . . . . Working with Brian, and *SMiLE* particularly, I would say, was The Brian

TWENTY YEARS LATER: LOOKING BACK AT 2004

Wilson Band's apex. And it surpassed any of our imagination of what that journey of playing with Brian Wilson could ever become. It was magical on levels that you couldn't really put into words. It has to be the most magical time I've ever been on a stage. It was definitely not to be topped.'

Jim Hines: 'I would say that particular moment, that first night, was the height of it all for me, in terms of a live performance . . . It was a validation also, just for me personally, of all the skill set that I had accumulated over my career, all the different roads I had gone down. It all led to that. It all led to this. Like my awareness of myself as a musician was fully realized, in that setting. My personal feelings about that are simply gratitude that I got to be there, that I got to be that guy. The man brought me the greatest musical experience of my life. I got a Grammy hanging on my wall. I got to see the world. All the top-of-the-mountain dreams I had as a kid.'

Bob Lizik: 'It's one of the things I'm most proud of that I've ever done. The fact that it was this monumental piece of music that people were dying to hear for decades, and I finally got to be part of pulling it off. And not just pulling it off. Pulling it off in a spectacular way . . . Playing with Brian has given me so many highlights: playing at the Queen's Jubilee, the Radio City show, Glastonbury. I feel blessed that I was part of it. Granted, it was Brian's [bass] parts. It was Carol Kaye and the other bass players [playing] it at the beginning. But I became part of musical history. And that can never be taken away. I'll always be there, and when anybody hears that album or sees the video, I'll always be there. Something I can pass on. I've told my grandkids about it. I've showed it to them and tried to explain how important it was to do this. To do it and to do it right.'

Probyn Gregory: 'I feel like I've been really honoured and extremely lucky to be in the right place at the right time, to be able to have been part of Brian Wilson's renaissance. And of course, *SMiLE* is a big part of that. If I look at the benchmarks along the way, lots of other people probably could have done what I did. I was lucky enough to be with the right people in The Wondermints, to be asked to be part of the Brian band. There have been people that have come and gone from the band, and I've been one of the few to make it through to the present, for which I'm extremely grateful. And I don't take any of that for granted.

I thank Brian. I thank Melinda. I thank The Beach Boys, for being who they are. I'm very sorry I never got to meet Carl or Dennis. But I'm really happy to be part of the Greater Beach Boys Family.'

Anna Dager: 'The music is so filled with details and wonderful harmonies and it's really emotional to listen to the music since it's connected to so many memories and feelings. One of my favourite songs on the album is 'Surf's Up' – just such a beautiful piece of music. To be able to play the song live and hear all the harmonies performed live was truly a blessing . . . It will forever be one of the greatest experiences in my life. The music was great, and we had so much fun playing all those gigs around the world, I met people who are now friends for life (one of my dearest friends on earth!) and it was also an adventure for my family! I'm so honoured that I got to play this wonderful music together with a legend, Brian Wilson, and that I got to experience so much fun all around the world!

Malin-My Wall: 'The music of SMiLE has a special place in my heart for many reasons, means a lot to me. I still listen to it from time to time. It's one of the most beautiful and interesting pieces I ever played in that genre (if you could put SMiLE in a genre). It's a masterpiece and I am so grateful I got to be a part of this journey!'

Viktor Sand: 'I am thankful for it . . . It gives you something you can't get anywhere else. No one can take it away from me.'

Nelson Bragg: 'It was the most important musical accomplishment of my life. There was the pinnacle, the top of the mountain in my musical world since I started playing music. This was it. This was "the peak." The SMiLE concerts were as good as it ever got. It's like when you think about things that you'll be remembered for, and you know, "Yes." I'll be remembered for being in Brian's band, the band that played SMiLE and recorded it for the world to discover.'

Taylor Mills: 'It was the top of the mountain. What challenge, what a surprise, what excitement, what a moment in time. Everything was magic surrounding it and it was truly beyond special. It was the thrill of a lifetime to be a part of it. Don't make me cry . . .'

★ ★ ★ ★

Ray Lawlor: 'I listened to it recently; I had put it down for quite a while. And it's really vibrant. I can't imagine any greater sound than The Beach

TWENTY YEARS LATER: LOOKING BACK AT 2004

Boys circa 1966/1967. Part of the greatness of the record that came out in 2004, Brian's version of SMiLE, is that is that somehow, it got put together on this album without those Beach Boys vocals. And it still sounded spectacular. Can't believe I stayed alive to hear it. So many friends of mine didn't. Was it worth the wait? Of course. And then there's the incongruous part – how is this guy a friend of mine?'

★ ★ ★ ★

David Anderle *(in 2004):* 'The important thing in my mind is, from now on, is SMiLE gonna have an influence on the modern musicians? Is it going to have the impact now it maybe would have had in 1966?'

Nelson Bragg: 'I don't know about its impact. I think that the thrill of SMiLE has waned a little bit. But the excitement for the fans that were always there and the excitement for the people who always love that kind of music? That sixties eccentricities, melodic, vocal, adventurous. This will always be near and dear to our hearts. I would love a new generation that could rediscover it.'

Darian Sahanaja: 'At the time, I remember thinking, "The people here that showed up for our performances are really digging it. And I see grown men crying. I see ten-minute, fifteen-minute ovations. But the real test is the test of time." The first couple of months or year, we were in our honeymoon period. How does this record play after five years, ten years, fifteen years, twenty years? And I have to say that I still see many people to this day, twenty years later, being inspired by it. That gives me a lot of satisfaction. That makes me really proud of it. I'm so glad that twenty years later, it has some significance and meaning for people, and it's touching people. That's all anybody would want, really, when making any kind of art.'

Darian looks back at his essential work with typical modesty.

Darian: 'SMiLE has always been a Brian Wilson and Van Dyke Parks creation. My role was merely to facilitate and realize their ideas. I'm just lucky to have been at the right place at the right time. It's been wonderful to see people showing genuine gratitude towards my contribution, some even suggesting that along with being in the right place at the time that I was also the right person. I suppose if Brian and Van Dyke could place that much trust in me, then maybe I was.'

No maybe about it.

In 2004, right after the world premiere concert was over, Van Dyke was thrilled and relieved. *SMiLE* was now out in the world, and his and Brian's 'baby' had exceeded all expectations.

In 2012, Van Dyke said, 'the most amazing thing is how *SMiLE* has become an emblem of an age, generation, and of a spirit.'

While there is no question that *SMiLE* left permanent scars on both Brian and Van Dyke, I like to remember what he wrote in the concert program for *Brian Wilson Presents SMiLE*: '*SMiLE* has "snap, crackle, and pop". . . Brian has made a lasting contribution in this work.'

Which means Mr. Parks did too.

The music we love can do many things. It doesn't just enrich our lives. It is more than, as the cliché goes, 'the soundtrack of our lives.' Sometimes, it saves our lives.

In the October 18, 1966, issue of *Melody Maker*, in a word-association article, Brian Wilson said: 'Suicide: You can't solve anything by killing yourself. I mean, things can always get better . . .'

Jerry Weiss: 'In the dozen years I was on the road with Brian, I was by his side as he met so many fans during countless "meet and greets," in airports, in hotel lobbies, backstage in venues, and even restaurants. And I witnessed people of all ages telling Brian how his music saved their marriages, healed their physical illnesses, got them through life-altering surgeries, rescued them from anxiety and depression and gave them encouragement and hope. In his presence, many trembled, many cried as they opened their hearts to thank him. I was often brought to tears myself just listening and watching their reaction and Brian's.'

The last essay in the book, as Jerry notes above, speaks to the emotional superpower of Brian's music. Here's an eloquent telling of just one of those countless stories. It also indicates that for at least one young woman, who discovered *Brian Wilson Presents SMiLE* in 2019, the impact of the art was more than meaningful. It was life-changing in the best possible way.

'COLUMNATED RUINS DOMINO': *BRIAN'S MESSIAH*

by Charlotte Martin

MY *SMILE* JOURNEY BEGAN IN TEARS.

The music of Brian Wilson burst into my life in 2019. I remember that it was the last week of February. I was an insomniac, kept awake that particular night worrying about a life that was quickly spiralling out of control. I turned to entertainment to ease the tension of the late hour and stumbled upon the biopic *Love and Mercy*.

What did I know about Brian Wilson up to that point? I knew that he had a bunch of hits with The Beach Boys back in the 1960s. I knew that there were two songs of his I truly loved: 'In My Room' and 'God Only Knows,' that I, like any sensible music lover, had a healthy appreciation and awe for 'Good Vibrations,' and that at Christmas, The Beach Boys' arrangement of 'We Three Kings' is my absolute favourite rendition of that hymn. I also knew that those big hits about sun and fun and cars and girls didn't speak to my heart, pleasant as the sounds were. Not even the lush harmonies of a song like 'Don't Worry Baby' could get me through the incredibly difficult and often very painful first quarter century of my life.

When the biopic had first come out, it had been on an endless list of movies that sounded interesting but which I just never got around to watching. In 2016, the fiftieth anniversary of *Pet Sounds*, an NPR program to which I often listened did an album dissection episode on it one week in May to honour the occasion. I heard parts of songs, and that album, too, went on a list for future consideration, if I ever started listening to music regularly again.

But at that time, music wasn't as big a part of my life as it had been. For the first twenty years, music was everything. It was always playing in my room: Sixties and Seventies music, classical music, folk music, even opera. I played multiple instruments, even dabbled in composing and arranging. For a long time, I wanted music to be my whole life. But, on July 6, 2012, exactly a month short of my twentieth birthday, one of the people who loved me most, who cheered me on in my musical endeavours and shared his excellent musical tastes with me, died, and my joy in music was buried with him.

Until that night in February 2019, when desperate anxiety sent me searching for a late-night distraction. I stumbled upon that film, and I remembered that I never did get around to seeing it. Before the night was over, I had also listened to *Pet Sounds* for the first time.

It was like being struck by lightning. Like falling in love. I have never known, and I may never know, what it truly is like to fall in love with another person, but I know that's what happened then. I was struck by a force greater than anything I've ever experienced before. And I've never 'recovered.'

Before that week was over, not only had I listened to *Pet Sounds* again numerous times, but I had discovered something far greater: *Brian Wilson Presents SMiLE*. I scoured YouTube for every documentary I could find to tell me Brian's story. Including *Beautiful Dreamer*. Especially *Beautiful Dreamer*. I took to that one in particular, as the most artistic, aesthetically-pleasing documentary about Brian Wilson, but also as the one that explained most clearly to me what this whole *SMiLE* story was really all about. It helped me to begin to make sense of why I found so many conflicting results when I searched for *SMiLE* online. Most importantly, it told me the story that would, in May of that year, save my life.

I was a grad school student at the time, studying theology. My school was set in the cozy Hyde Park neighbourhood of Chicago, not far from Lake Michigan. I commuted by train from Indiana every day. My home life was chaotic, to say the least. But more on that in a moment. While that situation spiralled beyond any hope of control, I fell in love.

I remember one cold, drizzly March afternoon. I had a break between classes, or perhaps the pressure of my home life made me unable to focus on being in class that afternoon. I just remember that, despite the weather, I needed to take a walk. I walked as far as I safely could in every direction, listening to Brian's music. I remember listening to 'Don't Talk (Put Your Head on My Shoulder)' and having that sense of being drowned in honey, suffocated in velvet. Even now, I am overcome by the strings.

Sometimes I would play this alternate mix of ''Til I Die' that came from the *Endless Harmony* soundtrack, where the instruments are all added in one by one, leading up to the wave of harmonious vocals. I would listen to it at an unhealthy volume, letting it wash over me, clear my head. I would feel cleansed, even despite the mounting sense of hopelessness and despair.

No matter where I was or what I was doing, my thoughts would continually wander to this music, and to the story of the man who brought all of this music into the world. I felt it all so deeply in my heart, in a way that I've never experienced any music, or anything, really, before. The closest I could compare this feeling to is the way that Karen Carpenter's voice always tugs at my heartstrings. The Carpenters were my first musical love, but this was vastly more all-consuming.

My days would pass in wanting – needing – to hear this music. It became as necessary to me as the air I breathe. I couldn't understand it at the time – and, indeed, it would take me quite some time to even begin to come to any sort of understanding about this – but this music became my one sanctuary amidst a deepening crisis.

This crisis would reach its critical point one Monday in May 2019. As I said, my grad school was quite near Lake Michigan. On this cool, grey Monday, I went to the Lake. I intended to go into the Lake. I cannot swim.

I told no one. I left no note. It being grey and dreary, that particular spot was completely deserted. There was no one to stop me. No one to save me. I was alone.

As I prepared to enter the Lake, a thought struck me. I wanted to listen to two last songs, to say goodbye to life.

What was so wrong in my life, that would lead me to feel the need to say goodbye to it?

I could write an entire essay, actually an entire book, on the abuses – physical, emotional and psychological – that I suffered from my parents and other relatives. Suffice it to say that from the time I was three months old, I was being beaten. And it never stopped. My first quarter-century would continue much as it began.

However, a lifetime of abuse need not be detailed in this celebration of beauty and melody and harmony.

I only add one other relevant story: I really could have died at the age of nine, on Friday, September 7, 2001, when I nearly drowned at a classmate's birthday party. The circumstances of my rescue remain mysterious. Perhaps even miraculous. Before I was pulled out of the water, there was a beautiful golden glow under the water. And I felt someone holding me even before my classmate got there to fish me out.

And all of this and more brought me to the Lake on Monday, May 13, 2019.

As I was sitting on a rocky ledge that afternoon, my feet in the water, preparing to walk into it, knowing I need not walk too many steps before the Lake would claim me, knowing from that experience when I was 9 what drowning would feel like, knowing it would take a similar miracle to fish me out, and believing that would not happen, I felt the urge to listen to two final songs: 'Surf's Up' and 'Til I Die.'

My version of choice of 'Surf's Up' on that Monday afternoon was a recording from 1967, Brian alone at his piano. His voice is beautiful, the chords on the piano sublime. There is an intimacy to the performance. If I close my eyes, the music washes over me in waves. The final section, the chords over the moving bass notes in his left hand, the soaring of his voice, is like stepping outside after a bad storm. The heaviness of the air has lifted, but the skies are still grey. A dove takes flight. This was one final beautiful moment I wanted to grant myself. My last goodbye wasn't addressed to anyone in my life. It was said in my heart to the music that I had come to love, that had kept me from coming to the Lake months earlier.

One more song felt necessary: the aforementioned *Endless Harmony* version of ''Til I Die.' Again, sublime beauty, and fitting last words for someone who was nearing death. But this time I heard it in an entirely new way. When I had listened to this song before, I had related to the sense of being unmoored, the sense that I could just vanish in any moment. It felt different this time, though. Even now, I don't have the right words for what I experienced. 'Permanence' doesn't feel like it accurately describes the sense that filled my heart. But that line, 'These things I'll be until I die,' took on a new meaning to me. 'Until I die' didn't mean I had to die that day. That yes, I was living a life without stability, and maybe I would always feel that way. Maybe my life was never going to make sense. Maybe I was always going to feel adrift, with all the terror that entails. But, if Brian Wilson could survive what he was going through when he wrote this song, maybe I could, too. And not only did he survive, but he triumphed. I didn't believe in any triumph for myself, but I sure derived all my hope and strength from him.

Having listened to these songs, I stood up and started walking. Not into the water as I had intended, though. Away. I walked away from the Lake.

What was it in Brian's life and music that gave me the strength to continue to live? I have pondered this question many times in the intervening years.

The simple answer – which really isn't all that simple – is that I was able to draw strength from his music because I could trust his experience, the experience that led him to write such beautiful music. I could, even as a child, long before I became such a great fan of his music, trust a song like 'In My Room' because that's what I needed most, 'a world where I can go and tell my secrets to.' Later, I would come to trust a song like 'Midnight's Another Day,' because I felt like he was singing, not just about my chronic depression, but my spiritual anguish, as well. And a song like 'Love and Mercy'? My soul is at peace.

I was beginning to learn, and would learn in even greater detail, about how Brian suffered in his life. After hearing the infamous 'Help Me, Murry' recording, as well as reading an emotionally manipulative letter that Murry had written (after he had been fired as their manager), I realized that I knew what it was like to be raised by someone like him, because he is all three of the people most responsible for my upbringing. He had the physical abusiveness of my father and the mental and emotional abusiveness of my mother and grandmother.

I also understood what it is like, as Brian once was, to be kept in round-the-clock surveillance. For me, it wasn't a psychologist, but my mother who did everything she could to suffocate my spirit.

It's a wonder that Brian survived his 'nine years in prison.' And, sure, not all of our traumas were the same. But knowing about what he endured helped me to come to terms with the need to break out after twenty-six years in my own prison and, having done so, to take a deep breath of fresh air as I began my own life. These past five years have taught me to embrace and cherish the freedom of my mind and heart.

But, differences aside, perhaps the greatest similarity, the greatest reason that I realized I could trust his music, is because I knew what it was like to have my soul crushed repeatedly. Even now, I am no stranger to what it is to share myself, earnestly, creatively, to share some precious part of myself, only to have it rejected, to never be good enough. I know what it's like to find myself not understood by the people closest to me, the people I count on for approval, whose acceptance I so desperately seek. Whose love I can never have. I know intimately the heartbreak and loneliness of a song like 'I Just Wasn't Made For These Times'. And I know what it is to have great goals and dreams that I worked so hard for coming crashing down about me. I knew what it was to live with the feeling of having failed. Of being on the verge of something great and watching it all just completely falling apart in a matter of months. That's where my life was in May 2019.

That's why it was to Brian I addressed my final good-bye in my heart, in gratitude for the music that had made the last few months bearable until I just couldn't do it anymore. And that's why, while listening to those last two songs of his, when I felt the urge to continue to exist, I trusted that. My exact thought was, 'I want to live in the world where this beautiful music exists.' And I knew I could trust that because I knew that all those bad feelings weren't the end of Brian's story.

I had, by then, watched *Beautiful Dreamer* enough times to know that, while it took a very long time, and the road was never, ever easy, Brian triumphed over his adversity. He finished *SMiLE*. Not just for a studio recording, but for a live performance. In front of people. In front of a lot of people. The vulnerability and courage that took continues to inspire me to face my own life. That doesn't mean all of his problems suddenly vanished. Healing doesn't mean there are no scars.

Beginning that night, it is no exaggeration to say that every day for well over a year thereafter – sometimes more than once a day if I particularly needed it – I watched *Beautiful Dreamer*. Over and over and over again. At one point I had it practically memorized, because it became so comfortably familiar to me. It told me the story I needed, day after day, to affirm my decision to continue living. When things get bad, I still slip back into watching it as often as I need to in order to cope with the challenges of healing from my past. I'm estranged from my family. I found a new family, godparents who loved me, only to have my godfather die less than a year later. Sometimes I feel very unmoored and very fatalistic, even now. Those feelings, I think, never entirely leave you.

But thanks to the miracle of *Brian Wilson Presents SMiLE*, and the way that *Beautiful Dreamer* told me the story that has saved me, I am able to live through every day. I've even been able to watch as the spark of some of my old dreams have been reignited and a creative fire has begun to burn in my heart once more.

I recently heard someone say, 'God does not play games.'

I come from a religious background where God has often been depicted as very serious, quite frightening, really. And that hasn't done me well, because that's always been someone else, a really big Someone Else, to be afraid of failing, of letting down, of not measuring up to the unrealistic standard that I feel has been set for me. When I heard those words, though, I realized that what my heart has been searching for all along is the joyful God to whom the 'teenage symphony' that is *SMiLE* was written. This, perhaps, more than anything else, is why Brian's music, particularly 'Surf's Up,' was what I turned to that afternoon. And why *Brian Wilson Presents SMiLE* is the reason I am alive.

★ ★ ★ ★

The music saved me, inspiring the subtitle for this essay. A Messiah in strictly religious terms was the biblically prophesied deliverer of the Jewish people. A saviour for God's people. In Dr. Daniel Harrison's essay, he likens *Brian Wilson Presents SMiLE* to an oratorio. Perhaps the best-known oratorio is Handel's *Messiah*. For me, the music of *SMiLE* fulfils both messianic sensibilities.

I would never meet my musical liberator. But on July 24, 2022, I experienced something I never believed that I would be so fortunate to experience. I saw 'Heroes And Villains' performed live. It was the penultimate concert of his tour. The only time I would be in the same space as my hero. And to see that song performed live, knowing its story, knowing what role *SMiLE* had in my life . . . I was wearing my *Brian Wilson Presents SMiLE* t-shirt that day, as a symbolic representation of what it was that brought me to that moment. This sounds foolish to

SMiLE

some, I'm sure, but in a sense, I felt that song was for me, that in a deeply spiritual way, an inexplicable way, seeing that song performed live placed a seal on my life.

To borrow from my Catholic heritage, if my baptism into the Church of Brian Wilson was my walking away from the Lake after listening to 'Surf's Up,' then 'Heroes And Villains' in Tinley Park was my Confirmation. I wasn't around in 2001 when it was performed solo for the first time at the *All-Star Tribute to Brian Wilson*. I wasn't around for the premiere or subsequent tour of *Brian Wilson Presents SMiLE*. But I can say this: twenty-one years after it was first offered at Radio City, it was just as much of an out-of-body experience to hear it played live in Tinley Park. And my heart overflowed with love and gratitude as I gazed upon my hero. Many joyful tears were shed that evening.

The writer/producer of that Radio City tribute where Brian first played 'Heroes And Villains' as a solo artist . . . the filmmaker whose documentary told the story that helped save my life . . . a producer of *The Pet Sounds Sessions* box set, an essential part of my education when I began to study Brian's music . . . are all the same person. He's also the author of the landmark biography of Brian Wilson, updated in 2022 as *God Only Knows: The Story of Brian Wilson, The Beach Boys & the California Myth*. A volume that, in its original edition back in 1978 was so thorough in dissecting the reasons for the death of *SMiLE* in 1967 – and, more significantly, the collapse of Brian as an artist at that time – that I have come to think of it, and the subsequent 1985 update, as 'The Coroner's Report.' But, like a true Bible, the 2022 update does tell the tale of artistic Resurrection . . .

It is significant to me that *SMiLE* gave David's life meaning and *Brian Wilson Presents SMiLE* saved mine. Without *SMiLE* touching David's life as it did and sparking his mission, he would not have been there to tell the story of *Brian Wilson Presents SMiLE*. Indeed, *Brian Wilson Presents SMiLE* would not have even happened without him. And without *Beautiful Dreamer*, I wouldn't be here – finally pursuing my dream to be a writer.

Thank you, Brian - and David - for saving my life.

(Copyright 2024 by Charlotte Martin.)

(Charlotte Martin is a freelance writer who is currently working on her first novel.)

EPILOGUE

ALMOST IMPOSSIBLY, THE TWO SONGS THAT HAD PROPELLED ME ON MY *SMiLE* journey in 1971 were the two songs that saved Ms. Martin's life nearly a half-century later. And it's clear from her essay, a plethora of podcasts, and groups like The Lemon Twigs, that the hopes earnestly expressed above by Darian Sahanaja, Nelson Bragg, and the late David Anderle, have been realised: The music from the *SMiLE* era speaks powerfully to new generations.

Charlotte is less than half my age. But thanks to her, our story ends with a joyous tear and a very big *SMiLE*. And as Jimmy Stewart's character said in *Vertigo*, 'I'm responsible for you now. The Chinese say that once you've saved a person's life, you're responsible for it forever.'

The music of *SMiLE* is more than up to the job. The music will live forever, as will this remarkable story.

What Brian and his band did in 2004 was to present us with a miracle. *Brian Wilson Presents SMiLE* was the triumph of the artistic *and* human spirit. There was no dissension. There was no, 'This might not be commercial.' There was no record label saying, 'Hurry up.' There was no 'competition' with The Beatles.

There was just a composer, his collaborator and his band learning the music and presenting it to us, joyfully. Is *Brian Wilson Presents SMiLE* what we would have gotten in 1967? Of course not. But it is *the fulfilment of Brian's vision*. It is the healing of his broken artistic heart. And as we had long hoped, it freed him to fearlessly tackle new, ambitious, and artistically successful projects like *That Lucky Old Sun* and *Brian Wilson Reimagines Gershwin*.

In 2004, *Brian Wilson Presents SMiLE* was ecstatically received by those who celebrated Brian's artistic resurrection. Among those standing and cheering during the world premiere week in London were Sir Paul McCartney and Sir George Martin – applauding both the music and that Brian had the courage to revisit it and bring it to the world.

Does the beauty of the music surpass the regrets? What could have been. What might have been. And what *should* have been.

Usually, but not always.

That's because *Brian Wilson Presents SMiLE* wasn't exactly what he and Van Dyke had imagined in 1966. But the story of *Brian Wilson Presents SMiLE* is even more unimaginable.

So maybe, just maybe, the story had to play out exactly as it did, as if it was predestined. Maybe Brian had to be crucified on a musical cross for his 2004 *SMiLE* to bring us all together in a jubilant celebration of its resurrection, of *his* liberation.

Through this all, through getting to know Brian for all these years, I've come to believe that great art almost can't come from a 'normal' person. Whatever 'normal' means. It takes sensitivity and a rare sensibility; you have to understand the world in a different way to create art for the ages.

Brian Wilson feels and hears life differently than the rest of us. Unlike *anybody* else. And I think the circumstances of his life may have contributed to the fact that he created music of exquisite joy and beauty and, more than anything else, intensely harmonious feelings, because his life often lacked harmony.

I sadly conclude that the emotional abuse Brian suffered almost from the moment he could stand is what infused his art with a depth that knows no equal in modern times. That the happiness we feel from his songs has been, for him, a kind of balm. He expressed his melancholy in melody and simultaneously wrote such uplifting, happy music to make *himself* feel better. *Pet Sounds* speaks to generations because it came from the complex heart of such a troubled soul. 'Good Vibrations,' a song that most everybody knows and loves, maybe exists because nobody needed those 'good vibrations' in their life more than Brian did when he created it.

Laughter indeed is the best medicine, and nobody understood that better than Brian. The music he created for *SMiLE* was no accident. As for *Brian Wilson Presents SMiLE*, I know that when I listen to it in 2024, free of the trauma and drama . . . just listen to it as *music* . . . it has the exact effect that the creator intended.

Of course, it makes me cry too knowing what he went through, how

EPILOGUE

he had to suffer for our happiness. And then smile again remembering the pure happiness that completing *SMiLE* gave *him*.

There's something more than just a little biblical in all of that.

As we've repeatedly heard, *Brian Wilson Presents SMiLE* does cast a magical spell.

And so, twenty years after his most courageous, surprising, and important achievement, we can say with no hyperbole, Brian Wilson is one of popular music's most deeply revered figures. Indeed, it is no exaggeration to call Brian Wilson one of the most influential composers of the 20th *and* 21st centuries.

His work, especially *Pet Sounds* and *SMiLE*, will be studied in music schools as long as there are music schools. In fact, in the spring of 2024, I began teaching a brand-new class at the UCLA Herb Alpert School of Music. It is called 'Good Vibrations.' *SMiLE* is central to the course.

In a culture where Tik Tok trends change overnight, Brian and *SMiLE* have gone the distance.

I may have been the one who first said, 'If music is math, then Brian Wilson is Einstein.' But no comparisons are really necessary. He's Brian Wilson, an American composer, arranger and producer whose work has proved to be as powerful as faith, as heartfelt as love, and as profound as mercy.

Back in 1988, talking about his first solo album, Brian said that his goal with music was to 'cover us with love under the disguise of a record.' He has done that so many times, most especially with his 1966 trilogy—*Pet Sounds*, 'Good Vibrations,' and the music of *SMiLE*.

Back in 2002, in the liner notes of the *Brian Wilson Presents Pet Sounds Live* CD, in the credits, among others, Brian thanks 'The Beatles who originally inspired *Pet Sounds*. And, most importantly, God, for choosing me to carry his spiritual message to the world.'

Back on February 20, 2004, the first set of the concert began with an acapella Beach Boys classic from 1965: 'And Your Dream Comes True.' Choosing that song to open the show wasn't an accident. It was a deliberate, specific, and clever selection made by Darian in conversation with Melinda. And it fit perfectly because they knew what lay ahead. It was almost a musical Easter Egg.

They knew that about an hour later, everybody's dream *would* come true. They may have been nervous, but they had faith that Brian Wilson was about to do the bravest thing in his life, perhaps the bravest thing any musical artist has ever done.

He gave us *SMiLE*.

And near midnight, as we left the Royal Festival Hall following this very first show in London, Brian summed up how we were all feeling, the state of disbelief and deliverance.

Brian Wilson: 'Our *SMiLE* dream. It came true.'

The generosity of his inclusiveness is worth noting. As always, Brian was sharing the moment with those who loved him. Even though he was the composer, it wasn't just Brian's *SMiLE* dream. It was ours. All of us who believed in Brian. All of us who loved him unconditionally.

So, as we look back, regardless of the circumstances that led to the creation of this incomparable work of art, it is ultimately the art that survives and thrives, long after the 'origin' story has become a larger-than-life myth. Knowing that, what does *SMiLE*, in all of its iterations, mean to Mr. Wilson? This time, the artist answers.

Brian: 'My masterpiece . . . my masterwork . . . I think of myself as somebody who has left behind something people will cherish for a long time.'

Back in 1966, Brian said he was going to write 'a teenage symphony to God.'

And he did.

The completion, performance, recording, worldwide touring, and global acceptance of *Brian Wilson Presents SMiLE* immeasurably changed Brian, ushering in the happiest and most creative years of his post-Beach Boys life.

ACKNOWLEDGEMENTS

This book would not exist without the participation, help, and support of so many people.

First, thank you to everybody who did an interview in 2023, calling up memories from long-ago moments: Scott Bennett, David Bither, Nelson Bragg, Ky Cabot, Richie Davis, Probyn Gregory, Bob Harris, Jim Hines, Ray Lawlor, Randy Lewis, Bob Lizik, James Mathers, Glenn Max, Taylor Mills, Darian Sahanaja, Jean Sievers, Richard Sloan, Todd Sucherman, Mark Volman, Paul Von Mertens, Neil Warnock MBE, John Warren, Jerry Weiss, and, from The Stockholm Strings 'n' Horns – Anna Dager, Malin-My Wall, and Viktor Sand.

Thank you to everybody who sat with me in 2003-2004 for the interviews for *Beautiful Dreamer*. Your memories were invaluable in helping me understand what happened in the 1960s, making that film and this book come alive as *SMiLE* was dying and then being reborn. Especially helpful in 2023 were Danny Hutton, Carol Kaye, Mark Linett, David Marks, Durrie Parks, Don Randi, and Annie Wilson-Karges.

A prayerful moment to reflect upon those very special friends of Brian Wilson and *SMiLE* who we've lost: David Anderle, Derek A. Bill, Hal Blaine, Chuck Britz, David Crosby, Eva Easton-Leaf, Jeffrey Foskett, Bob Hanes, Billy Hinsche, Lauri Klobas, Philip Lambert, Robert Leaf, Larry Levine, Ronnie Lippin, Sir George Martin, Terry Melcher, Mike Melvoin, Paul Quarrington, Chip Rachlin, Phil Ramone, Markus Sandlund, Stan Ross, Derek Taylor, Michael Vosse, Timothy White, Paul Williams, David Wilczewski, Carl Wilson, Dennis Wilson, Melinda Wilson, and all the studio staff, engineers, assistant engineers, and AFM musicians who played on Brian's 1966 *SMiLE* recordings And, of course, everybody's favorite pirate – Nick (Nicky Wonder) Walusko.

SMiLE

Rest in Peace, all. I believe when they listen to *Brian Wilson Presents SMiLE*, they are smiling.

To my impeccable and obsessive copy editor, Aimee T. Perhach, my eternal gratitude for making sure that I wrote in the King's English, and for her tireless and peerless effort to make sure that every quote is right and every piece of punctuation is where it should be.

To Robert Flory, an immense 'thank you' for his essential help in historical research and especially for his work on the 'Brianistas' chapters. Your sourcing of relevant Wilsonian quotes was vital.

On the other side of the pond, a massive 'thank you' to my old compadre, Andrew G. Doe, the incredible Beach Boys and Brian Wilson historian. He did his best to make sure I got the knowable facts of *SMiLE* right with every possible subtlety. By your last count, my endless emails to you totaled well over 400. ☺

To David Barraclough, Greg Morton, Claire Browne, David Stock, and the team at Omnibus for believing in the importance of *SMiLE*.

As always, thank you to Robbie Leff, my lifelong musician friend who makes sure that my words describing music are both sharp and accurate. And my trusted friends, especially Kevin Gershan, who gave me invaluable feedback during the creation of this book.

To the essayists: *Howie Edelson*, whose words leave me in speechless appreciation . . . to *Tom Nolan*, for bringing it all back home . . . to *Harvey Kubernik*, who remembers it all . . . to *Debbie Keil-Leavitt,* whose piece focused on two of the most important people in my life, both of whom she introduced me to . . . to *Gary Pig Gold*, my old orange juice-drinking pal, for stirring up so many wonderful memories . . . to *Sylvie Simmons,* for sharing her beautiful writing and always special heartfelt point of view . . . to *Peter Carlin,* for knocking *my* socks off... to *Sean O'Hagan,* for telling his musical truth about Brian & *SMiLE* . . . to *David Scott,* for digging so deeply into the music . . . to *Andrew G. Doe* for reliving the big night so perfectly . . . to *Domenic Priore,* for bringing his special *SMiLE* and pop culture brilliance to this book . . . to *Dr. Daniel Harrison,* for writing an essay that is mostly above my head but still speaks to my heart . . . and lastly, to *Charlotte Martin,* for sharing her heart-rending story that brings the *SMiLE* mini-anthology to such a beautiful conclusion.

A special acknowledgement to all who have written about Brian Wilson

ACKNOWLEDGEMENTS

and *SMiLE* since the fall of 1966 and helped inspire this oral history, most especially the original mythmakers: Tom Nolan, Jules Siegel, and Paul Williams. And, of course, Derek Taylor.

Special Thanks to: Kingsley Abbott, Keith Badman, David Beard, Cindy Lee Berryhill, Alan Boyd, Harold Brook, Perry Cox, Will Crerar, Michael DeMartin, Lee Dempsey, Brian Diamond, Mark Dillon, Bertis Downs, Lee Eastman, Elliot Easton, Brad Elliott, Jason Fine, Bob Fitzgerald, Ali Gifford, Vince Gill, Caroline Graham, Mike Grant, Lucy Hall, Jonas Herbsman, Geoffrey Himes, Frank Holmes, Wayne Johnson, Elliot Kendall, Brent Kubasta, Richard Leaf, Susie Lidstone, Maurice Linnane, Peter Lynch II, Ed Mandelbaum, Sir Paul McCartney, Jeff McEvoy, Lauren Mele, Eddie Micone, Phil Miglioratti, Cam Mott, Sujata Murthy, Matt Pinfield, David Poleno, Bill Porricelli, Peter Reum, Ed Roach, Paul Rock, Jeff Rosen, Brad Rosenberger, John Scheinfeld, Jerry Schilling, Ken Sharp, Lewis Shiner, Tom Smucker, Tea Takaoka, Richard Waltzer, Russ Wapensky, Lenny Waronker, Don Was, Jimmy Webb, Richard Williams, Brent Wilson, Daria Wilson, Delanie Wilson, Dylan Wilson, Dash Wilson, and Dakota Wilson. And to all of my fellow 'Brianistas,' especially those who contributed their memories for this book.

To Jasper Dailey, the man who showed us what the *SMiLE* sessions looked like.

To Jonathan Anderle – for everything.

To Mark London – for your perfectly-realized designs.

To Jean Sievers – who manages to make everything work.

Thank you to the dear Gloria Ramos for nearly forty years of friendship and support...and for taking such good and kind care of Mr. Wilson. A real Guardian Angel.

To Ray – We got there!

To Vicki – who loves *SMiLE* and taught me how to smile every day.

To Darian – You are the man. Always.

To Melinda – for giving Brian the support he needed to step back into the world of music, providing him with what he called 'emotional security.' And apropos of this book, without Melinda, there would almost certainly never have been *Brian Wilson Presents SMiLE*. So we all owe her our eternal thanks.

To Van Dyke – You're such a special artist and friend. And your 2004 interview was spectacular. So glad you didn't want to do a new one.

SMiLE

To Brian, for trusting me with your *SMiLE* memories and for sharing your music and soul with the world. Everybody loves you for having the courage to bring your magnificent *SMiLE* music to the world.

This book is dedicated to Brian & Van Dyke for having the artistic courage and creativity to bring the brilliant *SMiLE* music to life in 1966 and to them and Darian Sahanaja for *finally* completing it.

Brian autographing the concert program, designed by Mark London, after the world premiere on February 20, 2004.

SELECTED BIBLIOGRAPHY

BOOKS

Heller, Joseph, *Catch-22,* Simon & Schuster, 1961.

Leaf, David, *The Beach Boys and the California Myth,* Grosset & Dunlap, 1978.

——, *God Only Knows: The Story of Brian Wilson, the Beach Boys & the California Myth,* Omnibus Press, 2022.

——, *The Making of Pet Sounds,* Capitol Records, 1996.

Priore, Domenic, *Look! Listen! Vibrate! Smile!,* rev. ed., Last Gasp, 1995.

——, *Smile: The Story of Brian Wilson's Lost Masterpiece,* Sanctuary, 2005.

Seigel, Jules, *Record,* Straight Arrow Books, 1972.

White, Timothy, *The Nearest Far Away Place: Brian Wilson, the Beach Boys, and the Southern California Experience,* Henry Holt, 1994.

Williams, Paul, *Brian Wilson & The Beach Boys: How Deep Is the Ocean? Essays and Conversations,* Omnibus Press, 1997.

ESSAYS

Leaf, David, 'When You Wish Upon a Star . . .', concert program for *Brian Wilson Presents SMiLE,* 2004.

Wilson, Brian, 'Music Is God's Voice,' liner notes for *The Beach Boys SMiLE Sessions,* Capitol Records, 2011.

LINER NOTES

Leaf, David, *Brian Wilson Presents SMiLE,* **Nonesuch Records, 2004.**
——, *Good Vibrations: Thirty Years of The Beach Boys,* **Capitol Records, 1993.**
——, *The Pet Sounds Sessions,* **Capitol Records, 1996.**

PERIODICALS

Aquarian Drunkard
Austin Chronicle
Beach Boys Stomp!
Beat
Beat Instrumental
Billboard
Billboard 1967 Talent Directory
Cheetah
Creem
Disc and Music Echo
Endless Summer Quarterly
Fabulous 208
Forbes
Goldmine
Guardian
Hit Parader
Los Angeles Times
Melody Maker
Mojo
Mojo '60s
Musician
New Musical Express
Newsweek
Open Sky
Pet Sounds
Record Collector
Record Mirror
Rolling Stone
Sounds
TeenSet
Time
Uncut
West

SELECTED BIBLIOGRAPHY

TELEVISION AND RADIO DOCUMENTARIES AND PROGRAMS

An All-Star Tribute to Brian Wilson, **written by David Leaf, 2001.**
The Beach Boys: An American Band, **Malcolm Leo, 1985.**
The Beach Boys: The Best Summer of Our Lives, radio documentary, **written by Ken Barnes, 1976.**
The Beach Boys: Pet Sounds, episode of *The Classic Album Series,* **Matthew Longfellow and Martin R. Smith, 2010.**
The Beach Boys SMiLE **Sessions webisodes, Capitol Records, 2011.**
The Beach Boys Story, **BBC Radio documentary, written by Bob Harris, 1974.**
Beautiful Dreamer: Brian Wilson and the Story of SMiLE, **David Leaf, 2004.**
Brian Wilson: A Beach Boy's Tale, **Morgan Neville, 1999.**
Brian Wilson: I Just Wasn't Made for These Times, **Don Was, 1995.**
Brian Wilson: Long Promised Road, **Brent Wilson, 2021**
Endless Harmony: The Beach Boys Story, **Alan Boyd, 1998.**
Pet Stories, **John Anderson, 2003.**

PODCAST

Goyer, Nate, 'Ep413: Mike Love of The Beach Boys,' *The Vinyl Guide, 2023.*

COURT DECISION

Love v. Associated Newspapers, Ltd., **611 F.3d 601 (9th Cir. 2010).**

WEBSITES

https://www.bellagio10452.com
https://brianwilson.com
https://leafprod.com

PICTURE CREDITS

Page xv Photo by K Mazur/Getty Images.

Page xvi Courtesy the David Leaf Collection.

Page xx Photo by Jasper Dailey/Copyright 1997 David Leaf Productions, Inc. All rights reserved.

Page xxx Courtesy the David Leaf Collection.

Page 209 Photo by Jon Furniss/Getty Images.

Page 213 Photo from the world premiere concert by Hayley Maden/Getty Images.

Page 235 Courtesy the David Leaf Collection.

Page 243 Courtesy the David Leaf Collection.

Page 248 Photo by Mike Marsland/Getty Images.

Page 262 Photo Courtesy BriMel.

Page 265 Courtesy the David Leaf Collection.

Page 270 Courtesy the David Leaf Collection.

Page 278 Photos by Jeff McEvoy, All Rights Rseserved.

Page 297 Photo by Jasper Dailey/Copyright 1997 David Leaf Productions, Inc. All rights reserved.

Page 314 Photo by Ron Wolfson/Getty Images.

Page 318 Photo by Mike Marsland/Getty Images.